The Reception of Walter Pater in Europe

The Athlone Critical Traditions Series:
The Reception of British Authors in Europe

Series Editor. Elinor Shaffer
School of Advanced Study, University of London

Published volumes

Volume I: *The Reception of Virginia Woolf in Europe*
Edited by Mary Ann Caws and Nicola Luckhurst

Volume II: *The Reception of Laurence Sterne in Europe*
Edited by Peter de Voogd and John Neubauer

Volume III: *The Reception of James Joyce in Europe*
Edited by Geert Lernout and Wim Van Mierlo

Volume IV: *The Reception of Walter Pater in Europe*
Edited by Stephen Bann

Volume V: *The Reception of Ossian in Europe*
Edited by Howard Gaskill

Forthcoming volumes in the series include

The Reception of Lord Byron in Europe
Edited by Richard Cardwell

The Reception of H.G. Wells in Europe
Edited by Patrick Parrinder and John Partington

The Reception of Jonathan Swift in Europe
Edited by Hermann Real

The Reception of Walter Pater in Europe

Edited by Stephen Bann

thoemmes

First published 2004 by
Thoemmes Continuum

The Tower Building, 11 York Road, London SE1 7NX
15 East 26th Street, New York, NY 10010

British Library Cataloguing-in-Publication Data
A catalogue record for this book is available from the British Library.

ISBN: 0826468462

Library of Congress Cataloguing-in-Publication Data
The reception of Walter Pater in Europe/edited by Stephen Bann.
p.cm.—(The Athlone critical traditions series)
Includes bibliographical references and index.
ISBN 0-8264-6846-2
1. Pater, Walter, 1839–1894—Appreciation—Europe. 2. Pater, Walter, 1839–1894—
Translations—History and Criticisms. 3. European Literature—English influences. 4. Pater,
Walter, 1839–1894—Influence. I. Bann, Stephen. II. Series.

PR5137. E87. R43 2004
824.8—dc22   2004051659

Typeset by Tradespools, Frome, Somerset
Printed and bound in Great Britain by The Cromwell Press, Trowbridge, Wiltshire

Contents

Series Editor's Preface

The reception of British authors in Britain has in good part been studied; indeed, it forms our literary history. By contrast, the reception of British authors in Europe has not been examined in any systematic, long-term or large-scale way.

It is the aim of this Series to initiate and forward the study of the reception of British authors in continental Europe, or, as we would now say, the rest of Europe as a whole, rather than as isolated national histories with a narrow national perspective. The perspectives of other nations greatly add to our understanding of individual contributors to that history. The history of the reception of British authors extends our knowledge of their capacity to stimulate and to call forth new responses, not only in their own disciplines but in wider fields and to diverse publics in a variety of historical circumstances. Often these responses provide quite unexpected and enriching insights into our own history, politics and culture. Individual works and personalities take on new dimensions and facets. They may also be subject to enlightening critiques. Our knowledge of British writers is simply incomplete and inadequate without these reception studies.

By 'authors' we intend writers in any field whose works have been recognized as making a contribution to the intellectual and cultural history of our society. Thus the Series includes literary figures, such as Laurence Sterne, Virginia Woolf and James Joyce, philosophers such as Francis Bacon and David Hume, historians and political figures such as Edmund Burke, and scientists such as Charles Darwin and Isaac Newton, whose works have had a broad impact on thinking in every field. In some cases individual works of the same author have dealt with different subjects, each with virtually its own reception history; so Burke's *Reflections on the French Revolution* (1790) was instantaneously translated and moulded thinking on the power struggles in the Europe of his own day; his youthful 'Essay on the Feeling of the Beautiful and Sublime' exerted a powerful influence on aesthetic thought and the practice of writing and remains a seminal work for certain genres of fiction. Similarly, each of Laurence Sterne's two major works of fiction, *Tristram Shandy* and *A Sentimental Journey*, has its own history of reception, giving rise to a whole line of literary movements, innovative progeny and concomitant critical theory in most European countries.

While it is generally recognized that the receptions of Byron and Scott in Europe were amongst the most extensive of British authors, that of Walter Pater may be hardly known, and surmised to be very small; yet a minor writer at home may be a major one abroad. The extent of reception, moreover, may not be a true index of its interest. The movement and style that Pater forwarded, through his own writings, and his personal influence over such figures as Oscar Wilde, while he himself lived quietly as a don in Oxford, came to more open and florid bloom abroad. If an English writer, Vernon Lee

(Violet Paget), who lived and published in Italy, was the first (in the 1880s) to make him known (and this kind of individual, personal intervention by a fellow countryman is a mode of reception worth attending to in itself), the effect was felt (in some cases paraded, in others masked) by leading figures such as d'Annunzio in Italy, Hofmannsthal in Austria, and Proust in France. Indeed, it was a liberating and formative influence in the life and work of the great Portuguese poet Fernando Pessoa, whose secret yet flamboyant literary life was carried out through his three poetic heteronyms or personae.

The research project examines the ways in which selected authors have been translated, published, distributed, read, reviewed and discussed on the continent of Europe. In doing so, it throws light not only on specific strands of intellectual and cultural history but also on the processes involved in the dissemination of ideas and texts. The project brings to bear the theoretical and critical approaches that have characterized the growing fields of reader response theory and reception studies in the last quarter of the twentieth century and into the twenty-first century. These critical approaches have illuminated the activity of the reader in bringing the text to life and stressed the changing horizons of the reading public or community of which the reader is a part. The project also takes cognizance of the studies of the material history of the book that have begun to explore the production, publication and distribution of manuscripts and books. Increasingly, other media too are playing a role in these processes, and to the history of book illustration must be added lantern slides (as in the popular versions of both Scott's and Dickens's works), cinema (whose early impact forms an important part of our H. G. Wells volume), and more recently television (as recounted in the Jane Austen volume). Pater's art-historical writings have a history in images as well as in prose style, as his passages on Leonardo's 'Mona Lisa' (only the best-known example) show. The study of material history is also concerned with the objects that form durable traces of the vogue for a particular author, which may be parts of himself (as with the macabre story told in our Shelley volume of the wish to possess the poet's heart), or items of his wardrobe (as with Byronic shirtsleeves), or mementos of his characters such as Wedgwood plates depicting scenes of Sterne's Maria. The significance of such cults and cult objects requires further analysis as the examples multiply and diversify.

The Series as published by Continuum Books is open-ended and multi-volumed, each volume based on a particular author. The authors may be regarded according to their discipline, or looked at across disciplines within their period. Thus the reception of philosophers Bacon and Hume may be compared; or Hume may be considered as belonging to an eighteenth-century group that includes writers like Swift and Sterne, historians and political figures such as Gibbon and Burke. As the volumes accumulate they enrich each other and our awareness of the full context in which an individual author is received.

The Swift volume shows that in many places Swift and Sterne were received at the same time, and viewed sometimes as a pair of witty ironists, and sometimes as opposites representing traditional satire on the one hand (Swift) and modern sentimentalism on the other (Sterne), and equally or diversely valued as a result. These chronological shifts, bringing different authors and different works into view together, are common to the reception process, so often displacing or delaying them into an entirely new historical scene or set of circumstances. The kaleidoscope of reception displays and discovers new pairings and couplings, new milieux, new matches and (as Sterne might say) mismatches; and, of course, new valuations. Sterne even seems to be the occasion of a new literary history that wends its way far from the monuments of realism erected to Scott. Pater's reception suggests the route, not obvious yet by now seen as a major one, from Aestheticism to Modernism.

In period terms one may discern a Romantic group; a Victorian group; a *fin-de-siècle* and an early Modernist group. Period designations differ from discipline to discipline, and are shifting even within a discipline: Blake, who was a 'Pre-Romantic' poet a generation ago, is now considered a fully fledged Romantic, and Beckford is edging in that direction. Virginia Woolf may be regarded as a *fin-de-siècle* aesthete and stylist whose affinities are with Pater or as an epoch-making Modernist like Joyce. Terms referring to period and style often vary from country to country. What happens to a 'Victorian' author transplanted to 'Wilhelmine' Germany? Are the English Metaphysical poets to be regarded as 'baroque' in continental terms, or will that term continue to be borrowed in English only for music, art and to an extent architecture? It is most straightforward to classify them simply according to century, for the calendar is for the most part shared. But the various possible groupings will provide a context for reception and enrich our knowledge of each author.

Division of each volume by country or by linguistic region is dictated by the historical development of Europe; each volume necessarily adopts a different selection of countries and regions, depending on period and on the specific reception of any given author. Countries or regions are treated either substantially, in several chapters or sections where this is warranted, for example, the French reception of Sterne, Woolf or Joyce (and nearly all English-language works until after the Second World War pass first through the medium of French language and the prism of French thought), or on a moderate scale, or simply as a brief section. In some cases, where a rich reception is located that has not been reported or of which the critical community is not aware, more detailed coverage may be justified, for example, the reception of Woolf in the different linguistic communities of the Iberian peninsula. In general, comparative studies have neglected Spain in favour of France, Germany and Italy, and this imbalance needs to be righted. Brevity does not indicate lack of interest. Where separate coverage of any particular country or region is not justified by the extent of the reception, relevant material is incorporated into the bibliography and the timeline, as with the Russian reception of Pater. Thus an early translation may be noted, although there was subsequently a minimal response to the author or work, or a very long gap in the reception in that region.

This kind of material will be fully described in the database (see below). It is, of course, always possible, and indeed to be hoped and expected that further aspects of reception will later be uncovered, and the long-term research project forwarded, through this initial information. Reception studies often display an author's intellectual and political impact and reveal effects abroad that are unfamiliar to the author's compatriots. Thus, Byron, for example, had the power of carrying and incarnating liberal political thought to regimes and institutions to whom it was anathema; it is less well known that

Sterne had the same effect, and that both were charged with erotically tinged subversion; and that Pater suggested a style of aesthetic sensibility in which sensation took precedence over moral values. Woolf came to be an icon for women writers in countries where there was little tradition of women's writing. By the same token, the study of censorship, or more broadly impediments to dissemination, and of modes of circumventing control, becomes an important aspect of reception studies. In Bacon studies, the process of dissemination of his ideas through the private correspondence of organized circles was vital. Certain presses and publishers also play a role, and the study of modes of secret distribution under severe penalty is a particularly fascinating subject, whether in Catholic Europe or Soviet Russia. Irony and aesopian devices, and audience alertness to them, are highly developed under controlling regimes. A surprising number of authors live more dangerously abroad than at home.

Translation itself may provide a mode of evading censure. As French 'l'art pour l'art' had come to Britain through 'pseudo-translation', that is through works by British writers masquerading under pseudonyms suggestive of 'dangerous' foreigners such as Baudelairean French poets and Scandinavian naturalists, so the implications of Pater's writings were lived out in impersonations and translations in other countries. His own form of the 'imaginary portrait' became a major vehicle for such life-rewriting. It may not be wholly surprising, then, that Pater became an icon of liberation, both artistic and political, for the Catalan anti-Franco movement.

New electronic technology makes it possible to undertake reception studies on this scale. An extensive database stores information about editions, translations, accompanying critical prefaces or afterwords, illustrations, biographies and correspondence, early reviews, important essays and book-length studies of the authors, and comments, citations and imitations or reworkings, including satire and pastiche by other writers. Some, as often Pater, live in the echoes of their style as understood in another language. Some authors achieve the status of fictional characters in other writers' works; in other cases, their characters do, like Sterne's uncle Toby, Trim and his own alter ego Yorick; or even their characters' family members, as in the memorable novel by a major Hungarian contemporary writer chronicling the early career of the (Hungarian) grandfather of Joyce's Leopold Bloom.

The recording of full details of translations and translators is a particular concern, since often the names of translators are not supplied, or their identity is concealed behind pseudonyms or false attributions. The nature of the translation is often a determining factor in the reception of a work or an author. The database also records the character and location of rare works. Selected texts and passages are included, together with English translations. The database can be searched for a variety of further purposes, potentially yielding a more complete picture of the interactions of writers, translators, critics, publishers and public across Europe in different periods from the Renaissance to the present.

Dr Elinor Shaffer, FBA
Director, Research Project
Reception of British Authors in Europe

Acknowledgements

The Research Project on the Reception of British Authors in Europe is happy to acknowledge the support of the British Academy, the Leverhulme Foundation, the Arts and Humanities Research Board and the Modern Humanities Research Association. We are also greatly indebted to the School of Advanced Study, University of London, where the project was based during the early preparation of this volume; and to the Institute of Germanic Studies, Institute of English Studies, Institute of Romance Studies and the Institute of Historical Research, with whom we have held a series of seminars and colloquia on Reception Studies since 1998, where some of the contributors to this volume presented early versions of their chapters and benefited from discussion.

We acknowledge gratefully the advice and guidance of the Advisory Board of the Project, which has met regularly since the launch of the Project. We also acknowledge the indispensable services of the staff of the Project during the preparation of this volume: the AHRB Research Fellow, Dr Wim Van Mierlo; the Assistants to the Project, Miss Monica Signoretti and then Mr Lachlan Moyle; and during 2003, Mrs Charlotte Pattison Reuter. Finally, our debts to a variety of individuals and institutions across Europe are too extensive to be fully acknowledged.

We acknowledge the valuable initiative of the International Walter Pater Society, whose conference on 'Reading Pater at the Millennium', held at Christ Church College, Oxford, in July 2000, placed the issue of Pater's European reception firmly on the map. A special session on the European reception of Pater concluded the proceedings, at which the Series Editor, the Editor and Dr Robert Vilain gave presentations. Dr Richard Hibbitt gave invaluable editorial help in the later stages of the preparation of the manuscript and provided the index. Dr Paul Barnaby advised on the composition of the timeline, which has been expertly compiled by Dr Stefano Evangelista. We are also indebted to Dr Evangelista for his scrupulous checking of the bibliographical entries. Thanks are owing also to Dr Alessandra Tosi, the project's MHRA Research Associate, and to Dr Rachel Polonsky, who supplied the brief bibliography of work in Russian relating to Pater.

List of Contributors

Maurizio Ascari is a lecturer in English literature at the University of Bologna. He is the author of *In the Palatial Chamber of the Mind: Comparative Studies on Henry James* (1997) and *La leggibilità de male: genealogia del romanzo poliziesco e del romanzo anarchico inglese* (1998). He has also edited and translated works by Henry James, Katherine Mansfield, Jack London and William Wilkie Collins.

Stephen Bann is Professor of History of Art at the University of Bristol, and a Fellow of the British Academy. He organized a conference on Pater at the University of Kent at Canterbury in 1994 to mark the centenary of Pater's death. The proceedings appeared in vol. 17 of *Comparative Criticism*, edited by Elinor Shaffer (1995), under the title *Walter Pater and the Culture of the Fin de Siècle*. He has also published extensively on the tradition of English aesthetic criticism, from Ruskin to Pater and Adrian Stokes. His most recent publications are *Parallel Lines: Printmakers, Painters and Photographers in Nineteenth-Century France* (2001), which was awarded the R. H. Gapper Prize for French Studies in 2002, and a monograph on the *Arte Povera* artist Jannis Kounellis (2003).

Jorge Miguel Bastos da Silva completed his undergraduate and graduate studies in the Faculty of Letters of the University of Oporto, where he now teaches English literature and culture. He has conducted research in that field, as well as in those of translation studies and utopian studies. He has published books on English Romantic poetry, *O véu do templo: contributo para uma topologia romântica* (1999), and the reception of Shakespeare in Portuguese Romanticism, *Shakespeare no romantismo português: factos, problemas, interpretaçoes* (2004), as well as an anthology of utopian chapbooks, *Utopias de cordel e textos afins* (2004).

Benedetta Bini is Professor of English Literature in the University of Tuscia (Viterbo). Her publications include *L'incanto della distanze: ritratti immaginari nella cultura del decadentismo* (1992), various essays on Pater, Wilde, Vernon Lee, William Wetmore Story, and late nineteenth-century travel writing. She has also edited and translated Wilde's *The Picture of Dorian Gray* (1991), Henry James's *The Figure in the Carpet* (2002), and edited Elizabeth Gaskell's *Crowley Castle* (2003) and a selection of Mary Cholmondeley's short stories (*Il gradino più basso*, 2003). She is currently working on *fin-de-siècle* fiction.

Elisa Bizzotto teaches English language and literature at the University of Venice-Ca' Foscari and the University of Trento. She has published essays on Pater, Wilde, Meredith and Dowson, and is the author of *La mano a l'anima: ll ritratto immagginario fin de siècle* (2001), which covers the imaginary portrait genre from Dante Gabriel Rossetti to Joyce and Woolf. She has recently completed an Italian translation of short stories by Dante Gabriel and Christina Rossetti, and is currently working on Vernon Lee and on European Decadence.

Bénédicte Coste teaches English at Stendhal University in Grenoble and is currently completing a dissertation on Pater in the Faculty of Psychoanalysis. She has published articles on psychoanalysis, Emily Brontë and Pater. Her French translation of a selection of Pater's texts was published under the title *Walter Pater: textes esthétiques* in 2003.

Emily Eells is *maître de conférences* at the University of Paris X – Nanterre. Her research on Proust and nineteenth-century British art and literature is presented in *Proust's Cup of Tea: Homoeroticism and Victorian Culture* (2002). Her recent publications on Anglo-French cultural exchange include 'Images of Proustian Inversion from Ruskin' in *Ruskin and Gender* (2002), and an article on Charlotte Brontë's use of French. She is now working on Proust's translation of Ruskin's *The Bible of Amiens*.

Stefano Evangelista is a junior research fellow at Merton College, Oxford, where he is working on Modernism, gender and the classics. He gained his doctorate from St Anne's College, Oxford, with a thesis on Pater's romantic Hellenism. He has published several articles on Pater, John Addington Symonds and Benjamin Jowett, and is currently writing a book on Pater and the Greeks.

Jacqueline A. Hurtley is a Professor of English Literature at the University of Barcelona and Head of the Department of English and German. Her PhD dealt with English literature in Spain following the Civil War and her *José Janés: editor de literatura inglesa* (1992) was awarded the Enrique García y Díez Research Prize by the Spanish Association for Anglo-American Studies (AEDEAN). She contributed to *Ireland in Writing: Interviews with Writers and Academics* (1998), and to *The Reception of Virginia Woolf in Europe* (2002), and is working to complete a biography of the founder of the British Council in Spain, Walter Starkie.

Wolfgang Iser is Professor Emeritus at the University of Constance, Germany, and a professor of English at the University of California, Irvine. His recent publications include *The Range of Interpretation*. He is working on a book entitled *How to Do Theory*.

Piotr Juszkiewicz is an Assistant Professor of Art History in the Adam Mickiewicz University in Poznan. His publications include: *Wolnosc I metafizyka: o tradycji artystycznej twórczosci Marcela Duchampa* (Freedom and metaphysics: on the artistic tradition of Marcel Duchamp) (1996), *Melacholia Jacka Malczewskiego* (Jacek Malczewski's 'Melancholy') (2002) and *Od salonu do galerii: Krytyka artystyczna I historyczna zmiana* (From salon to gallery: art criticism and historical change), in *Artium Quaestiones*, 13 (2002). He is working on Polish art criticism after 1945.

Martina Lauster is Professor of German and Director of the Centre for European Nineteenth-Century Studies at the University of Exeter. She works mainly on nineteenth-century literature in a European perspective, and is currently finishing a study on journalistic sketches (both written and graphic) of the 1830s and 1840s. Other interests include the essay as a literary form, the sonnet, the post-Christian ethic, dandyism and the aesthetics of 'l'art pour l'art'.

Maria Teresa Malafaia teaches English culture and visual culture at the Faculty of Letters, University of Lisbon. She has published widely on Victorian culture and gender and on Pre-Raphaelite art. She is currently engaged in the study of Victorian women essayists and representations of gender and race in the British Empire. She also works at the ULICES (University of Lisbon Centre for English Studies) where she is one of the coordinators of *Anglo-Saxónica*.

Martin Procházka, Professor of English, American and Comparative Literature, is the Head of the Department of English and American Studies at Charles University, Prague. He is the author of *Romantismus a osobnost* (Romanticism and personality, 1996), a critical study of English Romantic aesthetics, Coleridge and Byron. His forthcoming book, *Romantismus a romantismy* (Romanticism and romanticisms), written jointly with Zdenêk Hrbata, deals with principal distances in European and North American Romanticism. His work in progress is focused on heterogeneous forms and themes of heterogeneity in eighteenth-century literature and landscape gardening. He has published articles on Shakespeare, Romanticism and poststructuralism, and translated Byron's *Manfred* into Czech. He is the founding editor of an international academic journal, *Litteraria Pragensia*.

Ulrike Stamm lives and works in Berlin. Her study *'Ein Kritiker aus dem Willen der Natur: Hugo von Hofmannsthal und das Werk Walter Paters* appeared in 1997, when she also published an article on Pater as bridge between Romanticism and Modernism in *Nineteenth Century Prose*. Her more recent publications have been concerned with the Oriental travel accounts written by German female authors in the nineteenth century, on which she is preparing a book-length study.

Mihály Szegedy-Maszák has been Professor of Cultural History at Eötvös University, Budapest, since 1981. He has been a member of the Executive Council of the International Comparative Literature Association since 1991 and is currently a Vice-President. He is the author of books on the subject of Romanticism and realism, narratology and historical poetics, as well as a study of a nineteenth-century Hungarian novelist. He has been Visiting Professor at the University of Indiana on several occasions.

Lists of Essays by Pater

There is no current critical edition of Pater's complete writings. The great majority of his essays were originally published in the form of articles for newspapers and periodicals, and a few were delivered as lectures. Most of them were gathered together in collections in the course of his lifetime, and appeared in a number of editions before and after his death. Others were published posthumously. Macmillan and Co. acted as his publishers throughout his lifetime and continued to produce subsequent editions of his work. The original format chosen by Pater was succeeded by the 'Library Edition' (from 1910) and the 'Pocket Edition' (from 1924), with consequent changes in pagination.

In the only critical edition in English of any Pater work to date, Donald L. Hill chooses to follow the 1893 text of *The Renaissance*, which would have been the latest version of the full collection to be seen through press by Pater himself, since he died in 1894. However, Hill points out that even this text contains 'some errors'. (See Walter Pater, *The Renaissance: Studies in Art and Poetry: The 1893 Text*, edited, with textual and explanatory notes, by Donald L. Hill, Berkeley: University of California Press, 1980, p. x.) For the purposes of this volume, we can reasonably assume that the editions used by most of Pater's European readers were those that appeared around and subsequent to this date. It would serve little purpose to refer to earlier editions, or to the original periodical publications of the essays, though it is evident that some early readers would have had access to them.[1] Pater published in a range of periodicals: the *Fortnightly Review* was his most frequent outlet, while *Macmillan's Magazine*, *Contemporary Review* and *New Review* also featured several of his essays. Charles Shadwell's helpful preface to Pater's posthumous

---

[1] A clear example of reference to Pater's original periodical publications is the notice referring to his recent death, and recommending 'the last articles of Walter Pater' ('les derniers articles de Walter Pater') which appeared in T. de Wyzewa's running feature on foreign periodicals in the widely read *Revue des deux mondes* (15 August 1894, 935–38). A much earlier reference in a French periodical, which may indeed rank as one of the first records of Pater's European reception, is the notice dated 16 February 1876 in the chronicle of the sumptuous print connoisseurs' journal *L'Art* (Deuxième année, Vol.IV, p. 218). This signals the fact that Pater, 'the author of a remarkable volume of Essays on the art of the Renaissance' ('l'auteur d'un remarquable volume d'essais sur l'art de la Renaissance') has just published 'an admirable study of the Greek myth of Demeter and Persephone' ('une admirable étude sur le mythe grec de Demeter et Persephone') in the *Fortnightly Review*. The essay in question had appeared in the *Fortnightly Review* in January/February 1876. The chronicler of *L'Art* comments: 'The subject is no less brilliantly treated from an artistic point of view than in the literary respect' ('Le sujet n'est pas moins brillamment traité au point de vue artistique que sous le rapport littéraire').

Miscellaneous Studies (London: Macmillan, 1895, pp. vi–xiv) should be consulted for fuller bibliographical details.

The following abbreviated list will enable today's readers to appreciate the chronological sequence of the separate texts that formed the contents of Pater's essay collections. Individual essays often played an important part in disseminating his ideas. They are dated separately below, and grouped beneath the titles of the successive collections. Entries provide the dates of first publication, or delivery as a lecture where appropriate.

1873 *The Renaissance: Studies in Art and Poetry*
Preface (1873)
Aucassin and Nicolette (retitled 'Two Early French Stories' in 2nd edn)
    (1872)
Pico della Mirandola (1871)
Sandro Botticelli (1870)
Luca della Robbia (1873)
The Poetry of Michelangelo (1871)
Leonardo da Vinci (1869)
The School of Giorgione (1877: added to 3rd edn 1888)
Joachim du Bellay (1873)
Winckelmann (1867)
Conclusion (1868)

1887 *Imaginary Portraits*
A Prince of Court Painters (1885)
Denys l'Auxerrois (1886)
Sebastian van Storck (1886)
Duke Carl of Rosenmold (1887)

1889 *Appreciations: with an Essay on Style*
Style (1888)
Wordsworth (1874)
Coleridge (1866, revised 1880)
Charles Lamb (1878)
Sir Thomas Browne (1886)
'Love's Labour's Lost' (1878)
'Measure for Measure' (1874)
Shakespeare's English Kings (1889)
Aesthetic Poetry (based on 'Poems by William Morris', 1868)
Dante Gabriel Rossetti (1883)
Feuillet's 'La Morte' (1886)
Postscript (1889: first published as 'Romanticism', 1876)

1895 *Greek Studies*
A Study of Dionysus (1876)
The Bacchanals of Euripides (1889)
The Myth of Demeter and Persephone (1875)
Hippolytus Veiled (1889)
The Beginnings of Greek Sculpture (1880)

The Marbles of Aegina (1880)
The Age of Athletic Prizemen (1894)

1895 *Miscellaneous Studies*
Prosper Mérimée (1890)
Raphael (1892)
Pascal (1895)
Art Notes in North Italy (1890)
Notre Dame d'Amiens (1894)
Vézelay (1894)
Apollo in Picardy (1893)
The Child in the House (1878)
Emerald Uthwart (1892)
Diaphaneitè (1864)

1901 *Essays from 'The Guardian'*
English Literature (1886)
Amiel's 'Journal in time' (1886)
Browning (1887)
'Robert Elsmere' (1888)
Their Majesties' Servants (1888)
Wordsworth (1889)
Mr Gosse's Poems (1890)
Ferdinand Fabre (1889)
The 'Contes' of M. Auguste Filon (1890)

Timeline: European Reception of Pater

Year	Translations	Criticism
1885		**Italy**: Vernon Lee's 'La morale dell'estetica: appunti sul nuovo libro di Walter Pater' (on *Marius the Epicurean*), in *Fanfulla della domenica*.
1890		**Italy**: Enrico Nencioni's review of *Appreciations*, in *Nuova antologia*.
1894	**Austria**: First German-language translation. Hugo von Hofmannsthal translates extracts from 'Leonardo da Vinci' in his article 'Über moderne englische Malerei', in *Neue Revue* (Vienna).	**France**: Théodore de Wyzewa's 'Les derniers articles de Walter Pater', in *Revue des deux mondes*.
		Austria: Hugo von Hofmannsthal's article 'Walter Pater', in *Die Zeit*.
1895		**France**: Wyzewa's 'Deux figures d'écrivains anglais: Walter Pater et James Anthony Froude', in *Revue des deux mondes*.
1896		**France**: Wyzewa's 'Un roman posthume de Walter Pater' (on *Gaston de Latour*), in *Revue des deux mondes*.
1897		**Poland**: Leon Winiarski's series of five sketches on Pater, in *Prawda* (through 1901).
		Russia: Z. A. Vengerova's 'Val'ter Peter', in *Cosmopolis*.
1898	**France**: First French translation. 'Sebastian van Storck' (Georges Khnopff), in *Mercure de France*.	**Russia**: Vengerova's 'Val'ter Pater, 1839–94', in *Entsiklopedicheskii slovar*.
1899	**France**: First translation of *Imaginary Portraits* (Georges Khnopff).	

Year	Translations	Criticism
	Translation of 'Leonardo da Vinci' (Richard Irvine Best and Robert Darles), in *Mercure de France*.	
1900		**Germany**: Rudolf Kassner's *Die Mystik, die Künstler und das Leben: über englische Dichter und Maler im 19. Jahrhundert*.
1902	**Germany**: First translation of *The Renaissance* (Wilhelm Schölermann).	**Germany**: Rilke's review of the German translation of *The Renaissance*, in *Bremer Tageblatt*. **Italy**: Ulisse Ortensi's 'Letterati contemporanei: Walter Horatio Pater' (on *Marius* and *Imaginary Portraits*), in *Emporium*.
1904	**Germany**: First translation of *Greek Studies* (Wilhelm Dobbe).	**France**: Marcel Proust alludes to *Imaginary Portraits* and *Miscellaneous Studies* in the introduction to his translation of Ruskin's *The Bible of Amiens*.
	First translation of *Plato and Platonism* (Hans Hecht).	
		Hungary: Sándor Hevesi's 'Új görög renaissance', in *Magyar Szemle*.
1906		**Hungary**: Miháli Latkóczy's review 'Walter Pater: Griechische Studien', in *Egyetemes Philologiai Közlöny*.
1907	**Czech Lands**: First Czech translation of *Imaginary Portraits* (Jiří Živný)	
1908	**Russia**: First Russian translation of *Imaginary Portraits* and 'The Child in the House' (P. Muratov).	
1909	**Poland**: First Polish translation of a selection of Pater's essays (Stanisław Lack), including passages from *Plato and Platonism, Greek Studies, Imaginary Portraits* and *The Renaissance*.	**Italy**: Federico Olivero's 'Walter Pater ed i suoi studi sul Rinascimento', in *Studium*.
		Poland: C. J.'s (possibly by Cezary Jellenta) two short essays on Pater, in *Literatura i Sztuka*.

Year	Translations	Criticism
	'Luca della Robbia' (Maria Rakowska), in *Sfinks* (1909–10) 'Leonardo da Vinci' (possibly by Maria Rakowska), in *Literatura i Sztuka.*	
1910	**Poland**: Translation of 'Pico della Mirandola' (Maria Rakowska), in *Sfinks*.	**France**: Raymond Laurent's *Etudes anglaises*, containing a long essay on Pater.
1911	**Bohemia**: First Czech translation of *Marius* (Anna Fišerová), with an afterword by Miloš Marten First translation of *The Renaissance* (Máša Dvořáková).	**Norway**: Lorentz Julius Holtermann Eck dissertation (Oslo), 'Walter Pater'.
1912	**Hungary**: First translation of 'Sebastian van Storck' (Piroska Reichard), in *Budapesti Szemle.* **Italy**: First translation of *The Renaissance* (Aldo de Rinaldis). **Russia**: First translation of *The Renaissance* (S. G. Zaimovskii).	**Hungary**: Piroska Reichard's 'Walter Pater', in *Budapesti Szemle.* **Italy**: Reviews of De Rinaldis's translation of *The Renaissance* by Roberto Longhi, in *La Voce*, and by Giuseppe Severio Gargano, in *Il Marzocco.*
1913	**Bohemia**: New Czech translation of *The Renaissance* (Jan Reichmann). **Hungary**: First translation of *The Renaissance* (Károly Sebestyén). **Italy**: First translation of *Imaginary Portraits* (Aldo de Rinaldis). **Norway**: First translation of *The Renaissance* (Ingeborg von der Lippe Konow).	**Germany**: E. J. Bock's 'Walter Paters Einfluß auf Oscar Wilde', in *Bonner Studien zur englischen Philologie.* **Italy**: Emilio Cecchi's '*Ritratti immaginari* di W. H. Pater', in *La Tribuna.* Giulio Caprin's 'Critica e immaginazione: i *Ritratti immaginari* di W. Pater', in *Il Marzocco.*
1914	**Hungary**: First translation of *Greek Studies* (László Kőszegi).	**Italy**: Federico Olivero's *Studi sul romanticismo inglese.*
1917	**France**: First translation of *The Renaissance* (Firmin Roger-Cornaz).	

Year	Translations	Criticism
1918		**France**: Paul Souday's review '*La Renaissance*', in *Le Temps*. Régis Michaud's *Mystiques et Réalistes Anglo-Saxons*, including a chapter on Pater's paganism. **Italy**: Federico Olivero's *Nuovi saggi di letteratura inglese*.
1922	**France**: First translation of *Marius* (E. Coppinger).	
1923	**France**: First translation of *Plato and Platonism* (Samuel Jankélévitch). **France**: Charles Du Bos delivers series of lectures on Pater to audiences in André Maurois's apartment.	**France**: Georges Duthuit's *Le Rose et le Noir, de Walter Pater à Oscar Wilde*.
1924	**Austria**: 'Sebastian van Storck' (H. H. Voight). **France**: 'Vézelay: Essai d'histoire d'art religieux' (L. Vignes). **Portugal**: Excerpt from 'Leonardo da Vinci' (Fernando Pessoa), in *Athena: revista de arte*.	**France**: Madeleine Cazamian's review article on the French translations of *The Renaissance* and *Plato and Platonism*, in *Revue anglo-américaine*.
1925		**France**: Mary Duclaux's 'Souvenirs sur Walter Pater', in *La Revue de Paris*. **Italy**: Vincenzo Golzio's 'Walter Pater critico d'arte', in *L'arte*.
1926		**France**: Gabriel Mourey's 'Marcel Proust, John Ruskin et Walter Pater', in *Le Monde nouveau*.
1927		**Italy**: Vittorio Lugli's 'Una visita a Ronsard', in *Il Baretti*. **Germany**: Hans Hecht's 'Walter Pater: eine Würdigung', in *Deutsche Vierteljahrsschrift für Literaturwissenschaft und Geistesgeschichte*.

Year	Translations	Criticism
1928		**France**: Ramon Fernandez's 'Note sur l'esthétique de Proust' (comparative study of Pater and Proust), in *La Nouvelle Revue française*.
1929		**Poland**: Zbigniew Grabowski's *Walter Pater: Życie-dzieło-styllz*.
1930	**France**: New translation of *Imaginary Portraits* (Philippe Neel).	**Italy**: Mario Praz's *La carne, la morte e il diavolo nella letteratura romantica* (*The Romantic Agony*). **France**: Charles Du Bos's 'Sur *Marius l'Épicurien* et Walter Pater', in *Le Roseau d'or*.
1931		**France**: Albert Farmer's *Le Mouvement 'esthétique' et décadent en Angleterre, 1873–1900*, and *Walter Pater as a Critic of English Literature: A Study of Appreciations*. Louise Rosenblatt's *L'Idée de l'art pour l'art dans la littérature anglaise pendant la période victorienne*.
1938	**Spain**: First Catalan translation of *The Renaissance* (Marià Manent).	
1939	**Italy**: First translation of *Marius* (Linda Storoni Mazzolani).	**Germany/Switzerland**: Rudolf Borchardt's 'Walter Pater zu seinem hundertsten Geburtstag', in *Sonntagsblatt der Basler Nachrichten*. **Italy**: Federico Olivero's *Il pensiero religioso ed estetico di Walter Pater*.
1941	**Hungary**: New translation of the description of the *Mona Lisa* (József Szigeti) and translation of an extract from 'A Prince of Court Painters' (Piroska Reichard), included in the anthology of English literature *Az angol irodalom kincsesháza* (ed. Gábor Halász).	
1942	**Spain**: First Castilian translation of *Imaginary Portraits* (J. Farrán y Mayoral).	

Year	Translations	Criticism
1943		**Italy**: Marialuisa Gengaro's 'La "critica immaginativa" di Walter Pater (1839–1894)', in *La Nuova Italia*.
1944	**Italy**: *Pater: scelta e traduzione* (Mario Praz), including passages from *The Renaissance, Imaginary Portraits, Miscellaneous Studies, Marius* and *Greek Studies*. New translation of *Imaginary Portraits* (Praz), including 'The Child in the House' and 'Apollo in Picardy'. **Spain**: First Castilian translation of *Marius* (Agustín Esclasans).	
1945	**Spain**: First Castilian translation of *The Renaissance* (J. Farrán y Mayoral).	
1946	**Germany**: First translation of *Imaginary Portraits* (Ernst Sander). **Italy**: New translation of *The Renaissance* (Mario Praz). **Spain/Argentina**: First Castilian translation of *Plato and Platonism* (Vicente P. Quintero).	
1950	**Netherlands**: *De levende gedachten van Walter Pater* (R. van Brakell Buys).	
1951		**Germany**: Wilhelm Vollrath's *Verschwiegenes Oxford: Matthew Arnold, Goethe u. Walter Pater, Fellow of Brasenose*.
1960		**Germany**: Wolfgang Iser's *Walter Pater: die Autonomie des Ästhetischen*.
1961		**Finland**: Aulis Kurkinen's *Imagery in Walter Pater*. **France**: Germain d'Hangest's *Walter Pater, l'homme et l'œuvre*. **Italy**: Dario Gazzoni-Pisani's *Walter Pater: critico d'arte*.
1963	**France**: 'L'Ecole de Giorgione' (Robert André), in *La Nouvelle Revue Française*.	**France**: Robert André's 'Walter Pater et Marcel Proust', in *La Nouvelle Revue française*.

Year	Translations	Criticism
1967	**Hungary**: New translation of 'Leonardo' (István Jánosy), in his *Hagyomány és egyéniség* (a selection of English essays).	
1970	**Italy**: Revised reprint of the 1939 translation of *Marius*, with an essay by Mario Praz.	
1972		**France**: Germain d'Hangest's 'La place de Walter Pater dans le mouvement esthétique', in *Etudes anglaises*. **Italy**: Mario Praz's *Il patto col serpente* (containing two essays on Pater).
1976	**Netherlands**: 'Leonardo da Vinci' (H. Martens).	
1982	**Romania**: *The Renaissance* (Iolanda Mecu). **Spain**: New Castilian translation of *The Renaissance* (no translator acknowledged).	**France**: John J. Conlon's *Walter Pater and the French Tradition* (publ. USA). **Italy**: Roberto Barbolini's *Il sileno capovolto. Socrate nella cultura fin de siècle: Nietzsche, Pater e d'Annunzio*.
1985	**France**: *Essais sur l'art et la Renaissance* (Anne Henry), including passages from *The Renaissance, Appreciations, Plato and Platonism* and *Greek Studies*.	
1987		**Germany**: Hildegard Hummel's 'Reflexe der ästhetischen Konzeption Walter Paters im Werk Rudolf Borchardts', in *Germanisch-Romanische Monatsschrift*. **Portugal**: Maria Teresa Malafaia's '*Marius the epicurean: his sensations and ideas* – Marius e Psyché ou a reconciliação das polaridades', in *Anglo-Saxónica*.
1992	**France**: New translation of *Marius* (Guillaume de Villeneuve).	**Italy**: Benedetta Bini's *L'incanto della distanza: ritratti immaginari nella cultura del decadentismo*.

Year	Translations	Criticism
	L'Enfant dans la maison (Pierre Leyris), includes 'The Child in the House', 'Emerald Uthwart', 'Apollo in Picardy' and 'Hippolytus Veiled' *Walter Pater: La Renaissance et l'esprit de la modernité* (Hélène Bokanowski), translation of the 'Preface' and the 'Conclusion'	
1993	**Netherlands**: 'Sebastian van Storck' (Iain Macintyre).	**Portugal**: Maria Teresa Malafaia's 'Cultura e identidade: ou a forma como Edward Said nos recorda Walter Pater', in *Actas do XVI Encontro da Associaçäo Portuguesa de Estudos Anglo-Americanos*.
1994	(Centenary of Pater's death) **Italy**: New translation of *Imaginary Portraits* (Franco Marucci), also including 'An English Poet' and 'Apollo in Picardy'. Translation of *Greek Studies* (Vittoria Caterina Caratozzolo).	
1995	**Italy**: First translation of *Gaston de Latour* (Franco Marucci).	
1996		**Italy**: Elisa Bizzotto and Franco Marucci's (eds.), *Walter Pater (1839–1894). Le forme della modernità. The Forms of Modernity* (proceedings of the International Conference on Pater held in Venice in December 1994).
1997	**Spain**: New translation of *Marius* (Rafael Lassaletta).	**Austria/Germany**: Ulrike Stamm's *'Ein Kritiker aus dem Willen der Natur': Hugo von Hofmannsthal und das Werk Walter Paters*.
1998	**France**: Authoritative edition of *Plato and Platonism* (Jean-Baptiste Picy). **Netherlands**: *Imaginary Portraits* and 'Apollo in Picardy' (Gerlof Janzen). **Poland**: First full translation of *The Renaissance* (Piotr Kopszak).	**Russia**: Rachel Polonsky's *English Literature and the Russian Aesthetic Renaissance*.

Year	Translations	Criticism
1999	**Italy**: *Walter Pater critico di Shakespeare* (Maria Luisa de Rinaldis), contains 'Love's Labours Lost', 'Measure for Measure' and 'Shakespeare's English Kings'. **Spain**: New translation of *The Renaissance* (Marta Salís).	**Hungary**: Aladár Sarbu's 'The Lure of Lacedæmon: A Note on Pater and Modernism', in Péter Szaffkó and Tamás Bényei (eds.), *Happy Returns: Essays for Professor István Pálffy*.
2001	**Italy**: New translation of *Marius* (Alberto Rossatti).	**Italy**: Elisa Bizzotto's *La Mano e l'Anima: il ritratto immaginario fin de siècle*. **Germany**: Thomas Lütkemeier's *Chez soi: The Aesthetic Self in Arthur Schopenhauer, Walter Pater and T. S. Eliot*.
2003	**France**: Bénédicte Coste's *Walter Pater: textes esthétiques* **Spain**: 'Style' (Luis Martínez Victorio).	

Introduction

Stephen Bann

Taking stock of Walter Pater's European reception through this collection of essays has been an instructive, but by no means a simple assignment. Here is an author whose reputation in his native country has survived a long series of peaks and troughs, readjustments and reappraisals. An editorial in the *Times Literary Supplement* for 5 August 1939 asserted hopefully: 'Time has almost dissolved the grosser misunderstandings of Pater' (Bertocci 1955, 178). But this onset of confidence was without any doubt premature. Scarcely had the Second World War come to an end when the reputation of Pater in his own country went into a virtual eclipse, heralding what Bénédicte Coste describes in this volume as his 'relative disappearance from the English canon in the third quarter of the twentieth century'. Any broad-based account of the subsequent revival of interest in Pater in the English-speaking world would be bound to acknowledge that it was the American academy that then came to the fore. It had already in the prewar period provided one of Pater's most thoughtful defenders in the person of the ex-Balliol undergraduate and brother-in-law of Bernard Berenson, Logan Pearsall Smith. It would return to the lists in restoring his damaged reputation from the 1970s onwards.[2] According to Harold Bloom's confident prediction at the outset, Pater not only deserved recognition for his role as a harbinger of Modernism, but merited a stake in the future as Postmodernism's 'valued precursor' (Bloom 1974, xxxi). Reverberations from this weighty judgement can be detected in many of the more recent European writings on Pater that are discussed here.

In the shadow of Ruskin and Wilde

For the half-century following Pater's death, such a conviction of his lasting importance was rarely to be found. In Europe, as in Britain, the pattern of Pater's reception was at first a chequered one, though this was for different reasons, and European reservations persisted on the whole for a briefer period. This was due in part to the great difficulty (also apparent in the English-speaking world, but to a lesser degree) of extricating Pater's distinctive and personal contribution from the overbearing proximity of two roughly contemporary figures who easily surpassed him in posthumous fame: John Ruskin and Oscar Wilde. In the case of France, for example, the devoted

---

[2] A helpful interim report on this process is provided by R. M. Seiler of the University of Calgary in his bibliographical article, 'Walter Pater Studies: 1970–1980' (Dodd 1981, 84–95).

exegesis pioneered by Robert de la Sizeranne's *Ruskin et la religion de la beauté* (1898) was followed up directly by a spate of translations in the first years of the new century. This could be said to have cut off Pater's oxygen. At least it hindered his own more modest body of work from being considered in its own right. As Emily Eells records here, Mallarmé took good note on his visit to Oxford of 1894 that 'the most consummate prose-writer alive live[d] there'. But no palpable results emerged from this recognition. Nor had they done so a decade before in response to Paul Bourget's almost equally admiring tribute.

Eells clearly shows, however, that there were more covert strategies at work among French writers. As we may now conclude on the basis of her research, Proust, for one, would have had his own reasons for depreciating Pater's importance by comparison with the achievement of Ruskin. Eells's essay uses manuscript sources, and detailed comparison between the texts of both authors, to indicate how Pater surreptitiously functioned as an 'occult influence' for Proust, though his actual name was sedulously excised from the drafts of *A la recherche du temps perdu*.

The conflation of Pater's work with the overwhelming legacy of Ruskin has also proved a factor inhibiting his reception in other European countries. No European critic has come forward to assume with Bloom's degree of confidence the task of uncoupling him from his Victorian predecessor, and promoting him as 'the father of the Anglo-American Modernism' (xxxi). Ruskin's widespread European reputation survived into the twentieth century with a remarkable tenacity, largely as a result of the fact that his writings on the social role of art and architecture became the textbook for advanced artists and designers of many persuasions. Several of the essays in this collection refer accordingly to the impact that his ideas still possessed in Europe after the turn of the century. As Mihály Szegedy-Maszák indicates, the high prestige of the Arts and Crafts movement in Hungary (and Central Europe generally) developed as a necessary counterweight to the growing hegemony of Germany. Thus it continued to provide a conduit for Ruskin's message, but allowed little room for the acknowledgement of Pater's less practice-orientated contribution to contemporary culture. This habit of viewing Pater in the shadow of Ruskin has died hard, and indeed seems to have survived until quite recently among members of the European artistic establishment. In France, according to Bénédicte Coste, Pater was dismissed as no more than a 'Ruskinian epigone' by the most influential French art historian of the last generation, André Chastel.

Such reluctance to extricate Pater's legacy from that of Ruskin, whether as a result of mere ignorance (on the part of Chastel) or (in Proust's case) cunning literary subterfuge, was however by no means universal. From the first years following his death, there were European readers who studied Pater attentively, and were able to recognize his differences not only from Ruskin, but from any other possible competitor in his chosen domain of aesthetic and critical writing. It was in Italy, no doubt, that this conviction of the distinctive character of his contribution proved most durable. On the face of it, the explanation is a simple one. Pater devoted a large and important section of his writings to the study of Italian art, and enabled the Italians to rediscover aspects of their national heritage through the intermediacy of his poetic prose.

Lionello Venturi's pioneering history of art criticism, published in 1948, acclaimed Pater as 'the most notable exponent of idealist art criticism'. Maurizio Ascari's essay for this collection breaks new ground in focusing on the successive stages through which Pater's contribution to art criticism – an aspect only rarely stressed in the English-speaking literature – has been acknowledged and then assimilated by Italian critics and art historians.

All things told, any lingering confusion there may be in distinguishing the contributions of these two prime exponents of 'Aesthetic criticism' has probably been less detrimental in its consequences than the distorting effect on Pater's reputation brought about by a retrospective identification with his one-time disciple, Oscar Wilde.[3] Although Wilde's trial and subsequent disgrace took place shortly after Pater's death, his rehabilitation both as an author and as an exemplary figure striving for social and sexual freedom could be shown to have had more than incidental implications for the repute of his more closeted mentor. To the extent that Wilde was gradually elevated almost to the status of a Christ-like martyr born out of his time, his mentor emerged in the unflattering guise of a *sotto voce* John the Baptist.

This is in fact the precise image used to qualify their relationship when the satirical diatribe entitled *Le Rose et le noir* was published in 1923. Relying for the most part on the abundant but often unreliable material provided by Pater's biographer Thomas Wright, the young French critic Georges Duthuit here contrived to present Wilde as a living exemplar of Pater's ideas, while poking fun simultaneously at what he characterized as Pater's hesitant attempts at transgression. Duthuit's purpose was certainly not to lionize Wilde by comparison with Pater, but rather to ridicule master and pupil alike. But his book can perhaps be viewed as a foretaste of how the rising generation of the interwar period would indeed tend to elevate the former at the latter's expense. Wilde would accrue credit on the basis that he had been courageous enough to follow his own instincts, and had suffered catastrophically for doing so. Pater, by contrast, would come across as a half-hearted figure, who tried to camouflage his forbidden desires beneath the pallid veils of fiction.

Duthuit's case will be examined later in this introduction, since his hostility is a product of his privileged, though indirect, knowledge of Pater's Oxford reputation. Yet the invidious comparison with Wilde that Duthuit promoted was also taken up by other commentators who, unlike Duthuit, focused their attention not on Pater's life but on his texts. Marguerite Yourcenar, to take one telling example, seems to have much resented the suggestion by a publisher's reader that her *Mémoires d'Hadrien* would invite direct comparison with *Marius the Epicurean* (Bann 2002, 56–7). She argued that Pater's fictional representation of the ancient world was quite lacking in the firm historical basis that was her own safeguard as a novelist, and that her older friend Charles Du Bos's excessive regard for Pater was a sign of weakness. In view of her

---

[3] Bertocci cites an article from an English-speaking source published in 1932 in which it was stressed that Pater was 'becoming detached more and more from Wilde and even the Victorian age' (Bertocci 1955, 188). This must however presumably be set against the tradition of a close identification, no doubt even more persuasive in the European context, over the intervening period.

own personal interest in the historical development of same-sex relationships, she coupled this disregard for Pater with a much more sympathetic interest in the life and work of Wilde.[4]

In the English-speaking world, it has to be said, the tendency to mummify great writers and artists in copious biographies has continued to work to the benefit of Wilde and to the detriment of Pater. Wilde's stock has climbed to ever new heights, partly as a result of the popular success of the outstanding biography by Richard Ellman. On the other hand, Michael Levey's *The Case of Walter Pater* (Levey 1978) – the first biography to be published since the early efforts of A. C. Benson and Thomas Wright – indicated that, lacking the animus of a Georges Duthuit, a conventional biographer of Pater would end up with precious little substance to satisfy the reader. In the absence of any significant documentary evidence for his later life, the fictions that Pater invented, and the myths that he embroidered, are all there is to flavour the thin gruel on which readers avid for biographical particularities hope to slake their thirst. Successive attempts to 'out' Pater in recent years have also had to confront, from their varying levels of sophistication, the tantalizing ambiguity of his life story. Strong readings there have certainly been, in the Bloomian sense of the term. But, if we are inclined to accept Bloom's own formulation – that Pater successfully evacuated Ruskin's aestheticism of its moral content – this undercover return of a new variety of moralism flies in the face of Pater's achievement as a writer and thinker.

Yet the very fact that such new emphases have brought about a certain polarization of Pater criticism in the English-speaking world is all the more reason for giving more close attention to the long-term history of his reception throughout Europe. Without any doubt, the European balance sheet has been, and remains, extremely positive. But it should also prove extremely relevant to any global reassessment of Pater's reputation as it stands today. Judged by the high quality of the critical insights and interpretations that Pater has generated in Europe over the past century, the record compares, indeed, more than favourably with the very intermittent attention paid to him in his native country. This may well be for the reason that – discounting one or two cases of personal contact between our diffident author and representatives of the following generation – the European experience of Pater was gathered almost exclusively from the reading of his texts. Thus it was Pater's unusual literary construction of subjectivity, rather than its coefficient in biography, that proved to be of overriding interest to Hofmannsthal, to Pessoa, and no doubt also to Proust, who was not devoid of ideas of his own about the oblique relation of an author's persona to the experience of his writings. Admittedly, the lure of Pater's Oxford milieu, to which non-native writers like Du Bos, Duthuit and Pearsall Smith reacted in their very different ways, did acquire a mythic character for those few foreign adherents (or assailants) who had the chance to acquaint themselves with it.

---

[4]   See Yourcenar 1929. Nigel Saint mentions that the theme of sexual ambivalence that is 'prominent in this early essay' is toned down in the second version published by Yourcenar in 1982, 'Wilde rue des Beaux-Arts' (Saint 2000, 53).

For the majority of European commentators, however, Oxford's reputation played no major role in determining Pater's legacy.

Pater's legacy in Europe

Taking into account, then, the relative lack of biographical (or more broadly cultural) interest attaching to him, it would surely be wrong to think of Pater as having been overmuch disadvantaged in the European domain by the comparison with Ruskin and Wilde. The very success of both Ruskin and Wilde in having their names attached to some of the most wide-ranging social and cultural movements of the modern age has arguably turned out to be a double-edged triumph. Whilst it has encouraged the diffusion of their fame, it may also have entailed the oversimplification of their respective messages. Each in turn has come to stand for a whole climate of modern opinion. On the other hand, Pater's highly individual legacy – being fundamentally wedded to the reading of his books – is for that reason more easily traceable in terms of the intricate history of their translation and critical interpretation. Whether we choose to consider those countries that have had a long history of Pater studies – particularly Italy and France – or countries where his works have impinged in a more piecemeal or conjunctural fashion, this process of reception turns out to be significant in a variety of different ways.

It will come as no surprise that the different patterns of response are in close accord with the historical development of the European national cultures, especially as regards the major issue of their respective receptions of Modernism. In some countries featured here, for example Portugal or Czechoslovakia in the first quarter of the twentieth century, the record of Pater's reception comes down essentially to a question of specific modernist writers who responded very positively to aspects of Pater's message. The side of Pater that comes to the fore in these cases is thus in accordance with the logic of the historical and cultural context; as often as not, his role in critical discourse is tailored to the needs of literary polemic, or harnessed to major projects of national regeneration, that reflect a particular time and place. Yet simultaneously in some other countries – Italy being the prime example – such individual acts of appropriation by a succession of writers come to appear more than just isolated phenomena. In the long run, they start to add up, and contribute to the formation of an identifiable tradition of Pater studies.

Even in the case of Italy, which arguably has the longest and fullest record of engagement with Pater's work, such a tradition has not been without occasional interruptions. What we can take stock of now is the gradually formed product of the large number of different impulses and inflections given to Pater studies in Italy over a period of more than a century, beginning in the author's own lifetime. It would be misleading to imply that Pater's Italian reception exhibited any profound consistency across the decades. Yet, as Elisa Bizzotto justly points out in her wide-ranging essay, its development still has a special coherence from the Italian point of view. This is because the rising interest in Pater has closely paralleled the birth of English studies as an academic discipline in Italian universities. To the extent that English studies became, over the twentieth century as a whole, more and more firmly entrenched within the Italian academy, Pater's work also began to merge successfully with the body of contemporary Italian literary culture. One can only conclude that the continuing, lively interest in new critical editions and translations of Pater that is so marked a feature of the Italian scene is a manifest symptom of this assimilation. It is never just a matter of resurrecting yet another little-known English piece of writing.

From the outset of this collection of essays, then, we can take it for granted that Italy offers exceptionally rich materials for tracking the fortunes of Pater's work throughout Europe. The French engagement with his work, starting as it does with the signs of what Emily Eells calls 'occult influence' – and following quite a different pattern of assimilation – proves to be hardly less significant. But before we summarize briefly the contrasts between these two national scenes, it is worth making some preliminary conclusions about Pater's reception outside the Latin world that he esteemed so highly. It would be wrong to underplay the evidence of Pater's reception in the German-speaking countries, or, more broadly speaking, in the linguistic communities of Central Europe both within and adjoining the former Austro-Hungarian Empire. Here Pater's impact has proved, at particular times and in the case of specific authors, surprisingly intense.

As early as 1894, the year of the writer's death, the Austrian Hugo von Hofmannsthal was already acknowledging his debt to Pater, and enthusiastically seeking to spread the knowledge of Pater's writings to his own ever-widening intellectual circle. This attachment to Pater on Hofmannsthal's part was justified by a thorough acquaintance with his major writings, and a desire to identify with what Hofmannsthal took to be the main focus of his ideas. As Robert Vilain has argued elsewhere, Pater's reception in the cultural centres of the German-speaking world was encouraged by the conjunction of three major factors working simultaneously: the reaction against Naturalism in German literature itself, the accompanying tendency towards a certain anglophilia, and the strong revival of interest in the Italian Renaissance. All three strains met together in the person of the young Hugo von Hofmannsthal (Vilain 2002, 63).

Moreover this intense preoccupation with Pater's writings permeated Hofmannsthal's work on a deeper level than such receptivity to certain key ideas would of itself warrant. As Ulrike Stamm demonstrates here, the Austrian writer's meditation on the famous 'Conclusion' to *The Renaissance* created an inner ferment whose effects can be detected in the fine nuances of his choice of language, as well in the close attention that he pays to the philosophical underpinning of his early poetic work. For several years subsequent to the composition of these early poems, Hofmannsthal's high opinion of Pater's work continued to receive an airing both in his critical reviews and in his personal correspondence. Hofmannsthal ultimately made no secret of the fact that that he had some reservations about *Marius the Epicurean*. But he never ceased to hold *Imaginary Portraits* in the highest esteem.

Evidence is also produced in the essays that follow of Pater's reception, on a rather different level, by various writers living in Hungary and former Czechoslovakia. I have to confess at this point that for the majority of the Slavic countries – Serbia, for example – it has not proved possible to find any very significant source for the study of his reception, whether it be through translations or through critical commentaries. Even Russia is absent from the group of essays, though a listing of a small number of relevant Russian entries may be found in the concluding bibliography.[5] However, Poland has emerged as a striking exception to this rule. In his essay, Piotr Juszkiewicz underlines the importance for Polish letters of Pater's contribution to the ethos of the 'Young Poland' movement of the turn of the century. This was signalled in part by a number of short translations of his essays, but more notably by a number of absorbing critical discussions that centred upon Pater's notion of subjective agency in history. As Juszkiewicz concludes, the premature death of Stanislaw Brzozowski unfortunately cut short the writing career of the Polish critic who had most appreciated and identified with the psychological aspects of Pater's work.

There would be no point in trying to elicit a common pattern from these various strands of Central European reception. But it is worth stressing that German writers in the strictest sense of the word did not play a very significant role in Pater's diffusion. Wolfgang Iser makes it clear in his contribution that, in Germany as opposed to Austria, Pater never really figured as a figure of central importance. An exception should be made for the highly important essay of 1939 by Rudolf Borchardt (originally published in Basel and analysed here by Martina Lauster). Apart from this, however, there would appear to have be no interwar discussion of Pater in a specifically German context that is worth investigating. Borchardt himself, we can say, is the exception that proves the rule. His intense preoccupation with Pater can be attributed to a great extent to his own close personal involvement with Hofmannsthal.

Nor has Pater's work succeeded in acquiring much greater prominence in the development of the postwar cultural debate in Germany. Iser's study of 1950 remains another noteworthy exception to the rule, but in this light it is revealing to adduce the specific reason why he originally undertook to write on such a comparatively disregarded literary figure. What comes out of Iser's retrospective view in the essay that follows is the important point that his critical strategy at the time was addressed to the general, worldwide situation in postwar literary studies. There was nothing exclusively German, or indeed specifically European, about the dilemma that he was trying to address. Iser was thus seeking to find a middle way between the old-fashioned but persistent tradition of 'life and letters' still current in Europe, and the discipline of close reading pioneered by the New Criticism. Pater's texts, for all their relative obscurity in the German context, enabled him to plot an alternative direction to these well-trodden paths.

Patterns of reception in Italy and France

I will continue, then, by looking in more detail at the course that Pater's reception has taken in Italy and France, the two countries where it has proved both durable and significant over a long period. This is attested even in the

---

[5]   See p. 279. I am greatly indebted to Dr Rachel Polonsky for providing this information about Russian translations of Pater. These did not, however, in her estimation, provide material substantial enough for a full essay.

recent past by the admirable critical editions of individual works that have been published in both countries over the past decade. Although the need has been well recognized for over twenty years, there still exists no standard critical edition of Pater's works in their original language. With the exception of *The Renaissance* (published in a useful critical edition by Donald L. Hill in 1980), the book texts still in circulation are mainly those of the frequently reprinted Library and pocket editions that entered production during and shortly after the author's lifetime (see Dodd 1981, 74–83). There is no equivalent in English to Franco Marucci's translation and edition of *Imaginary Portraits*, which came out in 1994 and ranks as the third Italian publication of this work in the course of the century, nor of Paola Colaiacomo's recent critical edition and translation of *Greek Studies*. Jean-Baptiste Picy's annotated French edition of *Plato and Platonism* could be seen as an even more surprising recent development, since it is not primarily directed at French students of English literature. It puts the emphasis on the quality of Pater's thought as being philosophically important in its own right, rather than simply as a representative product of a certain nineteenth-century historical mentality.

This comparison between recent editions apart, there is undoubtedly still a genuine disparity between the responses to Pater in Italy and France, as they have developed over the years. The appearance of successive translations has followed a quite different rhythm in the two countries, and as a result the major critical discussions have rarely taken a parallel course. Italy was without question the first European country to welcome and (we might say) domesticate several aspects of Pater's work, although (as Benedetta Bini reminds us) it is more accurate to conceive of this process extending through a succession of regional focuses, rather than provoking any simultaneous nationwide response. Pater's fame spread from 'the hills around Florence', in the first instance, to be celebrated at a rather later stage in the salons of Rome. It was however to be in Naples, finally, that the first translations of *Imaginary Portraits* and *The Renaissance* were published, in 1912 and 1913 respectively.

Indispensable as the go-between who first established Pater's name in Italian literary circles was the English writer and Florentine resident Vernon Lee (Violet Paget) who had kept in touch with Pater since meeting him in Oxford in 1881, and (as Bini recounts) made a sadly fruitless attempt to acquaint him with the Roman intelligentsia during his Italian visit of 1883. In 1894 – the year of Pater's death, and also of the publication by Hofmannsthal of his German translation of the famous passage on the Mona Lisa from 'Leonardo da Vinci' – the critic Angelo Conti showed his colours by placing an epigraph from Pater at the beginning of his study of the Venetian painter Giorgione, the subject of a second memorable essay in *The Renaissance*. By 1900, when the Roman author Gabriele d'Annunzio published his novel *Il fuoco* (*The Flame*), with its thinly disguised contemporary aesthetes as protagonists, Pater had become securely established in Rome as a new critical voice enshrining a special significance for the devotees of the Italian *fin de siècle*.

The Paterian vogue in Italy had thus run well ahead of the availability of translations into Italian. Moreover the Neapolitan editions of 1912/13 were not followed up – with the exception of a reprint of de Rinaldis's *The Renaissance* in 1925 – until *Marius the Epicurean* was finally published in Italian in 1939. In France, the first years of the same period were marked by a dearth of public references to Pater in the press, despite the existence of a few translations and a number of essays on his work. Emily Eells's deductions about the unacknowledged debt of Proust to Pater have been mentioned earlier. She also cites pioneering articles in the *Revue des deux mondes* by Théodore de Wyzewa dating from 1890 and 1894, and Georges Khnopff's translation of *Imaginary Portraits* which appeared in 1899. Yet these publications seem to have generated very little further interest at the time. Certainly the approving remarks made with reference to Pater by Paul Bourget, and then by Mallarmé after his Oxford meeting of February 1894, cannot compare with the adulation offered up in the same years by d'Annunzio and his circle. Significantly, Eells's second main focus for the early period, apart from Proust, is a little-known but extraordinary essay by the young writer Raymond Laurent, published after his suicide in Venice in 1910. This would seem to have achieved virtually no public circulation. Pater's critical fortunes in France only began to pick up in 1917 with the publication of the French translation of *The Renaissance*, which was followed by that of *Marius the Epicurean* in 1922.

Whether or not Ruskin's prior claim on their attention was partly responsible, the French had kept their distance from Pater in the twenty years that followed his death. But they would compensate for this omission with a new and intensive attention to both translated and untranslated works from the mid-1920s onwards. Pater's collection of essays entitled *Greek Studies*, which had not been translated anywhere, but whose influence was already perceptible in d'Annunzio's *Il fuoco*, was to exert a lasting fascination on André Gide (Bann 2002, 59). It was moreover a young Catholic critic in Gide's circle, Charles Du Bos, who made it his mission to explain to his fellow countrymen the greatness of *Marius*, still by general consent (as Hofmannsthal well recognized) Pater's most problematic as well as his lengthiest work.[6]

Du Bos and Duthuit: conflicting French views of Pater in the 1920s

There could hardly be a more telling sign of ambivalent reactions to Pater among the French critics of this generation than the fact that Du Bos's major, and frankly admiring, essay on *Marius* – delivered as a lecture in André Maurois's apartment in February 1923 (Du Bos 1946, 229) – was conceived in the same year as Georges Duthuit's satirical denunciation of Pater and Wilde, *Le Rose et le noir*. The former was at first intended as part of a book-length study of Pater, provisionally entitled *Walter Pater, ou l'ascète de la beauté*, which would have incorporated discussion of the 'Pater–Wilde problem' (Bertocci 1955, 189). But its central aim would certainly not have been biographical. As the existing essay makes clear, Du Bos's intention would have been to follow through the entire corpus of Pater's writings, with the aim of demonstrating the 'spiritual evolution of Pater from the "Conclusion" of *The Renaissance* to

---

[6] Gide placed *Marius* among what he called 'pseudo-novels of genius', a category which also included *Tristram Shandy* and *A la recherche du temps perdu* (Bann 2002, 59).

Marius and *Plato and Platonism*' (186). In this scenario, Wilde would only have played a supporting role.

Duthuit, on the other hand, paid very little attention at all to Pater's writings – and he actually mistook the publication date of *The Renaissance*, crediting it to 1870 rather than 1873. Instead, he spent much of the time raking through the motley mass of vaguely compromising materials that had been brought together in Thomas Wright's compendious biography of 1907. In particular, he lent far too much credence to the testimony of the egregious Richard Jackson, who seems to have virtually blackmailed Wright into ascribing him a prime position in Pater's personal life.[7] Having convicted Pater of being 'the father of all the English aesthetes to come'[8] (Duthuit 1974, 69), Duthuit then pressed on to the conclusion that Pater's favoured successor was the doomed figure of Oscar Wilde: 'Dorian Gray Wilde is the Messiah announced by John the Baptist Pater'[9] (93). Duthuit's recent editor, the very level-headed Yves Bonnefoy, could be excused for ranking this tirade as 'certainly the least satisfying of [his] works' (12).

Yet, as Bonnefoy astutely points out, the venom that seems, for no apparent reason, to have poisoned Duthuit's pen is in fact the sign of no mere whimsical antagonism. Seemingly the factor common to both Du Bos and Duthuit – the common fund of experience that governed their diametrically opposed points of view – was the point that both had a significant indirect acquaintanceship with Pater's milieu, but at one remove from Pater himself. Proust also had this sort of connection, through his close friendship at one period with the former Oxford undergraduate Douglas Ainslie. This young Scottish aristocrat's respect for Pater, whom he had known when a student, may indeed have inveigled his defiantly Ruskinian friend into tempering (however covertly) his allegiance to the prophet of the earlier generation (Bann 2002, 60–62). Du Bos himself was half-British, and had been a student at Oxford, where he began his apprenticeship in Pater studies a short time after the writer's death. He was also a personal friend of Vernon Lee whose proselytizing on Pater's behalf was certainly not restricted to the circle of her Florentine friends, but extended to her many American connections and, in this case, to Pater's self-appointed champion in the Salons of Paris.

Duthuit, on the other hand, appears to have been profoundly influenced – and not only in his sceptical view of Pater – by the radically independent views of a little-known (and virtually forgotten) English mentor, Matthew Prichard, who also had personal experience of Pater's Oxford milieu. What comes across today as the surprisingly crude and biased polemic of *Le Rose et le noir* is probably a faithful reflection of Prichard's quite violent repudiation of

---

[7]   This is the conclusion that emerges from the extensive correspondence between Jackson, Wright and his publisher, held in the collection of the Harry Ransom Center, University of Texas at Austin. In mitigation, it appears that Jackson was seriously unwell at the time when he was bombarding Wright with material.

[8]   'Il était le père de tous les esthètes anglais à venir.'

[9]   'Dorian Gray Wilde est le messie annoncé par Jean-Baptiste Pater.' This punchline is already being prepared on the first page of Duthuit's book, when he pours scorn on Pater for trying to establish his relationship to the northern French painter of the same name, the master and blood relation of the great Watteau (1974, 39).

what he saw as the dated theories and irretrievably provincial customs of the leaders of the English avant-garde. The targets that Prichard handed down to Duthuit included the nineteenth-century pioneers of the Aesthetic movement, as well as those whom he regarded as their contemporary avatars, such as Clive Bell and Roger Fry (Duthuit 1974, 57). A pronounced anglophile at this early period of his life, the young Duthuit became an intimate member of the circle of the Sitwells towards the end of the 1920s.

What can be put in the balance to offset Duthuit's apparently so negative judgement on Pater is the significant part then being played by his mentor Prichard in the contemporary revival of interest in the Byzantine world. This would also become a major theme in Duthuit's early writings – and one that he applied in a positive spirit to the art of the contemporary world. As Matisse's cherished son-in-law, and a brilliant writer on the Fauvist movement, Duthuit forcefully championed a view of plastic art polemically opposed to notions of the role of representation that had been current since the Renaissance. His aim, as he described it, was seeing Byzantium 'from a Hellenic angle' (1974, 120). Such a commitment to some of the most progressive modern painting of his day makes it understandable that Duthuit should have poured scorn on what seemed to him the outworn nostrums of 'l'art pour l'art', and vented his spleen on the two culprits of *Le Rose et le noir*.

It would be wrong to represent Duthuit and Du Bos as being in any real sense in dialogue with one another, despite the close chronological coincidence between their writings on Pater. As far as can be seen, Du Bos took no notice of Duthuit's attack. Both critics were however contributing in their very different ways – Du Bos as a member of a close-knit and socially influential literary group, Duthuit from the dandyfied position of an outsider – to the continuing public revaluation of Pater in French modernist culture. Pater's long period as an 'occult influence' had by the mid-1920s been superseded by a more public phase.

What Du Bos and Duthuit held in common, then, was the personal link, albeit at one remove, with the Oxford and London milieu in which Pater had moved. Here Duthuit was probably more in tune with the view of Pater among many of his fellow Oxonians, who viewed him (in the words of the historian Sir Charles Oman) simply 'as a *poseur*, not at all as a leader of thought' (Oman 1941, 209). Du Bos's most significant personal contacts, by contrast, succeeded in embellishing his own experiences at Oxford, where his initial reaction to Pater's work had been no more than lukewarm. His devotion finally flourished when he began to frequent literary London in the early 1920s. Thus his diary for May 1923 records 'an exquisite lunch' with Edmund Gosse at the Marlborough Club, at which they 'spoke a great deal' of Pater (Du Bos 1946, 279–80). A foreign visitor to England whom he encountered on the same trip was none other than 'the young and sympathetic Italian Mario Praz', 'a great friend of Vernon Lee' (274, 276).

Du Bos – already linked by friendship to Vernon Lee who had recommended the young Praz to call and introduce himself, as well as being the valued correspondent of Hofmannsthal – was thus at the centre of a uniquely cosmopolitan forum for Pater studies in the 1920s. Equally at home in London and Paris, with literary friends in Florence and Vienna, he had elaborated from the basis of his Oxford experience the material for what would eventually be a close identification with the master. His profound obeisance to Pater in the essay conceived in 1923 begins by citing Bach and Beethoven as the synaesthetic equivalent to the prose style of *Marius*. It ultimately concludes with a truly Paterian peroration:

> Pater's spirit is like one of those cathedrals that one enters at the fall of day, at the hour when no one is there any more, which then invade you with the feeling of some sort of crowded assembly; and Pater himself always moved forward in his spirit as one proceeds in a cathedral, with slow, hesitant and silent steps. *Marius the Epicurean* remains the great office that he celebrated, in a voice beyond reproach, each of whose inflections penetrates to the very heart of our most intimate retreats, and which seems always to evoke appearance, on the altar, of the Holy Sacraments that it dares not set there itself. (Du Bos 1930, 42–43)[10]

I have spent some time in developing the contrasted cases of Du Bos and Duthuit because their contemporaneous, and yet radically opposed, attitudes to Pater are closely (and revealingly) related to their knowledge of Pater's milieu. Perhaps the only other European critic of this second generation who took so much trouble to acquaint himself with Pater's academic and personal background was the Austrian Rudolf Kassner, who (as Wolfgang Iser points out) travelled to Oxford and met Jowett, seizing the opportunity at the same time to speak to some of Pater's former students. Kassner saw it as his prime aim to restore Pater to his rightful place in the panorama of an English proto-modernist formation already marked by the international significance of the Pre-Raphaelites. As early as 1900, he appears to have been trying to undertake for Germanic culture the role of interpreter of the British scene that Robert de la Sizeranne – with his Ruskinian *parti pris* – was performing for the French. Here again Hofmannsthal provided the main stimulus. He had been the first to introduce Kassner to Pater, and he generously acknowledged the achievement of Kassner's synoptic studies in spreading the knowledge of his work.

Iberian echoes

Outside Italy, France and Austria (in particular the German-speaking areas), the impact of Pater in the period that concluded with the Second World War was considerably more fragmented. With regard to the Iberian countries, there were no translations of his books into Catalan or Spanish up to the very eve of the war, and there has been not one single book by Pater published in Portuguese to date. Any original influence of Pater's writings had therefore to

---

[10]   'L'esprit de Pater ressemble à une de ces cathédrales où l'on entre à la tombée du jour, à l'heure où il n'y a plus personne, et qui vous envahissent alors du sentiment de je ne sais quel recueillement peuplé; et Pater lui-même s'est toujours avancé dans son esprit comme on avance dans une cathédrale, à pas lents, retenus et silencieux. Marius l'Epicurien demeure le grand office qu'il y célébra, d'une voix sans reproche, dont chacune des inflexions pénètre jusqu'au coeur de nos plus intimes retraites, et qui semble toujours appeler l'apparition, sur l'autel, du Saint-Sacrement qu'elle-même n'ose y dresser.'

be by way of the reading of the original texts or – more likely in the case of Portugal, where French literary culture was dominant during the early part of the century – through the growing stock of French translations. But it would be wrong to conclude that nothing of interest emerges in tracing Pater's reception in Spain, or indeed in Portugal. In the case of the translations into Catalan, the urgency of the political circumstances at the time when these texts were released points to a timely revaluation of the Paterian concept of subjectivity that was diametrically opposed to the traditional British interpretation. In Portugal's case, the fact is that their most celebrated modernist poet showed a vigorous interest in the polemical advancement of a Paterian aesthetic.

Indeed, as Maria Teresa Malafaia and Jorge Miguel Bastos da Silva have revealed after their examination of his private papers, Fernando Pessoa fully intended to tackle a Portuguese translation of *The Renaissance* at an important stage in his career. Though this did not come to fruition, Pessoa's version of the famous description of the Mona Lisa from the 'Leonardo' essay – evidently the sole early published translation of Pater into Portuguese – served a strategic purpose in testifying to the esteem in which he held 'the greatest of European aesthetes'. This translation appeared in the magazine *Athena*, co-edited by Pessoa, in 1924. Two years earlier, however, he had already invoked the heritage of Winckelmann and Pater in writing a pseudonymous defence of the poems of the 'only Portuguese aesthete', António Botto, in the face of vocal contemporary criticism. Pessoa insisted on this wider European dimension with the intention of deflecting the critical debate from a mere moralistic condemnation of Botto's homoerotic verse. From Pessoa's point of view, Botto's poetics could be portrayed as an exemplary modernist practice following in the lineage of Pater.

Pessoa's intense interest in Pater was in part a reflection of his own isolated position in Portuguese letters, and served as a means of connecting the singularly few likeminded individuals who deserved his support. In a quite different but comparable way, Jacqueline Hurtley associates the interest in Pater's work shown by Catalan intellectuals with the project of one figure in particular, the 'prime mover of early twentieth century doctrine', Eugenio d'Ors. Though d'Ors referred to Pater in passing as early as 1908, it was thirty years later when, following the initiative of one of his disciples, the Catalan translation of *The Renaissance* was finally published, to be followed in the space of a few years by a Castilian translation of the same work, and Castilian translations of *Imaginary Portraits* and *Marius*. Where Pessoa had been fascinated by the Hellenic and pagan sides of Pater's creed, d'Ors's follower Carles Riba saw him as a kind of mediator through English culture of the legacy of the classical world, who could thus make a direct contribution to the self-assertion and search for cultural identity of the Catalan bourgeoisie. Pater's translator into Catalan, Marià Manent, immersed himself in a wide range of English and French sources, reading Du Bos as well as Eliot on Pater, in the period when the Civil War in Spain was drawing to its close. The war culminated of course, in November 1938, with General Franco's occupation of Barcelona.

Something of the same uncanny timeliness, though in a different political context, was infused into the essay on Pater that Rudolf Borchardt published in the *Basler Nachrichten* in August 1939. Borchardt was, as Martina Lauster describes him here, an 'ultra-conservative', German-Jewish writer, who had learnt from Hofmannsthal to cherish the example of the 'sublime Englishman', but whose thinking had developed in new directions as the political climate of Germany began to deteriorate. Initially he had been quite willing to express his discovery of Pater purely in terms of individual self-fulfilment ('we thought we found ourselves again'). By 1939, however, he had evolved to an extreme nationalist position, believing that collective military action represented the only way in which his fellow countrymen might 'tense and purify' themselves.[11] In the 1939 essay, the vocabulary of Pater's 'Conclusion' to *The Renaissance* was employed, very much against the grain, to give ideological support to such militaristic ideals.

Borchardt's cult of Pater presents a different order of interest, nonetheless, in so far as it testifies to a strong sense of the deep interconnections between German and English culture – something that could hardly have seemed acceptable to public opinion in either nation at the time. He rightly detected in the very Oxford milieu that had nurtured Pater's ideas a profound immersion in the classic texts of nineteenth-century German science and philosophy. In terms of his highly tendentious reading, the destiny of Pater's writings was, in one sense, to give back to Germany the quintessence of what German culture had provided in the first place.

Martina Lauster acknowledges in this context the pertinence of a question which only the close examination of Borchardt's German translation can clarify. How far does Borchardt modify, or distort, Pater's meaning in accordance with what is – when all is said and done – an opportunistic transformation of the original text? Her answer, with regard to the crucial passages drawn from the 'Conclusion' is categorical (and hardly unexpected). Some of the small modifications of vocabulary that Borchardt introduced could reasonably be seen as adjustments to the cultural expectations of a German audience. But others undoubtedly served the questionable purpose of bolstering up the level of Pater's 'martial appeal', whether by the loading of individual phrases, or by the simple omission of passages that might have seemed too feeble to pass muster.

This collection of essays on Pater's reception does not claim to give systematic attention to the levels of accuracy with which his texts have been translated into the different European languages. That the aim of providing better, and so implicitly more accurate, translations of already published books has frequently proved a powerful motive may be seen, for example, in the Italian case. As Maurizio Ascari explains, Mario Praz believed that his predecessor de Rinaldis had entirely failed to create 'an equivalent of Pater's style'. Praz published his own translations of *Imaginary Portraits* and *The Renaissance*, in 1944 and 1946 respectively. But inevitably a time came when these translations, in their turn, were regarded as outmoded. This was the

---

[11]   This seemingly unlikely kinship between art criticism and the development of German militarism is however anticipated in the character of the earlier Aesthetic movement around Stefan George. Though Pater's work was not explicitly championed there, it is possible that he might still have been a secret cult hero for the George circle (see Osterkamp 2001).

justification of Franco Marucci when he published his Italian translation of *Imaginary Portraits* in 1994.

As for the detailed level of comparison with Pater's original writing, there are pertinent comments in a number of the following essays that relate to the specific choice of terms in the translated versions. Jacqueline Hurtley focuses especially on the nuances of the translation of Pater's works into Catalan and Spanish, singling out for attention examples like Marià Manent's Catalan version of 'Pico della Mirandola'. Her conclusion in this particular case is that Manent's choice of vocabulary occasionally betrays a simple inadvertence to the special connotations invested in one of Pater's words; what is more, his translation can be faulted for showing a consistent lack of attention to the rhythmic character of Pater's carefully wrought prose. It would probably be possible to make similar points about many, if not all, of the translations that are listed here. Following another line of enquiry, it would be no less revealing to look closely at the ways in which Pater's characteristic phrases have sometimes acquired a veiled form of representation in the texts of other writers. Here Pater becomes an intertextual presence in the poetry of Hofmannsthal – and the prose of Proust. Borchardt's is surely not the only case where the translator's ideology has been illicitly imposed on Pater's text, though there could be few impositions so flagrant as causing the author of the frankly non-militaristic 'Emerald Uthwart' to strike a warlike posture.

Pater in politics and the Academy

Over the period that concluded with the Second World War, there were two major, and contrasting, developments in the reception of Pater's work. On the one hand, there was a progressive deepening of the understanding of the many aspects of Pater's legacy in the two countries where his cult had firmly taken root. In Italy, these decades were perhaps not so fulsome in their response as in the period of celebration around 1900, when the Roman love affair with English Decadence had been at its height. But they culminated with the translation of *Marius* in 1939, by which time Praz's major revival of the entire oeuvre was getting under way. Moreover, as Maurizio Ascari has shown, the appearance of the first Italian translation of *The Renaissance* in 1925 initiated a particularly fruitful concentration on Pater's role as an art critic, with Paterian aesthetics being analysed not simply on a retrospective basis but with a view to being incorporated wholesale into the contemporary critical debate. In France, also, despite the withering tone of Duthuit's polemic of 1923, the high profile of Pater's writings in the literary circles where both Du Bos and Gide moved was a significant pointer to further development. Together with the new availability of translations of the major works, Pater's prestige prepared the ground for the substantial academic studies that started to celebrate his reputation at the outset of the 1930s.

Among the nations of Central Europe that had briefly acquired independence as a result of the Versailles settlement, it was undoubtedly Poland that stood first and foremost in engaging with some of the central ideas in Pater's work. This level of interest, which had peaked in the first quarter of the century, also led to Pater's writings being absorbed in their turn within the corpus of academic studies. As previously mentioned with reference to Piotr Juszkiewicz's essay, the 'Young Poland' movement was a dominant force in Polish culture between the late 1890s and 1918. Its members were particularly engaged with the question of the autonomous value of art, and were thus attracted to the art and literature of the Aesthetic movement. Ruskin and Wilde may have been considered as the preeminent representatives of this distinctive phase of English culture. Wilde, in particular, acquired an emblematic status for his concept of the critic as artist. But Pater's special contribution was also being carefully assessed as early as the 1890s. The Polish socialist Leon Winiarski, who was residing permanently in France at the time, provided an extensive introduction to Pater's work in two articles that appeared in the Polish press in 1897 and 1899. His initially hostile reaction to Pater's 'cynicism' was quite reversed in the second article, which lauded the distinctive concept of the 'imaginary portrait' as well as explicating the significance of *Marius* in an original and intelligent way.

Ten years later, in 1909, Polish translations of selected essays from Pater's work appeared for the first time in both Lvov (under Austrian rule at this point) and Warsaw (under Russia). If the premature death of the most outstanding critic of the 'Young Poland' movement effectively prevented this initial diffusion of Pater's writing from being followed up, Pater was not for that reason ignored in interwar Poland. In 1929, a full-length book, based on a doctoral dissertation, was published in Poznan by Zbigniew Grabowski, who had studied at the Jagellonian University of Cracow with a distinguished historian of English literature. As Juszkiewicz puts it, this marked the end of Pater's involvement in 'the immediate context of Polish literary tradition' and his inclusion 'in the domain of literary history and the history of criticism'.

Throughout all the differing national contexts in which Pater's work was received, a transition of this kind inevitably took place, sooner or later. For a certain period of time, within a spectrum of European cultures where patterns of reception were inevitably disparate, Pater had habitually played a role as an actual, or potential, model for critical practice. In certain cases, such as Poland, Spain and Germany, his distinctive portrayal of subjectivity was for a time annexed to a mass political programme. Then, at a later point, he tended to become more primarily an object of academic and historical study. However this inevitable transition has not always been as clearly defined as the previous remarks would suggest. There has been evidence of considerable temporal overlaps, when the overall shift is traced across Europe as a whole. The moment of the 'Young Poland' movement was past by 1918, but the 'Noucentisme' of the Catalan intellectuals who espoused Pater's ideas on the connection between art and life extended into the period of the Spanish Civil War and beyond. In Italy, the phase of reception that followed the piecemeal adaptation of specific aspects of Pater's legacy was dominated, from the 1930s onwards, by the figure of Mario Praz. And of him, it can certainly be said that, though he performed the double role of a scholar and translator in making the major works of Pater available, his own personal charisma also helped to invest Pater's image with a special kind of aura. Praz's Pater could not be confined to mournful biographical repositories such as Thomas Wright's two volumes. In Elisa Bizzotto's account, the period of 1930 to 1950 in Italian Pater studies thus lies between two phases which could justly be labelled 'pre-Praz' and 'after Praz'. Obviously, the period 'after Praz' is still benefiting from the fact that notable pupils of the master, like Paola Colaiacomo, continue to take the lead in initiating the discussion of aspects of Pater's work.

Yet the French Paterians also deserve recognition for initiating a series of sound academic studies of Pater that have continued, in virtually unbroken succession, since the 1930s. Whilst British literary critics were still raking over the warm coals of the Aesthetic movement (and in that process trying to exorcise 'the grosser misunderstandings of Pater'), the French universities had already begun to place him firmly within the canon of literary history. In Louise Rosenblatt's doctoral dissertation of 1931, Pater was given his rightful place as (in Bénédicte Coste's words) 'the official British exponent of art's for art's sake'. In the same year, Alfred Farmer complemented his doctoral dissertation on the Aesthetic movement in Great Britain with a special study of Pater's *Appreciations*, the important collection which, despite the inclusion of crucial essays like 'Style', had always received less attention than the familiar canon of *Imaginary Portraits*, *The Renaissance* and *Marius*. Farmer became in turn the supervisor of Germain d'Hangest, whose lengthy dissertation of 1961 ranked for several years as unquestionably the most thorough and extensive survey of Pater's 'Life and Work' in any language.

It would be wrong to conclude, however, that even such thoroughly well researched and serious academic studies as these have made it possible to draw a line under Pater's achievement. One of the discoveries of the last few decades has been the fact that Pater's work appears to be intrinsically resistant to any such form of recuperation. So it continues to pose timely issues that are integral to the contemporary theory and practice of literature and the arts. The fact that such studies are often, though not exclusively, situated in the Academy – at least where criticism is concerned – marks an irreversible difference from the more free-floating literary and cultural scene of the early nineteenth century. But this necessary relationship to academic debate can hardly be seen as untrue to the example of Pater himself, whose situation of being half in and half out of the Academy must always have been integral to the special appeal of his writings.

In pursuance of this point, it is valuable to reflect once again on Wolfgang Iser's contribution to this collection, and to recall his decision to write his seminal study in the immediate postwar period in terms that emphasized Pater's unusual status as a critical writer. For Iser, the bleak alternatives that he himself faced as a scholar and critic in this period were, as I mentioned, the well-trodden path of 'life and works' with its positivist underpinning, and on the other hand the linguistic discipline of the 'New Criticism', which programmatically insisted on excluding extraneous factors, and treated the art work as an autonomous object. Pater's continuing attraction lies, according to Iser, in the fact that his practice conspicuously avoids these two, potentially restrictive methodologies. In attempting to devise a 'blueprint for an aesthetic existence', he also offers an example and an incentive for critical practices dedicated to overriding such a dichotomy. Iser has of course continued to underline in his more recent writings the capacity of Pater's thought to transcend its temporal limits, and remain closely in tune with the changing times.

From such a perspective, it should come as no surprise that the academic work of contributing essayists is frequently listed in these surveys, and that one of the more substantial essays focuses specifically on the 'academic reception' of Pater in France. When Bénédicte Coste considers the difficulties that have been experienced in finding a place for Pater within the academic curriculum of the French universities, she is inviting us to draw our conclusions from the current compartmentalization of the Arts and Humanities. Is Pater a novelist, or a critic?, we may ask. If a critic, is he a literary critic, or an art critic? If an art critic, then does his almost exclusive focus on artists of the Renaissance mean that he also has something to say to art historians? If, in the French philosopher Picy's terms, he turns out to have valuable things to communicate to philosophers, then how does his original view of ancient philosophy square with the fact that he is, inevitably, a product of the Hellenism of the Victorian age? These are, of course, questions that can receive no definitive answer, here or elsewhere. They are at the same time valid symptoms of a certain collective impulse towards the ideal of 'transdisciplinarity' over the past few years, a tendency perhaps more honoured in the breach than in the observance. The progress of reception studies in general demonstrates that no author's reputation is ever set in stone. Both major and minor literary figures have their message renewed in unexpected ways, and the process continues both inside and outside the sphere of the Academy. This panorama of Pater's European reception indicates how one British author, despite his legendary discretion, has contrived to reappear continually in a variety of different guises. On his own account and for his foreign readers, he has fulfilled the expectations aroused by that enigmatic epigraph to *The Renaissance*: 'Yet shall ye be as the wings of a dove.'

1 'The sterile ascetic of beauty': Pater and the Italian *fin de siècle*

Benedetta Bini

The hills around Florence

Although Violet Paget (better known by her androgynous pseudonym of Vernon Lee) wrote several letters of introduction for her distinguished friend, Walter Pater does not seem to have made any use of them – and his visit to Rome in 1883 remains, even today, a complete mystery. Nor did his sister Hester throw much light on the matter when she thanked Miss Paget for her thoughtfulness:

> Walter enjoyed his visit to Rome very much. He was very obliged for the introductions you sent him and was very sorry he had no time to use any. A month is a short time to see much of Rome. He found he had to give all his time to the galleries and churches and was so tired in the evening he was quite unfit for social intercourse. (Pater 1970, 48)

This blank – one of the many, as we know – is particularly regrettable. Pater had already visited Ravenna, Pisa and Florence in 1865 with C. L. Shadwell, but the mystery surrounding this second trip to Italy, following the publication of *The Renaissance*, and at a time when Pater was engaged in writing *Marius the Epicurean*, deprives us of an important clue in tracing his presence in the Roman *fin-de-siècle* intellectual society. The particular physiognomy of Vernon Lee as a writer, critic and influential figure, and especially her remarkable role in introducing the 'new' British culture to the Italian literary and artistic *milieux* of the 1880s and 1890s would have made his stay and his meeting with some of his admirers particularly rewarding to all. Although she moved to the famous Villa il Palmerino on the outskirts of Fiesole only in 1889, Miss Paget had been living first in Rome for two winters, and then in Florence since 1873, devoting herself to her invalid half-brother, the poet and translator Eugene Lee-Hamilton and to her researches in the still untilled field of what later became *Studies of the Eighteenth Century in Italy* (1880). This brilliant work which made her known in England and elsewhere was translated into Italian in 1881. Then only twenty-four, from that moment on she was to become a pivotal figure in the cosmopolitan social life which gathered in Italy at the turn of the century, especially in Venice, Florence and Rome (Gunn 1970; Colby 2003). It was a peculiar mixture of artists, writers, men and women of letters, who had either made Italy their permanent home, like Robert Browning and Elizabeth Barrett Browning, William Wetmore Story (Bini 2004) and others, or had, like Henry James, the habit of spending long periods of time in Italy.

In Florence the Anglo-American community was particularly numerous (McComb 1966), and like any colony of cultured expatriates inevitably prone to gossip, social rivalries and intellectual misunderstandings: nothing is probably more significant than the long quarrel about aesthetics (Wellek 1970) which for many years divided two troublesome neighbours, Bernard Berenson and Vernon Lee, living at an uncomfortably short distance from each other on the hills around Fiesole (Samuels 1979). Then there were her Italian friends: the Baroness Elena French-Cini, the writer and *émigré* Giovanni Ruffini, well known in England for his novel *Doctor Antonio* (1855) (Corrigan 1962), the critic Enrico Nencioni, the painter Telemaco Signorini, Pasquale Villari and his English wife Linda, the cosmopolitan 'cortegiano moderno' (Praz 1944) Carlo Placci, friend of Berenson (Pantazzi 1961), and many others. For the 'expatriates', the occasional visitors from abroad, and her Florentine friends, the very opinionated and eccentric Vernon Lee was to become, probably more than any other figure of the time, a many-faceted *trait d'union* in the history of cross-cultural relations: introducing people and ideas, mixing stereotypes and discoveries, enchanting the mixed Florentine society with the unique gifts of her conversation. And, inevitably, making enemies. From the story of her life, friends and relations, a fascinating portrait emerges of the – somehow inevitably distorted – mirroring of one culture within another. At the same time, her acquaintance and friendship with some of the Italian *literati* made her presence invaluable in the still provincial cultural life of the young Italian nation, in which the glorious season of English Romanticism was still considered the one and only acme of 'modern' artistic and critical achievement and which opened very slowly but with eager innocence to a new understanding of English culture. If it is true that the circle which gathered around her was the successor of the group which in the 1850s and 1860s had found its identity around the Brownings and the Trollopes (Pantazzi 1961), then it is also true that the shift of two or three post-Risorgimento decades makes this Anglo-Italian colony a very revealing and significant paradigm of the profound changes that Italian culture and society were undergoing in those years: reflecting, and reinterpreting, that great period of transformation involving the whole of Europe known as Decadence.

It was into this circle of learned anglophiles and romantic italophiles that Vernon Lee was to introduce the new trends of contemporary English literature and culture (Zorn 2003): first and foremost among others, the name of Walter Pater would soon be circulating.

Vernon Lee had managed to meet Walter Pater in the summer of 1881 at Oxford. Although in a letter to her mother she remembers him as a 'heavy, shy, dull looking brown moustachioed creature over forty, much like Velasquez' Philip IV, lymphatic, dull, humourless' (Lee 1937, 78), there is no doubt about the impression that his critical approach to the Renaissance and the style of his imaginative prose had already left on her mind. As is known, a real friendship was soon to develop between them, with Pater obviously considering Miss Paget a young and gifted scholar. *Belcaro: Being Studies on*

Sundry Aesthetical Questions (1881) seemed to prove that Vernon Lee had abandoned forever the teaching of Ruskin in connection with which she had been gently quoted by Robert Browning in 'Asolando' ('"No, the book / Which noticed how the wall growths wave", said she, / "Was not by Ruskin". / I said, "Vernon Lee?"').

As a matter of fact, Vineta Colby's definition of Lee as a 'puritan aesthete' (1970), alternating between the two modes of aesthetic reception, is very apt, and it will have its bearings on the early reception of Pater in the Italian cultural world. In Lee's next collection of essays on the Renaissance, *Euphorion* (1884), she included a dedication to Pater ('in appreciation of that which, in expounding the beautiful things of the past, he has added to the beautiful things of the present') which definitely put her among the true and enthusiastic followers and emulators of the master, as, later, would her remarkable writings on the *genius loci* (Bini 2003) and her short stories, so obviously reminiscent of the indelible trace left by her reading of *Imaginary Portraits*.

Vernon Lee's shift towards Pater is highly significant. This is not only because it follows a tendency in criticism, typical of *fin-de-siècle* redefinition of taste, which she shared with John Addington Symonds, Swinburne, Oscar Wilde, Herbert Horne and others. But it is also because she took on the role of disciple of a new aesthetic *credo* in her actual writing on Pater, marking her position in the Italian cultural *milieu* as the clever and up-to-date 'correspondent' on English literary matters, at a time when the name of John Ruskin was still well known and respected among the Italian reading public (Praz 1937). In fact, Vernon Lee had started as early as the mid-1870s to contribute to various Italian literary papers. *La rivista europea*, edited by Angelo de Gubernatis, had published her articles dealing with both Italian and English cultural issues: on the leading novelists of England, but also on the need for the Italians to have more respect for their own past greatness. She subsequently went on to write for other journals such as the famous *Fanfulla della domenica* (the cultural supplement to *Il fanfulla*, edited by Ferdinando Martini) which was soon to become one of the most relevant periodicals in turn-of-the-century Italy.

Although (or maybe because) Pater's presence in Lee's work is so pervasive as to act as a kind of general subtext, only a few direct comments on her mentor can be found in her writings. It was in the *Fanfulla della domenica* that, in 1885, she produced a lengthy article ('Ethics into Aesthetics: Notes on Walter Pater's New Book')[1] on *Marius the Epicurean* in which she reveals her admiration 'awakened by the subtlest of thinkers and by the more artistic of writers in contemporary England'[2] and goes on to remember the success of *The Renaissance*, the 'wonderful *rêverie* on Monna Lisa', before introducing the lesson of *Marius*, seen as the figure of moralized aesthetics:

> Physical beauty, which is to say symmetry, purity and loveliness in the material world, finds its equivalent in the strength, temperance and chastity

---

[1] 'La morale nell'estetica. appunti sul nuovo libro di Walter Pater.'
[2] 'destata dal più sottile pensatore e dallo scrittore più artista dell'attuale Inghilterra' (1).

of the moral world. This thought is not new, nay, it is very ancient: it was the dominating intuition of Greek art and poetry, a teaching that was after all essentially platonic, and that it was utterly important to recall in our times, when the desire for a sensation which should be *new and unique* as Pater himself had once defined it, made the search for malady and moral death analogous to the search for physical beauty.[3]

Vernon Lee was later to mention *Marius* again, in the dedication of her collection of essays *Juvenilia* to her friend Carlo Placci. Her attitude to the novel seems rather romantic, lingering on the 'aesthetic, classic, Goethian days' (1) evoked by the novel and its being 'the Lehrjahre of an antique Wilhelm Meister: but a Wilhelm Meister simpler, purer, more dignified than the hero of Goethe' (8). Given the status of Vernon Lee and the relevance of the journal where she wrote, it is legitimate to assume that the review of *Marius* must have left an impression on its readers, especially those who were to become Miss Paget's good friends and frequent visitors to Il Palmerino. It is not a surprise, then, that a journal like *Nuova antologia* – in which a section ('Notizie di Scienza, Letteratura ed Arte') was devoted to a brief updating on the European literary world – should have informed its readers in 1889 not only that Robert Browning was buying a house on the Canal Grande in Venice but also that:

> Messrs. Macmillan & Co. publishers in London are about to bring forth a new book by Mr. Walter Pater, entitled *Appreciations*.[4]

Moreover:

> The May issue of *Macmillan's Magazine* contains a piece by Mr. Freeman on *The Difference between Towns and Boroughs* and an essay on *The Bacchanals of Euripides* by Mr. Pater.[5]

Concise though they are, these notes are illuminating in as much as they tell us that Pater was no longer an unknown name, but that his fame had by that time already reached Italy's literary world, although the first translation of *The Renaissance* and *Marius* were only to appear in 1912 and 1939 respectively. Not many people were able to read in English: Italian society was still very much French-oriented in its taste, and all the new literary fashions arrived from Paris. English poetry had been widely translated and would continue to be, and only a small group of cultured people were able to read texts in the

---

[3] 'il bello fisico, cioè la simmetria, la purezza e venustà nel mondo materiale, possiede il suo equivalente nella forza, la temperanza, la castità nel mondo morale. Pensiero non nuovo, anzi antichissimo, intuizione dominante dell'arte e della poesia greca; insegnamento in fondo essenzialmente platonico, e che era importantissimo richiamarci ai nostri tempi, quando il desiderio della sensazione *nuova ed unica*, come l'aveva una volta definita lo stesso Pater, ha fatto ricercare come analogo della bellezza fisica la malattia e la morte morale' (2).

[4] 'Gli editori Macmillan & Co. di Londra stanno pubblicando un nuovo libro del signor Walter Pater, intitolato *Apprezzamenti*' (16 November).

[5] 'Il numero di maggio del *Macmillan's Magazine* contiene uno scritto del Signor Freeman su *La distinzione fra città e borghi* e uno studio su *Le baccanali di Euripide* del Signor Pater' (1 May).

original. Nevertheless, the slow process of de-provincialization of Italian culture – of which the new approach to English literature and criticism was a relevant factor – dates from this period. It reached its acme with d'Annunzio, coinciding also with the slow fading of Ruskin's supremacy in favour of other, and more modern, sensibilities, although it was to receive its decisive impetus more from the prestige of the new trends in European visual arts (Pre-Raphaelites and Symbolism) than from the challenge of the written word.

After Pater's death in 1894, Vernon Lee was to remember her master and friend in the final chapter of her *Renaissance Fancies and Studies* (1895). Here, as elsewhere, she pays homage to the name with which 'I began my first book on Renaissance matters', thus acknowledging the presence of Pater as a constant guide in her work, and then goes on to draw a comparison between the author and the character of Marius:

> He began as an aesthete, and ended as a moralist. By faithful and self-restraining cultivation of the sense of harmony, he appears to have risen from the perception of visible beauty to the knowledge of beauty of the spiritual kind, both being an expression of the same perfect fittingness to an ever more intense and various and congruous life (255–56).

These words, variously reinterpreted, would echo frequently in the next few years in which the figure of Pater became little by little more visible in the cosmopolitan culture of the *fin-de-siècle* society in Italy.

A good friend of Vernon Lee and a frequent visitor at Il Palmerino was Enrico Nencioni, the first Italian man of letters destined to play an important role in the reception of Pater. Nencioni is a very interesting transitional figure in the literary landscape of that period, which is marked by a slow assimilation of more advanced cultural and intellectual trends from abroad (Sormani 1975): his criticism, commended by Croce for his 'most precious gift [...] sureness of taste', was later damned with faint praise as 'the effusion of a fervent and happy lover of art' (Cicognani 1943, 371). If in the 1890s he was not 'a critic in the rigorous sense of the word' – indeed nobody was yet, apart from de Sanctis – and if it is true that his approach to the arts was still in many respects impressionistic and honestly bourgeois (Praz 1943), his role in introducing English contemporary literature and thought to the Italian world cannot be denied or underestimated.

Enrico Nencioni was for twenty-three years private tutor in a number of Italian aristocratic milieux, living for many years in Siena with Count Gori Pannilini's family and meeting there some interesting and famous figures of expatriates such as William Wetmore Story, Walter Savage Landor and the two Brownings. It was only when Ferdinando Martini asked him to join the staff of the *Fanfulla della domenica* that Nencioni moved to Rome, where he came in contact with some of the leading writers of the time like Luigi Capuana and Matilde Serao. From 1883 he lived in Florence, where he was appointed professor at the Istituto Superiore di Magistero (secondary school for girls), renewing his acquaintance with Vernon Lee. At the same time he began to define a more visible role for himself as a lecturer, a translator (Coleridge and Swinburne), a literary critic with a strong interest for French and English contemporary literature, and a poet with a perceptive ear. Among his manuscripts there was found a long list of authors 'imitandi e traducendi':

especially Hugo, Bourget, James, V. Lee, Hawthorne, Ruskin and Pater (Angeli 1999). He was later to write for some of the more influential 'new' magazines of the time, the international journal *Nuova antologia*, the *Cronaca bizantina*, directed by Angelo Sommaruga, the *Domenica letteraria* and other periodicals, becoming a close friend of several important figures like Angelo Conti, Angiolo Orvieto (founder in 1896 of the magazine *Il Marzocco*) and Gabriele d'Annunzio. The latter had passionately devoured his essays while still at school at the Collegio Cicognani in Prato and was later to dedicate to him his *Elegie romane*, besides writing two articles in his memory when Nencioni died in 1896. The *Saggi critici di letteratura inglese* (*Critical Essays on English Literature*), a collection of essays and reviews previously written for the *Nuova antologia*, were published posthumously in 1897 with the preface by Giosuè Carducci, the main poetical voice of post-unity Italy, Nobel prize winner for poetry in 1907 and a lifelong friend. In these essays Nencioni shows a lively curiosity and a firm grasp of English themes and figures: as early as 1867 he had published an essay in the *Nuova antologia* in which, introducing to the Italian reader the poetry of Robert Browning, he had criticized the Italian lack of curiosity with regard to English literature, especially when compared to the craze which surrounded other influences from abroad:

> In Italy, where everything that comes from France, novel and poetry, criticism and history, is read voraciously, little or nothing is known of modern and contemporary English literature. With the exception of Byron, Walter Scott, Macaulay, the names of the great poets, novelists, critics and historians who in our century have flourished and are flourishing in England are, generally speaking, new names in Italy, while perhaps of all foreign literatures the one that can be studied with the greatest profit by Italians is the English.[6]

The essay is illuminating in that it states very clearly what was to be for many generations the trend – and, if you like, the paradox – of Italian cultural society: full of anglophiles, but at the same time strangely reluctant to approach English culture except on a very superficial level, and apparently indifferent to its formal and critical developments. This explains also the scanty direct comments we find in those years relating to Pater and his work, even in such a favourable milieu as the one that Vernon Lee had created around herself, where the magic of Pater did not go unnoticed.

There were, of course, a few notable exceptions, like Nencioni himself. In his reviews and essays for the various periodicals of the time he showed remarkable insight and passion in introducing new English and American literary voices to the Italian public: Rossetti, Whitman, Tennyson, Swinburne and, later on, even Henry James, at a time when the American author was still

---

[6] 'In Italia, dove si legge avidamente ogni scritto che viene di Francia, romanzo e poesia, critica e storia, poco o nulla si sa della letteratura inglese moderna e contemporanea. Se ne eccettui Byron, Walter Scott, Macaulay, i nomi dei grandi poeti, dei grandi romanzieri, dei critici e degli storici che nel secol nostro han fiorito e fioriscono in Inghilterra sono, generalmente parlando, nomi nuovi in Italia: mentre forse di tutte le straniere letterature quella che con maggior profitto potrebbe studiarsi dagl'Italiani è la inglese' (1).

relatively unknown on the Continent. His friendship with Vernon Lee, who always considered him a very good friend and who dedicated to him the second edition of her *Studies of the Eighteenth Century in Italy* (1907), was helpful in widening his circle of English expatriates and providing him with new means to investigate the contemporary English world of letters. In two reviews of Lee's works (*Euphorion* and *Juvenilia*) in the *Nuova antologia* Pater is mentioned on the one hand as having influenced the style of Miss Paget with his 'meditative calm and lucid control',[7] and on the other as having contributed, together with Ruskin, Symonds and Lee herself, to the admirable new trend of English studies on Botticelli. Only in 1890 did Nencioni deal directly with Pater, and this was in his review of *Appreciations*, once again from the pages of *Nuova antologia*. After acknowledging the value of *The Renaissance*, Nencioni characterizes Pater's role as a critic:

> For him a painting, a character, a plant, a poem, have a special value and deserve to be analysed only for their faculty to procure us a distinct and unforgettable impression of pleasure. He is in the world of criticism what Dante Gabriel Rossetti was in the world of poetry: a refined, aristocratic, and if the word did not often have an odious meaning, I would also say a fine and delicate *dilettante*.[8]

Characteristically, Nencioni sees what he calls 'dilettantismo' and 'pessimismo' as the two main currents of contemporary literature. Pater is one of the most exquisite representatives of the first category, argues Nencioni, adding that the author shares with all the other aesthetic critics the vice of expressing ideas, which are sometimes far from being original, in an oracular tone. Having stated the limits of Pater's work, Nencioni expresses his appreciation for all the essays in the volume, among the most beautiful and perfect of modern English prose, and goes on to remark that

> The greatest of modern and contemporary critics in Europe are in their writings – even in their most scholarly and philosophical pages – artists of the word; able to produce real *works of art*: such are Wilhelm Schlegel, Carlyle, Ruskin, Michelet, Sainte-Beuve, Taine, Renan.
>
> How is it that in our country, apart from a very few and commendable exceptions, a book of literary, artistic or historical criticism is vulgarly written [. . .] without life, or warmth or colour, without grace: grey and boring like a slate roof in November? I think that the reason lies, at least in part, in this. The Italian critic has the dread of being taken for a *poet* – he is afraid of being accused of not being sufficiently serious and scientific. This is absurd. Any real criticism is – or should be – a resurrection, an interpretation of life.[9]

---

7 'calma riflessiva e lucido ordine' (81).

8 'Per lui un quadro, un personaggio, una pianta, una poesia, hanno speciale valore e meritano essere analizzati solo in quanto hanno facoltà di procurarci una distinta e indimenticabile impressione di piacere. E' nel campo della critica quel che fu Dante Gabriele Rossetti nel campo poetico: un raffinato, un aristocratico, un delicatissimo *dilettante*' (415–16).

9 'I più insigni critici moderni e contemporanei di Europa sono nei loro scritti, anche nelle più dotte e filosofiche pagine, artisti della parola; e fanno veramente

Nencioni's lucid awareness of the necessity for a different critical approach is what really drives him to write this review: although not completely without flaws, Pater's image slowly emerges as the model of a new style of criticism. It was in this role that his fame was to assert itself in the 1890s and especially in the Roman *fin-de-siècle* artistic circles. For the moment, however, apart from the insights of Nencioni, he remains the fascinating but slightly dangerous essayist whose influence, although elusive, is in the process of emerging from behind the scenes to capture the attention of Vernon Lee, Placci and others. Understandably, more attention is given to Pater's gifts as a new interpreter of the Renaissance than as a narrator: the more subversive aspect of *Marius* and of the *Imaginary Portraits* seems to have been overlooked – or, in the case of Lee, just very deftly interwoven into her own writing. Soon Pater would become a name in a selected group of authors who would be cited as participating in the new trend of the aesthetic essay: even, perhaps, slightly neutralized in the process and reduced to an icon of the cultivated traveller. Nothing is more revealing of this new habit than a review of Vernon Lee's *Euphorion* by the cosmopolitan Carlo Placci (Cambieri Tosi 1984) for the *Fanfulla della domenica* in 1884:

> Who has enjoyed more fully a reading of texts from the Elizabethan age than those who have had as companions Symonds to order them and Swinburne to reproduce the impressions thereof? What lesson of architecture has been more fascinating than the one you have received wandering along the Canal Grande with a book by Ruskin on your knees? What guide more attractive than a chapter of Pater to help us understand with pleasure a dance by Botticelli?[10]

Had he written this review a few years later, Placci would have added to this list of names that of the eccentric architect and connoisseur Herbert P. Horne, editor of the *Century Guild Hobby Horse*, a frequent visitor to Italy and from 1904 a permanent resident in Florence (Fletcher 1970). A collector of primitives, Renaissance furniture, Old Masters' drawings, Horne was to buy Palazzo Corsi in Via dé Benci and bequeath it and his collection to the Foundation which still bears his name. His *Botticelli: Painter of Florence* (1908), profoundly influenced by his friend Walter Pater, would be the final and

---

opere d'arte: tali Guglielmo Schlegel, Carlyle, Ruskin, Michelet, Sainte-Beuve, Taine, Renan.
Come va che da noi, fatte pochissime e più lodevoli eccezioni, un libro di critica letteraria, artistica, o storica, è quasi sempre scritto barbaramente [. . .] senza vita, senza calore, senza colorito, senza allettamento veruno, grigio ed uggioso come un tetto di lavagna in novembre? Io credo che derivi, almeno in parte, da questo. Il critico italiano ha una sacrosanta paura di passar da *poeta* – e che gli si addebiti di non esser abbastanza serio e scientifico. Ed è un assurdo. Ogni vera critica è, o dovrebbe essere, una resurrezione, una interpretazione di vita' (417–18).

10 'Chi ha gioito più pienamente d'una lettura di testi dell'epoca elisabettiana di quelli che hanno avuto a compagni il Symonds per ordinarli, e il Swinburne per riprodurne le impressioni? Quale lezione d'architettura è stata più affascinante di quella che avete ricevuto vagando pel Canal Grande con il libro di Ruskin sulle ginocchia? Quale guida più attraente di un capitolo del Pater, per aiutarci a contemplare con più piacere una danza del Botticelli?' (10).

definitive critical statement that put Botticelli back into the canon (Kermode 1985). Indirectly, it served the same function for Pater himself.

This new cult of the painter of 'The Birth of Venus' was soon to become, significantly, the theme of a novel, although a minor one. In his *Un furto* (*A Theft*, 1890), Carlo Placci tells the story of an amateur art historian who steals a painting, convinced it can be attributed to Botticelli. The hero is described as reading

> with admiration the fine sentences of Vernon Lee, Pater and other English writers [...] these critics possessed extraordinary gifts of intuition and a real love for the Quattrocentisti; moreover, they sometimes were able to find the right epithets to define the temperament, and paint the style of the various artists of that age.[11]

Another kind of literary presence, however, was needed to embody more fully these aspects of Pater's work: and this could only be the controversial and highly gifted figure of d'Annunzio. It was only when his star began to rise in the firmament of *fin-de-siècle* Italian literature that the figure of Pater seemed to emerge more clearly, even though – perhaps inevitably – reduced to a useful stereotype of the decadent.

Very revealing in this context is Nencioni's review in the *Nuova antologia* in 1889 ('Two New Novels'[12]), of d'Annunzio's *Il piacere* (*The Child of Pleasure*) and Matilde Serao's *All'erta sentinella!* (*Look out, sentry!*). Here, and for the very first time, Pater is seen not only as an author but as the major influence on the characterization of d'Annunzio's first hero:

> Many have been quoted as being the models for d'Annunzio: Gautier, Flaubert, Goncourt, Mendès, the *Quattrocentisti*, the Pre-Raphaelites, Keats, Shelley, Rossetti, Alma Tadema, Michetti [...] and nobody has mentioned Pater [...] *Il piacere* has more affinities with his *Marius the Epicurean* than with any other novel, poem or painting. But what does that prove? Perhaps d'Annunzio does not even know Pater's novel; and the affinity derives only from the kindred similarity of the two temperaments.[13]

The statement, although almost hidden in a minor review of the time, seems relevant for two reasons. First, it reveals in Nencioni the ability to detect the presence of a dialogue between two texts that stem from different cultures. Secondly, it forms a significant transition between two ways of interpreting

---

[11] 'delle belle frasi di Vernon Lee, di Pater e di altri inglesi [...] questi critici possedevano un'intuizione straordinaria, un vero amore per i Quattrocentisti; inoltre, sapevano qualche volta trovare giusti epiteti per caratterizzare l'indole, e dipingere la maniera dei diversi artisti di quel tempo' (118).

[12] 'Due nuovi romanzi'.

[13] 'Si sono citati molti *modelli* del D'Annunzio: e Gautier, e Flaubert, e Goncourt, e Mendès, e i quattrocentisti, e i Preraffaelliti, e Keats, e Shelley, e il Rossetti, e Alma Tadema, e il Michetti [...] e nessuno ha ricordato il Pater, col cui *Marius the Epicurean Il piacere* ha più affinità che con qualsiasi altro romanzo, poema o pittura. Ma ciò che prova? Forse il D'Annunzio non conosce neppure il libro del Pater; e la somiglianza deriva solo dall'indole consimile dei due ingegni' (664).

Pater, shifting ideally to d'Annunzio and the cultural climate of the Roman *fin de siècle*.

If Florence had been the first literary scenario for the introduction of Pater's work into Italy, Rome would prove to be the perfect visual setting for its – however elusive – canonization.

The lure of Rome

Had d'Annunzio read *Marius* by the time that he composed *Il piacere*? He might have done. We know that some of Pater's works were present in his library. They are heavily underlined, although it is difficult to establish the date of his actual reading. The eclectic and ambitious young poet from Pescara was a voracious reader, and at that stage of his apprenticeship was particularly fascinated by the English 'movimento estetico': Swinburne, Wilde and Pater are the names always mentioned as being fundamental in his approach to – and discovery of – modernity (Anceschi 1976). Cultural life in post-unity Rome was experiencing a moment of great and creative excitement and it was especially the fate of the visual arts to fall under the spell of European Symbolism and take the lead in the battle against what seemed the old and dusty supremacy of Realism, the vulgarity of *Verismo*, the uninspiring legacy of positivism (Damigella 1981).

New magazines like *Il Convito* and *Cronaca bizantina* were emphatically advocating a different approach to art and criticism, gathering under their banners the best talents of that generation: painters, sculptors, writers, critics, who all looked at the great artistic movements in Europe and especially at the English experience as the fertile example to imitate (Frandini 1972). The first Esposizione Internazionale di Belle Arti which took place in Rome in 1883, and the turmoil which followed, were probably a watershed in the definitive rejection of academic taste. Three years later, the group *In Arte Libertas*, founded in 1886 by the painter Nino Costa in the premises of an historical meeting-place for artists, the Caffè Greco in Via Condotti (Angeli 1930), had been conceived as an imitation of the Pre-Raphaelite brotherhood. The names of its members – Cellini, Coleman, Sartorio and others – are the same that would be found gathering round *Il Convito*, one of the most representative magazines of the literary and artistic tastes of Roman *fin de siècle*. Nino Costa had always had close contacts with the English artistic milieu: his lifelong friendship with Frederic Leighton dated from 1849, and he himself had exhibited at the Grosvenor Gallery in 1862. It was probably through him that the first real knowledge of the Pre-Raphaelites' work had reached the artistic circles in Rome, whereas it was through Angelo Conti's reading of Ruskin that the attraction to the Brotherhood and the revaluation of Botticelli found its intellectual justification (Piantoni 1972; d'Anna 1996). Other painters like Cabianca, Carlandi and de Maria had worked in London in the 1880s, bringing back new ideas and suggestions which they were to use as a weapon in the same battle against Naturalism, the medievalism of the Pre-Raphaelites and the classical inspiration of Alma Tadema and Frederic Leighton. These two painters, it is worth remembering, had lived and worked in Italy. The fact that the debate around the figurative arts was so central to the

Rome of the 1880s–90s paved the way for the emergence of Walter Pater as the hidden *maestro* of a new theory of art and of a new way of interpreting history – and memory.

It was through the vogue of the Pre-Raphaelites, to whom he had been introduced by Nencioni, that d'Annunzio had first discovered that English aesthetic world which was to be so influential on the anglophilia of his Roman years (Sborgi 1990), shared with the entire artistic and intellectual milieu with which he had come in contact. Between 1890 and 1892 the annual exhibitions of the *In Arte Libertas* group had showed for the first time works by D. G. Rossetti and Burne-Jones (who in the same years was drawing the mosaics for the Protestant Church of S. Paolo dentro le Mura in Rome). Although it was only in 1893 that the Biennale di Venezia presented a more complete survey of the Pre-Raphaelites, their style was a continuous source of imitation and questioning; and various contributions to *Il Convito* (1895) by the charismatic painter Giulio Aristide Sartorio on Dante Gabriel Rossetti and English painting would represent an important milestone. Sartorio especially highlighted the last phase of the movement, with its more explicit Symbolist turn, and associated it with Pater as well as Swinburne, Burne-Jones and Morris.

Rome, then, was significantly receptive towards English culture and art at this moment. Gabriele d'Annunzio was quick to capture the spirit of the times, and transform what for others was a simple source of ideological inspiration into something more complex. Pater, as we shall see, is the figure in the carpet in his first phase, coinciding with the publication of *Il piacere* (*The Child of Pleasure*, 1889), *Le vergini delle Rocce* (*The Maiden of the Rocks*, 1896), *Il fuoco* (*The Flame*, 1900) and some essays in the pages of *Cronaca bizantina*, *Il Convito* and *Il Marzocco* (Oliva 1979). Although the extent of d'Annunzio's celebrated anglophilia, and its consequences, exceed the scope of this chapter, this is the broad and colourful scenario – made of imitations, contaminations, forgeries and social rituals – in which we have to start our quest for the traces of Pater in Italian *fin-de-siècle* art and aesthetics. The quest is not easy – or maybe it is all too easy. The continual reference to English Aestheticism, Symbolism and Decadence seem to point to the hidden master and at the same time to blur his figure on an ideal canvas that is crowded with other names: the great *fin-de-siècle* wave of anglomania submerges Pater's profile and it is only indirectly that we can detect his presence.

As early as 1887, from the pages of *La Tribuna*, d'Annunzio had tried his hand at what was in all likelihood a little imaginary portrait (Vita–Finzi 1978) of a young and unknown English poet, Adolphus Hannaford ('Un poeta d'autunno', 'An Autumn Poet'), follower of the aesthetic school which stemmed from Hunt, Millais, Rossetti and Swinburne. With a different surname, Adolphus Jeckyll will appear again in *Il piacere*: one of the many evocative English names, in the Roman world of 1887, that surround the figure of the hero. Right from the start the novel reveals its paradigmatic aspect in being deeply pervaded by an English atmosphere, which reflects both the upper-class rituals of the Roman anglophile society and the vivid impression left on d'Annunzio's creative mind by his encounter with the poetry of Keats and Tennyson, on the one hand, and on the other with the language – both poetic and figurative – of the Pre-Raphaelites, Alma Tadema and others.

But it is not in the flowery and eclectic bric-à-brac of the setting, nor in the continuous allusions to themes and figures of the English decadence that significant traces of Pater will be found, other than in a vague reference to the aesthetic vogue which he was rather hazily believed to have initiated. Rather, in some more oblique but relevant way, Pater's figures and themes seem to run under the surface of d'Annunzio's sumptuous fictions. Andrea Sperelli, a man of the present and of the past, is the first character to embody that concept of analogy which was so crucial for d'Annunzio and which had probably been inherited from the great lesson of the master. Nencioni had been very perceptive in pointing to Marius as the predecessor of Sperelli: a character which seems to be at least in part conceived by d'Annunzio as an imaginary portrait of a hero who is the last of a noble family, 'the ideal type of the young Italian gentleman in the nineteenth century, the legitimate champion of a lineage of noblemen and elegant artists, the last scion of an intellectual race'.[14] This hero belongs to an age of transition, as the famous *incipit* of the novel makes clear, when the season is seen in the moment of its natural and symbolic death: 'The year was, rather softly, dying'.[15] A similar inclination to create an anti-naturalistic hero seems to have driven d'Annunzio along lines that were strangely similar to Pater in the latter's creation of Marius, despite some obvious dissimilarities.

If Andrea Sperelli can be considered one of the many embodiments of the spirit of the age (more, as Nencioni conceded, because of the analogy between his temperament and that of Marius than because of any evidence of a direct influence) there is no doubt that it was only when the much-respected *doctor mysticus* Angelo Conti (see Maurizio Ascari's essay, pp. 35f.) introduced d'Annunzio to the reading of Pater that the first real impact of the master could be sensed. Conti's *Giorgione* (1894) attacked the 'frozen inquiry' of positivism in favour of an idea of the critic's mission as being similar to that of the artist, and consecrated Pater's famous statement that 'all art constantly aspires towards the condition of music' which from that moment was to echo innumerable times in *fin-de-siècle* criticism. This was to be in spite, perhaps, of the more perceptive and detailed insight into Pater's text which finally arrived in the work of Federico Olivero (1914, 1918) and of course Mario Praz.

D'Annunzio was deeply impressed by the direct reading of Pater under the guidance of the *doctor mysticus*: his review of Conti's work ('Note su Giorgione e su la Critica', 'Notes on Giorgione and Criticism') which appeared in *Il Convito* in 1895 pays homage to 'That rich and delicate stylist, Walter Pater, who has died recently, and who was until now unknown in Italy'[16] (and thus overlooking Vernon Lee's and Nencioni's earlier discoveries). The same

---

[14]   'L'ideal tipo del giovin signore italiano nel XIX secolo, il legittimo campione d'una stirpe di gentiluomini e di artisti eleganti, l'ultimo discendente d'una razza intellettuale' (35–6).

[15]   'L'anno moriva, assai dolcemente' (5).

[16]   'Quello stilista delicato e ricco che fu Walter Pater, morto di recente, ignoto in Italia fino a oggi' (73).

review was published six years later as an introduction to *La beata riva: trattato dell'oblio* (1900), Angelo Conti's definitive critical work which was, again, to prove extremely influential on d'Annunzio's idea of the role of style and criticism in the system of the arts of *fin-de-siècle* aesthetics. What is even more revealing is the way in which Pater's figures and ideas appear to surface, although intermittently and endlessly interwoven with the other great texts of European decadence (from Nietzsche to Séailles, from Schopenhauer to Barrès), in the two novels by d'Annunzio which follow *Il piacere*.

In the prose-poem *Le vergini delle rocce* – a true repertory of decadent imagery and thought – the figure of Claudio Cantelmo is seductively evocative, as the title itself suggests, of Pater's myth of Leonardo – he is the belated hero in whose physiognomy, like a palimpsest, the past writes and rewrites itself in a manner which is strikingly reminiscent of Pater's reworking of memory and history in *Marius* and the *Imaginary Portraits*. At the same time the metamorphosis of Plato into the aesthetic thinker, and the predominance of the figure of Socrates in *fin-de-siècle* thought, find their way into the novel through d'Annunzio's familiarity with Pater's *Greek Studies*. The dying Socrates who, fascinated by the sensuality and beauty of life, renounces the certainty of knowledge is not only derived from Nietzsche but, in the context of the novel, he is more significantly the result of the imaginative reworking of the figure of Winckelmann (Marabini Moevs 1976; Lorenzini 1989) as Pater had portrayed him in *The Renaissance*. Claudio Cantelmo is at the same time Socrates and Leonardo, in a play of free association of images and themes which makes *Le vergini delle rocce* such a unique point of intersection of the various influences simultaneously at work in d'Annunzio's text. The landscape, following the precepts of Symbolist aesthetics and revealing itself in the double paradigm of rocks *versus* garden, is openly evocative of the 'country of pure reason or half-imaginative memory' that Pater had explicitly described in his essay on Giorgione: 'That great moribund ancestry added to that land of rocks a sort of mournful beauty.'[17] Time itself has in the novel a strange, definitely Paterian echo: the present is touched by the shadow of a previous life, by the fate of repetition and by that perpetual return to the past (Raimondi 1989) which was one of the themes that Pater had so meaningfully reworked into the fabric of his essays and narratives.

It is again in the pages of *Il fuoco* – in which the discourses on art and its languages, art and life dominate the entire formal and thematic structure of the novel – that the presence of *The Renaissance* can be traced, although obviously mediated by Angelo Conti, and as always combined with a whole array of powerful influences from Nietzsche and European Symbolism: it is indeed a 'splendid accumulation of material', as Henry James (1968, 340) described it. The *locus classicus* of *fin-de-siècle* imagery, Venice, is the rich and golden canvas from which the novel seems to draw its meaning and life. Its colours, form and light, as d'Annunzio evokes them, owe much to the lure of 'The School of Giorgione' (1980), but they especially conjure up the figure of the painter himself: and it is his *fuoco giorgionesco* as Pater had de- and re-constructed it,

---

[17] 'Quella grande stirpe moribonda aggiungeva a quel paese di rocce una specie di funebre bellezza' (45).

that casts a spell on the themes which weave closely around the three characters. The novel itself, in its rhapsodic texture (Lorenzini 1989, 1194), seems to fulfil the concept of *Anders-streben* from which Pater derived the famous concept of music as the ideal of art which had become, as we know, the generative metaphor of the decadent idea of art. 'Look', he said, pointing to the silent level of the lagoon, creased here and there by the passage of a breeze. 'Do not these infinite lines of silence aspire to become music?' (361)[18]

D'Annunzio's poet Stelio Èffrena, in his search for the perfect art, offers the reader in his description of Giorgione's *The Concert* a fascinating reworking of Pater's text, mixing it with the evocation of Socrates' death in *Le vergini delle rocce* which again takes its source from *Greek Studies*:

> [E]merging from the warm shadow like the expression of desire itself, we see the youth with the plumed hat and the unshorn locks, the fiery flower of adolescence, whom Giorgione seems to have created under the influence of a ray reflected from the stupendous Hellenic myth whence the ideal form of Hermaphrodite [...] He knows that he is master of the life that escapes both the others; the harmonies sought after by the player seem only the prelude to his own feast. He glances sideways intently as if turning to I know not what fascinates him, and that he would fascinate.[19] (62)

It is to *Greek Studies* and specifically to the chapter on 'The Myth of Demeter and Persephone' that we have to return again to discover one of the last, and most intriguing, rewritings of Pater's influence into d'Annunzio's novels. The powerful, mournful myth of Persephone does not only act as the major influence on Stelio Èffrena's art: it also lends its features to the great actress Foscarina, 'nocturnal creature', described by d'Annunzio in a long *crescendo* which can be read as a final apotheosis and metamorphosis of Pater's Mona Lisa:

> Thus, with an unlimited vastness and through endless time, the outlines of human age and substance seemed to widen and perpetuate themselves [...] the very genii of the place consecrated by poetry breathed over her and girded her round with alternate visions [...] regions furrowed with blood, laboured by pain, transfigured by a dream or lighted by an inextinguishable smile, appeared, receded, and melted away behind her head.[20] (106–7)

---

18 'Guarda' egli disse, indicando la taciturna pianura lagunare che qua e là si corrugava al passaggio dell'aura. 'Queste infinite linee di silenzio non aspirano a divenir musica?'
19 'Ma è pur quivi, emerso fuor della calda ombra come la espressione stessa del desiderio, il giovanetto dal cappello piumato e dalla chioma intonsa: l'ardente fiore d'adolescenza, che Giorgione sembra aver creato sotto un riflesso di quello stupendo mito ellenico donde sorse la forma ideale d'Ermafrodito [...] Egli sa d'essere padrone di quella vita che sfugge ad ambo gli altri, e le armonie ricercate dal sonatore non gli sembrano se non il preludio della sua propria festa. Il suo sguardo è obliquo e intenso, rivolto a una parte come per sedurre non so qual cosa che lo seduca' (247).
20 'Così in una vastità senza limiti e in un tempo senza fine pareva ampliarsi e perpetuarsi il contorno della sostanza e dell'età umana [...] i genii stessi dei luoghi consacrati dalla poesia alitavano sopra di lei, la cingevano di visioni alterne

Again, Persephone blends in with the mood of enchantment that arises, first of all, from the physical geography of Venice and its dead waters, and is transformed, imperceptibly, into a Paterian sense of death.

> [D]uring the afternoon we went to visit Torcello. I had already begun living in the myth of Persephone in those days, and the work was being slowly formed within me, so that I felt as if I were gliding on Stygian waters and passing into the regions that lie beyond them. Never had I known a purer and sweeter foretaste of death, and that feeling had made me so light that I could have walked on the meadow of Asphodel without leaving a footprint.[21](20)

Symptomatically, *Il fuoco* is also the novel in which the presence of the master himself as a source of endless suggestion is evoked beneath the fictional disguise of Daniele Glauro, 'fervent and sterile ascetic of beauty' (30).[22] Though this is an obvious reference to Angelo Conti, the figure of the aesthetic critic seems at the same time a coded homage to Pater and the influence that he exerted on the first, fertile period of d'Annunzio's controversial career.

It is with this passing reference to Daniele Glauro that this essay must end. From Pater's mysterious visit to Rome in 1883, to his virtually ending up as a fictional character, we seem to have come full circle. *Il fuoco* was published in 1900: at the beginning of the new century, new critical eyes would soon look with profound insight into Pater's work and his achievements.

[...] i paesi rigati di sangue, travagliati dal dolore, trasfigurati da un sogno o rischiarati da un sorriso inestinguibile, apparivano, lontanavano, dileguavano dietro la sua testa' (283).

[21] 'nel pomeriggio andammo a visitare Torcello. Come in quei giorni io avevo già incominciato a vivere nel mito di Persefone e l'opera andavasi formando in me segretamente, mi sembrava di navigare su le acque stigie, di trapassare nel paese *di là*. Non avevo mai avuto un più puro e più dolce sentimento della morte; e quel sentimento mi rendeva così leggero che avrei potuto camminare senza lasciare orma su la prateria d'asfodelo' (212).

[22] 'fervido e sterile asceta della bellezza' (225).

2 The fortune of *The Renaissance* in Italian art criticism, 1894–1944

Maurizio Ascari

My essay will focus on the reception *The Renaissance* had in Italy in the period between the *fin de siècle* – when the novelty of Pater's aesthetic gospel reached the country through outstanding decadent writers such as Angelo Conti and Gabriele d'Annunzio – and the cultural watershed of the Second World War. In the fifty years between 1894 and 1944 Pater played a major role in Italian art criticism and aesthetic thought, thanks to a process of diffusion pivoting on Aldo de Rinaldis's translation of *The Renaissance* in 1912. This critical itinerary will bring us into contact with art critics as noteworthy as Roberto Longhi, but it will only marginally touch upon the works of Gabriele d'Annunzio and Mario Praz, which are discussed by the two other Italian contributors to the present volume.

In order to establish right from the start some basic co-ordinates I have decided to begin with a backward glance from the postwar period, when Lionello Venturi published his *Storia della critica d'arte* (*History of Art Criticism*, 1948) where he concisely traced the estrangement of art history from its original idealistic drive and its subsequent rebirth. In assessing the theoretical grounds of his discipline, Venturi highlighted the fracture that took place in the nineteenth century between 'the progress achieved in the publication of documents and in their philological commentary'[1] on the one hand and the immaturity of aesthetic judgement on the other. In the positivist period historical disciplines tended more and more towards the discovery and definition of facts, almost forgetting 'the ideas from which they started in order to interpret them'.[2] In Venturi's words, 'the new historians were philologist-historians who rejected and despised philosopher-historians'.[3] Art history thus became a matter of classification akin to natural history, a mode of thinking that reached its climax with Taine's cultural determinism. But, as Venturi put it: 'After so to speak touching the bottom, aesthetics resurrected at the beginning of our century.'[4]

---

[1] 'il progresso raggiunto nella pubblicazione dei documenti e nel loro commentario filologico' (10).
[2] 'le idee da cui erano partiti per interpretarli' (11).
[3] 'i nuovi storici furono storici-filologi, e rifiutarono e spregiarono gli storici-filosofi' (11).
[4] 'Dopo aver così toccato il fondo, l'estetica risorse nel principio del nostro secolo' (12).

In the eyes of the Italian art critic, Pater – who strove to define beauty in concrete terms and to penetrate the personality of the artist – played such a major role in this process that he is described as 'the most notable European follower of idealist art criticism'.[5] Venturi labelled Pater's essays on Botticelli, Luca della Robbia, Leonardo and Giorgione as masterpieces and his remarks are an apt introduction to the present critical overview insofar as the history of Pater's Italian reception is closely intertwined with the critical reception of Botticelli, Leonardo and Giorgione, three painters whose temperament was in harmony with the turn-of-the-century aestheticizing tendency.[6]

The influence of Pater on Italian Decadentism

The literary formation of the young Angelo Conti took place at the beginning of the 1880s in the intellectual milieu of the Roman review *Cronaca bizantina*. Conti met Gabriele d'Annunzio in 1882 and that year marked the beginning of a friendship that was fundamental for the cultural growth of both writers. In 1894 Conti was assigned to the Gallery of the Academy in Venice and produced a monograph devoted to Giorgione (*Giorgione*, 1894), which was soon followed by a Catalogue of the Galleries in Venice (*Catalogo delle gallerie di Venezia*, 1895). Back in Florence, in 1896 Conti started to contribute to the newly created review *Il Marzocco*, and after spending a period in Rome he settled in Naples in 1904, where he first directed the National Museum and then from 1925 the Art Gallery in Capodimonte.[7]

1900 may be regarded as the annus mirabilis of Aestheticism in Italy, since in that year Conti's treatise *La beata riva* was published with a preface by d'Annunzio, while the novelist used his friend as a model for the character of Daniele Glauro in *Il fuoco*. The critic Pietro Gibellini is right in defining the two texts as 'a diptych both symmetrical and complementary',[8] reminding us that the actress Eleonora Duse (a friend of Conti's, and d'Annunzio's theatrical muse) wrote in that year, "'Send me the *Beata riva*, and send me *Il fuoco*. I wish to read the books of the two brothers who resemble one another so much and so little.'"[9] The aesthetic premises of *La beata riva*, however, are to be found in the previous volume Conti wrote on Giorgione, where the influence of Pater is apparent, as Ezio Raimondi remarks:

---

[5]   'il maggiore continuatore europeo della critica d'arte idealistica' (319).

[6]   The nineteenth-century rediscovery of Botticelli after a long period of oblivion is explored by Frank Kermode in the first chapter of *Forms of Attention* (1985), Chicago: University of Chicago Press.

[7]   Various books help to contextualize Angelo Conti within the wide spectrum of Italian Decadent culture: Walter Binni (1961) *La poetica del decadentismo*, Florence: Sansoni; Sandro Gentili (1981) *Trionfo e crisi del modello dannunziano: Il Marzocco, Angelo Conti, Dino Campana*, Florence: Vallecchi; Ricciarda Ricorda (1993) *Dalla parte di Ariele: Angelo Conti nella cultura di fine secolo*, Rome: Bulzoni; Laura Romani (1998) *Il tempo dell'anima: Angelo Conti nella cultura italiana tra Otto e Novecento*, Rome: Studium.

[8]   'un dittico fatto di simmetria e di complementarità' (Gibellini 2000, xv).

[9]   "'Mandatemi la *Beata Riva*, e mandatemi *Il Fuoco*. Voglio leggere i due libri dei due fratelli che tanto e così poco si somigliano'" (Gibellini 2000, xv).

Conti's Aestheticism, with the same spirit of his old essay on Giorgione, derives from Pater's idea that 'all art constantly aspires towards the condition of music' and reshapes it in a lyrical-speculative form which is taken from Kant and Schopenhauer, with the added ingredient of an almost priestlike stupor.[10]

In his recent study on Conti, Giorgio Zanetti repeatedly explores the affinity between the thought of Pater and Conti, insisting on the role Conti's friend Vernon Lee (alias Violet Paget) played as a mediator between them (1996, 27). Already on 10 May 1885 Lee published an article entitled 'La morale nell'estetica: appunti sul nuovo libro di Walter Pater' ('Morals in Aesthetics: Notes on Walter Pater's Latest Book') in *Fanfulla della domenica*, the weekly supplement of the Roman newspaper *Fanfulla*. Although in those pages Lee dealt mainly with *Marius the Epicurean*, she also commented on the role Pater's *The Renaissance* played within the aesthetic movement, the spirit of which was described by the critic as follows:

> that spirit was a craving for the beautiful, the new, for the most refined or most stunning things, something that could charm, titillate or shake the imagination – the desire of aesthetic sensations, emotions, visions, or if you prefer hallucinations. They wanted the beautiful at any cost, and the beautiful included – for the bizarre character of all the times of imaginative fervour – also the horrible, the loathsome, I would almost say the ugly.[11]

Lee regarded Pater as the interpreter of this cultural phase, the thinker who was able to capture its ambivalent soul and its love for syncretism, offering 'a mystical description of it in that stupendous *rêverie* he wrote about the Mona Lisa'.[12]

A similar aesthetic temper presided over the birth of Conti's volume on Giorgione, which was intended as a sort of pamphlet against the dominant tendency in art criticism of the nineteenth century – i.e. *scientific criticism*, focusing on data and the formative influence of the environment. Against this dry erudition, marked by a technical knowledge that discouraged readers and was unable to address the fundamental issues of life, Conti advocated a form of *poetic criticism*, capable of establishing an inspired continuity with the artist's creativity and to probe the depths of his/her soul. In Conti's eyes, the 'dubious and fatal criticism which aims at catalogues'[13] should make way for

---

[10]   'L'estetismo del Conti, con lo stesso spirito del suo vecchio saggio su Giorgione, prende le mosse dall'idea del Pater secondo cui "tutte le arti aspirano a raggiungere la condizione della musica" e la riprospetta in una forma lirico-speculativa mutuata da Kant e da Schopenhauer con l'aggiunta di uno stupore quasi sacerdotale' (132).

[11]   'quello spirito era la brama del bello, del nuovo, della cosa più raffinata o più stordente ancora, che potesse invaghire, o stuzzicare o scuotere l'immaginazione: il desiderio della sensazione, dell'emozione, della visione, o se preferite, dell'allucinazione estetica; si voleva ad ogni costo il bello, includendo nel bello, per una stranezza di tutte le epoche di fervore immaginativo, anche l'orribile, lo schifoso, direi quasi il brutto' (2).

[12]   'una mistica descrizione in quella pagina di stupenda *rêverie* che scrisse intorno alla Monna Lisa' (2).

[13]   'dubbia e funesta critica di cataloghi' (11).

'the operation which penetrates the meaning of forms and attains the essence of things'.[14] After beautifully enunciating these concepts in his prologue, Conti – the apologist of enthusiasm, poetry in art and the sense of life – elaborated them in the third chapter of his work: 'La musica della pittura' ('The Music of Painting'), which is introduced by the epigraph from Pater, 'All art constantly aspires towards the condition of music' (33).

Against the positivist tendencies of the late nineteenth century, Conti devised a form of aesthetics that goes beyond the idea of the symbol, preaching instead an alchemical process of transfiguration of nature into art whose catalyst is music – the 'mysterious link between the various art forms'.[15] Starting from this assumption and referring back to the aforementioned epigraph, which represents the core of Pater's aesthetics, the prose of the Italian critic reads as a sort of imaginary dialogue with his English *confrère*. One would be tempted to claim that while writing down these sentences Conti was actually mentally translating Pater's dictum into his own language and redefining it in the course of this process:

> All arts aspire to something which goes beyond the material symbol. But why should one say *all arts*? Could not one say – or better, should not one, in order to be more precise – say *art*? In fact all arts, in the diversity of their languages, are united in the supreme aim to satisfy the metaphysical tendency of human nature. And art, which is one only, is the aspiration and the prayer of the world.
>
> Again, one should not say *all arts*, because there is an art which, having almost succeeded in freeing itself from the material symbol and having a mysterious physical nature, can be considered as pure art. Indeed, no form of human expression can exceed the power of music in representing the religious sentiment of humanity.
>
> Therefore I will state the following principle: all arts tend to free themselves from the symbol (that is to say to deny themselves) and imply a constant aspiration towards music.[16]

This passage represents a careful and insightful meditation on a translation problem that both Aldo de Rinaldis and Mario Praz subsequently abstained

---

[14]   'alla operazione che penetra il significato delle forme e giunge all'essenza delle cose' (11).

[15]   'legame misterioso delle varie forme artistiche' (36).

[16]   'Tutte le arti aspirano a qualcosa che va oltre il simbolo materiale. Ma perché dire *tutte le arti*? Non si potrebbe, anzi non si dovrebbe, per maggiore esattezza, dire *l'arte*? Tutte le arti infatti, nel loro così diverso linguaggio, si ricongiungono nello scopo supremo di soddisfare la tendenza metafisica della natura umana. E l'arte, che è una sola, è l'aspirazione e la preghiera del mondo.

Non si dovrebbe dire *tutte le arti*, anche perché c'è un'arte la quale, essendo quasi riuscita a liberarsi dal simbolo materiale e della quale il fondamento fisico è misterioso, può essere considerata come l'arte pura. Dopo la musica manca infatti ogni altra manifestazione al sentimento religioso dell'uomo.

Io pongo dunque il seguente principio: tutte le arti tendono a liberarsi dal simbolo (cioè a negare se stesse) e contengono una costante aspirazione verso la musica' (36).

from tackling in their respective translations of Pater's essay on Giorgione, as is shown by their versions of Pater's celebrated pronouncement:

> *Tutte le arti aspirano costantemente a raggiunger la condizione di musica.* (de Rinaldis 1912, 146)
> *Tutte le arti aspirano costantemente alla condizione della musica.* (Praz 1944, 43)

Choosing to be ambivalent, Pater employed the term art in the singular, but the resources of his language would have enabled him to opt for the plural, had he wished, so as to point out the individual character of each art. We should not forget that according to Pater 'the sensuous material of each art brings with it a special phase or quality of beauty, untranslatable into the forms of any other' (Pater 1893, 136) and that he valued this principle so much as to define it as 'the beginning of all true aesthetic criticism' (136). By using 'art' in the singular Pater seemed to reassert – in the name of the *Anders-streben*, i.e. of the tendency of each art to overcome its limits in order to achieve the effects of another medium – that unity of art he elsewhere denied. This may seem a matter of nuances, but it is far from marginal, since, as we shall see, the role of Pater in the Italian aesthetic debate at the beginning of the twentieth century was also linked to the problem of defining a common denominator of art.

Although the theories of Pater and Conti have much in common, both implying an *Anders-streben* pivoting on music, they also reveal some interesting differences. The religious dimension of Conti's aesthetics, which became apparent in his last works, devoted to Virgil and Saint Francis, is a case in point. Moreover, relying on Schopenhauer and Lessing, Conti distinguished music from the other arts because of its temporal development – 'Music is the least impure of the arts, because it lives only in time and its symbol is fleeting.'[17] He likewise asserted that all the arts tend 'to acquire the power to speak to the inner dimension, immediately – this represents their aspiration to attain the condition of music.'[18] Yet Conti often reverted to Pater:

> In lyrical poetry too, more than in any other art forms, one can see that the ultimate aim of art is to express its intimate aspiration to approach music and to free itself from the symbol. Indeed, in lyrical poetry the symbol is transformed and attains such a high degree of ideality that, in the supreme moments of inspiration, we see words lose their literary meaning and take on a musical one.[19]

One is tempted to read between these lines a passage where Pater described the perfection of lyrical poetry as dependent on 'a certain suppression or

---

[17]   'La musica è l'arte meno impura, perché vive solo nel tempo e il suo simbolo è fugace' (37).

[18]   'ad acquistar la potenza di parlare all'intimo, *immediatamente*; in ciò consiste la loro aspirazione a raggiungere la condizione di musica' (37).

[19]   'Anche nella poesia lirica si vede, più che in ogni altra forma artistica, che scopo supremo dell'arte è di esprimere la sua intima aspirazione ad avvicinarsi alla musica e a liberarsi dal simbolo. Nella lirica infatti il simbolo si trasforma e raggiunge un tal grado d'idealità che, nei momenti supremi dell'ispirazione, vediamo la parola perdere il senso letterario ed assumere un senso musicale' (37).

vagueness of mere subject, so that the meaning reaches us through ways not distinctly traceable by the understanding' (1893, 144).

These are the Paterian principles Conti applied to the analysis of Giorgione's work, aiming to refute the 'artistic Darwinism'[20] of German origin which dominated criticism at that time, but curiously Pater was not mentioned by Conti in his epilogue 'L'arte e la critica' ('Art and Criticism'), where he not only started a polemic against the Italian critic Adolfo Venturi, but also eulogized Eugène Müntz, Gabriele d'Annunzio and Gabriel Séailles. One could safely conclude that Pater was so omnipresent in the book that further mention was hardly needed – at least in the eyes of the initiated to whom it was addressed.

As early as 1895 d'Annunzio himself reviewed the volume – under the title 'Note su Giorgione e su la critica' ('Notes on Giorgione and on Art Criticism') – for *Il Convito*, a Roman literary journal that was directed by Adolfo de Bosis. The *Imaginifico*, as the writer styled himself, did not abstain from reshuffling this material as part of the preface to *La beata riva* and his commentary provides a good introduction to Conti's aesthetic criticism since it helps us to see it in the context of the turn-of-the-century methodological debate:

> Thus by repudiating the biographical method that was practised by Sainte-Beuve, as well as the sociological and geographic one that was practised by Taine and the more recent complex methods of psychiatry which derive from the former, he regarded the art work *per se*, out of time, not only as isolated from common life, but also as detached from the particular life of its creator.[21]

In this respect the impenetrable obscurity which surrounded Giorgione's biography was a blessing for Conti, as d'Annunzio explained: 'the mythical and dream-like atmosphere Giorgione seems to breathe as a semi-god in a cloud of fire is more favourable to the imaginations of the poet and the philosopher, since it allows the wildest raptures of thought and sentiment'.[22] These words are a symptom of a fully decadent attitude and may remind us not so much of Pater as of Oscar Wilde, who revisited Pater's method in 'The Critic as Artist' (1890), wondering 'Who, again, cares whether Mr. Pater has put into the portrait of the Mona Lisa something that Leonardo never dreamed of?' (Wilde 1966, 1028). Wilde judged Pater's description of the painting as one of the highest instances of criticism precisely because 'It treats the work of art simply as a starting-point for a new creation' (1029). Likewise, d'Annunzio wrote in his preface to *La beata riva*:

---

[20] 'darwinismo artistico' (38).

[21] 'Così ripudiando il metodo biografico praticato dal Sainte-Beuve come quello sociologico e geografico praticato dal Taine e i più recenti metodi complicati di psichiatria che dai primi derivano, egli considera l'opera d'arte *in sé*, fuori del tempo, non soltanto isolata dall'esistenza comune, ma anche distaccata dall'esistenza particolare dell'artefice che l'ha prodotta' (vii).

[22] 'l'atmosfera mitica e quasi di sogno, in cui Giorgione sembra respirare come un semidio in una nuvola ignea, è favorevole alle imaginazioni del poeta e del filosofo, permette le più sfrenate ebrezze del pensiero e del sentimento' (xii).

Does Angelo Conti manage in those ways to show us the true essence of Giorgione's art? One can legitimately doubt that. But who cares? Perhaps we are not facing Giorgione, but we are certainly facing a chosen spirit who, thinking and feeling with deep sincerity, is trying to communicate with all the virtues of the word the emotions he felt before those forms of beauty that in his eyes represent the purest and brightest expression of life. Is he not thus offering us a pleasure far superior to that we would be given by some detailed and cold pages of scientific documents? Let us read the chapter where he comments and illustrates the formula of that delicate and rich stylist, Walter Pater, who has recently died and who was unknown in Italy until today – *All art constantly aspires towards the condition of music* – Here the metaphysical tendency, which is so strong in him, finds its natural outlet.[23]

Conti's criticism was legitimated by d'Annunzio in the name of a rarefied impressionism which can be ascribed to Pater. Likewise in *La beata riva* Conti himself asserted that the task of criticism consists of 'divulging, through an invention, the invention of the artist. All else is vain.'[24]

Although Pater is not included in the list of acknowledgements which introduces *La beata riva* – 'The things I wrote in the present work derive from Plato, Immanuel Kant and Arthur Schopenhauer'[25] – Conti paid homage to the critic in the Appendix, 'L'Arte delle Muse'[26] ('The Art of the Muses'):

As all the arts aspire, according to the happy intuition of Pater, to attain the condition of music, music, which is the synthesis of them all, aspires like the others to free itself from its sensible element in order to attain the condition of musical silence in dance.[27]

By combining Pater's thought with that of Schopenhauer, Wagner and Nietzsche, Conti created a complex metaphysical system of the arts where two

---

23   'Riesce Angelo Conti per tali modi a mostrarci la vera essenza dell'arte giorgionesca? È lecito dubitarne. Ma che importa? Noi non ci troviamo forse davanti a Giorgione, ma certo davanti a uno spirito eletto il quale, pensando e sentendo con profonda sincerità, cerca di comunicarci con tutte le virtù della parola le emozioni da lui provate al conspetto di quelle forme della bellezza che per lui rappresentano la più pura e più luminosa manifestazione della vita. Non ci offre egli così un piacere assai superiore a quello che ci potrebbero dare alcune pagine di documentazione scientifica precise e fredde? Leggiamo il capitolo in cui egli comenta e illustra la formula di quello stilista delicato e ricco che fu Walter Pater, morto di recente, ignoto in Italia fino a oggi: – *All art constantly aspires towards the condition of music*, tutte le arti aspirano costantemente a raggiungere la condizione di musica. – Qui la tendenza metafisica, che è in lui così forte, trova il suo natural campo' (xviii–xix).

24   'nel far conoscere, mediante una invenzione, l'invenzione dell'artista. Tutto il resto è vano' (202).

25   'Le cose da me scritte nel presente lavoro derivano da Platone, da Emanuele Kant e da Arturo Schopenhauer' (1).

26   A shorter version of this essay had originally been published in *Il Marzocco* on 10 September 1899 with the title '*Il ritmo della musica*' (The rhythm of music).

27   'Come tutte le arti aspirano, secondo la felice intuizione del Pater, a raggiungere la condizione di musica, la musica, che è la sintesi di tutte, aspira come le altre a liberarsi dal suo elemento sensibile, per raggiungere nella danza la condizione di silenzio musicale' (228).

opposites such as music and silence meet, generating with their alternation the breath of the world. 'If in nature mystery has a voice, this voice is music'[28] wrote Conti, insisting in a prophetic and inspired style on the link between music, the depths of the human soul and the rhythmic totality of the universe:

> Each sound, each wave of sounds has the power to call our spirit, to wake it up and to make it perceive the identity between its own life and the life of things. Every sound, every wave of sounds speaks to the deepest part of our being, and in the intervals, which are true islands in the sea of sounds, makes us hear the voice of silence. In the pauses the sounds keep silent, the noises of existence keep silent and the silence of life appears. In time as well, that is to say in the texture of phenomena, it is possible to conceive of the essence of music only in the succession of silence between intervals of sound, that is to say in the apparition of silence in the form of rhythm. Rhythm generates sounds and gives voice to mystery, wakes up the tumult of existence and the silence of life within ourselves. It is the sign of what runs to death and of what is eternal and infinite.[29]

This passage testifies to the vast metaphysical implications Conti's aesthetic theory acquired in *La beata riva*.

Although it is difficult to assess to what extent Conti contributed to Pater's celebrity in Italy, it must be noted that when in 1902 Ulisse Ortensi published a biographical and critical essay on Pater, 'Letterati contemporanei: Walter Horatio Pater' ('Contemporary Writers: Walter Horatio Pater'), he glossed over *The Renaissance* in order to focus on *Imaginary Portraits* and *Marius the Epicurean*. Since the article was published in an art magazine (*Emporium*), could we perhaps attribute Ortensi's choice to the fact that Pater was known primarily as the author of the former volume? A lawyer turned librarian to satisfy his vocation for *belles lettres*, Ortensi translated many poems from the English and also published several essays on foreign literatures. This may explain his interest in Pater as a writer rather than as an art critic.

And yet it is to another literary critic we owe the first article that specifically dealt with Pater's volume, Federico Olivero's 'Walter Pater ed i suoi studi sul Rinascimento' ('Walter Pater and his Studies in the Renaissance', 1909).[30] Olivero taught English literature at the University of Turin and his view of

---

[28] 'Se nella natura il mistero ha una voce, questa voce è la musica' (230).

[29] 'Ogni suono, ogni onda di suoni ha la virtù di chiamare il nostro spirito, di risvegliarlo e di fargli sentire la identità fra la sua stessa vita e la vita delle cose; ogni suono, ogni onda di suoni parla alla parte più profonda del nostro essere, e negli intervalli, vere isole nel mare dei suoni, ci fa sentire la voce del silenzio. Cessano nelle pause i suoni, tacciono i rumori dell'esistenza e appare il silenzio della vita. Anche nel tempo, cioè a dire nel tessuto dei fenomeni, non è possibile concepire l'essenza della musica se non nel succedersi del silenzio fra gli intervalli sonori, cioè a dire nella apparizione del silenzio in forma di ritmo. Il ritmo genera i suoni e dà una prima voce al mistero, sveglia in noi il tumulto dell'esistenza e il silenzio della vita, è il segno di ciò che corre verso la morte e di ciò che è eterno ed infinito' (231–2).

[30] This study was published in a small university review – *Studium* – but an abstract was also printed. A copy of this pamphlet is kept at the Biblioteca dell'Accademia delle Scienze di Torino and this made it possible to include it in this itinerary.

Pater is much more analytical and objective, albeit less creative and fertile than Conti's. Pater's criticism is here described as the effort to analyse the impression a work of art produces in the viewer, identifying the particular quality (such as Leonardo's *chiaroscuro* or Buonarroti's *incompleteness*) which triggers this aesthetic emotion. Pater did not, according to Olivero, conceive painting as an end in itself, but as a starting point from which to explore the psychological condition of the artist. As a result he came to regard the Renaissance as a movement guided by an idealistic, rather than a formalist, tendency and Olivero argued that the novelty of Pater's critical insight lay precisely in his perception of the Renaissance as an 'intense aspiration towards the ideal'.[31]

Far from identifying the Renaissance with a simple longing for classical culture, Pater emphasized its forward-looking dimension, describing it as a prelude to Romanticism, on account of its sadness, pathos and spleen. Pater thus dwelt upon the veil of melancholy and thoughtfulness which weighed on Pico della Mirandola and Winckelmann, as well as on the obscure torment that underlay various masterpieces. Michelangelo's poetry and sculpture are a case in point, since they were interpreted by Pater as symbols the artist devised in order to render his complex and controversial psychology: 'every image is suffused with spirituality, it is an *idea* rather than an *aesthetic form*'.[32] While acknowledging the importance music had in Pater's aesthetic system as the art where form and matter most intimately interfuse, Olivero underlined Pater's interest in psychology and his view of the Renaissance artist's quest for perfection as a desire to capture the essence of life. In this respect, Botticelli may be considered as a subtle psychologist, whose greatness was due not to the intensity but to the singularity of his expression, while Luca della Robbia excelled in conveying a sense of intimacy, Du Bellay anticipated the Romantics' inexplicable sadness and Winckelmann was a precursor of Goethe.

Angelo Conti's 'Leonardo pittore'[33] ('Leonardo the Painter', 1910) brings us back to the more familiar territory of art criticism. Conti opened his essay by focusing on the relationship between Leonardo and his master Verrocchio, to reassert the difference between these two artists and to deny the possibility to learn or teach art, which should be regarded by critics as a gratuitous miracle, for 'Only nature can generate artists, and humans at most can help them find the means to express the word they are destined to pronounce in the world.'[34] Indeed, Conti aimed at disproving the formative influence of the environment in order to emphasize the individual creative power:

---

[31]   'intensa aspirazione verso l'ideale' (11).

[32]   'ogni immagine è irradiata di spiritualità, è un'*idea* più che una *forma estetica*' (8).

[33]   The essay was published in *Leonardo da Vinci: conferenze fiorentine*, a collection of writings including pieces by Benedetto Croce and Edmondo Solmi. In the long critical bibliography published as an appendix to his introductory essay, Solmi did not mention Pater and described the works of Houssaye, Müntz, Gronau and many others as biographies 'di scarso o di nessun giovamento' ('of little or no value', 1910, 48), while he praised without reserve the volume Séailles had written on the painter.

[34]   'La natura sola genera gli artisti, e l'uomo al più può aiutarli a trovare i mezzi d'esprimere la parola ch'essi son destinati a pronunziare nel mondo' (84).

Perhaps it is not yet possible to prevail over a so-called school of scientific criticism which is founded on the mistake I hinted at and which is caught up in the net of chronological prejudice. To those who still believe in the influences bearing on the spirit of geniuses and in the necessity of a classification in art as well as in botany, we can triumphantly reply with Leonardo that the artist generates his works *as things do* [. . . .] A painting, a statue, a building must be born like forests and appear like dawns.[35]

This passage strikes a characteristic note in the prose of Conti, who perceived a mystic link between nature and art (incidentally, in 'The School of Giorgione' Pater did not hesitate to analyse park scenery as a work of art). Yet in addition to this refusal of a determinist approach to art, the essay reveals a far more interesting affinity with Pater, due to Conti's emphasis on the creative action of time, intended both as the corrosive effect of which Leonardo's *Last Supper* is the emblem and as the inverse phenomenon, i.e. the poetics of the unfinished. In this respect Conti compares Leonardo's *Adoration of the Magi* to Michelangelo's sculpture:

There are ideas and feelings that the plastic arts cannot represent but with perfunctory means, by taking advantage of what is commonly called *the unfinished*. The unfinished is often a marvellous means of expression for the human genius. It is a reversal of the means nature itself uses to purify and consecrate human masterpieces through the centuries. In this case nature proceeds by elimination, while in the unfinished artwork genius operates in a state of supreme concentration.[36]

One is reminded of the essay Pater devoted to Michelangelo, where the critic identified the sculptor's love for 'unwrought stone' (1893, 80) as the essence of his sweetness and the secret which infused life into his creations. Likewise, Conti's attitude to the Mona Lisa is redolent of Pater's celebrated description:

Looking at the eyes of Monna Lisa del Giocondo, I saw them palpitate in rhythm, in harmony with the music of her smile. I did not know the painting yet, and I was thinking of Leonardo. I thought I could see him, while in his Florentine studio he was waiting for the arrival of the smiling

---

[35] 'Non è forse ancora possibile vincere una così detta scuola di critica scientifica, fondata sull'errore già accennato e chiusa nella rete del pregiudizio cronologico. A coloro che ancora credono alle influenze sugli spiriti geniali e alla necessità in arte di una classificazione come in botanica, noi possiamo trionfalmente rispondere con Leonardo che l'artista genera le sue opere *qual fanno le cose*. . . . Un quadro, una statua, un edifizio debbono nascere come le selve e apparire come le albe' (85).

[36] 'Vi sono idee e sentimenti che le arti plastiche non possono rappresentare se non con mezzi sommarii, se non giovandosi di ciò che comunemente si chiama *l'incompiuto*. L'incompiuto è spesso un mezzo meraviglioso di espressione per il genio umano: è, a rovescio, il mezzo stesso che la natura adopera per purificare e per consacrare nei secoli i capolavori degli uomini. In questi la natura procede per eliminazione, nell'opera rimasta incompiuta il genio lavora in uno stato di concentrazione suprema' (91–92).

sphinx. A little later she entered and sat close to the window [. . . .] He sat too, and after taking the silver lyre he had built with his own hands, he started to sing. The beautiful woman, hearing the melodious hymn, smiled, while in the far distance the Arno grew richer in sparks. Then he started to paint, and after the first strokes an invisible orchestra of lutes resumed the interrupted song. The woman smiled with a queenly calm: her instincts of conquest, of ferociousness, all the heredity of the species, the voluptuousness inherent in seduction and in setting a trap, the gracefulness of deceit, the goodness which hides a cruel intent, all that appeared and disappeared alternatively behind her smiling face and fused in the poem of her smile.[37]

Conti's rhapsodic treatment of the painting betrays the influence of Pater, as is shown by the link between the enigmatic smile of the Mona Lisa and the musical stimulus that produced it according to the legend, as well as by the interpretation of the Mona Lisa as a simulacrum that embodies with the impossible density of an oxymoron the multifaceted collective experience of the human genus. Zanetti emphasizes the importance Pater's description of the Mona Lisa had for Conti, who did not regard memory as a faculty pertaining to the individual, but rather as a quasi-mystical heredity of the species, a subconscious power which can explain the mysterious resurgence of genius (1996, 378–9).

In order to understand the cultural debate which marked the beginning of the century, providing the backcloth against which Pater's reception took place, it may be useful to assess the distance which divides Conti's thought from an important collection of essays by Benedetto Croce – the most important Italian philosopher of that time – also published in 1910: *Problemi di estetica e contributi alla storia dell'estetica italiana* (*Problems of Aesthetics and Contributions to the History of Italian Aesthetics*). Although Croce in turn rejected what he termed as 'empirical aesthetics', whose ideal is zoology or botany, the philosopher likewise disagreed with the decadent attitude of Conti and d'Annunzio (a position he saw as deriving from the 'mystical aesthetics' of the Romantics) in order to advocate what he called 'aesthetics of pure intuition'. Croce's disapproval of the opposite tendencies which had fought for supremacy at the end of the nineteenth century is proved by the following excerpt:

---

[37] 'Guardando gli occhi di Monna Lisa del Giocondo, li vidi palpitare in ritmo, in armonia con la musica del suo sorriso. Il quadro m'era ancora ignoto, e pensavo a Leonardo. Mi pareva vederlo, mentre nel suo studio fiorentino aspettava l'arrivo della sfinge ridente. Poco dopo ella entrava e si sedeva accanto alla finestra. . . . Anch'egli si sedeva, e, presa la lira d'argento che s'era fabbricata con le sue mani, cominciava a cantare. La bella donna, udendo la laude melodiosa, sorrideva, mentre l'Arno da lungi diveniva più ricco di scintille. Poi cominciava a dipingere, e, dopo i primi tocchi una orchestra invisibile di liuti riprendeva la canzone interrotta. La donna sorrideva in una calma regale: i suoi istinti di conquista, di ferocia, tutta l'eredità della specie, la volontà della seduzione e dell'agguato, la grazia dell'inganno, la bontà che cela un proposito crudele, tutto ciò appariva alternativamente e scompariva dietro il volo ridente e si fondeva nel poema del suo sorriso' (93–94).

Aestheticism and historicism are the twin products of the degeneration of criticism conceived as interpretation of the work of art. One cannot deny that aesthetes are artistic souls, but they are also empty. While looking anxiously for Art, they do not grasp any concrete and precise artwork. Historicists are anti-artistic souls, who throw themselves on any artworks in order to dissect them, analyse and compare them with one another and with other facts; but despite having so many contacts with them, they never get in touch with what makes them art, something that only a spiritual act of aesthetic synthesis can capture.[38]

The distance between Croce's aesthetics – which is rigorously grounded in philosophy – and Pater's impressionism is quite apparent. Furthermore, in a chapter on Conti's critical vision, Croce wrote: 'The real critic is not looking for the man himself, but for the soul of the artist',[39] and went on to define *Sul fiume del tempo* (*On the River of Time*, a collection of essays Conti published in 1907) not as a 'book of criticism', but rather as a 'book of art' – that is to say a hybrid and artificial mixture 'of hyperbolized impressions, contrivances based on analogy, imaginative subtleties and intellectual meditations'.[40] By imitating Pater's rarefied manner, the Italian decadents produced what Croce regarded as a form of decorative writing devoid of real analytical value.

The Italian translation of *The Renaissance*

The first Italian translation of *The Renaissance* was made by Aldo de Rinaldis, who was already the author of important critical studies such as *Dell'idea di decadenza nell'arte italiana* (*Of the Idea of Decadence in Italian Art*, 1907) and *La coscienza dell'arte* (*The Consciousness of Art*, 1908), which triggered a heated controversy with Adolfo Venturi. De Rinaldis also engaged in intense activity as the curator of various Italian museums and at the height of his career he became director of the Borghese Gallery in Rome (1933).

Il Rinascimento: studi d'arte e di poesia was printed by the Neapolitan publisher Ricciardi in 1912 and it was followed one year later by the translation of *Imaginary Portraits*. De Rinaldis's long 'Preliminary Note' is particularly useful in assessing the first stage of Pater's reception, since the Italian scholar claimed that the English critic 'is still almost unknown to the Italians. Could it be because his name was not pointed out to us from France and no fragments of his prose came to us through the prose of some French

---

[38]   'Estetismo e storicismo sono le due degenerazioni della critica, in quanto interpretazione dell'opera d'arte. Gli estetisti sono anime artistiche, sì, ma vuote; cercando ansiosamente l'Arte, non s'impossessano davvero di nessuna concreta e determinata opera d'arte. Gli storicisti sono anime antiartistiche, che si gettano su tutte le concrete opere d'arte, le frantumano, le analizzano e le paragonano tra loro e con altri fatti; ma, pur avendo tanti svariati contatti con esse, non vengono mai in contatto con ciò che le fa arte, e che solamente un atto spirituale di sintesi estetica può cogliere' (51).

[39]   'Il critico vero non cerca il suo signor sé stesso, ma l'anima dell'artista' (48).

[40]   'di impressioni iperbolizzate, di escogitazioni analogiche, di sottigliezze immaginifiche e di riflessioni intellettive' (50).

translator?'[41] After stating that Pater's volume 'penetrated with difficulty into some small circles of lovers of foreign literatures'[42] – words which may hint at the milieu of Conti – de Rinaldis remarked that 'in an anthology of modern English literature, which was printed in Italy and edited by an Italian, there is no trace of the writer'.[43, 44]

De Rinaldis's translation is very good for the standards of the time and it is still a delightful read, since the critic was able to phrase his sentences with great elegance, adherence to Pater's thought and an underlying ease in communication. Superfluous ornaments, as well as obscure sentences, are rare, while the text is accompanied by erudite notes that redress wrong attributions and offer philological indications (concerning documents and paintings of recent discovery) in order to bridge the gap between Pater's perspective and twentieth-century art criticism.

It was in the Florentine literary journal *La Voce*[45] that the book was reviewed in the same year of its publication by Roberto Longhi, who was destined to acquire a major role in twentieth-century art criticism, but was then only in his early twenties and could boast as a claim to fame little more than the reputation of his two teachers – Pietro Toesca and Adolfo Venturi. Although Longhi's appreciation of de Rinaldis's version seems enthusiastic, in response to the affinity between writer and translator, the judgement he expresses on the volume is more conditional, for he deems Pater a *general* rather than an *aesthetic critic* (15).[46] According to Longhi, Pater's historical criticism is at its best in his 'almost essentially environmental essays on Pico and Winckelmann'[47] and in his literary essays; it is also acceptable when he deals with the figurative arts only because of the heroic nature of Renaissance art, which requires one to set it within a wider historical frame. On the other hand, while appreciating the theoretical import of the volume, notably 'the belief in the single expressiveness of art',[48] based on the 'repudiation of every metaphysical aesthetics and of every aspiration to pure beauty',[49] Longhi nevertheless laments Pater's tendency to base his analyses on the 'unstable and friable ground of psychology, which can at most reveal something about the

---

[41]   'è rimasto fin oggi quasi del tutto sconosciuto agli italiani. Forse perché il suo nome non ci fu additato dalla Francia e qualche frammento dell'opera sua non ci pervenne traverso la prosa di qualche traduttore francese?' (viii).

[42]   'pentrarono a pena qualche ristretta cerchia di cultori di letterature straniere' (viii).

[43]   'in un'antologia della moderna letteratura inglese, stampata in Italia a cura di un italiano, nulla è registrato o ricordato dello scrittore' (viii).

[44]   Perhaps de Rinaldis was alluding to Pietro Bardi's *Scrittori inglesi dell'Ottocento* (*English Writers of the Nineteenth Century*, 1912), which includes texts by Rossetti, Ruskin, Swinburne and Meredith, among others. While Arnold is at least mentioned in the Introduction (9), Pater does not feature in this text.

[45]   The journal had been founded in 1908 by Giuseppe Prezzolini and in 1912 was temporarily edited by Giovanni Papini.

[46]   Pater himself uses both terms, respectively at the end of his essay on Botticelli and at the beginning of his Preface to the volume.

[47]   'i saggi quasi essenzialmente ambientali su Pico, su Winckelmann' (15).

[48]   'la credenza nella singola espressività dell'arte' (16).

[49]   'ripudio d'ogni estetica metafisica e d'ogni aspirazione alla bellezza pura' (16).

arbitrary inventive originality of human beings, but nothing at all regarding their imaginative talents'.[50]

A more eulogistic review was written in the same year by Giuseppe Saverio Gargano, a literary critic who was particularly alert to the developments of decadent culture both in Italy and in Europe, and who had developed a special interest in English and American literature. Gargano also directed important literary journals such as *Vita nuova* (*New Life*, 1889–91) and *Il Marzocco* (in its first year of life, 1896), where his review of Pater's *Studi sul Rinascimento* appeared on 4 August 1912 under the title 'Walter Pater'.

After describing the book as one of the most original works of the end-of-the-century period, Gargano pointed out the fact that forty years separated its original publication from de Rinaldis's version, whereas various volumes of J. A. Symonds's monumental *Renaissance in Italy* (1875–86) had already been translated.[51] Gargano attributed this anomaly to the superfine quality of Pater's prose, which inevitably addressed an elite:

> The truth is he is a stylist and a man of subtle and deep culture, and these two qualities are not likely to gain all of a sudden the favour of the general public, who are oblivious to the imperceptible nuances of words and thoughts, precisely where the essence of the English aesthete lies.[52]

As Gargano underlined, the same unconventional character marked Pater's method, relying on subjective impressionism rather than historical objectivity. Far from being a dilettantish, undisciplined form of individual expression, however, Pater's aesthetic criticism was the fruit of a special temperament and a vast erudition, and in spite of those who believed in the definitive character of aesthetic judgement, it was not without a philosophical basis:

> This will not lead us to believe, I hope, that Pater is an enemy of philosophy. On the contrary, he is the most philosophic of aesthetic critics, and a leading figure, although his debt to French critics such as Sainte-Beuve, Théophile Gautier and Paul de Saint-Victor cannot be ignored. Yet he intends philosophy like Novalis, one of whose maxims he loves to repeat: *philosophiren ist vivificiren [to philosophize is to vivify]*. His aim is to extract an animated sense of life from literature and art. That is why style is a

---

[50]   'terreno smottato friabile della psicologia che ci rivelerà tutt'al più qualcosa della arbitraria originalità inventiva dell'uomo, ma nulla assolutamente delle sue doti fantastiche' (16).

[51]   John Addington Symonds (1879) *Il Rinascimento in Italia: le Belle Arti*, trans. Sofia Fortini Santarelli, Florence: Le Monnier; John Addington Symonds (1900) *Il rinascimento in Italia: l'era dei tiranni*, trans. Guglielmo de la Feld, Turin: Roux e Viarengo. Incidentally, unlike Symonds, Pater is not mentioned in Corrado Ricci's *Michelangelo* (1900), Florence: G. Barbera.

[52]   'Il fatto è che egli è uno stilista ed un uomo di una coltura sottile e profonda; e queste due qualità non sono fatte per insinuarsi d'un tratto nel gran pubblico a cui sfuggono le leggerissime sfumature della parola e del pensiero, nelle quali è appunto riposta l'essenza dell'arte dell'esteta inglese' (2).

capital question in his activities. To make the expression equal to the impression is a problem he always proposes to solve.[53]

Gargano described *The Renaissance* as an intentionally fragmentary text, remarking that its few inaccuracies as to biographical details or attributions did not alter its value because Pater's interest rested on his assessment of each painter's profile: 'You can see that the method of this critic is really philosophical, since he always strives to get to the elementary formulas which are the sources of genius.'[54] After expanding on Pater's essay on Leonardo, Gargano reserved a word of praise for de Rinaldis, who had brilliantly managed to recreate in his language the stylistic effects of the original. In conclusion, the critic reasserted the elitist nature of the volume, which did not aim at consecrating definitive judgements, but was destined to be appreciated by a narrow circle of adepts, while the crowd preferred the easy certainties of historical critics or of philosophers inclined to be dogmatic: 'But the crowd is satisfied with chronology, photographic descriptions and those general *a priori* ideas that metaphysics can always easily and uselessly formulate.'[55]

Interestingly, in 1912 Pater also received a small and ambiguous mention in a book by Emilio Cecchi, *Studi critici* (*Critical Studies*), a collection of short pieces the influential literary critic had published separately between 1909 and 1911. While reviewing Israel Zangwill's *Italian Fantasies* (1910), Cecchi's attention was curiously drawn by the cover of the volume – a rich floral Madonna which reminded him of Pater and his stereotypical disciple:

> one of those subtle intellects who enjoy looking in our primitives for the dawn of the recurring pagan laxity and gaiety. People who are Christian because they love spiritual experiences, because being a Christian or deluding oneself to be one, predisposes one to enjoy all the moral suavity of those Virgins who, waiting for an aesthete to reveal them, dream with their arms crossed, in shady Gothic cathedrals or peasant brotherhoods.[56]

---

53   'E con ciò non s'intenderà, spero, che il Pater sia un nemico della filosofia. Egli è al contrario il più filosofo dei critici estetici, ed è un caposcuola, quantunque non sia ignota la sua derivazione da alcuni critici francesi, dal Sainte-Beuve, da Théophile Gautier e da Paul de Saint-Victor, specialmente: ma egli intende la filosofia al modo di Novalis, una cui massima ama volentieri ripetere: *philosophiren ist vivificiren*, e il suo scopo è di estrarre dalla letteratura e dall'arte un animato senso della vita. E' perciò che lo stile è la questione capitale delle sue attività. Eguagliare l'espressione all'impressione è il problema che egli si propone di risolvere continuamente' (2).

54   'Voi vedete quale è il procedimento del critico: veramente filosofico, poiché cerca di arrivare sempre alle formule elementari dalle quali si è sviluppato il genio' (2).

55   'Ma per la folla bastano la cronologia, la descrizione fotografica e le idee generali aprioristiche che la metafisica può formulare facilmente ed inutilmente sempre' (3).

56   'uno di quegli intelletti sottili, che godono di ricercare nei nostri primitivi gli albori della ritornante mollezza e festosità pagana: cristiani per amor di esperienze spirituali, perché l'esser cristiano o illudersi di esserlo predispone a gustare tutta la soavità sentimentale delle Vergini che, aspettando l'esteta il quale le riveli, sognano con le braccia in croce, nella penombra delle cattedrali gotiche o delle confraternite contadine' (249).

This passage betrays a satirical undertone. Cecchi represented Pater ironically as an ultimately sterile poseur, somebody who deliberately and artfully fostered his precious emotional life as an end in itself, rather than experiencing it as the outcome of a sincere inner drive.

The dissemination of Pater's aesthetic gospel

One year later Lionello Venturi, the son of Adolfo Venturi, published a volume entitled *Giorgione e il giorgionismo* (*Giorgione and the Giorgionesque*, 1913), in which the young scholar pursued the research he had started with his first work, *Le origini della pittura veneziana* (*The Origins of Venetian Painting*, 1907). In dealing with Giorgione, Venturi could not refrain from tackling the problem of attributions, following in the footsteps of nineteenth-century critics such as Giovanni Battista Cavalcaselle and Giovanni Morelli, who analysed the hundreds of paintings that had been traditionally ascribed to the master in order to select a few credible ones. Cavalcaselle came forward with a list of ten titles, while Morelli drastically reduced it to the three paintings he regarded as the sole reliable starting point for further attributions. It was largely thanks to these two critics that the figure of Giorgione came out of myth and into reality, but Venturi also underlined the importance their preliminary activity had in paving the way for Pater's critical attitude:

> Giorgione realised a principle to which all the arts tend, and which is typically reached by music. According to this principle the subject of an artwork is pervaded by its form, and he put this into practice by freely choosing suitable subjects. And since a little earlier Crowe and Cavalcaselle had revealed as false the attribution of many works where this fusion took place, Pater deduced that Giorgione had handed down to his school the principle he had arrived at.[57]

Studi sul Rinascimento also featured in the bibliography of *Vita di Sandro Botticelli,* an essay Ettore Cozzani published in 1914 and whose affinity with Pater's critical attitude is apparent. Focusing on a marginal figure in the *Adoration of the Magi*, Cozzani identified it as Sandro Botticelli, or better, recognized it as 'the portrait of Sandro's *soul*'.[58] This quasi-mystical and irrational intuition – 'I am tempted to say that even certain documents and the critical inquiries of great scholars would no longer suffice to destroy this certainty'[59] – is the starting point for Cozzano's interpretation of Botticelli's works, where 'everything is pain and always pain'.[60] Like Pater, Cozzani

---

[57] 'Giorgione realizzò un principio cui tutte le arti tendono, e che è tipicamente raggiunto dalla musica, secondo il quale il soggetto di un'opera d'arte è compenetrato dalla sua forma; e lo realizzò con la libera scelta di soggetti adattati. E poiché Crowe e Cavalcaselle poco tempo prima avevano sbattezzato parecchie opere d'arte, in cui tale realizzazione si dimostrava, il Pater deduce che Giorgione trasfuse nella sua scuola il principio raggiunto' (326).

[58] 'il ritratto *dell'anima* di Sandro' (11).

[59] 'quasi non mi potrebber più distruggere tanta certezza documenti certi, e indagini critiche di maestri' (8).

[60] 'tutto è dolore e sempre dolore' (15).

insisted on the 'strange and subtle sweetness of that melancholy which represents his most original grace',[61] and he presented it as a musical theme recurring in the works of the painter: 'Yet no music (for all this panel is music, with a vast and concrete orchestration that only we moderns can understand to the full), no music has ever wound with a subtler melancholy through our open veins'.[62]

In addition to this synaesthetic tension, Cozzani's interpretation struck a distinctly Paterian note when he described Botticelli as a painter who both embodied the 'tormented modern spirit (modern with regard to us as well)'[63] and drew from the sources of classical poetry to capture 'in a brief fable the immanence of the forces and forms that recur in the inexplicable plot of life, which is love and pain'.[64] Cozzani thus explained Botticelli's classical modernity as a melancholy awareness of the transitory character of things, of the omnipresence of pain and moreover of an eternal *why* – a thirst for ultimate knowledge that is never to be quenched. Thus in the critic's eyes the central female figure in the *Primavera*, with her musical gesture, becomes an ineffable and mathematical emblem that represents the mystery of Botticelli without dispelling it:

> It is a mystical gesture, which is rooted in the unconscious will of the poet, who, living and creating in a musical ambience, can but express himself through musical lines. We all know that music is the most intense expression of mystery, because it is the more illogical, unreasonable, unlimited expression of the human spirit, and precisely for that reason it is also the most exact from a mathematical standpoint – like this hand, which can be studied in all its veins and sinews![65]

It is difficult to decide whether the musical dimension of these pages must be ascribed to the decadent temper of the early twentieth century or to the direct influence of Pater, but the lesson of this master remains an important antecedent also in the former case. Although in his title Cozzani prosaically promised to offer a life of Botticelli, he actually traced the portrait of a soul, an inner biography, almost an imaginary portrait *à la Pater*, as is apparent when one contrasts the book with the detached and factual monograph Igino Benvenuto Supino had devoted to this painter a few years before (*Sandro*

---

61   'dolcezza strana e sottile d'una malinconia che è la sua grazia più originale' (16).

62   'Eppure non mai musica (poiché tutta questa tavola è musica, con una vastità e concretezza di orchestrazione che soltanto noi moderni possiamo comprendere fino in fondo) non mai musica ha serpeggiato più sottilmente malinconica per le nostre vene aperte' (18).

63   'tormentato spirito moderno (moderno anche rispetto a noi)' (24).

64   'nella favola breve l'immanenza delle forze e delle forme nella inesplicabile vicenda della vita, che è amore e dolore' (47).

65   'E un gesto mistico, che ha la sua ragion d'essere nella inconscia volontà del poeta, il quale, vivendo e creando in un'atmosfera musicale, non può esprimersi che per linee musicali; e la musica, si sa, è la più intensa espressione del mistero, perché è la più illogica, irragionevole, illimitata espressione dello spirito umano, e appunto per questo la più matematicamente precisa, – come questa mano di cui si possono studiare le vene ed i tendini!' (52).

Botticelli, 1909) or with the anodyne book Adolfo Venturi subsequently wrote on the painter: *Il Botticelli interprete di Dante* (*Botticelli as an Interpreter of Dante*, 1921).

Predictably, Pater also features in *La critica e l'arte di Leonardo da Vinci* (*The Criticism and Art of Leonardo da Vinci*, 1919), where Lionello Venturi explored the critical tradition that had developed through the centuries around the figure of the artist. Venturi acknowledged not only Pater's 'rare critical sensibility'[66] but also a sort of intimate affinity between him and the Renaissance artist: 'The thread in Pater's mind is so subtle that it strangely reminds one of Leonardo's'.[67] That is why Pater's description of the Mona Lisa – 'a masterpiece apart in all the history of art criticism'[68] – has the power to cast such an intense spell. It is worth mentioning that while exploring late nineteenth-century criticism, Venturi lamented the indifference of Italian intellectuals such as Camillo Boito and Edmondo Solmi, who both wrote critical works on Leonardo, to the novelty of the 'refined interpretations'[69] of Stendhal and Pater.[70]

In the same year de Rinaldis wrote 'Il sorriso di Leonardo' (The Smile of Leonardo, 1919), where he compared the main Renaissance artists, discovering in Raffaello's faces a 'static serenity',[71] in those of Michelangelo a 'tormented passion'[72] and in those of Leonardo a 'subtle cerebral character'.[73] While de Rensis deemed Raffaello's Olympian calm distant from the modern spirit, he regarded the uneasiness of Michelangelo's figures and the irritating mystery of Leonardo's as powerful visual stimuli, which were still able to trigger strong responses in critics and public alike. De Rinaldis's interest in Leonardo was also due to the painter's posthumous involvement in what we might call an example of critical symbiosis – i.e. the interaction between the Mona Lisa and Pater's interpretation.

In de Rinaldis's eyes, Pater's reading of the Mona Lisa acquired the value of an *ur-ekphrasis*, a descriptive model that had the power to condition every subsequent interpreter: 'The later variations of poets are obviously included in the magic circle that was traced by Pater's fancy.'[74] As an example, de Rinaldis quoted d'Annunzio's celebrated poem 'Chimera' (1889, later republished as

---

[66] 'rara sensibilità critica' (137).

[67] 'Il filo anzi che conduce la mente del Pater è così sottile, che somiglia stranamente a quello di Leonardo stesso' (138).

[68] 'un capolavoro a parte in tutta la storia della critica d'arte' (138).

[69] 'raffinate interpretazioni' (141).

[70] In a footnote Venturi quoted Camillo Boito's *Leonardo, Michelangelo, Andrea Palladio: studii d'arte* (*Leonardo, Michelangelo, Andrea Palladio: Art Studies*, Milan: Hoepli, 1883); but the first two essays in this volume had already been published in 1879 as *Leonardo e Michelangelo: studio d'arte* (*Leonardo and Michelangelo: An Art Study*, Milan: Hoepli) and Boito's silence on Pater is explained even better by the original date these essays bear – respectively, 1872 and 1875.

[71] 'statica serenità' (265).

[72] 'tormentata passionalità' (269).

[73] 'cerebralità sottile' (269).

[74] 'Le posteriori variazioni dei poeti naturalmente rientrano nel cerchio magico tracciato dalla fantasia del Pater' (268).

'Gorgon'). In order to assess the unsettling power of Leonardo's painting (which was enhanced by Pater's interpretation), de Rinaldis chose to use as a litmus test the long passage where Bernard Berenson described in strongly emotional terms the contrast he felt between his first impression of the Mona Lisa as almost repugnant and his preliminary reading of Pater's prose, which had worked a sort of charm on him, making him oblivious to the real quality of the painting. The Italian critic also reminded his readers that when Berenson, sojourning in the Alps, had been informed of the theft of the Mona Lisa from the Louvre, he had felt almost relieved, as if he had got rid of a nightmare that had obsessed him (271). Ironically, de Rinaldis draws the conclusion that 'the certain proof of Leonardo's charm, rather than in new homages, lies in restless reactions like that!'[75]

The first Italian translation of *The Renaissance* was reprinted in 1925 and this event probably helped trigger a renewed interest in Pater's aesthetics, as is shown by 'Walter Pater critico d'arte' ('Walter Pater as an Art Critic'), an essay the art critic Vincenzo Golzio published at the time in a journal called *L'arte* (*Art*), which was edited by Adolfo Venturi. Pater was regarded by Golzio as a forerunner of modern criticism because of his refusal to believe in a universal notion of beauty, his will to consider 'each artist as an individual who is absolutely distinct from any other',[76] and his effort to single out the particular *active principle* which pertained to that artist alone. In other respects, however, Pater's method was closer to the nineteenth century, as was proved by his tendency to regard the artist as the product of his/her environment (Taine) as well as by his interest in temperament and biography (Sainte-Beuve) – and should therefore be defined as *psychological* rather than *aesthetic criticism* (63). Yet other important aspects of Pater's critical attitude were truly ahead of their times:

> Such is the case when he says that matter and content in themselves have nothing artistic, and that in order to produce an aesthetic emotion matter must be completely fused with form, leaving no residue; when he remarks that in the imagination every thought or sentiment is born together with its symbol or concrete equivalent. Here the principle of art as pure form and the genetic dependence of expressive form on content are already clearly outlined.[77]

Pater's interest in music as the art that realizes above any other this ideal fusion of matter and form induced Golzio to relate him to Romantic mysticism and Symbolism. Yet Pater's tendency to consider the work of art as a starting point

---

[75]   'la riprova sicura del fascino di Leonardo, più che in rinnovate laudi, è in reazioni smaniose come quella!' (271).

[76]   'ogni artista come un'individualità assolutamente distinta da tutte le altre' (63).

[77]   'Così avviene quando dice che la materia e il contenuto di *per se* stessi non hanno nulla di artistico, e che, perché l'emozione estetica si abbia, è necessario che la materia sia già fusa nella forma completamente senza lasciar residui; quando rileva che nell'immaginazione ciascun pensiero o sentimento nasce insieme al suo simbolo o equivalente sensibile. Qui troviamo già chiaramente espressi il principio dell'arte come pura forma e la dipendenza genetica della forma espressiva dal contenuto' (64).

to explore the invisible was also a potential danger, since it led the critic to lose himself in poetic *rêveries* that did not really contribute to our understanding of the artwork, being indifferent to its historical and aesthetic dimension. To illustrate this attitude, Golzio did not refer directly to Pater's highest example of *imaginative criticism* – his Mona Lisa – but to Wilde's paradoxical reading of it, resulting in the conviction that the aim of the critic is to see the object as in itself it really is not. Golzio presented Pater as the exponent of a Neoplatonic tradition going back to Winckelmann and Hegel, which considered classical sculpture as the art *par excellence* due to its power to elevate human beings to an ideal sphere.

Having underlined the elements of novelty in Pater's critical attitude, Golzio stressed his distance from the so-called literary critics, for Pater was far from indifferent to the treatment of pure line and colour, and by spiritualizing these figurative elements overcame the idea of art as the imitation of nature. Indeed although when Pater was faithful to his theoretical premises he lapsed into a form of psychological criticism, when he approached a painting relying on his instinct he produced 'true art criticism, as is shown by his intense sensibility to the particular language of figurative elements'.[78] Leonardo's *sfumato*, for instance, was regarded by Pater precisely as the *virtue* or *active principle* of the painter, whose art 'is all in a melancholy shadow submerging both the figure and the landscape, which are not estranged from one another, but intimately connected'.[79] Pater is thus presented in this essay as a theoretician who was influenced by Taine and Sainte-Beuve, by Neoplatonism and Romantic mysticism, although he was capable of surprisingly modern intuitions that qualify him as a forerunner of twentieth-century formalist critics, thanks to his sensibility to the figurative dimension.

In 1927 Raffaello de Rensis published a new edition of a volume that had appeared in 1910 with the following title: *Anime musicali: introduzione ai poeti musici – G. d'Annunzio, N. Lenau, E. Nencioni, I. U. Tarchetti (Musical Souls: Introduction to Poet Musicians – Gabriele d'Annunzio, Nikolaus Lenau, Enrico Nencioni, Igino Ugo Tarchetti)*. Compared with the previous edition, that of 1927 presents various additions that make it relevant to our critical itinerary, as is shown by its new title: *Anime musicali: la sensibilità musicale nei poeti, letterati, filosofi – Leonardo, d'Annunzio, Lenau, Giorgio Sand, Nencioni, Tarchetti, Oriani, Walter Pater (Musical Souls: The Musical Sensibility in Poets, Literati and Philosophers – Leonardo, Gabriele d'Annunzio, Nikolaus Lenau, George Sand, Enrico Nencioni, Igino Ugo Tarchetti, Alfredo Oriani, Walter Pater)*. As a musicologist linked to the philosophical school of Giovanni Gentile, de Rensis founded in 1908 the publishing house and the weekly journal *Musica (Music)* and in the same year he took part in the creation of the Association of Italian Musicologists. His name is also linked to the foundation of the Italian Institute for the History of Music in 1939.

---

[78] 'vera critica d'arte, come mostra la sua profonda sensibilità al particolare linguaggio degli elementi figurativi' (68).

[79] 'è tutta in un'ombra melanconica, in cui sono immersi la figura e il paese, non più estranei una all'altro ma intimamente collegati' (66).

The second edition of de Rensis's book may strike the reader as a rather incongruous enquiry into the musical sensibility of poets, novelists and philosophers belonging to different countries and epochs. This overview opens with Leonardo, who is included here both as a theoretician and as a painter. Wishing to fill a gap in the critical assessment of Leonardo's personality, de Rensis illustrated the role music plays in his system of the arts, where it features as a *younger sister* of painting due to its transitory character: "'Music, which is consumed while it is born, has a lower dignity than painting, which becomes eternal thanks to its glaze.'"[80] De Rensis also explored the influence of music on Leonardo's paintings, starting from the composition of the famous Mona Lisa, which was 'executed precisely in a musical ambience'.[81]

It is difficult to assess whether these considerations were inspired by Pater's essay on Leonardo, but what can be safely demonstrated is that Pater's aesthetics permeate the following chapter of the volume, where d'Annunzio is presented as an artist whose prose spontaneously tends to a musical flow and whose style translates into practice:

> Walter Pater's famous theory, claiming that art (any art), once it has achieved its ideal climax, its stage of perfection, does not allow one to distinguish the end from the beginning, the shape from its background, the subject from the expression, the image from the emotion.[82]

According to de Rensis, d'Annunzio embodied the decadent musical spirit that also presided over the creations of Wagner, but it is to Pater himself that the critic paid homage at the end of the 1927 edition. The chapter on Pater is almost entirely taken up by a long quotation from de Rinaldis's translation of 'The School of Giorgione' and it is curiously introduced by a rather laconic comment:

> There was a time when, mainly thanks to d'Annunzio, the theory of Walter Pater – that surprising singer of manifest beauties and enchanting discoverer of hidden ones – was met with great acclaim.
>
> *All art constantly aspires towards the condition of music*, he stated with a singularly bright intuition.[83]

Behind the Italian musicologist's insistent reassertion of Pater's message, one can perhaps sense the fear that Pater would be forgotten by the Italians as an

---

[80]   "'La musica, che si va consumando mentre ch'ella nasce, è meno degna della pittura che con vetro si fa eterna'" (21).

[81]   'eseguita appunto in un'atmosfera musicale' (28).

[82]   'la famosa teoria di Walter Pater, secondo la quale l'arte (qualunque arte); giunta al suo apice ideale, al suo stadio di perfezione, non lascia distinguere la finalità dal principio, la forma dallo sfondo, il soggetto dall'espressione, l'immagine dall'emozione' (31).

[83]   'C'è stato un momento, auspice in prima D'Annunzio, in cui la Teoria di Walter Pater, quel sorprendente illustratore di bellezze palesi e discopritore magico di bellezze nascoste, fece fortuna.
       Tutte le arti aspirano costantemente a raggiungere la condizione di musica, egli sentenziò e fu singolarmente intuitivo e luminoso' (97).

outdated decadent by-product. And yet de Rinaldis's translation had been reprinted only two years earlier. Be that as it may, de Rensis saw Pater as the initiator of an important aesthetic trend and treated him as the musical soul by definition.

A few years later Matteo Marangoni published *Saper vedere* (*How to See*, 1933), a purportedly popular work which is marked by a strong polemic vein. The book was not intended as an instance of art criticism, but rather as a method conducive to the development of a critical attitude, in other words as an introduction to aesthetics, with a definite didactic import. Marangoni wished to educate common people to a formalist appreciation of art or, better, to the *method of pure visibility*,[84] as it was called at the time: 'This new world that needs to be revealed is that of *form* as opposed to *content* – a dimension the laity do not know how to evaluate and even less how to fuse synthetically with content itself.'[85]

Formalists wished to exorcise that most evil of demons – the idea of subject, an accessory fact that in their opinion prevented an authentic appreciation of the work of art. Pater was implicitly – rather than openly – implicated in this debate by Marangoni, who claimed:

> The uninitiated always ask what a work of art means as a subject. This question should never be raised, but one should enjoy a painting or a statue as music, whose meaning is never brought into question. The artists themselves, painters or poets, would not in any case be able to translate their works into a logical meaning. The well-known maxim that all the arts tend towards music could also be interpreted in this sense. Only nowadays, as we shall see, do the figurative arts and poetry itself at last aspire to the abstraction and latitude of means which is typical of music.[86]

Here Marangoni reinterpreted the basic assumption of Pater's aesthetics, setting his theory at the origin of a contemporary critical attitude, but Pater's lesson also recurs in the volume in less eulogistic terms. This is how, for instance, Marangoni classified Pater's reading of the Mona Lisa:

> From the banal criticism of Vasari who counted the hairs in her eyelashes, one arrives at the celebrated opening of Walter Pater, which represents the

---

84 In this respect Marangoni quotes Lionello Venturi's 'La pura visibilità e l'estetica moderna' ('Pure Visibility and Modern Aesthetics', 1929), in *Pretesti di critica*, Milan: Hoepli.

85 'Questo nuovo mondo da rivelare è quello della *forma* – intesa nel senso di opposizione a *contenuto* – la quale il profano non sa valutare e tanto meno fondere in sintesi col contenuto stesso' (11).

86 'L'inesperto domanda sempre che cosa un'opera d'arte significa come soggetto. Questo non si dovrebbe mai domandare, ma godere invece un quadro o una statua come una musica, della quale nessuno chiede che cosa significhi. L'artista stesso, pittore o poeta, non saprebbe per lo più tradurre in significato logico la sua opera.
La nota frase che tutte le arti tendono alla musica potrebbe essere interpretata anche in questo senso. Ed oggi soltanto, come vedremo, anche le arti figurative, e la stessa poesia, aspirano finalmente alla astrazione e alla libertà di mezzi della musica' (21).

most illustrious example of *literary criticism*, i.e. a criticism that bears exclusively on contents and is blind to the figurative values, and is unable therefore to ascertain the synthesis of form and content in the absence of which a work of art does not exist.[87]

Not surprisingly, these words are followed by a quotation from Pater's description of the Mona Lisa, which is regarded by Marangoni as a likely example of pure poetry, but certainly not as pure art criticism, although in his last few lines Pater 'finally opens his eyes to look at his heroine',[88] proving that he could also feel 'the stylistic value of the painting'.[89]

In the hope of establishing a communication between art and the great public, Marangoni distanced himself from Pater and his decadent followers. Already in his introduction Marangoni disagreed with the elitist conception of art criticism Conti had expressed in *La beata riva* (Marangoni 1933, 6) and d'Annunzio had enthusiastically praised in his introduction to the volume. Pater's impressionist tendency had fructified in Conti's prose, generating highly personal interpretations where erudition took the ravishing colours of the critic's aesthetic temper. This tendency was firmly opposed by Marangoni, who called Pater to account with a view to refuting his method.

The witness this public prosecutor of art called to testify before his popular jury of readers was none other than Berenson, although Marangoni did not mention him openly and quoted *The Study on Criticism of Italian Art* (1916) unobtrusively in a footnote: 'If on the other hand I were expected to see the Mona Lisa with the eyes of the multitude, or even only with the admiration of a Walter Pater I know I would end by disliking it, as some of the most famous art historians confess.'[90] This attack did not appease Marangoni's anti-decadent wrath and he went on to contrast Pater's debased *literary* interest in classical and Renaissance art with the fields of interest of other literary critics who at least devoted their efforts more profitably to the present time 'with results which are far from negative, as on the other hand happened in similar cases in the past – and even a Walter Pater could prove that – when a long and mature experience was required to penetrate the formal values of art'.[91] Marangoni exemplified this statement by setting Baudelaire's inspired pages on contemporary painting against the rather feeble writings d'Annunzio had devoted to the Renaissance (162). In conclusion, although Marangoni seemed

---

[87] 'Dalla critica banale del Vasari che vi contava i peli dei cigli, si arriva al celebre squarcio di Walter Pater, che è il più illustre esempio di critica *letteraria*; critica esclusivamente contenutista, e cieca dinanzi ai valori figurativi; impotente quindi a scuoprire la sintesi di forma e contenuto, senza di che l'opera d'arte non esiste' (88).

[88] 'riapre gli occhi finalmente a guardare la sua eroina' (89).

[89] 'il valore stilistico del dipinto' (89).

[90] 'Se invece io dovessi, per esempio, vedere La Gioconda con gli occhi della moltitudine, o anche soltanto con l'ammirazione di un Walter Pater, sento che arriverei ad averla in uggia, come lo confessano alcuni persino dei più illustri scrittori d'arte' (160).

[91] 'con risultati tutt'altro che negativi, come avveniva invece in passato in simili casi – e persino Walter Pater potrebbe provarcelo – quando alla penetrazione dei valori formali occorreva una lunga, maturata esperienza' (162).

to attach a certain value to Pater's *Anders-streben* theory, conceiving it as a starting point for a formalist aesthetics, he vehemently rejected Pater's *literary* approach to the work of art as virtually indifferent to its strictly pictorial dimension.

The canonization of Pater in Italy at the time of the Second World War

The monumental study Federico Olivero devoted to the English critic, *Il pensiero religioso ed estetico di Walter Pater* (*The Religious and Aesthetic Thought of Walter Pater*, 1939), is liable to produce a very different effect from Marangoni's formalist perspective. In fact Olivero wished to harmonize Pater's aesthetics with Catholic orthodoxy and in so doing he occasionally distorted it. Given Olivero's syncretic approach to Pater's work, it is not easy to isolate a section where he specifically deals with *The Renaissance*. Chapter XX 'Le arti' ('The Arts') is probably the most relevant to Pater's aesthetics, but its tone is set by a debatable opening statement: 'In art Pater searches for a sincere and convinced religious spirit.'[92] Starting from this weak premise, Olivero adopted a biased interpretative strategy in order to prove that 'religiosity and the aesthetic sobriety of form'[93] are 'the qualities Pater supremely values'[94] in a work of art. Olivero's fundamentally conservative approach to Pater's thought is often correct as far as paraphrase can go, but it is also unable to grasp its elements of transgression and innovation.

It must be recognized that by the 1940s Pater had acquired the status of a classic and his interpretations of Botticelli, Giorgione and Leonardo had become almost taken for granted among art critics, something hinted at *en passant* without any need to insist. This is the impression one gets when reading Sergio Bettini's monograph on Botticelli (*Botticelli*, 1942), where Pater plays the role of an unavoidable antecedent, a critical milestone:

> From Walter Pater's essay onward the observation of the particular psychological reality of these figures who are conscious of a 'sense of displacement or loss about them – the wistfulness of exiles' becomes a commonplace. It is as if they unwillingly answered a call to life and at that threshold lingered, already tired and disappointed in their obligation to live and act (but how briefly), as if on their first appearance they were greeted mournfully by the artist who had to impress them with reality, thus making them mortal.[95]

---

[92] 'Il Pater cerca nell'arte uno spirito religioso sincero, convinto' (325).
[93] 'la religiosità e l'ascetica sobrietà della forma' (334).
[94] 'le qualità che il Pater supremamente apprezza' (334).
[95] 'Dal saggio di Walter Pater in poi è ovvia l'osservazione della particolare realtà psicologica di codeste figure "conscie d'un senso di abbandono e di vuoto nel loro animo: tristezza di esuli", quasi sorgessero a malincuore alla vita e su quella soglia sostassero già stanche e deluse di dover vivere e agire (ma quanto poco); e al loro apparire s'accompagnasse l'accorato saluto dell'artista che ha dovuto imprimerle nella realtà, farle perciò mortali' (17).

Bettini grounded his analysis on Pater's fundamental intuition and underlined that the primordial *absence* of Botticelli's figures produces a double effect. On the one hand it isolates his figures from the surrounding space: 'the images are set against a background which is less and less defined from a spatial point of view'.[96] On the other hand it triggers a similar separation on a narrative level:

> It is obvious that Botticelli's primordial 'sentiment of exile' provokes the detachment of images not only from every environmental reference, but also from every narrative situation, and in the end it is what nourishes the slow and gradual uncoiling of his myths.[97]

Botticelli thus achieves a sense of 'suspended religiosity which presages something out of the present',[98] simultaneously enhancing the rhythmic/musical value of the painting and frustrating any narrative tension towards a subject:

> all this apparent construction of space is no more than the form of a complex and articulated rhythmic unity, and this apparent description of a fact is the creation of a fable – a real fable, an ornamental dance of fancy, a rhythmic animation which does not imply any narrative.[99]

Pater's canonization as a lay patron saint of art criticism is definitely proved by Marialuisa Gengaro's essay 'La "critica immaginativa" di Walter Pater (1839–1894)' ('The "Imaginative Criticism" of Walter Pater, 1839–1894'), which appeared in the Florentine journal *La Nuova Italia* in 1943. Gengaro, who belonged to the school of Paolo d'Ancona and taught history of art criticism at the University of Milan, opened her study with a comparison between the monumental and joyous creative inspiration of Ruskin, always ready to proselytize, and the shy attitude of Pater, who 'never wanted to become the head of a school, who did not create a philosophical doctrine, since he did not feel the need to know that his ideas were shared by other people',[100] and who moreover had a melancholy temper which prompted him 'to seek in works of art what life could not offer him'.[101] Although his desire to grasp the fleeting joy of the present is a sign of his temperamental kinship with Wilde, 'Pater tried to realize this theory in the purely intellectual field, while Wilde translated it into the field of action, and therein

---

[96]   'le immagini vengono a porsi sopra un fondo sempre meno individuato spazialmente' (17).

[97]   'È ovvio, che il primordiale "sentimento d'esilio" botticelliano sollecita il distacco delle immagini non soltanto da ogni determinazione ambientale, ma anche da ogni situazione narrativa; e alla fine è ciò che nutre il lento, graduale costituirsi dei suoi miti' (18).

[98]   'religiosità sospesa e presaga fuor del presente' (18).

[99]   'tutta codesta apparente costruzione di spazio non è che la forma d'una complessa e articolata unità ritmica, e codesta apparente descrizione d'un fatto è la creazione d'una favola –: una vera favola: danza decorativa della fantasia; animazione ritmica senza narrazione' (19).

[100]   'non volle mai farsi capo di una scuola, non creò una dottrina filosofica sentendo la necessità che altri condividessero le sue idee' (3).

[101]   'a cercare nelle opere d'arte quello che la vita non gli poteva offrire' (3).

lay the danger.'[102] Following this train of thought, Gengaro described Pater as 'the purity of Wilde's thought',[103] therefore establishing a curious correlation between him and Angelo Conti, who was famously defined by Giuseppe Antonio Borgese as 'the innocent side of the d'Annunzio cult'.[104]

While expanding on Pater's aesthetic theory, as well as on his interest in Greek art and philosophy, Gengaro mentioned Nietzsche, Wagner and Baudelaire. The scholar was not afraid of pointing out the limits of Pater's imaginative criticism and stressed his tendency to rely on Vasari's attributions and accounts instead of 'determining the intrinsic value of the work of art from a formal point of view'[105] with criteria such as dating and school. Refusing to consider Pater as an outmoded exponent of literary criticism, Gengaro explained his impressionist approach as 'a new creation that is inspired and suggested by the work of art with which the critic comes into contact'.[106]

Gengaro also referred to Pater's reception in Italy, emphasizing the conflict of methods that marked the beginning of the century:

> In Italy, Angelo Conti, who opposed the formalism that dominated contemporary criticism, came very close to Walter Pater's theory, although in practice he was closer to the inspired and mystical tone of Ruskin. Thus he lapsed into that literary or aestheticizing criticism that Benedetto Croce stigmatized for its failure to combine historical interpretation and aesthetic evaluation.[107]

Although critics like Golzio had set Pater within the frame of the naturalist and psychological tradition of Taine and Sainte-Beuve, Gengaro preferred to focus on the influence of French Symbolism. While Ruskin's critical stance was circumscribed by the idea of truth, Pater conceived art not as the imitation of nature, but rather as a 'symbol or image of the infinite we perceive through the veil of nature',[108] due to the Neoplatonic and symbolist essence of his thought, which was akin to Baudelaire's. Showing a critical sensibility that vibrated in sympathy with that of Pater and openly disagreeing with Olivero's thesis, Gengaro declared:

---

[102]   'Pater cercò la realizzazione di questa teoria nel campo puramente intellettualistico, mentre Wilde la tradusse nel campo dell'azione: e qui era il pericolo' (3).

[103]   'la purezza del pensiero di Wilde' (3).

[104]   'l'innocenza del dannunzianesimo' (Gibellini 2000, xxi).

[105]   'determinare il valore intrinseco dell'opera d'arte dal punto di vista formale' (4).

[106]   'una nuova creazione, ispirata e suggerita dall'opera d'arte con cui il critico viene a contatto' (4).

[107]   'Angelo Conti, in Italia, in opposizione al formalismo imperante nella critica a lui contemporanea, si è avvicinato di molto alla teoria di Walter Pater; sebbene, poi, in pratica, si sia accostato maggiormente al tono ispirato e mistico di un Ruskin, cadendo proprio in quella critica letteraria o estetizzante bollata da Benedetto Croce, dove l'interpretazione storica e la valutazione estetica non potranno mai coincidere' (5).

[108]   'simbolo, immagine, di ciò che attraverso il velo della natura traspare dell'infinito' (5).

We are far from art as it was intended by Ruskin or Tolstoy. Art is no longer a means of communication, neither between a human being and God nor between humans, but the eternal and full act of faith in the proclaimed mystery of human existence and of the human destiny both on this earth and beyond it.[109]

It is worth noting that Gengaro specifically dealt with the five essays of *The Renaissance* that had played a major role in the Italian reception of the book, those on Botticelli, della Robbia, Giorgione, Leonardo and Michelangelo. To underline the creative element of Pater's critical writings, Gengaro quoted Wilde, who found it impossible to visit the Mona Lisa at the Louvre without murmuring Pater's hymn to that female mystery and thus saw the painting becoming more beautiful 'on account of the new creation that added to the first'.[110] Yet what Gengaro regarded as the climax of Pater's aesthetic thought – his *ars poetica* – was his essay on Giorgione, which interfuses 'all the particular manifestations of the Romantic spirit that spread from Nietzsche's Germany through symbolist France and fully bloomed when it came into contact with the art of Renaissance Italy'.[111]

It was towards the end of the war that Mario Praz edited his seminal volume on Pater (*Pater*, 1944), an anthology including a new translation of Pater's essays on Botticelli, Leonardo and Giorgione, as well as his notorious Conclusion to *The Renaissance*. Since the link between Pater and Praz will be mentioned in the next chapter, I shall merely take this anthology as the endpoint of our itinerary. In his introduction, Praz dealt with the influence of Pater on Italian culture, notably on Conti and d'Annunzio. The critic also expanded on the difficult task of translating Pater and remarked that 'the persuasive force of his sentences resides rather in a delicate allure, in an impalpable charm, than in a concrete logical chain of terms'.[112] Yet de Rinaldis's elegant translation did not seem to meet with his approval. Praz criticized the text both for its frequent inaccuracies and its stylistic tone, suggesting that de Rinaldis 'strove, as far as we can see with no result, to create an equivalent of Pater's style'.[113] Praz's volume was an important event in Pater's reception and it was followed soon after in 1946 by a new complete translation of *The Renaissance*, again by Praz; but Pater's reception in postwar Italy is part of another story.

What this critical enquiry intends to show is the vitality of the impact Pater's aesthetics had not only on Italian decadents at the turn of the century

---

[109]   'Siamo ben lungi dall'arte come l'intendeva un Ruskin o un Tolstoi: l'arte non è più mezzo di comunicazione, né dell'uomo con Dio, né dell'uomo con l'uomo, ma l'eterno e pieno atto di fede al proclamato mistero dell'esistenza umana e del destino dell'uomo su questa terra e al di là' (5).

[110]   'per la nuova creazione che si aggiungeva alla prima' (6).

[111]   'tutte le particolari manifestazioni dello spirito romantico, che, diffusosi dalla Germania Nietzschiana, attraverso la Francia simbolista, trova la sua più evidente esplicazione a contatto con l'arte del Rinascimento italiano' (7).

[112]   'la forza suasiva delle sue frasi sta più in una delicata lusinga, in un impalpabile incanto, che in una vera e propria concatenazione logica di termini' (xxi).

[113]   's'è sforzato, a parer nostro invano, di creare uno stile che rispondesse a quello del Pater' (xxi).

but also on Italian art critics on a wider scale. One has to recognize that it is sometimes difficult to distinguish the lesson of Pater from that of other thinkers, like Schopenhauer in the case of Conti, or Conti himself with regard to later Italian critics (for example, Bettini). The creative mind was famously defined by Henry James in one of his Prefaces as an 'intellectual *pot-au-feu*' (James 1909, xvii) and this ironic image reminds us that whatever enters our brain inevitably changes its nature, acquiring a new taste. In the absence of precise textual clues such as quotations or bibliographical notes, the process of tracing influences and allusions rests on the personal sensibility of the critical detector and inevitably reveals an arbitrary component. This does not prevent one from acknowledging the widespread, albeit discreet, presence of Pater in the aesthetic thought of early twentieth-century Italy. Pater's rarefied and imaginative prose, his theoretical edifice and his keen pictorial sensibility became an anti-positivist (and at times anti-historicist) model for many critics of aesthetic or formalist creed, even when they criticized what they saw as his limits in order to advocate more advanced positions.

3 Pater's Reception in Italy: a General View

Elisa Bizzotto

The history of Walter Pater's reception in Italy covers more than a hundred years and in several senses parallels the birth and development of English studies in the country. Originating at the end of the nineteenth century, when a number of pioneering scholars introduced Pater's work into the most advanced cultural circles, Pater's fame increased moderately in the first decades of the twentieth century to be firmly established by the early 1930s through the dominant personality of Mario Praz. The undisputed father of Italian research in the field of Anglo–American literature, Praz virtually monopolized Paterian criticism in Italy for the subsequent fifty years, until his death in 1982. Only after this date was the figure of Pater gradually approached from a plurality of viewpoints that have determined his relative popularity at present. At the same time, such a reassessment of the writer could also be seen as corresponding to an increasing interest in English studies displayed by Italian culture at large.

Yet the launching of Pater's fortune in Italy was not strictly speaking a wholly national process. It was, in fact, fundamentally · indebted to an Englishwoman, Violet Paget, generally known by her *nom de plume* of Vernon Lee (1856–1935). Lee represented one of the most extraordinary figures of cultural mediation at the Italian turn of the century, and her Florentine residences attracted *fin-de-siècle* artists and cultured eccentrics. Some of these personalities were regular contributors to the most avant-garde Italian magazines of the time, urging post-Risorgimento Italy to join the European cultural debate. In *Fanfulla della domenica*, a literary Roman weekly characterized by professed attention to foreign influences, Vernon Lee's article 'La morale nell'estetica: appunti sul nuovo libro di Walter Pater'' ('Morals in Aesthetics: Notes on the New Book by Walter Pater'), a review of *Marius the Epicurean* and the first mention in Italy of a work by Pater appeared on 10 May 1885, only two months after the publication of the novel in Britain and more than fifty years before its first Italian translation.

Lee's influence in the initial diffusion of Pater's work in Italy has been discussed in detail in the essay by Benedetta Bini (this volume, Chapter 1). In the context of this broad survey, it should be said that her *Fanfulla* piece testifies to close familiarity with Pater's novel and sets it within the framework of his whole output, with intra- and extra-textual references that must have seemed too learned and specialized for the Italian readership of the time, even for the clique of connoisseurs the periodical could count on. Lee introduces

Pater's work by concisely summarizing *The Renaissance* and explains how the writer managed to overcome the juvenile aestheticism of his *succès de scandale*. *Marius* is presented as a more mature creation, imbued with a sober and saner philosophical attitude and a more serene approach to life. In the novel, Pater's earlier spontaneous impulse towards beauty seems mitigated by a pervasive moral drive. But whilst such an evolution is successfully enacted in fiction, Lee wonders whether there is any possibility of merging the two aspirations in real life. She eventually recognizes that the roads to beauty and to goodness, if seldom coincident, are often parallel and can both lead to a wiser and fuller existence. Pater's ultimate merit is that of having shown how they necessarily coexist in the highest minds.

Lee's passion for Pater was transmitted to one of the most assiduous presences in her Florentine circle, Enrico Nencioni (1837–96), a minor poet in the decadent vein and an enthusiast for English literature. Nencioni had been introduced to this through his youthful connection with the community of British expatriates in Tuscany, among whom were the Brownings and Walter Savage Landor, and through his constant presence in later years at the house-parties of the British colony in Florence. A regular contributor to *Fanfulla della domenica* and other prominent *fin-de-siècle* Italian periodicals, in one of these, *Nuova antologia*, Nencioni wrote a review of d'Annunzio's novel *Il piacere* (*The Child of Pleasure*) (1889) and seized the occasion to briefly compare it to *Marius the Epicurean*. Nencioni claimed that *The Child of Pleasure* bore more resemblance to *Marius* than to any other current literary or pictorial model it had been associated with by critics due to the stylistic analogies between the two works. Although he admitted that d'Annunzio would not necessarily have read Pater's book, he recognized a tendency of the two writers to bask in their stylistic prowess. Their inclination to overreach themselves often resulted in redundant and artificially strained writing.

In the following year, Nencioni dealt with Pater more extensively and directly in a review of *Appreciations* – written once again for *Nuova antologia* – that had actually been called for by Lee, as attested in a letter of 5 October 1889:

> Dear Nencioni, I do wish you to write a beautiful article on my poor and illustrious friend Pater. I believe that some of his writings, *Marius the Epicurean* and his last beautiful study on Plato, would do a mountain of good to Italian youths. For example, what an antidote to d'Annunzio Pater's spiritual career – I should almost say his *pilegrim's progres* [sic] – would be, starting from Swinburne's morbid aestheticism and being gradually purified in Plato's sublime moral aestheticism. Such a development of the sense of beauty until encompassing spiritual matters and recognizing in physical beauty the organic symbol of vigour, of moral cleanliness, of harmony in man as a whole![1]

---

[1]   'Caro Nencioni, desidero proprio che faccia un bellissimo articolo sul mio povero e illustre amico Pater. Credo che certi suoi scritti, *Marius the Epicurean* ed il suo bellissimo ultimo studio su Platone farebbero un monte di bene ai giovani italiani. Che contravveleno ad un d'Annunzio, per esempio, non sarebbe la carriera spirituale, direi quasi il *pilegrim's progres* [sic] del Pater, principiando dal morboso esteticismo Swinburniano, e appurandosi man mano nell'altissimo esteticismo

The article – 'W. Pater: *Appreciations*' – was promptly produced. Here Nencioni pinpointed the fundamental continuity between Pater's criticism in *The Renaissance* and in the later volume, noticing how both were founded on the centrality of the notion of pleasure provoked by the contemplation of beauty. But despite Nencioni's admiration for Pater's technique (he called him 'an artist of the word'),[2] which he saw as alien to the sapless prose of Italian critics, he reiterated the idea that his style lacked spontaneity, since it tended to state platitudes in an oracular tone. Such observations did not prevent Nencioni from invariably interspersing his writings with the major tenets of Paterian criticism, although he chose Pater as the explicit subject of his study in the two unique circumstances that have been mentioned. For example, Nencioni's essay 'La lirica del Rinascimento' ('The Lyric Poetry of the Renaissance', 1892) almost embarrassingly echoed Pater's 'Pico della Mirandola', but the derivation was never admitted to. Yet if Nencioni's attitude to Pater is not easy to accept, his crucial role in establishing the writer's early fame in Italy cannot be denied. He was, significantly, the prime connection between Pater and Gabriele d'Annunzio, who remained a lifelong advocate of Nencioni's critical assessment.

A further and closer mediating figure helped d'Annunzio appreciate the work of 'that rich and delicate stylist: Walter Pater'.[3] His Paterian reception was in fact assisted by Angelo Conti (1860–1930), an eager Paterian admirer within his Roman entourage. An art and literary critic bound as a museum director to a peripatetic career, Conti sensitively absorbed the varied artistic stimuli his job could offer. Characterized by a retiring individuality very similar to Pater's own, Conti was an amphibious critic–artist eclipsed by d'Annunzio's flamboyant personality and impressive talent as, to some extent, Pater had been by Wilde. Yet his *Giorgione* (1894), an essay displaying a clear Paterian derivation, proved instrumental in inspiring d'Annunzio with the central motifs of his novel *Il fuoco* (*The Flame*, 1900).

Far from influencing d'Annunzio alone, *Giorgione*, and even more unquestionably Conti's subsequent, more ambitious theoretical volume, *La beata riva: trattato dell'oblio* (*The Blessed Shore: A Treatise on Oblivion*, 1900), fixed the canons for much *fin-de-siècle* artistic debate in Italy. Patently dependent on Pater as it was – although here as elsewhere Conti never mentioned his source – *La beata riva* nonetheless proved Conti to be more than a slavish transcriber of English aestheticism. In fact, while he shared some pivotal themes and critical tenets of Pater's production (artistic hybridism, the superiority of music, the critic as artist, the notion of style), he adapted their most radical formulations to the contemporary Italian frame of mind. The Italian culture of the time was obviously peripheral if gauged in relation to European standards. It still relied on the high-Romantic stances and idealistic philosophy that had triggered the Risorgimento and on the values endorsed

---

morale di Platone; questo sviluppo del senso della bellezza finché si estenda alle cose dello spirito, e riconosca nella bellezza fisica il simbolo organico del vigore, della pulizia morale, dell'armonia in tutto l'uomo!' (Nardi 1985, 175–76).

2   'Un artista della parola' (Nencioni 1890, 702).

3   'Quello stilista delicato e ricco che fu Walter Pater' (d'Annunzio 1895, 73).

by the bourgeois ruling class and by Catholic morality. Conti's tenets thus appear characteristic of other *fin-de-siècle* Italian literati, who, despite a professed penchant for European aestheticism, tended to reinterpret over-sensualistic or hedonistic models in the light of a vague Platonic ideal or a languid mysticism. This is exactly the same charge Mario Praz would lay against Nencioni many years later (Praz 1972, 333–34).

The last expression of what might be termed Conti's Paterian trilogy was the essay 'Leonardo pittore' ('Leonardo the Painter', 1910) that confirmed his continuing partiality to Pater's critical output. By contrast, Pater's fiction was mostly neglected by Conti, and in those years it was only Ulisse Ortensi (1863–1935), a lesser scholar, who focused on *Marius the Epicurean* and *Imaginary Portraits* in the article 'Letterati contemporanei: Walter Horatio Pater' ('Contemporary Literati: Walter Horatio Pater') published in *Emporium* (1902). Ortensi's is indeed the first Italian commentary on *Imaginary Portraits*, and for all the errors the essay contains (for instance, *Marius* bears the date 1881, and Pater is said to have had just one sister, the one who accompanied him during his first Italian visit), it offers no negligible comment on the texts, that are summarized and discussed naively though perceptively. After a biographical preamble (essentially based on Edmund Gosse's 'Walter Pater'), Ortensi claims the greatness of *Marius* and signals some basic thematic analogies between the novel and *Imaginary Portraits*, whose protagonists – he notes – live a life that is 'a vague tragedy ending abruptly after many uncertainties and always with a subtle irony'.[4]

In the immediate prewar period interest in Pater's fiction was also stirred by Aldo de Rinaldis (1881–1948), a Neapolitan art critic and museum director who translated *The Renaissance* (*Il rinascimento*) in 1912 and rendered the first Italian version of *Imaginary Portraits* (*Ritratti immaginari*) in the following year. The former text was reviewed by Roberto Longhi (1890–1970) in 1912 in a short contribution to *La Voce* – the famed Florentine cultural magazine which took a militant line against positivism. Longhi stressed the value of Pater's criticism, centred as it was on artistic individuality and avoiding a rigid historical approach though maintaining a basically historical stance. Unique in his appraisal, Longhi even extolled de Rinaldis's work as showing 'a congeniality between author and translator'.[5]

Longhi's article was matched by Giuseppe Saverio Gargano (1859–1930), a literary critic whose comment on de Rinaldis's achievement appeared in another important Florentine periodical of the time, *Il Marzocco*, to whose foundation Gargano himself had contributed along with d'Annunzio. Anti-positivistic and anti-naturalistic, *Il Marzocco* proclaimed a close adherence to European aestheticism – a position evident in Gargano's piece. Another distinguished scholar, and in fact one of the fathers of Anglo-American studies in Italy, the Florentine Emilio Cecchi (1884–1966), wrote an article on de Rinaldis's *Il rinascimento* in the Roman newspaper *La Tribuna* on 3 July 1912.

---

[4] 'Una vaga tragedia, che finisce bruscamente, dopo molte incertezze e sempre con un po' di sottile ironia nella sua conclusione' (Ortensi 1902, 25).

[5] 'Una congenialità tra autore e traduttore' (Longhi 1912, 902).

A year later Cecchi reviewed de Rinaldis's second Paterian tour de force. His '*Ritratti immaginari* di W. H. Pater' ('Walter Pater's *Imaginary Portraits*') first appeared in *La Tribuna* on 5 August 1913 and was reprinted in the collection *Scrittori inglesi e americani* (*English and American Writers*) in 1935, followed by several later editions, the last in 1976. Cecchi spotlights the originality of Pater's fictional invention, described as 'a new form all of his own'[6] and seen as the ideal expression 'in which the spirit of historical reality [is] exalted to the intensity of revelations seemingly typical of poetry and music'.[7] Pater – Cecchi states – chooses figures akin to his personality, partaking of the inner conflict that makes him both dissatisfied with immediate reality and incapable of setting himself free. Uneasiness and frustration are inborn in the writer as they are in Watteau and Sebastian van Storck, and this possibly accounts for Cecchi's appraisal of the first and third portraits as the best in the collection. In particular, the third imaginary portrait appears as an even more exemplary demonstration of Pater's creative and expressive powers, conflating a masterly historical representation with a pervasive lyricism. 'Sebastian van Storck' does not just fictionalize Pater's own dilemmas, but enacts the conflicts of the whole aesthetic movement.

The journalist and critic Giulio Caprin (1880–1958) also reviewed the 1913 translation of *Imaginary Portraits* in *Il Marzocco* but, like Cecchi, did not spend a word to comment on de Rinaldis's merits or faults. Considering, however, Giorgio Zanetti's reference to an unpublished letter from Cecchi to Bernard Berenson of 6 January 1913 (Zanetti 1996, 340), in which the sender ironically commented on Longhi's favourable opinion of de Rinaldis's *Rinascimento*, one suspects that Cecchi did not esteem *Ritratti immaginari* highly either. And possibly Caprin's silence as regards the same issue should be interpreted likewise. In the article 'Critica e immaginazione: *i Ritratti immaginari* di W. Pater' ('Criticism and Imagination: W. Pater's *Imaginary Portraits*', 1913) he praised instead the peculiar quality of Pater's stories, seen as critical assessments rather than fictional expressions. Pater's imaginative-aesthetic criticism, never free of a philosophic impulse towards the absolute, is based – Caprin explains – on the sympathy an artistic object or personality can stir in him. This is patent in the Watteau portrait, where Pater conveys his perception of the painter's temperament as one that shares with himself 'a marvellous tact of omission'.

What strikes one as the most obvious feature of this initial stage of Pater's Italian reception is the prevailing interest in Pater's œuvre from scholars and critics contributing to the Florentine debate or otherwise having a formative background in Florence. At the time Florence was the place of publication of numerous magazines that seemed particularly eager to absorb Pater's work. The Florentine intelligentsia, low-profile as compared to the complacent Roman or Milanese circles, traditionally enjoyed familiarity with international literary tastes thanks to the foreign cultural enclaves that had been settling in Tuscany ever since the Romantic heyday. An effect of such open-mindedness

---

[6]   'Forma nuova e tutta sua' (Cecchi 1913, 152).
[7]   'Dove lo spirito della realtà storica [si esalta] a quella intensità di rivelazioni che sembra propria della poesia e della musica' (Cecchi 1913, 152).

and intellectual diversity was an inclination to encourage young people coming from all over Italy who professed a desire for novelty and wished to adhere to contemporary European trends. The militant criticism of Florence hailed Pater as a representative of current literary standards – the very same standards they themselves revealed when collaborating with non-Florentine magazines, as is evident in Cecchi's pieces in *La Tribuna* or Nencioni's contributions to *Nuova antologia*.

Yet Rome too, the capital of the recently unified kingdom, seemed rather receptive towards Pater. This was despite the fact that its cultural cliques – worldly and eager to entertain the *nouveaux-riches* galvanized by d'Annunzio – tended to view him from a more superficial and fashionable perspective. Conversely, Pater provoked virtually no interest in Milan, the cultural centre of the north. Here an increasing emphasis on productive activity contrasted with the Byzantine indolence of Rome and the aesthetic composure of Florence. Moreover, the Milanese literary sets were still deeply involved in the belated expressions of the Scapigliatura, a minor *fin-de-siècle* movement that succumbed to the most morbid features of Decadence, while tending to embed them in realistic contemporary contexts. This work, which often bordered on regional literature, was very far from the sophistication demanded by an author like Pater.

Despite the recognition of Florence and Rome as the cultural poles of Pater's Italian reception, the first Paterian translations were published in Naples and were the work of the Neapolitan de Rinaldis. There is, however, a suggestion that they were prompted by one of the figures more directly involved in Florentine and Roman cultural life and in the launching of Pater in Italy. Giorgio Zanetti indicates that it was Angelo Conti – then the director of the picture-gallery of the National Museum in Naples – who proposed the translations of *The Renaissance* and *Imaginary Portraits* to the Ricciardi publishing house (Zanetti 1996, 18). As a friend and occasional collaborator of Conti's, de Rinaldis was possibly chosen as translator for his expertise in art history, seen at the time as Pater's almost exclusive domain.

Even if de Rinaldis was not a specialist in English literature, his rendering of Pater's texts is generally accurate – however blatantly outdated it now seems – and pays attention to the linguistic range and syntactical structures of the original text. In his version of *Imaginary Portraits*, based on the 1887 text, the lexis is precise but far from the expressiveness of the English, and there seems to be little evidence for Mario Praz's claim – given below – that the translation was full of mistakes. Inaccuracy emerges, for example, in the misdating of entries in the Watteau portrait (August 1706 instead of 1705, March 1716 instead of 1715, or May ['maggio'] instead of March ['marzo']), rather than in crucial points of the text, so that no fundamental misapprehension occurs. An overall lack of fluency is however evident.

De Rinaldis's interest in Pater is confirmed by a paper he delivered at a conference for the fourth centenary of Leonardo's death in 1919. This piece 'Il sorriso di Leonardo' ('The Smile of Leonardo') proves obviously derivative and appears as an interesting counterpart to Conti's earlier essay on the same subject. Similar in his approach to Pater's work from the point of view of art history was Vincenzo Golzio (1896–1981), whose long article 'Walter Pater critico d'arte' ('Walter Pater as an Art Critic') in the Roman magazine *L'arte* (1925) provided a fine assessment of Paterian art criticism.

Also in the interwar period, a cursory contribution to Paterian reception was provided by Alfredo Galletti (1872–1962), an Italianist and proto-comparatist. Galletti referred to Pater's Rossetti essay in the piece 'Dante Gabriele Rossetti e il Romanticismo Preraffaellita' ('Dante Gabriel Rossetti and Pre-Raphaelite Romanticism') included in his collection *Studi di letteratura inglese* (*Studies of English Literature*, 1918) and in so doing offered one of the very rare Italian comments on *Appreciations*. A propos of *The House of Life*, Galletti cited this dense passage from Pater as an example of well-turned criticism:

> The dwelling-place in which one finds oneself by chance or destiny, yet can partly fashion for oneself; never properly one's own at all, if it be changed too lightly; in which every object has its associations – the dim mirrors, the portraits, the lamps, the books, the hair-tresses of the dead and visionary magic crystals in the secrets drawers, the names and words scratched on the windows, windows open upon prospects the saddest or the sweetest; the house one must quit, yet taking perhaps, how much of its quietly active light and colour along with us! – grown now to be a kind of raiment to one's body, as the body, according to Swedenborg, is but the raiment of the soul. (*Appreciations*, 214)

The excerpt was translated into Italian, possibly by Galletti himself,[8] since the text of *Appreciations* did not yet exist in the language – and indeed has never been translated since, apart from the three essays on Shakespeare included in Maria Luisa de Rinaldis's collection (1999), which will be mentioned later. Interestingly, Galletti proved incorrect in some of his chronological references, as when he dated *Appreciations* back to 1880. This inaccuracy seems to substantiate further the impression that in the first period of Pater's Italian reception – from the 1890s to the years immediately subsequent to the First World War – few scholars focused attention on Pater's fiction, and even fewer on his literary criticism, thus leaving the field potentially open to dilettantes and those with only an approximate knowledge of the original. His oeuvre was rather seen from the point of view of the (at least superficially) more facile and modish theories of the figurative arts, possessing the additional merit that it celebrated the glorious Italian art of the past and aided its dissemination outside the country. This aspect should not be disregarded, especially when one reflects on how young a nation Italy actually was at this stage (unity having been gained as recently as 1870), and consequently how strong was the Italian quest for European identity and recognition.

---

8   Here is the Italian version: 'È l'abitazione in cui uno ritrova per volere del destino, ma che egli può in parte edificarsi da sé; non veramente e interamente sua, poiché può mutare con troppa facilità, ma in cui ogni oggetto ha i suoi ricordi: gli specchi appannati, i ritratti, le lampade, i libri, le trecce delle donne morte, i magici cristalli visionari negli stipi secreti, i nomi e le parole incise sulle finestre, le finestre aperte sulle visioni più tristi e più liete: la casa che diventa come una veste del corpo, a quel modo che, secondo lo Swedenborg, il corpo non è che una veste dell'anima' (Galletti 1918, 220).

An exception to the common trend that saw Pater first and foremost as an art critic was provided however by Vittorio Lugli (1885–1968), a professor of French literature at Bologna University, who focused on the impact of French culture on Pater in an essay entitled 'Una visita a Ronsard' ('A Visit at Ronsard's') published in the Turin literary magazine *Il Baretti* (1927). This essay considers the substantial Paterian corpus dealing with French subjects and *Marius the Epicurean*, relating them both to the Ronsard chapter in *Gaston de Latour* by highlighting common motifs, such as the force of modernity, the cyclic nature of history and the epiphanic power of art. Passages from 'Modernity' are translated to support Lugli's idea that in *Gaston*, as in *Marius* at an earlier point, Pater was attempting to achieve 'the total and conclusive work of art, in which his previous words reappeared and were put together to achieve a greater significance'.[9]

If Lugli's merit lies basically in the fact that he offered an unprecedented Italian evaluation of Pater's unfinished novel – one that would however pass unnoticed for many years more – he also displayed a subtle critical talent and an enlightened and forward-looking approach. He cleverly suggested that Pater's fiction as a whole could be seen as a series of imaginary portraits set in different transitional or decadent ages, discussing the example of Ronsard as the ideal protagonist of Pater's narrative output. Ronsard could be seen as a hero in retirement who has discovered, over time, the religious value of art. The neglect of this essay by Lugli proves yet again that the contemporary Italian intelligentsia could not cope with an all-encompassing evaluation of Pater's multifarious oeuvre. Pater had been assimilated either as an acute interpreter of Italian Renaissance – by contrast with Ruskin, for instance, who was viewed as highly prejudiced – or as an idiosyncratic novelist in the aesthetic or decadent lineage (though this was a less readily accepted facet of his work). Any synthetic appraisal of the author as a versatile figure embodying the art connoisseur, the literary critic and the creative writer was scarcely acceptable in the Italian cultural milieu, distant as it was, despite its attempts to conform, from the canons of contemporary European taste.

To offer a comprehensive view of Pater's output a less provincial-minded scholar was needed. This was left to Mario Praz (1896–1982), whose well-known international fame and experience as a writer contributed to shaping a novel image of Pater in Italy. Praz's groundbreaking *La carne, la morte e il diavolo nella letteratura romantica* (*The Romantic Agony*, 1930) offered an innovative discussion of Pater's works that avoided false prudery and placed them high among the artistic expressions derived from European Romanticism that eluded traditional chronological definitions, and were epitomized in the movement known as Decadence. Of this movement, Pater was one of the initiators, in Praz's view. The impact of Praz's criticism in this domain has been enormous, and his work still remains a cornerstone of *fin-de-siècle* studies. It has, moreover, had the effect of determining the canons of Pater's Italian reception over a long period, though there has been a general tendency towards revisionism over the last two decades.

---

[9] 'L'opera totale e conclusiva, ove naturalmente riapparivano le parole già dette in tempi diversi, e raccolte ora per la più completa significazione' (Lugli 1927, 147).

An early attempt at undermining Praz's hegemony in the field of Paterian criticism was made by Federico Olivero (1878–1955), holder of a chair of English literature at the University of Turin. As early as 1909, Olivero had published an article entitled 'Walter Pater ed i suoi studi sul Rinascimento' ('Walter Pater and his Studies on the Renaissance'), although his more ambitious works were to appear in the 1930s. *Letteratura inglese moderna* (*Modern English Literature*) (1930), a study so punctilious as often to stray on the verge of pedantry, devotes two pages to Pater, discussing *Marius the Epicurean* and *Imaginary Portraits*. With regard to *Marius*, Olivero essentially highlighted the merging of the subgenre of the historical novel with the currents of Symbolism, whilst viewing the *Imaginary Portraits* rather simplistically as elaborate renderings of the struggle between aesthetic or metaphysical thinking and the hardships of life. By and large, however, Olivero succeeded in summing up some of the essential traits of Pater's fiction.

Olivero's major contribution to the field of Paterian criticism was *Il pensiero religioso ed estetico di Walter Pater* (*Walter Pater's Religious and Aesthetic Thinking*, 1939), a massive study comprising the whole of Pater's œuvre, and to some extent following in Praz's wake in so far as the writer was considered as a multi-faceted artist. This monograph included practically every issue related to Pater's work, often grounding it in biographical details (for which the author drew copiously from Thomas Wright rather than A. C. Benson), though tending also to general description and summary. Nonetheless the book remains in most respects a typical product of the early Italian criticism of Pater, following the line of Nencioni to some extent. It appears outdated – especially when compared with Praz – in its sanitizing tendency to reconcile the aesthetic with the spiritual. 'The aim of *Marius*' – Olivero contends – 'is to proclaim Christianity as the only way of Salvation',[10] and thus religion is foregrounded as the author's final choice. Pater was in this reading ultimately seen as a moralist, even though he was attracted by beauty and occasionally by the macabre. No sign of decadent morbidity or personal frustration could be detected in these attractions, as certainly had been the case for Praz. Pater's desire for beauty, as Olivero interpreted it was a longing for perfection. He justified the sinister undertones that suffused the writer's work by asserting that they were typical of the Romantic episteme, and shared, for example, by Mérimée and Lamb. More worthy of record is Olivero's interpretation of Pater's texts as partially autobiographical creations. His criticism of Pater's imaginary, or – as he calls them – 'self'-portraits (a definition covering a broad spectrum of Pater's writings) is suitably expanded to encompass fictional and historical figures, such as Gaston de Latour, Sebastian van Storck, Pascal, Amiel, Chateaubriand and Florian Deleal.

In the same year that Olivero's volume appeared, a further proof of the interest raised in Italy by Pater was provided by the first translation of *Marius the Epicurean* (*Mario l'epicureo*) by a young classical scholar, Lidia Storoni Mazzolani. Prompted by Cesare Pavese – as Storoni Mazzolani revealed in the 1970 reprint – this translation was issued for the centenary of Pater's birth and

---

[10]   'Lo scopo di *Marius* è di proclamare il Cristianesimo come unica via di Salvazione' (Olivero 1939, 3).

arrived to bridge a considerable gap, since hitherto the novel could have been read only by the minority fluent in the English language, or approached through the French translation. Much appreciated for its exactness and its verbal intensity, the 1939 *Marius*, which was carefully but not substantially revised in 1970, endured as an achievement standing on its own until 2001.

This 1939 translation was prefaced by Storoni Mazzolani herself. She wrote a discerning piece in which Pater's role as a proto-decadent was rejected and emphasis was laid on the greater maturity and artistry displayed in the novel as compared to *The Renaissance* and *Imaginary Portraits*, 'the books that have mostly contributed to the legend of Decadent hedonism still surrounding the author, endowing him with the character of a precursor of an immoral aestheticism, that perhaps least corresponds to the deepest truth of his spirit'.[11] Strangely enough, the reprint of the text in 1970 supplemented Mazzolani's original introduction with an essay by Mario Praz that was quite at odds with the translator's own tenets. Praz's piece brought together some of his previous writings in a clever patchwork that spotlighted the disturbing facets of Pater's œuvre. One passage alone explained that 'in *Marius the Epicurean* [Pater's] epicureanism tended towards the deep, noble emotions of a life which itself had to become a masterpiece as complete as a work of art, rather than towards satisfying experiences and easy pleasures'.[12] *Pace* Praz, after *Marius* began to be more widely circulated as a result of this translation, a more unbiased and complex image of the writer gradually gained acceptance.

It seems as though Storoni Mazzolani's translation of *Marius* was born under an anti-Fascist star. In addition to Pavese's endorsement, it was printed by the Einaudi publishing house, which maintained a well-known oppositional stance towards the Fascist regime. Besides, as she again revealed in the 1970 edition, Storoni Mazzolani was introduced to Einaudi by Leone Ginzburg, then its managing director and a victim of Fascist persecution a few years later. By showing the Empire in the first stages of decadence, *Marius* could not have appeared (even to the more innocent readers) as properly speaking an apotheosis of things Roman. It could therefore be seen as an indirect critique, however bland, of Fascist principles and propaganda, both notoriously founded on a modern identification with Imperial Rome. Yet it seems that this topic has not been discussed any further – not even on the one occasion when Storoni Mazzolani looked back at the 1939 *Marius*, in a note to the 1970 reprint that explained why she dedicated her later edition to Pavese and Ginzburg. It was not raised in an anonymous review in *Giornale storico della letteratura italiana* (1940) that rapidly moved away from the issue of Storoni Mazzolani's translation in order to focus on 'the more solemn commemora-

---

[11] 'I libri che più hanno contribuito alla leggenda di edonismo decadente che circonda ancor oggi l'autore, attribuendogli il carattere di caposcuola di un estetismo immoralistico, il meno aderente forse alla verità profonda del suo spirito' (Pater 1939, 9).

[12] 'In *Marius the Epicurean* questo apparente epicureismo si precisava come rivolto non a esperienze comode e a godimenti di facile accesso, ma alle emozioni profonde e nobili d'una vita che doveva mirare ad essere essa medesima un capolavoro non meno completo di un'opera d'arte' (Pater 1970, xxiii).

tion'[13] of Pater's centenary that was provided by Olivero's *Il pensiero religioso ed estetico di Walter Pater*. A second anonymous review published in 1941 in *La Civiltà Cattolica*, the official organ of the Italian Jesuits, by contrast gave its approval to Storoni Mazzolani's translation, and described *Marius* as 'a philosophical study [...] embroidered on reality'.[14] This article explicitly eschewed the crucial question of the sincerity of the protagonist's conversion, since, as was made clear, there were no clues for giving a categorical answer. The reviewer simply judged Pater's aesthetics in *Marius* as 'neither immoral nor amoral',[15] though the final assessment was that of 'a novel not to be recommended to youths'.[16]

If Olivero and Storoni Mazzolani were never again to deal with Paterian subjects, Praz kept on discussing Pater, either as a main topic or in relation to Decadence at large. Praz, however, invariably recycled verbatim passages from *The Romantic Agony*, and from subsequent writings of the 1940s, without substantially modifying his earlier judgements. His later texts on Pater are in part a collage of excerpts from previous works, with the writer appearing as a proto-decadent in whose personality Eros and Thanatos coexisted, thus triggering deep conflicts in life and art. Such a notion is systematically reiterated in his 1966 essay on Pater and Rossetti entitled 'Due padri del Decadentismo' ('Two Fathers of Decadence'), which claimed to be presenting Germain d'Hangest's *Walter Pater: l'homme et l'œuvre* to the Italian public, but in fact revisited Praz's own long-established opinions on the English *fin de siècle*.

Praz's leading role in the history of Pater's Italian reception had been consolidated through his translations of *Imaginary Portraits* (1944), of *The Renaissance* (1946), and of a series of extracts from sundry works entitled *Pater: scelta e traduzione* (*Pater: Selection and Translation*, 1944). These versions, published by three different houses (respectively the Roman De Luigi, the Neapolitan ESI, and the Milanese Garzanti), were designed to be painstakingly accurate, by contrast with the imprecision of de Rinaldis's earlier attempts, but they also implicitly drew attention to the inexperience of Storoni Mazzolani by giving a sample translation of an excerpt from *Marius*. As Praz rather superciliously conceded in his introductory pages to *Pater: scelta e traduzione*,

> we do not feel like putting too much blame on Aldo De Rinaldis, who [...] has tried – vainly, in our opinion – to create a style corresponding to Pater's. In his versions frequent mistakes contribute to obscuring the comprehension of the text. And we must praise Lidia Storoni Mazzolani, who has been able to give *Marius the Epicurean* a decent Italian form, despite her inability to avoid some misunderstanding.[17]

---

13   'Più solenne commemorazione' (Anon. 1940, 251).
14   'Uno studio filosofico, ma ricamato sulla realtà' (Anon.1941, 67).
15   'L'estetica del Pater non solo non è immorale, me neppure amorale' (Anon. 1941, 67).
16   'Non è un romanzo da suggerirsi ai ragazzi' (Anon. 1941, 67).
17   'Non ci sentiamo di biasimar troppo Aldo de Rinaldis che nelle sue versioni ... s'è sforzato, a parer nostro invano, di creare uno stile che rispondesse a quello del Pater – versioni in cui purtroppo gli errori frequenti contribuiscono a render più

To be fair, if Praz's translations still deserve credit, those of de Rinaldis can by no means be slighted, especially when one takes into account the pioneering task that he was performing. Yet so distinguished was (and is) Praz's reputation that his *Il rinascimento* still functions today as the standard (the received, one might say) rendering of Pater's work. No more modern version has been attempted. And his *Ritratti immaginari* constituted the only Italian version of *Imaginary Portraits* until 1994, when Franco Marucci brought out his enhanced and up-to-date translation.

Praz's *Ritratti immaginari* carefully conveys the tone and atmosphere of the original, and is evidently the product of a profound connoisseur of the English language. If de Rinaldis's version sometimes sounds awkward and dull, Praz's very seldom does. Correspondingly, Praz's translation sounds smoother and closer to the style of the original, being characterized by harmoniously flowing rhythms and by an appropriate choice of words. Its modernity, and de Rinaldis's datedness, stand out when both are compared to Marucci's text.

Praz's decision to incorporate 'Apollo in Picardy' and 'The Child in the House' into the 1887 text, whilst de Rinaldis only translated the four imaginary portraits of the original edition, testifies to his acute understanding of the genre. This is confirmed by the introduction to the volume. Here we find some of Praz's most unbiased assessments of Pater, which successfully combine a penchant for philological details with a clever analysis of the writer's historicism and a lucid overview of the imaginary portrait mode. The conflating of biography and fiction in the genesis of the imaginary portrait is skillfully underlined by Praz. Indeed this brief prefatory essay could be said to represent the apex of his comprehension of Pater. Praz's perceptive remarks on the numerous anachronisms in the *Portraits* still stand out as being among the most convincing indications of the writer's peculiar use of historical detail. 'What Pater wants to convey', says Praz, 'is not history, but the historical climate. His figures are held up to the light, they are expressions of the quintessence of a country or a culture. They are psychological corollaries of a milieu. His method is that of a poet, not of a historian.'[18]

In the collection *Pater: scelta e traduzione* (1944), Praz brought together a miscellany of passages apparently chosen with no other criterion than that of exemplifying Pater's beautiful prose. It was probably with this purpose in mind that he supplemented his introduction (as usual, a melange involving extracts from previous writings) with the unique passage, partially quoted above, on the difficulties of translating Pater. The excerpts Praz elected as epitomizing Pater's style were taken from *The Renaissance* ('Sandro Botticelli',

---

oscura la comprensione del testo; e dobbiamo dar lode a Lidia Storoni Mazzolani che pur non riuscendo a evitare qualche fraintendimento nella sua traduzione di *Mario l'epicureo*, ha saputo dare al romanzo una decorosa veste italiana' (Pater 1944a, xxi).

18   'Ciò che il Pater vuol rendere non è la storia, ma il clima storico; le sue son figure viste contro luce, sono espressioni della quintessenza d'un paese, d'una cultura, corollari psicologici d'una premessa ambientale. Il suo procedimento è quello d'un poeta, non d'uno storico' (Pater 1944b, 14).

'Leonardo da Vinci', 'The School of Giorgione' and 'Conclusion'), *Imaginary Portraits* ('A Prince of Court Painters' and part of 'Denys l'Auxerrois'), *Miscellaneous Studies* ('The Child in the House' and part of 'Emerald Uthwart') and 'the best pages' of *Marius*, though, as mentioned earlier, not in Storoni Mazzolani's translation, but in Praz's own. Most importantly, he provided Italian versions of still untranslated essays from *Greek Studies* (parts of 'The Myth of Demetra and Persephone' and of 'Hippolytus Veiled').

At this early stage in the postwar period, Pater was still however traditionally approached from the perspective of art criticism. In 1948 the art historian Luigi Grassi enthusiastically reviewed Praz's translation of *The Renaissance* in 'Walter Pater e il Rinascimento', and defended the originality of Pater's subjective – otherwise described as 'idealistic' or 'romantic' – criticism as opposed to the positivistic school of Giovanni Morelli. In 1954 Giuseppina Fumagalli (1884–1966) dealt cursorily with Pater in her essay 'Leonardo: ieri e oggi' ('Leonardo: Yesterday and Today'), where she traced the history of Leonardo's European reception with a special focus on the turn of the century. Fumagalli saw Pater's Leonardo piece as the first successful attempt to consider the painter's interpretative freedom towards his subjects as one of his greatest merits. But she also envisaged in Pater's analysis the potential risk of transfiguring Leonardo into a decadent artist and was critical of the Mona Lisa passage, in which she perceived outdated and even comical undertones, involving an interpretation that was fundamentally misguided even though it paved the way for Freud. Later pieces comparable to Fumagalli's are Sandra Migliore's exhaustive volume on Leonardo's reception by decadent culture, *Tra Hermes e Prometeo: il mito di Leonardo nel Decadentismo europeo* (*Hermes and Prometheus: The Myth of Leonardo in European Decadence*, 1994) and Rita Severi's essay 'The Myth of Leonardo in English Decadent Writers' (1992) that will be discussed below. Migliore, an art historian, devotes the first chapter of her study – 'Walter Pater e la fondazione del mito' (Walter Pater and the Foundation of the Myth') – to Pater, regarding him as the initiator of the Leonardo mania in the *fin de siècle*.

In 1963 Dario Gazzoni-Pisani published a monograph entitled *Walter Pater: critico d'arte. Con particolare riguardo agli 'Studi sul Rinascimento'* (*Walter Pater as an Art Critic: With Particular Attention to 'Studies on the Renaissance'*). This is evidently a young man's work: detailed, yet mainly descriptive and on occasions imprecise. Croce and Praz are frequently cited as supporters of the author's view of Decadence; a period to which – he claims – Pater belongs without qualification. Gazzoni-Pisani's text enjoyed only modest recognition and remains mostly unknown to Italian critics of Pater.

After Praz another great anglicist, Giorgio Melchiori, turned his attention to Pater, even though incidentally. The occasion was provided by an essay on Henry James and Hopkins collected in *The Tightrope Walkers: Studies of Mannerism in Modern English Literature* (1956), and the assimilation of the three figures stemmed from the consideration that they all adopted 'a style which prefigured an age of instability not yet existing in fact' (Melchiori 1956, 12). In Pater Melchiori identified the common formative connection between James and Hopkins, whose concept of beauty was shaped by the Paterian ideals of strangeness as an enhancing factor and the quest for rare and beautiful moments within the flux of time. Moreover, the definition of Euphuism in

Marius the Epicurean, perceived by Melchiori as a 'passionate love of form, and more specifically of words' (23), suited the styles of Hopkins and James alike: they contrived to 'represent a different phase of sensibility from that which dominated the middle period of the nineteenth century' (25), not least thanks to Pater's exemplary prose.

In the 1960s Praz's mentor, the one-time Paterian critic Emilio Cecchi, had something further to say about Pater in an article published in *Corriere della sera* and entitled 'Splendori e miserie del decadentismo inglese' ('Splendour and Misery of English Decadence', 1963), where the writer was seen as one of the most eminent figures of European criticism in the nineteenth century, the other select members of the group being de Sanctis and Sainte-Beuve. Cecchi argued that Pater resembled more a mystic or an ascetic (a 'Platonic aesthete', as he puts it) than an artist. In Cecchi's view he represented the restrained and sanitized trend in English Decadence and became a haunting presence for the major Modernist writers (Yeats and Conrad being cases in point).

Continuity between Pater and Modernist literature was also signalled by Umberto Eco in *Le poetiche di Joyce* (*The Poetics of Joyce*, 1966). Eco argued that Joyce's concept of epiphany derived from the 'Conclusion' to *The Renaissance* and showed how Pater's 'analysis of the different moments of epiphanization of reality proceeds in an analogous way to Joyce's analysis of the three criteria of beauty'.[19]

On the whole, the 1940–1970 period, concomitant with Praz's most committed Paterian years, could appropriately be termed the dark passage of Pater's Italian reception. Apart from Prazian criticism, virtually all the studies devoted to Pater at that time seem to have stemmed from an occasional interest, instilled by the necessity of studying him as a significant formative presence for other artists. This is the distinctive feature of the appraisals by Melchiori and Eco. By contrast, Pater continued to attract the attention of art historians – such as Fumagalli or Grassi – but they suggested no innovative readings of his work.

As we could have anticipated, Praz was still active on the Paterian front, though not saying anything particularly new. His translations of *Imaginary Portraits* and *The Renaissance* were reprinted respectively in 1964 and in 1965, both by ESI, and characteristically contained no corrections or improvements. Even their introductions and detailed annotations were republished to the letter. In 1972 Praz published *Il patto col serpente* (*The Pact with the Snake*), a second volume on 'Romanticism' intended as a sequel to *The Romantic Agony*, though in fact a gathering of essays from over a thirty-year span that focused on various artists and recurring themes of the European *fin de siècle*. In a section devoted to the fathers of aestheticism, he inserted two essays on Pater, the former being the 1962 'Due padri del decadentismo' and the latter, entitled 'Walter Pater', consisting in a deft collage of writings from 1944 to 1970.

---

[19] 'L'analisi dei vari momenti del processo di epifanizzazione del reale procede in modo fortemente analogo all'analisi joyciana dei tre criteri della bellezza' (Eco 1966, 44).

Almost contemporaneous with Praz's book was an appealing article by the writer and essayist Roberto Barbolini, 'Socrate e le pertinenti brame di Nietzsche, Pater e d'Annunzio' ('Socrates and the Relevant Longings of Nietzsche, Pater and d'Annunzio, 1975), published in the Turin journal *Il Verri* and later developed into the volume *Il sileno capovolto. Socrate nella cultura fin de siècle: Nietzsche, Pater e d'Annunzio* (*The upturned Silenus. Socrates in* fin-de-siècle *Culture: Nietzsche, Pater and d'Annunzio*, 1981). Barbolini had come across Pater while investigating how the figure of Socrates had been interpreted by European *fin-de-siècle* culture and saw as a feature of Pater, Nietzsche and d'Annunzio their common interest in the motif of the eternal return. The article refers to several of Pater's works (the essays on Giorgione and Leonardo, *Marius*, 'Denys l'Auxerrois', 'Apollo in Picardy' and *Plato and Platonism*) in order to underscore the crucial themes of decadent culture that are to be found in them. Barbolini also discusses the presence of Socrates in *Plato and Platonism* and in *Marius*, where the philosopher represents respectively a rhetorical invention and a personification of the motif of the eternal return. Barbolini finally envisages Socrates as a Paterian alter ego, possessing like the writer a composite personality that condenses mysticism and sensuality through the blending of the Apollonian and the Dionysian spirit. A similar reading of Paterian texts was adopted in a study by Maria Teresa Marabini Moevs, *Gabriele d'Annunzio e le estetiche della fine del secolo* (*Gabriele d'Annunzio and* fin-de-siècle *Aesthetics*, 1976), that also mapped the Socratic presence in Pater, d'Annunzio and Nietzsche.

Mario Praz died in 1982, and it is no coincidence that in the following years a new interest in Pater gradually developed in a number of young scholars who were concerned to pinpoint the centrality of the writer in relation to Decadence at large. Isabella Nardi, an Italianist, could not escape focusing on Pater in her monograph *Un critico vittoriano: Enrico Nencioni* (*A Victorian Critic: Enrico Nencioni*, 1985). Nardi established Pater's pivotal role in Nencioni's work by explaining how his criticism was constantly modelled on the portrait typology (the 'medaglioni' which are the basis of Nencioni's fame) and on Pater's theoretical tenets, often at the risk of plagiarism. Another Italianist, Ricciarda Ricorda, concentrated on a reassessment of Angelo Conti and delineated his role as an intermediary between Pater and *fin-de-siècle* Italian culture in *Dalla parte di Ariele: Angelo Conti nella cultura di fine secolo* (*On Ariel's Side: Angelo Conti in* fin-de-siècle *Culture*, 1993), and in the reprint of Conti's essay on Leonardo which she edited in 1990. Two other scholars, Sandro Gentili and Giorgio Zanetti, have worked on Conti and so indirectly helped to draw attention to Pater even among people from outside the field of English studies. Both their texts, respectively 'Il ruolo di Angelo Conti' ('The Role of Angelo Conti', 1981) and *Estetismo e modernità: saggio su Angelo Conti* (*Aestheticism and Modernity: An Essay on Angelo Conti*, 1996), refer frequently to Pater's fiction and criticism.

In 1981 a lecturer in English literature, Gabriella Micks La Regina, contributed to a conference on Heraclitus with a paper entitled '"All things give way, nothing remaineth": Walter Pater and the Heraclitean Flux' that illustrated Pater's interpretation of Heraclitean doctrine over time, starting from his first publication, 'Coleridge's Writings', and finishing with his last volume, *Plato and Platonism*. In the interval, Micks considered the

'Conclusion' to *The Renaissance* and *Marius the Epicurean*, and she was particularly deft at pointing out the difference in the handling of Heraclitus' thought between *Marius* and *Plato and Platonism*. Taken as a whole, Micks's essay reveals a deep understanding of Pater's philosophical stances, and represents an original contribution to Paterian reception in Italy. Confirmation of Micks's stimulating approach to Pater came also from her essay 'Dante Gabriel Rossetti e Walter Pater: House of Life e House Beautiful nella *Waste Land* vittoriana' ('Dante Gabriel Rossetti and Walter Pater: House of Life and House Beautiful in the Victorian *Waste Land*', 1982). Here Micks aimed at reconstructing the relationship between Rossetti and Pater as two fundamental influences on the *fin-de-siècle* and early twentieth-century literature. She mapped out the profound analogies in the two writers (for example, the cult of beauty, the search for formal perfection, the acute sense of the transience of worldly things, the aspiration to isolating choice moments within the temporal flux) and discussed Pater's evaluation of Rossetti in his eponymous 1883 essay. Micks's close reading of this text is usefully contextualized within the framework of Pater's whole oeuvre. An interesting point is her suggestion that Rossetti's novella 'Hand and Soul' may have been an inspirational nucleus for *Imaginary Portraits*.

A few years later, a young scholar, Luisa Villa, wrote an engaging contribution to the study of Paterian reception in Italy – 'Verso/Attraverso *The Hill of Dreams*: Walter Pater, Arthur Machen, l'oggetto estetico e la decadenza' ('Towards and through *The Hill of Dreams*: Walter Pater, Arthur Machen, the Aesthetic Object and Decadence', 1988). Essentially she viewed Pater's work from a Bloomian perspective, adopting psychoanalytic notions and referring to the latest international Paterian criticism (Harold Bloom, Gerald Monsman and Linda Dowling). Villa concentrated on narcissism and on the progressive construction of an autonomous culture of decadence, preparing for her analysis of Arthur Machen's novel *The Hill of Dreams* by a comparison with 'The Child in the House' and other examples of Paterian 'portraiture'. By so doing, Villa confirmed Pater's role as a mediator between aesthetic and decadent discourses, and as a catalyst in the establishment of the latter. Yet the principal merit of Villa's dense essay lay in its attempt to reconsider Pater in a way that was independent of Praz's stance. This is essentially what other Italian scholars would succeed in achieving over the next few years.

A claim to a new critical interpretation of Pater was also put forward in an article on visual fiction in Pater, Wilde, and Firbank, written by Rita Severi in 1989: 'Words for Pictures: Notes on Iconic Description in Pater, Wilde, and Firbank'. Less exhaustive than Villa's as far as Pater is concerned, Severi's piece offered even so an interpretation of selected excerpts from *The Renaissance* and *Imaginary Portraits* which focused on the value of these works in creating the canons for aesthetic appreciation. A discussion of Wilde's quasi-dogmatic acceptance of Pater's critical principles was the follow-up. Further evidence of Severi's compelling interpretation of Pater was provided when her article 'The Myth of Leonardo da Vinci in English Decadent Writers' was published in *Achademia Leonardi Vinci* (1992). This charted the influence of 'Leonardo da Vinci' in the shaping of the *fin-de-siècle* Leonardo myth.

The 1990s finally witnessed an increasingly enthusiastic and broadly based rediscovery of Pater's œuvre in Italy. Reasons for this awakening of new interest are essentially to be found – as has already been suggested here – in the natural development and diffusion of English studies throughout the country, though they also reflect the renewal of attention to Pater displayed by critics both in America and elsewhere in Europe. Pater has thus been approached once again from a variety of perspectives: either as a late high-Victorian (a continuer of Arnold, also of Ruskin and even of the Romantics), or as the most immediate predecessor and disturbing presence sensed in the works of Hopkins, Wilde, Yeats, Joyce, Eliot and Woolf (just to mention those cited most often). Less frequently he has been seen as an artist to be assessed in the context of gay studies, as one who provides new clues about the relationship between individuality and power. Sporadically, he has also been acclaimed as a precursor of postmodernism.

The obvious novelty of the 1990s in this connection was that Pater gradually became a specific and almost exclusive subject of research for scholars of English literature, his genuine significance being thus finally recognized in these terms. He was accepted primarily as a creative writer whose talent had led him to experiment with a variety of writing modes, whilst the reductive perception of him as an art critic first and foremost – often an amateurish one at that – finally faded from view. Despite this tendency, his criticism has never been so highly valued as in these later years.

Paul Tucker was among the first to contribute to this new perception of Pater. Half-English (and English by education), Tucker had long been teaching in Italy, and was the only presence connected with Italian scholarship at the second international Pater conference held at Oxford in 1988. On this occasion, he delivered a paper on 'Pater as a "Moralist"' which was published in the conference proceedings in 1991. In more than one way Tucker may be seen as having performed a task similar to that of Vernon Lee as a cultural mediator in the field of Pater studies. Tucker, as an Englishman living in Italy, has contributed to the elitist academic zone of Italian culture in much the same way as Lee took her place within the select intellectual circles of her times. What is more, the topic of Tucker's Oxford paper strikingly re-echoes Lee's 'La morale nell'estetica' and, not accidentally, his analysis opens with a reference to Lee as having granted Pater 'the status of "moralist"' after the publication of *Marius*, which is seen as a revisionist text challenging the most radical tenets of *The Renaissance* (Tucker 1991, 107). For his part, Tucker notes that criticism since the 1950s has considered Pater as a moralist *tout court*, however ambivalent and damaging the implications. Tucker's own stance is less simplistic. His assessment of Pater as a moralist lays stress on the necessity of defining the precise nature of the writer's moral conflict by investigating the different ethical imperatives to be found in his works.

A few years after the Oxford conference, Tucker strengthened his noteworthy reading of Pater in publishing '"A Whole World of Transformation": Landscape and Myth in Walter Pater's MS fragment on Corot' (Bizzotto and Marucci 1996). Focusing on the visual–literary interconnections in the writer's oeuvre, the piece propounded a close analysis of disjointed passages from an undated project of an essay on Corot which Tucker chose to put in the company of Pater's other writings of the 1870s from the basis of meticulous philological research. A textual comparison between the Corot fragments and the published essays, moreover, allowed him to trace the influence of the novel disciplinary practice of anthropological studies in Pater's work.

Reassessments of Pater have also been undertaken by other Italian critics. One of these is Paola Colaiacomo, who has chosen to focus on the classical element in the writer – an aspect generally slighted by Paterian scholars in Italy – in her study 'Walter Pater e i greci' ('Walter Pater and the Greeks', Bizzotto and Marucci 1996). As the editor of the first Italian version of *Greek Studies*, translated by Vittoria Caterina Caratozzolo (1994), Colaiacomo has also been instrumental in promoting the Italian diffusion of Pater's less-famed critical pieces – a role she played again when she gave support to the publication of Maria Luisa de Rinaldis's *Walter Pater critico di Shakespeare* (*Walter Pater as a Shakespearian Critic*) in 1999. Based on the original edition of *Appreciations* (1889), the latter volume presents the first Italian translations with parallel texts of the essays 'Love's Labours Lost', 'Measure for Measure' and 'Shakespeare's English Kings' and complements them with a detailed foreword discussing Pater's Shakespearian criticism in the light of some of the typical tenets of his work. These range over such topics as Pater's tendency to detect a 'formula' or leitmotif in each work he considers, the pictorial quality of his descriptions, and his proclivity to conceive of criticism as a gallery of portraits and self-portraits, from the point of view of both artist and critic alike. Another interesting point is brought out when de Rinaldis suggests that Pater anticipates reader-response criticism when he stresses the centrality of the receiver in his approach. In a similar vein, Colaiacomo's prefatory essay for the translation of *Greek Studies* is a very dense discussion of Pater's writings that highlights his conflictual relation to such predecessors as the Romantic poets (Wordsworth, Coleridge and Keats) and Ruskin, whose tenets he grafted onto his own work at the *fin de siècle*, thus paving the way for Modernism. Colaiacomo's interpretation of the 'study' mode employed in *The Renaissance* and *Greek Studies* as a complementary and corresponding typology to the 'portrait' is also a convincing point, and deserves more extensive consideration.

These volumes were accompanied by a number of new translations of Pater's works or reprints of previous Italian versions. As has already been noted, in 1994 Franco Marucci published his *Imaginary Portraits* (*Ritratti immaginari*), adding 'Apollo in Picardy' ('Apollo in Piccardia') and the first Italian version of 'An English Poet' ('Un poeta inglese') to the four tales of the 1887 edition. Marucci is also the author of the first Italian translation of *Gaston de Latour* (1995). Concurrently, there has been a revival of Praz's translations. His *Ritratti immaginari* was reprinted by the Milanese publishing house Adelphi in 1980 and 1994, while another Milanese publisher, Abscondita, issued a new edition of the 1946 *Rinascimento* in 2000. Finally, in 2001 Alberto Rossatti provided a new translation of *Marius* (*Mario l'epicureo*), edited by Viola Papetti.

Rossatti's text is a careful piece of work which recognizes the necessity of modernizing the Italian of Storoni Mazzolani's earlier translation while remaining faithful in its rendering of Pater's ornate prose. A major tendency of Rossatti is to shorten and punctuate Pater's longest sentences that were left in their extended form by Storoni Mazzolani. In so doing, Rossatti achieves greater clarity and fluidity, though on occasions he loses the peculiar lingering flavour of Pater's style. Another merit of Rossatti's edition is the extensive use of explanatory notes, including both the translator's own and the commentaries in both the principal English editions and the previous Italian version of the novel. This solution proves particularly successful for a text which comprises such a thick web of erudite references as often to discourage its reading. Rossatti's translation seems therefore to aim at the diffusion and popularization of *Marius*, as is in fact in the spirit of Rizzoli's BUR editions – paperback pocket classics having considerably influenced the circulation of culture in Italy over the last fifty years.

The precision of Rossatti's translation was remarked on by Franco Marucci in a review titled 'Bellezza, modernità' ('Beauty, Modernity', 2001), published in *Alias*, the cultural supplement of *Il Manifesto*, where he commented favourably on Viola Papetti's editorial work. Indeed, Papetti's foreword to *Marius* underscores some fundamental leitmotifs of Pater's novel and œuvre (for example, the relation between face and mask, the Medusa icon, childhood and the house), thus offering hints at an engaging thematic reading. Also Marucci's extensive review aims at fulfilling an introductory function to Pater's work, being in the first place an all-encompassing piece on *Marius* and on the writer's idiosyncratic variety of fictional essay. In discussing this later topic, Marucci argues that Pater's novel may be seen as a response to the inadequacy of the canons regulating high-Victorian fiction at the approach of the turn of the century. He then maps out the main stages of Pater's reception and underlines the complexity and polyvalence of a writer who necessarily prompts conflicting critical interpretations.

The intricacies of *Marius* have also tempted other Italian critics. Fresh interest in the novel has been shown by Maria del Sapio, who has interpreted it from Bloomian and postmodern stances in 'Pater, Amleto e Marco Aurelio: il racconto della crisi' ('Pater, Hamlet and Marcus Aurelius: The Telling of a Crisis', Bizzotto and Marucci 1996). According to Del Sapio, *Marius* can be envisaged as a text incorporating and rewriting other texts – essentially *Hamlet* and Marcus Aurelius' *Memories*, but also Montaigne's *Essays* and Pascal's *Thoughts*. As a prototypical and emblematic figure of crisis, moreover, Hamlet seems to underlie the construction of such characters as Marius and Marcus Aurelius. His inner torment, just like theirs, posits itself as both exemplary of his age and symptomatic of modernity and the three are thus reminiscent of the multi-faced Mona Lisa: timeless and a synthesis of her epoch. Del Sapio's 'La Sfinge e la Chimera: miraggi di pienezza nella biblioteca *fin de siècle*' ('The Sphinx and the Chimera: Mirages of Plenitude in the *fin-de-Siècle* Library', 1995) is based on comparable assumptions. Here again Del Sapio elucidates her idea of modernity in Pater as an 'endless hermeneutics'[20] with reference to *Marius*, to the mythological *Imaginary Portraits* and to the Gioconda description.

A different but equally attractive interpretation of *Marius*, appreciating the novel in the light of the chivalric ideals that enjoyed a revival during the Victorian age, has been offered by Mario Domenichelli. If *Marius* was devised as an answer to the misguiding perils of the 'Conclusion' to *The Renaissance* – Domenichelli explains in '*Marius the Epicurean*: l'educazione del gentiluomo'

---

[20]   'Ermeneutica infinita' (del Sapio 1995, 166).

('*Marius the Epicurean*: A Gentleman's Education', Bizzotto and Marucci 1996)
– then it can been understood as 'the Paterian, and aesthetic version of a
gentleman's education'.[21] In this perspective, Marius's death comes more as a
crowning exemplum of Stoic renunciation and virtue than as an unconvincing
case of assent to Christianity.

Again, in the field of Pater's fiction, Benedetta Bini has focused on the
portrait formula in her original essay on the imaginary portrait genre, *L'incanto
della distanza: ritratti immaginari nella cultura del decadentismo* (*The Enchantment of
Distance: Imaginary Portraits in Decadent Culture*, 1992), analysing a series of
Decadent short stories over a period of fifty years and seeing in Pater's
Imaginary Portraits the exemplary expression of a peculiar typology of *fin-de-
siècle* short fiction. In a subsequent study, '*Genius loci*: il pellegrinaggio di
Emerald Uthwart' ('*Genius loci*: Emerald Uthwart's Pilgrimage', Bizzotto and
Marucci 1996), Bini concentrates on a short story generally overlooked by
Italian criticism and interprets it as a concluding segment to the circle that had
been commenced by 'The Child in the House', likewise set in England and
legibly autobiographical. Except for the unfinished *Gaston de Latour*, no
further fictional creation will follow in Pater's corpus, as the ending of
'Emerald Uthwart', with the protagonist's death and his wordless tombstone,
metaphorically foretells. Another essay by Bini, 'Alle origini del ritratto: "An
English Poet" di Walter Pater' ('At the Origins of the Portrait: Walter Pater's
'An English Poet' 1993), represents a unique Italian commentary on Pater's
unfinished story and discusses its vague mythological framework in the light of
his later mythological portraits.

Parallel and to an extent complementary to Bini's may be considered Elisa
Bizzotto's writings. Bizzotto has devoted close attention to the portrait
formula and wrote her first essay on the protagonists of *Imaginary Portraits* – 'A
Paradigmatic Reading of *Imaginary Portraits*' (Bizzotto and Marucci 1996) –
considering the recurring motifs in Pater's characterizations from a variety of
perspectives, though fundamentally inspired by Laurel Brake's studies on the
writer. A matching piece was devoted to Pater's female characters in 'Madri e
amanti: le figure femminili nei *Ritratti immaginari* di Walter Pater' ('Mothers
and Lovers: The Female Figures in Walter Pater's *Imaginary Portraits*')
published in *Il lettore di provincia* (1998). Subsequently, Bizzotto focused on the
influence of Giorgionesque art in 'Denys l'Auxerrois' and *Marius* in the piece
'Echi di Giorgione nella narrativa di Walter Pater' ('Giorgionesque Echoes in
Walter Pater's Fiction') in *Paragone* (1998), and contrasted Pater's mythological portraits 'Denys l'Auxerrois', 'Duke Carl of Rosenmold' and 'Apollo in
Picardy' with Wilde's 'The Portrait of Mr W. H.' in 'The Legend of the
Returning Gods in Pater and Wilde' (2000). The re-emergence of the
imaginary portrait typology in Wilde has been the first step towards Bizzotto's
development of a longer study, *La mano e l'anima: il ritratto immaginario fin de
siècle* (*Hand and Soul: The fin-de-siècle Imaginary Portrait*, 2001), devoted to the
different re-readings of the imaginary-portrait formula by artists writing in the
aesthetic-decadent vein and following the Modernist tradition.

---

[21] 'La versione pateriana, ed estetica, dell'educazione del gentiluomo' (Bizzotto and
Marucci 1996, 137).

If research by Bini and Bizzotto has stemmed from Pater and reached further into Wilde and the *fin de siècle*, a prolonged interest in Wilde has conversely led Giovanna Franci backwards to Pater, whom she has considered under a Bloomian light. Franci's essay 'Pater e Wilde: profeti di una nuova sensibilità estetica' ('Pater and Wilde: Prophets of a New Aesthetic Sensibility', Bizzotto and Marucci 1996) underlines Wilde's serene admission of the Paterian influence within himself, and traces back to Ruskin the origins of the aesthetic icon of the critic–artist conceived of by Pater and popularized by his most famous disciple. A young colleague of Franci's at Bologna University, Maurizio Ascari, has by contrast arrived at Pater by way of Henry James, of whose work he is one of the most valued contemporary Italian critics. His article 'The Mask Without the Face: Walter Pater's *Imaginary Portraits*' (1999) takes off from James's famed definition of Pater to discuss 'the pervasive and mutable character' of the imaginary portrait that 'lies at the intersection of autobiography, biography, the short-story, myth, the history of art, of ideas, of manners, of events' (98). Once he has acknowledged the deep-seated hybridism of Pater's mode, Ascari proceeds to include the bulk of the writer's work within this formula, and finally interprets Pater's concept of history as 'a succession of imaginary portraits, of fictional biographies' (111). An analogous approach to Pater through James has led Michela Vanon Alliata to reflect on the androgynous stereotype as evinced by the two writers, and to compare their literary productions with Burne-Jones's figurative output, in 'A Strange Passion: James, Burne-Jones, Pater and the Androgynous Ideal' (Bizzotto and Marucci 1996).

Many essays mentioned in this excursus in 1990s Paterian criticism – Tucker's '"A Whole World of Transformation"', Colaiacomo's 'Walter Pater e i greci', Domenichelli's '*Marius the Epicurean*: l'educazione del gentiluomo', Bini's '*Genius loci*: il pellegrinaggio di Emerald Uthwart', del Sapio's 'Pater, Amleto e Marco Aurelio: il racconto della crisi', Franci's 'Pater e Wilde: profeti di una nuova sensibilità estetica', Bizzotto's 'A Paradigmatic Reading of *Imaginary Portraits*', Vanon Alliata's 'A Strange Passion: James, Burne-Jones, Pater and the Androgynous Ideal' – were delivered at the international conference held in Venice in December 1994 for the centenary of Pater's death. The event sanctioned the revival of interest in Pater in Italy and initiated a kind of domino effect on the production of subsequent writings on the author. Following on in its wake have been translations, essays and dissertations centring on Pater. Furthermore, there have been university courses devoted to him, thus stimulating the relative popularity that still seems characteristic of the present moment. Pater has now more often than not achieved his entrée into the Italian academic world.

The Venice conference stemmed from an idea of Franco Marucci, a specialist in Victorian literature and a famed Hopkins scholar. It is essentially through his interest in Hopkins that Marucci developed his curiosity about aestheticism and Pater, in the first place through having had to reckon with him as an inescapable cultural presence in the last decades of the nineteenth century. Marucci's Paterian criticism primarily, though not exclusively, focuses on the writer's fiction and its relationship with the visual arts, a fine example being the article 'Alcune considerazioni sul ritrattismo letterario' ('A Few Considerations on Literary Portraiture', 1996), where passages from

'Sebastian van Storck' are taken as exemplifications of ekphrasis. But he has also devoted his attention to Paterian art criticism in 'Ruskin, Pater e il Rinascimento sfaccettato' ('Ruskin, Pater and Multi-Faceted Renaissance', 1994), where he underlines several points of contact between Pater's and Ruskin's notions of the Renaissance, despite the notorious absence of any reference to his predecessor on Pater's part. According to Marucci, 'a comparison of their critical and historical evaluations of Raphael, Leonardo and Michelangelo shows Pater continually correcting and adjusting the ideas of his unacknowledged master' (Marucci 1994, 130).

Generally unnoticed aspects of Pater's work, such as in 'L'aforisma nel secondo ottocento inglese: Arnold, Pater e Wilde' ('Aphorism in the Second Half of the Nineteenth Century: Arnold, Pater and Wilde') published in *Annali di Ca' Foscari* (1997), have also been the objects of Marucci's study. Moreover, the introductions and afterwords to his translations read as lucid commentaries on Pater's œuvre, setting it in the context of the English and European literature of the time, but also indicating previous influences on the writer and subsequent derivations. In his version of *Imaginary Portraits* Marucci devotes a few substantial pages to exploring this hybrid subgenre and indicates the alternate thematic repetition of the four canonical tales plus 'Apollo in Picardy', which – he suggests – 'more distinctively rhyme according to the scheme abab(b)'.[22] He insists on the innovative value of Pater's portrait formula, both on a generic and a thematic level, as exemplified by his invention of a mythical method *avant la lettre*. Marucci's translation reveals close adherence to the text, and a concurrent richness in vocabulary and complexity in sentence structure that succeeds in retaining the peculiar qualities of Pater's prose. When compared to the previous version of *Ritratti immaginari*, Marucci presents a contrast to the clumsiness of Aldo de Rinaldis's work and the complacently decadent morbidity of Praz's.

Equally successful is Marucci's translation of *Gaston de Latour* (1995), the only Italian version of the text, published by the Venetian house Marsilio in a scholarly collection devoted to the classics of English literature. Based on the 1896 edition revised by Shadwell (here presented as a parallel text), this translation is characterized by verbal intensity and vividness, and by extensive textual and biographical annotations. In the introduction Marucci highlights the recurring features of Pater's fiction ('he has always written the same novel' and this is 'a deplorable limit for some critics'[23]) and indicates continuators of his essay–novel typology in Proust, Musil and Thomas Mann.

The latter observation has been emphasized also by Gaetano d'Elia, who in 'Pater tra saggismo e intento storiografico' ('Pater Between Essay-Writing and Historiographic Intent', 1996) agreed with Marucci's interpretation of *Gaston de Latour* as dissociating the author from aestheticism and denouncing 'the gross mistake and reductive perspective of those who presented Pater as the

---

[22] 'Rimano più distintamente fra loro secondo uno schema abab(b)' (Pater 1994b, 252).

[23] 'Pater infatti, e questo è un deplorevole limite per taluni critici, ha scritto sempre lo stesso romanzo' (Pater 1995, 12).

father of aestheticism in the past'.[24] Another review of Marucci's *Gaston* and a comprehensive commentary on Pater's Italian translations in the 1990s was written by Luisa Villa in *L'indice* in 1996. Villa's 'Walter Pater: *Studi greci* et al.' bore witness to the revival of interest in the writer, though it noted a difference between recent radical British and American re-readings and the Italian tendency to inscribe Pater within a canonical tradition, so that he becomes either a belated Romantic in the Wordsworth–Keats lineage or a pre-Modernist forerunner of Eliot and Proust. This fact – as Villa suggested – is due to Pater's 'unresolved prevarication between the fascination for the unusual (what exceeds the norm), and the anxious reaction that invariably disciplines the results of "transgression"'.[25] With characteristic insight into Pater's work, Ascari too reviewed the translations of the 1990s in 'Walter Pater in Italy at the Postmodern Fin de Siècle' (2001) published in *The Pater Newsletter*. On this occasion, he gave an extremely personal reading of Pater as an anticipator of postmodernism by stressing some of the special features of his aesthetic criticism, which prefers 'the subjective to the objective, symbolic and fictional elements to documentary evidence, myth to history, transition to stability, androgyny to polar gender identities, brevity to redundancy, the non-referential art of music to the didactic and anecdotal character of Victorian painting' (Ascari 2001, 22–23).

Within such an intense critical debate, the most central contribution to Pater's Italian reception is certainly the essay originally delivered by Franco Marucci at the 1994 conference. This piece, 'Walter Pater: The Forms of Modernity and the Modernity of Form' (Bizzotto and Marucci 1996), gives the conference and the eponymous volume their title, and represents an unprecedented assessment of the different Italian responses to Pater over more than a century. It maps out the crucial developments of Italian interest in the writer, reappraising, for instance, the long-forgotten figure of Olivero, and identifying Paterian influences in Francesco de Sanctis (a point endorsed to some extent by Cecchi's 1963 article on Decadence, as already noted). But it also comes finally to terms with the disturbing personality of Praz, who had hitherto lurked inevitably behind any critical estimation of Pater in Italy. Marucci describes his illustrious predecessor as 'himself a decadent of sorts' (Bizzotto and Marucci 1996, 15) and admits that his interpretation of the writer has long been in need of revision, flawed as it was in its incompleteness and partiality. What Marucci essentially finds fault with in Prazian criticism is its unreserved denial – excepting only the recognition of Pater's fascination with Winckelmann – of the classical-humanistic vein in the writer. By contrast, this aspect is, according to Marucci, central to his inspiration. Marucci's reading of Pater as a precursor of typologists of culture, anticipating Ernst Robert Curtius and Lotman in his historical approach, is also an aspect that proves interesting and original.

---

[24]   'Il grossolano errore e la prospettiva riduttiva di chi ha visto e presentato Pater in passato come il padre dell'estetismo' (Pater 1995, 24).

[25]   'Irrisolta divaricazione tra fascinazione per il particolare, inteso come ciò che eccede la norma, e la reazione un po' spaventata che sempre tende a disciplinare gli esiti della "trasgressione"' (Villa 1996, 20).

Other Italian contributors to the 1994 conference helped to bridge the gap that had been exposed by Marucci. In 'Pater's Critical Foresight: Style, Insight and Complexity' (Bizzotto and Marucci 1996) Valerio de Scarpis provided a 'close reading' of the essay on 'Style' that uncovered conflicting theoretical stances: 'finesse of truth and subjective polysemic impressions' as opposed to 'balanced organic structure, unity of design, stylistic identity' (219). In such a composite and ambivalent text, de Scarpis was able to perceive reflexes relating to Wilhelm Wundt's experimental psychology, but also the presence of proto-structuralist and epistemological tenets. The art historian Gloria Fossi finally focused on the Watteau portrait by analysing the paintings cited in the literary text and presenting a painstaking scrutiny of Pater's literary and iconographic sources in 'Le vite antiche di Watteau e il ritratto immaginario di Walter Pater' ('Watteau's Ancient Lives and Walter Pater's Imaginary Portrait', Bizzotto and Marucci 1996). Notable for its erudition, Fossi's essay also exemplifies the new direction in which Paterian studies have embarked over the last years. If the piece could seem a product of inheritance and continuity with the earlier stages of Pater's Italian reception, seeing the writer essentially as an art critic, in fact Fossi embeds her assessment within a novel context, viewing Pater's œuvre as a multi-faceted totality and avoiding awkward isolation of his texts on art from the intrinsic hybridism of his whole œuvre. All in all, Fossi does not forsake her art-critical vocation, but she proposes a more wide-ranging kind of criticism, which incorporates art, literature, history and fiction. Tellingly enough, she chooses to focus on 'A Prince of Court Painters' and 'Sebastian van Storck', rather than on *The Renaissance.*

The papers delivered at the conference were collected in *Walter Pater (1839–1894). Le forme della modernità. The Forms of Modernity* (1996) edited by Bizzotto and Marucci, the first Italian volume entirely devoted to Pater apart from Olivero's *Il pensiero religioso ed estetico di Walter Pater*, and the first ever comprehensive contribution to Italian studies of the writer, bringing together practically all the Italian scholars who had been or were at the time working on Pater. The book covered almost the whole range of Pater's oeuvre, with the sole outstanding exception – as Francesco Rognoni lamented in 'Nel nome del Pater' ('In the Name of the Pater', 1996) – of *Gaston de Latour* (though to be fair, Marucci's translation still remained unpublished at the time of the conference).

The range and polyvalence of the essays, a marked contrast to the monolithic impression conveyed by Prazian criticism, was underscored by the most interesting reviews of the volume that endorsed the novel status of Paterian research. Emma Sdegno's article in *Comparatistica* (1996) gave evidence of the varied nature of the contributions, as proved by the fact that the central question posited by the Conference, as to the value of Pater's modernity, seems to have been answered from two conflicting perspectives. The first viewed Pater as a figure assimilable to Victorianism, whilst the second considered him a precursor of modern and postmodern stances. Francesco Rognoni for his part paid tribute to the volume as a long-awaited evaluation of Pater in his previously mentioned article published in *La rivista dei libri*, where he reviewed the four Italian books devoted to Pater in the two-year period 1994–96 (the translations of *Greek Studies, Imaginary Portraits* and

Gaston de Latour, plus *The Forms of Modernity*) and introduced Denis Donoghue's *Walter Pater: Lover of Strange Souls* to the Italian public. Rognoni felt he could give a 'generational' account for the rediscovery of Pater by the Italian academic world in the 1990s. This meant that 'up to ten years ago, Pater was simply unavailable to Italian Anglicists: he was Mario Praz's property',[26] and only after Praz could he be reappraised. Hence, whilst Praz notoriously saw Pater as a Romantic, modern-day scholars, such as Marucci and Colaiacomo, have tended to consider him a precursor of the twentieth century. Rognoni himself distinguished two Modernist trends that possibly stemmed from Pater, one being the 'narrative use of myth [...] that anticipates Eliot, Joyce, Pound etc.',[27] and the other the tradition of 'the incessant activity of an omnivorous conscience, that discriminates everything in order to lead it back to itself. It is the conscience – or better the supreme imagination – of the late Henry James, of some Woolf, or of Wallace Stevens'.[28]

Unexpectedly and provocatively, however, in the end Rognoni claimed that Pater's texts should be appreciated for their intrinsic 'strange beauty', rather than judged as 'modern', or 'decadent', or 'outmoded'. And he selected a few examples of Paterian art to champion his idea of what it really means to enjoy Pater: essentially a solipsistic relishing of his enthralling imagery and enchanting prose. In other words, Rognoni's strategy for appreciating Pater appears once again to envisage the writer's persistent appeal to a select coterie of aesthetes or refined litterateurs. And despite Rognoni's disappointment at the fact that Pater's reception continues to be confined to the academic world, he senses that, on the most optimistic assessment, Pater can only be recommended 'to the choicest readers'.[29]

In Italian culture, in other words, Pater still remains a writer for scholars and enthusiasts, a writers' writer, unable to exit the salons or, more recently, the Academy. What has changed, if we compare this with Vernon Lee's *Fanfulla* readership – and this seems by no means an unimportant detail – is the way in which such a coterie of followers construes him. The present way is much more dialectical and even contradictory, invoking a kaleidoscopic range of discourses and attaining a complexity that, for the first time since Lee's Florentine days, has raised Italian criticism of Pater to the international level.

---

[26] 'Fino a un decina d'anni fa, molto semplicemente non era disponibile agli anglisti italiani, era proprietà di Mario Praz' (Rognoni 1996, 39).

[27] 'Il suo uso narrativo del mito [...] che anticipa il cosiddetto "metodo mitico" di Eliot, Joyce, Pound ecc.' (Rognoni 1996, 41).

[28] 'L'attività incessante di una coscienza onnivora, che tutto discrimina per tutto ricondurre a sé. È la coscienza – anzi, l'immaginazione suprema – dell'ultimo Henry James, di certa Woolf, o di Wallace Stevens' (Rognoni 1996, 41).

[29] 'I lettori più scelti' (Rognoni 1996, 41).

4 'Influence Occulte': The Reception of Pater's Works in France Before 1922

Emily Eells

1

Walter Pater's appreciation of French culture was not reciprocated by an immediate response to his work from across the Channel, where it was received with apparent indifference until well into the twentieth century. The closest equivalent of an obituary giving a portrait of the man and an overview of his work was not published until over thirty years after his death: Mary Duclaux's twenty-page 'Souvenirs sur Walter Pater' (1925) serves as precisely the kind of introduction an author needs to establish any renown abroad. Had it been published earlier, it would doubtless have benefited Pater's French critical fortune. But such was not the case, and when René Lalou described Pater's influence as 'occulte', he was using an adjective which applies particularly well to the early reception of his work in France (1926, 125). It went practically unnoticed there until the publication of the translation of *The Renaissance* in 1917,[1] followed five years later by the translation of *Marius the Epicurean*. And yet, by 1973, the French bibliography of work on Pater was twice as long as the corresponding Italian or German bibliographies (Court 1980, 407). This account of Pater's reception in France will therefore consider in what ways his early influence was 'occulte' and why his name was not established on the French literary scene until 1922.

Teodor de Wyzewski (1863–1917), the Polish-born translator and essayist on foreign literature who signed his work Théodore de Wyzewa, was the first French critic to write on Pater. He reviewed Pater's work in four separate articles published in the last decade of the nineteenth century in the *Revue des deux mondes*.[2] He first discusses Pater in an article dated January 1890, entitled 'La Renaissance du roman historique en Angleterre' ('The Renaissance of the

---

[1] Translated by Firmin Roger-Cornaz. For other French translations, see Best and Darles: 'Léonard de Vinci' (Pater 1899b); André: 'L'Ecole de Giorgione' (Pater 1963) and Henry: *Essais sur l'art et la Renaissance* (Pater 1985).

[2] See Seiler (1980, 297–303 and 376–80) for an English translation of extracts from de Wyzewa 1890 and 1896.

Historical Novel in England').[3] In it, he uses *Marius the Epicurean* as an example of how British writers revived Walter Scott's model, and in particular how Pater used ancient Rome as a framework to portray the sensitivities of characters from the past. Following a four-page summary of its plot, de Wyzewa favourably compares *Marius the Epicurean* to Joseph Henry Short-house's *John Inglesant*, extolling Pater's historical and philosophical expertise. De Wyzewa adds a muted footnote on Pater's prose style to gently criticize his tendency to favour the musical ring of a sentence over its meaning which, according to the critic, accounts for the unequal quality of some of the essays in *Appreciations*.

De Wyzewa's second article, published over four and a half years later, in August 1894, begins with the announcement that Pater has died. After a short comparison of Pater's and Leconte de Lisle's artistic use of language, de Wyzewa revises his earlier assessment of *Marius the Epicurean*, admitting that the novel is somewhat 'ennuyeux' ('boring'). He suggests that the novel's attempts to be original – a lack of plot, indecisive characters and an ungraspable philosophical thesis – might explain why it did not make a significant impact. He then goes on to review 'Notre-Dame d'Amiens' and 'Vézelay',[4] apparently to acquaint his French readers with an English writer's view of their culture. In an aside, he notes that Pater considered Watteau to be an embodiment of French seriousness, passion and profound poetry. De Wyzewa's article concentrates on Pater's interest in French cathedrals which render religious art freer than in other countries due to the way they combine piety and fantasy. He quotes at length from Pater's essay on Amiens, but only after cautioning that the French version cannot faithfully reproduce the musical phrasing and nuances of the original. He translates the passages which summarize Pater's argument that Amiens is a 'popular' cathedral, in the sense that it was built by and for the community.

In January 1895, de Wyzewa published a double obituary of Pater and the historian James Froude. Its five-page biographical section on the former is based on Edmund Gosse's article 'Walter Pater: A Portrait' which appeared in *The Contemporary Review* a month earlier (Gosse 1894), and presents him as a dilettante and a recluse.[5]

Finally, in November 1896, de Wyzewa devoted an eleven-page article exclusively to Pater and his posthumous novel *Gaston de Latour*. He believed

---

3   De Wyzewa's article might account for the brief reference Firmin Roz (1904, 216) makes to *Marius the Epicurean* in his review of Jonathan Nield (1904) *A Guide to the Best Historical Novels and Tales* (London: Elkin Mathews; New York: G. P. Putnam's Sons).

4   De Wyzewa's article is based on the first publication of Pater's essays under the heading 'Some Great Churches of France': 'Notre-Dame d'Amiens', *The Nineteenth Century*, 35 (March 1894): 481–88 ; 'Vézelay', *The Nineteenth Century*, 35 (June 1894): 963–70.

5   After the publication of de Wyzewa's third piece on Pater, an unsigned article in *The Saturday Review* praised the 'subtle and brilliant' French critic who had written 'beyond doubt the first adequate review of that extraordinary individuality which has yet appeared on the continent of Europe'. See 'A Cosmopolitan Frenchman' (1896).

that Pater's portrayal of Renaissance France would interest the French, but at the same time he predicted that its perfectly composed prose would make it impossible to translate, and indeed there is no French version to date. He regarded *Gaston de Latour* as Pater's most accomplished writing and, to prove this view, he translated long passages recounting Gaston's first communion, the impromptu visit of King Charles IX and Gaston's visits to Ronsard and Montaigne. De Wyzewa contends that Pater's wavering religious conviction might explain his inability to conclude the narrative of Gaston's spiritual journey. Anticipating Monsman's autobiographical interpretation of the work (1980), de Wyzewa reads Gaston's progression from an inherited allegiance to Catholic ritual to a fascination with the novelty of Protestantism, followed by a conversion to the profane religion of Aestheticism, as Pater's own 'confession' (de Wyzewa 1896, 468).

Georges Khnopff was Pater's first French translator. He began with Arthur Symons's chapter on Pater from *Studies in Two Literatures* (1897), which appeared in the *Mercure de France* in February 1898. The same journal published his translation of one of Pater's *Imaginary Portraits* – 'Sebastien van Storck' – in July 1898. The following year, the Mercure de France publishing house brought out Georges Khnopff's translation of all four of Pater's *Imaginary Portraits* – 'Un prince des peintres de cour', 'Denys l'Auxerrois', 'Sébastien van Storck' and 'Le Duc Carl de Rosenmold'.[6] Entitled *Portraits imaginaires*, the volume is dedicated to Pater's sisters and Khnopff's previously published translation of the Symons chapter serves as an introduction. *Portraits imaginaires* failed to make any apparent impact in France, though it has been suggested that the anglophile Marcel Schwob was inspired by Pater's original text to write his *Vies imaginaires* (1896).[7] Over twenty years later, in a review prompted by the publication of Emmanuel Coppinger's translation of *Marius the Epicurean*, Edmond Jaloux dismissed Khnopff's version of the *Portraits* as 'détestable'. He conceded, however, that 'Pater's prose certainly makes martyrs of its translators'.[8]

In September 1899, the *Mercure de France* published a translation by Richard Irvine Best and Robert Darles of Pater's chapter on Leonardo da Vinci from *The Renaissance*. Their translation is fairly accurate and faithful, at least until their concluding misrepresentation of Pater's conception of the relationship between the Italian and French Renaissance. They misconstrue Pater's image of Leonardo's last years on the banks of the Loire as a period when 'Italian art dies away as a French exotic' (1902, 128) by translating it with a phrase to the effect that Italian art blossoms again in France in the form of an exotic flower.[9] They also subtly modify Pater's discussion of sexual ambiguity in Leonardo's

---

[6] In 1930, the same four *Imaginary Portraits* were translated into French again and prefaced by Philippe Neel (Paris: Stock, Delamain et Boutelleau). Reprinted in 1985, with a postface by Mario Praz (Paris: Christian Bourgois).

[7] Anne Henry (1981, 230) makes this point.

[8] 'la prose de Pater est certainement un martyre pour les traducteurs' (Jaloux 1923, 2).

[9] 'l'art italien s'évanouit pour fleurir en France sous une forme exotique' (Pater 1899b, 605).

work. This was partly a consequence of translating from the almost gender-free language of English into the entirely gendered language of French. Their translation of Pater's description of a drawing representing a 'head' or 'face of doubtful sex' (1902, 115) necessarily adds a feminine element to the English version, given the French gender of the word for 'head': 'la tête'. But the translators could have retained the sexual uncertainty expressed in Pater's original if they had translated his second term – 'face' – with the masculine 'le visage',[10] rather than their choice of another feminine term, 'la figure'. These blemishes are not in themselves sufficient explanation of why 'Léonardo de Vinci' went unnoticed, and why it does not even appear in Germain d'Hangest's list of French translations of Pater's works (1961, 2: 329). The original version had however been noticed by Gabriel Séailles (1892), who praises Pater's 'delicate and subtle article'[11] in the annotated bibliography at the end of his long biographical monograph on Leonardo da Vinci.

During the years between the French editions of *Portraits imaginaires* in 1899 and *La Renaissance* in 1917, Pater's name did not figure prominently in France. His work was not imported there through the public channels of publication and critical reviews but, reflecting Pater's appeal to the individual, it was read and commented on in private.

2

Pater led a withdrawn life and did not try to publicize his works by travelling abroad on foreign lecture tours. The only direct contact he had with French literary circles was through visitors to Oxford, which was how he met Stéphane Mallarmé at the end of February 1894, when Mallarmé came to Oxford to give a lecture on 'Music and Literature'. Despite their common aesthetic interests, they reportedly spent their brief time together in complete silence. Mallarmé's notes on his stay in Oxford allude to 'the illustrious Walter Pater',[12] but say only this about him: 'I know that the most consummate prose-writer alive lives there.'[13] Paul Bourget echoed Mallarmé in an account of his visit to England in 1883, qualifying Pater as the 'most refined of contemporary English prose-writers'.[14] He praises Pater in the superlative as 'the most delicate of prosateurs alive, whose book on the Renaissance contains the loveliest pages ever to have been devoted to Leonardo da Vinci'.[15] In a

---

10   This is the word Anne Henry uses in her translation. See Pater trans. Henry 1985, 84.

11   'article délicat et subtil' (Séailles 1892, 545). Séailles's use of the word 'article' suggests that he is referring to the original publication of 'Leonardo da Vinci' in *The Fortnightly Review* (November 1869).

12   'l'illustre Walter Pater' (Mallarmé 1897, 321).

13   'J'y sais le prosateur ouvragé par excellence de ce temps' (Mallarmé 1897, 373). Conlon (1982, 139) gives a succinct account of Pater and Mallarmé's meeting.

14   'plus raffiné des prosateurs anglais contemporains' (Bourget 1906, 304). Bourget's impressions of Pater were added to the 1906 re-edition of his *Etudes et Portraits*.

15   'plus délicat des prosateurs actuels M. Walter Pater, dont le livre sur la Renaissance contient les plus belles pages qui aient jamais été consacrées à Léonard de Vinci' (Bourget 1906, 293).

footnote to an essay on Octave Feuillet written in 1886, Bourget introduces Pater as 'the admirable author of *Marius the Epicurean*' before citing his unbounded admiration for Feuillet's style.[16] Such laudatory comments on Pater were made in passing and therefore did not help to bring him to the French public's attention.

The minor French poet Marc-André Raffalovich (1864–1934) also met Pater in Oxford. In this instance, however, their ensuing friendship gives us an intriguing clue connected with the covert aspect of Pater's French reception. They corresponded over a two-year period (1884–86) during which Pater sent Raffalovich copies of his books with short notes tucked into them (Vernon, 1983). Pater reviewed Raffalovich's volume of poetry *It Is Thyself,*[17] but, as Pater's family destroyed his personal papers after his death, we can only speculate as to what kind of relationship he had with the author of *Uranisme et unisexualité: étude sur différentes manifestations de l'instinct sexuel* (*Uranism and Unisexuality: A Study of Different Manifestations of Sexual Instinct*).[18] Two years after Pater's death, Raffalovich became a Dominican and contributor to their Oxford-based journal *Blackfriars*, which published his 'Walter Pater: In Memoriam' in August 1928. Since Raffalovich used the pseudonym Alexander Michaelson and wrote the article in English, it in no way helped to further Pater's cause in France.

The indication concerning Pater's 'influence occulte' which Raffalovich left is in an article he published in *Blackfriars* in January 1928. He reports a conversation he overheard in which the use of the linguistic minimal pair 'myth' and 'miss' seems to insinuate that Pater was homosexual: '"Mr Pater, are you a man or a myth?" I once heard. Before Walter Pater had time to reply Mrs Meadows Taylor broke in: "Do you lisp, Miss Corelli?"' (Raffalovich 1928a, 24). On the next page of the article, Raffalovich makes an elliptical reference to an unnamed French reader of Pater, saying: 'I was once astonished by a French Jesuit, now membre de l'Académie, recommending *Marius the Epicurean* as spiritual reading. I am no longer astonished, and I revel in Walter Pater's spiritual growth' (Raffalovich 1928a, 25). He was undoubtedly referring here to Henri Bremond (1865–1933), the Jesuit priest and author of *Histoire littéraire du sentiment religieux en France depuis la fin des guerres de religion jusqu'à nos jours* who had been encouraged to stand for election to the *Académie française* by Maurice Barrès. Bremond came to England for his novitiate (1882–93) and became an avid reader of English literature.[19] He was particularly interested in Anglo-Catholicism and the Oxford movement, and wrote extensively on its leading figures.[20] He grew to

---

[16]   'Walter Pater, l'admirable lettré de *Marius l'Epicurien*' (Bourget 1912, 124).

[17]   Published in 1889 (London: Walter Scott). Pater's review appeared in *The Pall Mall Gazette* [London], 49 (5 April 1889), p. 3; reprinted in *Uncollected Essays by Walter Pater* (Portland, ME: for T. B. Mosher, 1903), pp. 87–91.

[18]   Published in 1896 (Lyon: A. Storck).

[19]   Bremond recalls devouring 'tous les romans anglais imaginables' ('all the English novels imaginable') during that time in England. Quoted in Goichot 1982, 39.

[20]   See in particular Henri Bremond, *Ames religieuses* (Paris: Perrin et Cie, 1902) and *L'Inquiétude religieuse* [first series] (Paris: Perrin et Cie, 1919).

be an intimate friend of the English Jesuit George Tyrrell who, in a letter to Bremond dated 22 January 1901, commended Pater:[21]

> Have you ever read *Marius the Epicurean* by Walter Pater? I'm in the middle of rereading it for the third time, with ever renewed admiration. Despite his over-worked preciousness (he's our Flaubert), I find his writing strangely alluring; he gives you that far-reaching, detached perspective on life which is so healthy and essential a tonic for people who, like me, have a tendency to take their role in the drama a little too seriously and not to see the divinely humorous side to it all.[22]

Tyrrell reiterated his recommendation to read Pater a year later, complimenting Bremond on his moralistic tale 'L'Ourse et le petit ours' (1902): 'Your "Little Bear" is a true delight to me; the moral is that of *Silas Marner* and its method that of Walter Pater in *Gaston de Latour* (which you must read if you haven't already done so).'[23] No trace of Bremond's response to Tyrrell is recorded, and the only echo we have of his reading of Pater is thanks to Raffalovich's disclosure. It is possible however that Bremond included Pater in a lengthy article he drafted in 1904 but never published on English literature at the end of the nineteenth and the beginning of the twentieth centuries. He might also have planned to discuss Pater in the work he outlined in 1907 on 'the *history of religious liberalism* in England'.[24] Pater's work could have served as an illustration of how educated British writers of the Victorian period had relinquished the dogma but retained a sense of Christianity. As I could find no explicit reference to Pater in either Bremond's manuscripts or his published works, the impact he had on Bremond remains a mystery. But Raffalovich's report that he advised reading Pater as a spiritual education illustrates how the latter's work reached the French through the informal network of hearsay. In addition, Bremond's comment on reading Pater

---

[21] In obituaries on Tyrrell published in *The Times* and *The Daily Mail* of 16 July 1909, Petre speaks of his 'intimate friend', the Abbé Bremond. See Maude Dominica Mary Petre (1912) *Autobiography and Life of George Tyrrell* (London: Edward Arnold) 2: 435.

[22] 'Avez-vous jamais lu *Marius l'Epicurien* de Walter Pater? Je suis en train de le relire pour la troisième fois avec une admiration toujours nouvelle. En dépit de sa préciosité laborieuse (il est notre Flaubert), je le trouve étrangement séduisant; il vous donne de la vie ce point de vue lointain et détaché qui est un tonique si sain et si nécessaire pour les gens qui comme moi ont tendance à prendre leur rôle dans le drame un peu trop au sérieux et à ne pas voir le côté divinement humoristique de tout cela' (Tyrrell 1971, 87). Tyrrell's letters were written in English, but as I could not consult them in the original, I am quoting here from the version published in French.

[23] 'Votre "Petit Ours" me ravit tout à fait; la morale est celle de *Silas Marner* et la manière celle de Walter Pater dans *Gaston de la Tour* (qu'il vous faut lire si vous ne l'avez déjà fait)' (Tyrrell 1971, 111). The letter is dated 23 February 1902. Tyrrell is referring to Henri Bremond (1902) 'L'Ourse et le petit ours', *Etudes* 90 (20 February): 553–60.

[24] '*l'histoire du libéralisme anglais*', manuscript note quoted by Goichot (1982, 46). See p. 40 for Goichot's section on Bremond's project to write on late Victorian and early Edwardian literature.

becomes part of a suggestive association between Anglo-Catholicism and homosexuality. Bremond's friend Tyrrell exchanged letters with Raffalovich in which they openly discussed 'unisexuality' and the church's attitude to it.[25] We also know that Raffalovich helped the Dominican Order to purchase Pater's house (64 St Giles, Oxford) after his death, which subsequently became part of Blackfriars Hall (Vernon 1983, 192–97). If that is concrete proof of how Raffalovich consolidated the link between Pater and Anglo-Catholicism, his remark that the academician recommended *Marius the Epicurean* as religious instruction remains tenuous – and tantalizing – evidence that some important *hommes de lettres* were reading Pater, albeit confidentially.

3

Marcel Proust figures among Pater's French readers and, even though he left very little explicit evidence about how much Pater he actually read, he contributed covertly to the reception of his works in France. Proust only refers to Pater twice in the several thousand pages of his printed text. In both instances Pater is relegated to a footnote in Proust's annotated translation of John Ruskin's *The Bible of Amiens*, published by the *Mercure de France* in 1904. In his accompanying introduction, Proust alludes to two *Imaginary Portraits* and two essays from *Miscellaneous Studies*, constituting the sum total of Proust's acknowledged reading of Pater. He outlines an enticing project he never pursued: 'What an interesting collection the landscapes of France seen through English eyes would make: the rivers of France by Turner, Versailles by Bonington, Auxerre or Valenciennes, Vézelay or Amiens by Walter Pater, Fontainebleau by Stevenson, and so many others!'[26] From this footnote, we can at least deduce that Proust had read 'Denys l'Auxerrois' and 'A Prince of Court Painters', probably in Georges Khnopff's translation, as well as 'Vézelay' and 'Notre-Dame d'Amiens', which he must have read in the original English, since the former was not translated into French until after Proust's death and the latter remains untranslated.[27] In the second footnote, Proust refers again to Pater's 'Notre-Dame d'Amiens' in the following annotation on Ruskin's discussion of the pure Gothic style: 'See the development of these ideas in Walter Pater's *Miscellaneous* (the article on "Notre-Dame d'Amiens"). I don't know why Ruskin's name is never cited in it.'[28] By embedding Pater in the footnotes to his translation of *The Bible of Amiens*, Proust seems to make him subordinate to, and dependent upon, Ruskin.

---

[25] See Thomas Michael Loome (1970) 'Tyrrell's Letters to André Raffalovich', 2 parts, *The Month* [London], 229 (February and March): 95–101 and 138–49.

[26] 'Quelle intéressante collection on ferait avec les paysages de France vus par des yeux anglais: les rivières de France de Turner; le *Versailles* de Bonington: l'*Auxerre* ou le *Valenciennes*, le *Vézelay* ou l'*Amiens* de Walter Pater, le Fontainebleau de Stevenson, et tant d'autres!' (Ruskin 1904, 68).

[27] Dr L. Vignes's translation of 'Vézelay' was published as a fifteen-page fascicule in 1924 and sold to raise money for the hospital in Avallon.

[28] 'Voir le développement de ces idées dans *Miscellaneous* de Walter Pater (article sur "Notre-Dame d'Amiens"). Je ne sais pourquoi le nom de Ruskin n'y est pas cité une fois. – (Note du traducteur)' (Ruskin 1904, 250).

For all that, the four short prose pieces Proust cites have particular affinities with his own work. Pater's 'A Prince of Court Painters' is set in Valenciennes and pens an 'imaginary portrait' of Watteau's student, Jean-Baptiste Pater. Writing shortly after the publication of Khnopff's translation of *Imaginary Portraits*, Proust probably drew on Pater's study of the artistic temperament in his own portrayal of Watteau as being bereft of passion and pleasure (Proust 1971, 665–67). In his essay on Vézelay, Pater highlights the basilica's Oriental features, which are also prominent in the following report Proust made of his visit there in 1903:

> Vézelay is a fantastic place, in a sort of Switzerland, all alone on a mountain towering over the countryside, visible from all directions from miles around, in the most strikingly harmonious landscape. The church is enormous and resembles a Turkish bath as much as it does Notre-Dame, built of alternately black and white stones, a delicious Christian mosque.[29] (Proust 1983, 351–52)

The cathedral, central to both Pater's 'Notre-Dame d'Amiens' and his 'Denys l'Auxerrois', serves as a structuring trope in Proust's multi-volumed *A la recherche du temps perdu*,[30] first published between 1913 and 1927. As Proust pointed out, Pater's essay on Amiens had developed ideas from both Ruskin's study of that cathedral and *The Seven Lamps of Architecture*. In particular, Pater reworked its chapter entitled 'The Lamp of Memory', devoted to the mnemonic dimension of architecture, demonstrating that a cathedral bears the traces of the passage of time: 'In architecture, close as it is to men's lives and their history, the visible result of time is a large factor in the realised aesthetic value, and what a true architect will in due measure always trust to' (1895, 114). Such an architectural manifestation of memory would not have been lost on Proust and it is hard not to see Paterian reflections on the fourth dimension of the church in Combray, namely that of time (Proust 1987–89, 1: 60). Pater's construction of the cathedral tower in Auxerre is the temporal framework of 'Denys l'Auxerrois'. In it, he describes the harmonious union of the town and the river Yonne with an allusion to Turner's *Rivers of France*. It is probably more than coincidental that Proust cites this work alongside Pater's in his footnote concerning English artists' views of France.

The only other explicit reference Proust makes to Pater (apart from the three times he mentions him in his correspondence)[31] can be found in his manuscript material. It dates from sometime after January 1908, following Proust's request that Alfred Vallette send him a copy of Khnopff's translation

---

29   'Vézelay est une chose prodigieuse dans une espèce de Suisse, toute seule sur une montagne qui domine les autres, visible de partout à des lieues, dans l'harmonie du paysage la plus saisissante. L'église est immense et ressemble autant à des bains turcs qu'à Notre-Dame, bâtie en pierres alternativement noires et blanches, délicieuse mosquée chrétienne' (Proust 1970–93, 3: 419). Letter to Georges de Lauris dated 8 or 9 September 1903.

30   For a developed discussion of this subject, see Frank 1979.

31   See Proust 1970–93, 4: 93; 8: 27; 16: 189. The first two references are discussed here; the third one is in a letter to Walter Berry, dated 21 July 1917, where Proust points out that his friend has the same first name as Pater and Scott.

of '*Portraits imaginaires* de Pater' (Proust 1970–93, 8: 27). In a long, thin notebook he used between 1908 and 1910, Proust included an allusion to Pater in some reading notes he jotted down on Thomas Hardy: 'A bit of Pater's "Denys l'Auxerrois" in Pierston and the island'.[32] This elliptical remark draws a parallel between Pater's 'imaginary portrait' and Hardy's *The Well-Beloved*, pointing to the way both works associate character and place. Moreover, Hardy's novel and Pater's short story are shaped by the same sense of repetition and return which permeates Proust's *A la recherche du temps perdu*. Proust erases Pater's name from these reading notes on Hardy when he rewrites them in *La Prisonnière*, and consequently Pater is never mentioned by name in the many volumes of his novel.

Proust's two footnotes referring to Pater and the sole occurrence of his name that I could find in his voluminous manuscripts in no way reveal his opinion of the Englishman's work. The only indication we have of what he thought of Pater is thanks to Douglas Ainslie, who was introduced to Proust in 1897 by the diplomat Robert de Billy. Judging from the short letters they exchanged over the following two years, they became friends.[33] Ainslie helped Proust to understand the English texts he was interested in and it is possible that these included Pater's untranslated work. In a tribute written after Proust's death in 1922, Ainslie relates a conversation they had in the year they met, which reveals their apparent difference of opinion concerning Pater:

> Quite frequently we would get into a discussion about the respective merits of Ruskin and Walter Pater. We know that Proust translated several parts of Ruskin's work. He did not want Pater's reputation to prevail over Ruskin's, and when I relayed to him what Pater had said to me once: 'I don't think that Ruskin could have discovered more about St Mark's than I did', he shrugged his shoulders and said: 'You see, we'll never agree on English literature.'[34]

---

[32] 'Un peu de "Denys l'Auxerrois" de Pater dans Pierston et l'île.' (N.A.Fr. 16637, f° 48 r°). This and subsequent references to Proust's manuscript material are quoted using the classification numbers of the Proust papers in the 'Cabinet des manuscrits' of the Bibliothèque nationale de France.

[33] See Bryant C. Freeman (1960) 'Six lettres à Douglas Ainslie', *Bulletin de la Société des Amis de Marcel Proust et des Amis de Combray* [Illiers-Combray, France], 10: 61–78. Ainslie reports on meeting Proust in Parisian salons, and he clearly enjoyed their conversations together, though he is cuttingly critical about Proust's written style when he compares it to that of Choderlos de Laclos: 'Proust's talent is the exact opposite of the sober and intense author of *Liaisons dangereuses*. His style is like a feather-bed; and Laclos's, like the rapier that rips it.' See Douglas Ainslie (1922) *Adventures Social and Literary* (London: T. Fisher Unwin), p. 263.

[34] 'Nous entamions assez fréquemment des discussions sur la valeur respective de Ruskin et de Walter Pater. On sait que Proust a traduit plusieurs parties de l'œuvre de Ruskin. Il ne voulait pas qu'on se prévalût de Pater contre Ruskin, et lorsque je lui racontai que Pater m'avait dit un jour: "Je ne crois pas que Ruskin ait pu découvrir dans Saint Marc plus de choses que moi", il haussa les épaules et dit: "Que voulez-vous, nous ne nous entendrons jamais sur la littérature anglaise"' (Ainslie 1923, 259–60).

How are we to interpret Proust's gesture and remark? Taken at face value, they are dismissive of Pater's work. Yet, as Ainslie's comment suggests, Proust's attitude might be a ploy to promote Ruskin and consequently his own translations. Proust might also be trying to cover up his relative ignorance about Pater's work, since, as we have seen, there is no concrete evidence that he read more than the four short prose pieces he cited. Another possibility is that Proust is covering his tracks and disguising the impact of Pater on his own work. Indeed, given the close resemblance his writing bears to Pater's, one could argue that Pater played a more influential role in his literary development than he admits.

As Proust left such limited evidence that he had read Pater, further comparative study of their work is necessarily interpretative and speculative. De Billy takes credit for introducing Proust to Pater's writing, but he is circumspect about how much he then actually read: 'I spoke to him of Walter Pater and his *Greek Studies*. I'm not sure that he read *Marius the Epicurean*.'[35] I could find no explicit reference to either *Marius the Epicurean* or *Greek Studies* in any of Proust's published or unpublished writings. Nevertheless, he might be borrowing from Pater's discussion of Giotto's symbolism in a passage from *Greek Studies* (1895, 97–99). He echoes Pater in both his use of the term 'symbol' to describe how Giotto represents an intangible attribute literally and his choice of Giotto's 'Charity' in the Arena chapel in Padua as an exemplary allegorical figure (Proust 1987–89, 1: 81). But, as J. Hillis Miller points out, the two authors are reflecting their reading of Ruskin, so this textual overlap does not constitute proof in itself that Proust was quoting Pater (Miller 1976, 110).

It is reasonable to assume that Proust knew de Wyzewa's articles on Pater, both because he was an assiduous reader of the *Revue des deux mondes* and because his father, Adrien Proust, was an important contributor to the journal at that time.[36] Proust would thus have acquired indirect knowledge of *Marius the Epicurean* and *Gaston de Latour*. It is also possible that Ainslie recommended A. C. Benson's monograph on Pater (1906); Benson knew Ainslie personally and relays his report of a comment that Pater had made to him, namely that he had discovered more about Venice than Ruskin. Although Benson does not name his source, Proust would have recognized that Ainslie had repeated the same remark to him. It is significant that Benson's book quotes almost all the passages which I have identified as possible intertextual sources from which Proust may have drawn. So Proust might not have read Pater directly but picked up his knowledge at second hand.

Proust's writing echoes Pater's, either consciously, though not openly admitting it, or innocently ignorant to what extent their preoccupations and sensitivities intersected. The affinities between Pater's and Proust's works are

---

[35]   'je lui fis connaître Walter Pater et ses *Etudes helléniques*. Je ne suis pas sûr qu'il ait lu *Marius l'Epicurien*' (Billy 1930, 128).

[36]   Adrien Proust's 'Epidémies anciennes et épidémies modernes : les nouvelles routes des épidémies' appeared in the *Revue des deux mondes*, 120 (1 December 1893): 641–80; see also his article 'Le pèlerinage de La Mecque et la propagation des épidémies', *Revue des deux mondes*, 129 (15 May 1895): 368–93.

numerous and are sometimes so close that Proust seems to be citing Pater's very words.[37] Trying to define their intertextual relationship raises the question of whether their resemblances are the result of textual genetics or of a common inheritance of germane ideas.

Proust never mentions 'Style' explicitly, but he appears to appropriate the aesthetic ideas Pater expounds in the essay to such an extent that his phrasing sometimes reads like a translated quotation from the English original. One such example is Proust's response to the question of whether he had any intention of translating Pater himself. That question was addressed to him in a circumlocutory way by Maurice Barrès in a letter dated 13 March 1904: 'I've been told that Pater made trips to France. Who will make them known to us?'[38] Proust's reply echoes 'Style' and its definition of creative writing as a 'translation from inward to outward' (1889, 31). He explains that after completing his translations of Ruskin, he hopes that he will have enough strength left to embark on his 'search for lost time': 'As for Pater, I shall certainly not be the one who translates him. I still have two Ruskins to do, and after that I shall try to translate my own poor soul, if it doesn't die in the meantime' (Proust 1989, 33–34).[39] Proust incorporates that same Paterian idea into his reflections on aesthetics at the end of *Le Temps retrouvé*, where the narrator refers to his writing project as a translation of the inner self: 'So that the essential, the only true book, though in the ordinary sense of the word it does not have to be "invented" by a great writer – for it exists already in each one of us – has to be translated by him. The function and the task of a writer are those of a translator' (Proust 1992, 6: 247).[40] In 'Style', Pater presents the

---

[37] Anne Henry (1981, 220–46) interprets these affinities as proof that Proust had read Pater's work. André (1963) argues that Proust was deeply influenced by Pater, although he gives no evidence that Proust had actually read Pater. An exchange of letters in *The Times Literary Supplement* in 1958 debates whether there is simply a 'curious affinity' between Proust and Pater, or whether Proust was actually influenced by Pater. Betty Miller raises the question, expressing surprise that it had not yet been addressed (*The Times Literary Supplement*, 25 April 1958, p. 225); Mario Praz responds that he discusses it in the Introduction to his Italian translation of 'The Child in the House' (*The Times Literary Supplement*, 6 June 1958, p. 313) and J. P. Hulin (*The Times Literary Supplement*, 18 July 1958, p. 409) points to the comparative work already published on Proust and Pater (Mourey 1926, 906–09; Fernandez 1928; Maranini 1933, 67–69). Hulin concludes with the unfounded assertion that Proust had read *Appreciations*, although he does concede that he cannot positively state whether Proust had read 'The Child in the House'. The debate remains open.

[38] 'On m'a dit que Pater avait fait des voyages en France. Qui nous les fera connaître?' (Proust 1970–93, 4: 88).

[39] 'Quant à Pater certes ce n'est pas moi qui le traduirai. J'ai encore deux Ruskin à faire, et après j'essaierai de traduire ma pauvre âme à moi, si elle n'est pas morte dans l'intervalle' (Proust 1970–93, 4: 93). Letter written on 13, 14 or 15 March 1904.

[40] 'je m'apercevais que ce livre essentiel, le seul livre vrai, un grand écrivain n'a pas, dans le sens courant, à l'inventer puisqu'il existe déjà en chacun de nous, mais à le traduire. Le devoir et la tâche de l'écrivain sont ceux d'un traducteur' (Proust 1987–89, 4: 469).

writer's idiom as a personal language forged to convey a subjective way of seeing: 'any writer worth translating at all has winnowed and searched through his vocabulary [. . .] and doing this with his peculiar sense of the world ever in view, in search of an instrument for the adequate expression of that, he begets a vocabulary faithful to the colouring of his own spirit, and in the strictest sense original' (1889, 11). Proust expands Pater's concept to include the way painters convey their particular way of seeing through colour:

> For style for the writer, no less than colour for the painter, is a question not of technique but of vision: it is the revelation, which by direct and conscious methods would be impossible, of the qualitative difference, the uniqueness of the fashion in which the world appears to each one of us, a difference which, if there were no art, would remain for ever the secret of every individual [. . . .] Thanks to art, instead of seeing one world only, our own, we see that world multiply itself and we have at our disposal as many worlds as there are original artists. (Proust 1992, 6: 254)[41]

The analogy Pater establishes in 'Style' between literature and architecture might have inspired Proust to compare his literary project to an architectural plan for a cathedral. More specifically, it can be argued that Proust quotes from Pater's essay in some of the footnotes to his translation of Ruskin's *Sesame and Lilies*. Indeed, Pater's definition of 'literary architecture' as an

> architectural conception of [a] work, which foresees the end in the beginning and never loses sight of it, and in every part is conscious of all the rest, till the last sentence does but, with undiminished vigour, unfold and justify the first (1889, 18)

is synonymous with Proust's point that Ruskin's work seems to be constructed according to a secret plan which is only revealed upon completion:

> at the end it is apparent that he has obeyed a sort of hidden plan, unveiled in the last pages, which imposes retrospectively a kind of order over the whole thing, which is made to look as if it builds up magnificently to the final apotheosis.[42]

In his own discussion of Flaubert's style in the literary criticism posthumously published under the title *Contre Sainte-Beuve*, Proust appears to be citing Pater's essay. He highlights the uniformly smooth, reflecting quality of Flaubert's prose, thus apparently elaborating on Pater's insistence that there is

---

[41]   '[l]e style pour l'écrivain aussi bien que la couleur pour le peintre est une question non de technique mais de vision. Il est la révélation, qui serait impossible par des moyens directs et conscients, de la différence qualitative qu'il y a dans la façon dont nous apparaît le monde, différence qui, s'il n'y avait pas l'art, resterait le secret éternel de chacun. [. . . .] Grâce à l'art, au lieu de voir un seul monde, le nôtre, nous le voyons se multiplier, et autant qu'il y a d'artistes originaux, autant nous avons de mondes à notre disposition [. . .].' (Proust 1987–89, 4: 474).

[42]   'à la fin il se trouve avoir obéi à une sorte de plan secret qui, dévoilé à la fin, impose rétrospectivement à l'ensemble une sorte d'ordre et le fait apercevoir magnifiquement étagé jusqu'à l'apothéose finale.' (Ruskin 1906, 62–63).

no 'surplusage' to it. The following English translation of what Proust wrote could be mistaken for a citation from Pater's 'Style':

> In Flaubert's style, [...] all the elements of reality are converted into the one substance, whose vast surfaces have a monotonous shimmer. No impurity remains. The surfaces have become reflective. Everything is depicted in them, but as a reflection, without this homogeneous substance being impaired. Whatever was different has been converted and absorbed.[43] (Proust 1988, 62)

This manuscript was written at approximately the same time as Proust's other references to Pater, which strengthens the argument that he had read 'Style'.

Assessing Pater's influence on Proust in this way engages in literary detective work which requires a wide-angle lens to gain an overview of both authors' œuvres as well as a magnifying glass to dissect their minute similarities and to decipher Proust's manuscript material. Although Pater's name does not figure in *A la recherche du temps perdu*, there are some possible traces of his presence in Proust's manuscripts, in addition to the one occasion when Proust refers explicitly to '"Denys l'Auxerrois" de Pater'. The evidence is sometimes limited to single words, but added together they constitute compelling proof that Pater contributed to Proust's creation. In these cases, Proust does not identify his source and tends to obliterate it as much as possible when he makes the rough draft into a definitive version. For example, Proust included what seems to be an unacknowledged reference to Pater's 'Notre-Dame d'Amiens' in the following manuscript passage written in the spring of 1909: 'She [Gilberte Swann] was planning to go to Amiens to see "the greatest of cathedrals". Thus, in that northern town, there was a "great cathedral" which was part of it, bare, outdoors, and an important thing for thinkers and writers.'[44] Since Proust rarely used inverted commas for emphasis, they probably indicate here that he is quoting from the opening line of Pater's essay: 'The greatest and purest of Gothic churches, Notre-Dame d'Amiens' (1895, 105). This reference to Amiens disappears from Proust's printed text, suggesting that Proust deliberately erased any traces of Pater's work in his own.

In a similar way, the preparatory versions of *A la recherche du temps perdu* offer some proof that Proust used Pater as one of the models for his fictitious writer Bergotte.[45] In the following rough draft, Proust's narrator expresses his

---

[43] 'Dans le style de Flaubert [...] toutes les parties de la réalité sont converties en une même substance, aux vastes surfaces, d'un miroitement monotone. Aucune impureté n'est restée. Les surfaces sont devenues réfléchissantes. Toutes les choses s'y peignent, mais par reflet, sans en altérer la substance homogène. Tout ce qui était différent a été converti et absorbé' (Proust 1971, 269).

[44] 'Elle [Gilberte Swann] devait aller à Amiens pour voir "la plus prodigieuse des cathédrales". Ainsi dans cette ville du nord, à même la ville, nue, dehors, il y avait une "prodigieuse cathédrale" qui pour des penseurs, des écrivains, était une chose importante' (Cahier 12, N.A.Fr. 16652, f° 101 r°). Proust translates the superlative of 'great' as 'la plus prodigieuse' to capture Pater's idea that the cathedral is imposing or extraordinary, thus avoiding the mistranslation 'la plus grande', which would have meant that Amiens was 'the largest' Gothic cathedral.

[45] For further discussion of this comparison, see Bann 2002, 60–62.

admiration for the book he is reading, which is ostensibly by Bergotte, though it resonates with references to Pater:

> I saw from a superb phrase which was too short that he loved cathedrals, which put him even higher in my esteem. By comparing them to inaccessible cliffs and symbolic prayer books, he exalted my imagination without satisfying it. He quoted from Ruskin's book, 'The Bible of Amiens'.[46]

Proust thus appropriates the allusion Pater apparently makes to Ruskin's *The Bible of Amiens* when he describes the cathedral as 'an open Bible, [...] the Bible treated as a book about men and women'(Pater 1895, 116) in order to ascribe it to Bergotte. The corresponding printed version of this passage retains Bergotte's particular interest in Gothic cathedrals but it deletes the specific reference to Amiens, thereby obscuring the double reference to Ruskin and Pater. The same manuscript passage reveals that Proust intended Bergotte to describe cathedrals as 'inaccessible cliffs' ('inaccessibles falaises'). That image might derive from the final paragraph of Pater's essay on Amiens, where the cathedral is compared to 'cliffs of quarried and carved stone'. In the final version of the text, Proust displaces the comparison and dissociates it from Bergotte, applying it to the narrator's description of the churchtower in the seaside resort of Balbec: 'I had read that it was itself a rugged Norman cliff round which the winds howled' (Proust 1992, 2: 272–73).[47] The winds beating against the churchtower in this final version might also find their source in the last paragraph of Pater's essay, which speaks of the 'grey, driving sea winds' (1895, 121).

There is further proof in the same Proust manuscript to back the argument that Bergotte has some Pater in him. Just before Bergotte cites *The Bible of Amiens*, there is a description of his writing which again reverberates with Paterian allusions:

> he spoke endlessly about the vain dream of life, and old myths which the thought of centuries slowly enriches, of the endless drifting of illusory, unfounded appearances, of splendid messages of love, of the sterile torment of thinking, of the incurable melancholy of the beautiful.[48]

When reworking this passage, Proust retains three of the subjects treated by Bergotte (rephrasing them as 'the vain dream of life', 'the inexhaustible torrent

---

[46] 'Je vis par une phrase superbe mais trop courte qu'il aimait les cathédrales ce qui les plaça plus haut encore dans mon esprit. En les comparant à d'inaccessibles falaises, et à de symboliques missels il exaltait mon imagination sans la contenter. Il citait du livre de Ruskin *The Bible of Amiens*' (Cahier 14, N.A.Fr. 16654, f° 80 r°). The transcription is simplified and does not include Proust's successive versions.

[47] 'j'avais lu qu'il était lui-même une âpre falaise normande où s'amassaient les grains' (Proust 1987–89, 2: 19).

[48] '[il] parlait sans cesse du vain songe de la vie, des vieux mythes qu'enrichit lentement la pensée des siècles, de l'écoulement sans fin, et sans vérité des illusoires apparences, des splendides messages de l'amour, du tourment stérile de penser, de l'incurable mélancolie du beau' (Cahier 14, N.A.Fr. 16654, f° 80 r° – simplified transcription).

of beautiful appearances', 'the sterile and delicious torment of understanding and loving') which have been identified as citations from Anatole France and Leconte de Lisle.[49] At the same time, Proust deletes the 'old myths which slowly enrich the thought of centuries' and 'the incurable melancholy of the beautiful', which might well have been inspired by Pater's work. The idea that old myths and legends have grown, and been enriched, through centuries of thought and experience could refer to 'Denys l'Auxerrois', whereas the 'incurable melancholy of the beautiful' echoes elements from Pater's depiction of the physiognomy of the area around Auxerre as 'not quite happy – attractive in part for its melancholy' (1887, 57). Although the final version eliminates these possible references to Pater, the description of Bergotte's prose still has a Paterian ring to it and seems to borrow elements from his essay on style. It also puts into practice the aesthetic precept Pater defined in 'The School of Giorgione', that all art aspires to the condition of music, when it uses the terms 'dolce' and 'lento' to describe how the narrator reads Bergotte's books as if they were a musical score (Proust 1987–89, 1: 95). Another hint of Bergotte's Paterian origins can be found on the same page of Proust's novel, where the young narrator explains that while reading Bergotte, he feels as if he were in the arms of 'un père retrouvé' ('a father found again'). Since the epithet 'père' is a Gallicization of Pater's name, Proust might be making playful use of translation to indicate that Pater is one of Bergotte's literary forefathers.

The opening section of Proust's novel – 'Combray' – has frequently been read as a transposition into French of Pater's 'The Child in the House'. Proust never cites this title, and although it was not translated into French until long after Proust's death,[50] it is plausible that he had read it, given that it appears in the same volume of *Miscellaneous Studies* as 'Notre-Dame d'Amiens' and 'Vézelay'. The similarities between 'Combray' and 'The Child in the House' are striking: like Pater, Proust makes the childhood house into a spatial representation of memory, so that the architectural structure is endowed with a temporal dimension. Pater writes of how Florian's soul gradually expanded into the house, which anticipates Proust's description of the narrator's bedroom at Combray: 'a room which I had succeeded in filling with my own personality' (Proust 1992, 1: 9).[51] Pater puts the mechanisms of associative memory into action, showing how colours, smells and sounds in the present have the power to evoke the past. The flowering hawthorn plays a central role in both the Paterian child's 'brain-building' (1895, 184) and in Proust's narrator's formative experience. Pater relates how Florian left the house aimlessly and happened upon a fragrant crimson hawthorn whose beauty aroused his senses. That coincidental event was a revelation for the boy, a kind of epiphany which is rehearsed every subsequent year with the reflowering of

---

[49]   See Proust 1987–89, 1: 93 and corresponding notes on pp. 1146–47.
[50]   The first French translation, by Pierre Leyris, was published in 1992, in a volume entitled *L'Enfant dans la maison*, which also contains 'Emerald Uthwart', 'Apollon en Picardie' and 'Hippolyte voilé'. In his preface, Leyris points out the resemblances between 'The Child in the House' and 'Combray'.
[51]   'une chambre que j'avai fini par remplir de mon moi' (Proust 1987–89, 1: 10).

the hawthorn, thus perpetuating a continuity of the past in the present. Proust's young narrator seems to follow in the Paterian child's footsteps when he finds himself in a chapel of branches formed by the hawthorn tree (Proust 1987–89, 1: 136).

There is potential evidence that Proust had read 'The Child in the House' in the same manuscript notebook where he has Bergotte allude to 'Notre-Dame d'Amiens'. In it, Proust works on the passage relating the summer afternoons which the young narrator spends reading in his bedroom (Proust 1987–89, 1: 82). He specifies in a phrase, rewritten several times, that the heat was 'perfumed with the fall of the lime-blossoms'.[52] This wording is reminiscent of a passage of Pater's 'The Child in the House' which foreshadows Proustian sensory memory:

> The perfume of the little flowers of the lime-tree fell through the air upon them like rain; while time seemed to move ever more slowly to the murmur of the bees in it, till it almost stood still on June afternoons. How insignificant, at the moment, seem the influences of the sensible things which are tossed and fall and lie about us, so, or so, in the environment of early childhood. How indelibly, as we afterwards discover, they affect us; with what capricious attractions and associations they figure themselves on the white paper, the smooth wax, of our ingenuous souls, as 'with lead in the rock for ever', giving form and feature, and as it were assigned house-room in our memory, to early experiences of feeling and thought, which abide with us ever afterwards, thus, and not otherwise. (1895, 176–77)

Proust deletes the lime-blossoms from the final version of his text, perhaps in a conscious effort to mask his Paterian source. At the same time, he metamorphoses Pater's 'murmuring bees' into 'buzzing mosquitoes' performing 'chamber music' in the narrator's bedroom. Further evidence in the same notebook speaks for the view that Proust deliberately obscured allusions to Pater. In the rough draft of a conversation about various authors which the narrator has with his friend Bloch, the latter admonishes peremptorily: 'Come on, don't repeat the idiocies [...] of those pitiful prigs.'[53] Proust uses 'cuistres' ('prigs' or 'pedants') in the manuscript here to replace 'cocos' ('oddballs') which he crosses out on the same folio. In the final version of this passage, however, he reverts to 'coco', when he has Bloch quote Leconte de Lisle – 'cet immense bonhomme' ('that imposing fellow') – and that author's alleged opinion that Bergotte is 'un coco des plus subtils' ('a most subtle oddball').[54] The terms 'coco' and 'immense bonhomme' can be traced back to Flaubert's letters to George Sand,[55] but 'cuistre' is not used in their correspondence, nor does it belong to Proust's vocabulary. However, Pater highlights his use of the French word in 'Style': 'Pedantry being only the scholarship of *le cuistre* (we have no English equivalent)' (1889, 10–11). Pater's phrase might have

---

52   'parfumée par la chute des fleurs de tilleul' (Cahier 14, N.A.Fr. 16654, f° 68 r°). This passage is reworked on f° 67 v°, where the lime-blossoms have disappeared.

53   'Allons ne répète pas les sottises de [...] ces très pitoyables cuistres' (Cahier 14, N.A.Fr. 16654, f° 77 r°).

54   Proust 1987–89, 1: 89.

55   See Proust 1987–89, 1:1146 (note 9 to p. 89).

prompted Proust to put the word 'cuistre' in the mouth of his pretentious pedant, Bloch, in which case, it can only be significant that he then deleted it when revising his work.

Proust's aesthetic tenets are so consonant with the ideas Pater expresses in *The Renaissance* that they sound like a translation of the original English version. In the 'Preface', Pater writes that 'the first step towards seeing one's object as it really is, is to know one's own impression as it really is' (1902, viii), which sets the agenda for Proust's literary enterprise. Paterian subjective criticism places sensitivity above intelligence: 'What is important, then, is not that the critic should possess a correct abstract definition of beauty for the intellect, but a certain kind of temperament, the power of being deeply moved by the presence of beautiful objects' (1902, x). Proust reiterates and condenses that idea to make it into the opening line of his essay on criticism, *Contre Sainte-Beuve*: 'Daily, I attach less value to the intellect' (Proust: 1988, 3).[56]

All the painters studied in *The Renaissance* have found their way into *A la recherche du temps perdu*, which might simply reflect a shared aesthetic taste, but could be an indication that Proust had read Pater's essays before they were published in volume form in French.[57] In these essays, Pater anticipates the temporal complexity of the Proustian moment when he shows how Giorgione's painting depicts the past and the future in an intense consciousness of the present. Proust refers to the 'école de Giorgione' (Proust 1987–89, 1: 384) in what is arguably a translation of Pater's chapter title 'The School of Giorgione', just as he imitates Pater's use of the adjectival form of the artist's name when he describes a sensuous woman as '[f]ollement Giorgione' ('wildly Giorgionesque') (Proust 1987–89, 3: 94).

Pater's chapter on Botticelli might have coloured Proust's depiction of Odette Swann, which likens her to Botticelli's Zipporah in the Sistine Chapel frescoes. In a working version of 'Un amour de Swann', Proust had initially focused on Odette's 'hot, pinkish and puffy'[58] cheeks, but he corrected that typescript to make her face 'pale with little red spots, her features drawn, with rings under her eyes'.[59] Two pages later in the same typescript, he confirms the correction, again transforming her original 'puffy' and 'excessively pink' complexion into the sickly one she has in the final version: 'Odette's pallid complexion, her too thin cheeks, her drawn features, her tired eyes' (Proust 1992, 1: 459–60).[60] It is possible that this correction was made after reading Pater's lines on Botticelli's 'wan' Madonnas (1902, 56). It is equally possible that Proust translated the adjective Pater used to describe them – 'peevish-

---

[56]   'Chaque jour j'attache moins de prix à l'intelligence' (Proust 1971: 211).

[57]   For a more extensive discussion of this subject, see Johnson 1980. According to Kenneth Clark, there is no doubt that Proust had read Pater's essays, which influenced his 'theories, [. . .] modes of perception and even [his] style'. See Pater 1961, 23.

[58]   'chaudes, rosées et bouffies' (N.A.Fr. 16734 f° 196 r°).

[59]   'pâles avec des petits points rouges, ses traits tirés, cernés' (N.A.Fr. 16734 f° 196 r°).

[60]   'le teint pâle d'Odette, les joues trop maigres, les traits tirés, les yeux battus' (Proust 1987–89, 1: 375).

looking' (1902, 56) – in order to apply it to Odette's eyes, which he describes as 'maussades' (Proust 1987–89, 1: 219). The fact that terms from Pater's chapter on Botticelli are used by Proust in his portrayal of Odette is persuasive – but not conclusive – evidence that he had read *The Renaissance*. He might simply have based his description of her on his own study of the Florentine painter's work, inspired most likely by Ruskin's drawing of 'Zipporah',[61] meaning that the textual similarities with Pater's version are just a further indication of how much they had in common.

Pater's chapter on the French Renaissance poet Joachim du Bellay concludes on a resoundingly Proustian note which confirms the deep affinity between Pater and Proust. Pater cites a passage from one of du Bellay's poems which epitomizes his work as well as the whole of the Pléiade school, and could serve as an anticipatory example of Proust's notion of the 'phrase-type'. The poem Pater quotes portrays an instance of involuntary memory which is richly suggestive in its Proustian overtones: a passing ray of light revives du Bellay's childhood memories in the Beauce, which is incidentally the same area of France where the Proust family spent some of their holidays. Pater recalls how du Bellay captures the fleeting moment when the remembrance of something past illuminates and transfigures the commonplace present:

> That has, in the highest degree, the qualities, the value, of the whole Pleiad school of poetry, of the whole phase of taste from which that school derives – a certain silvery grace of fancy, nearly all the pleasure of which is in the surprise at the happy and dexterous way in which a thing slight in itself is handled. [. . . .] One seems to hear the measured falling of the fans, with a child's pleasure on coming across the incident for the first time, in one of those great barns of Du Bellay's own country, *La Beauce*, the granary of France. A sudden light transfigures a trivial thing, a weather-vane, a windmill, a winnowing flail, the dust in the barn door: a moment – and the thing has vanished, because it was pure effect; but it leaves a relish behind it, a longing that the accident may happen again. (1902, 176)

Such intense personal experiences prefigure those arresting instances when Proust's narrator realizes that the object in front of him holds the truth and can be likened to Virginia Woolf's 'moments of being' or Joyce's secular epiphanies.[62] Pater thus heralds the modern novel and Proust follows his cue. But he left such faint traces of his reading of Pater that it is impossible to assess the extent of his debt. The only conclusion we can draw is that he contributed to Pater's reception in France in an occult way, by diffusing his ideas as if – and because they were – his own.

In addition, Proust contributed unwittingly to making Pater better known in France, as some early reviews of his novel included comparisons with the Englishman's work. Even before all the volumes of *A la recherche du temps perdu* were published, Gabriel Mourey (1926) wrote an article pointing out its close

---

61   Reproduced as the frontispiece of vol. 23 of Ruskin (1903–12) *The Works of John Ruskin*, ed. E. T. Cook and Alexander Wedderburn, London: The Library Edition.

62   This point has been made by Morris Beja (1971) *Epiphany in the Modern Novel*, Seattle: University of Washington Press, p. 231.

resemblances with *Marius the Epicurean*,[63] though he prefaces his discussion with the caveat that he is not sure if Proust knew Pater's novel or not. *A la Recherche* could be interpreted as a conscious or unconscious rewriting and continuation of *Marius*. Marius and Proust's narrator alike are haunted by a sense of lost time; they embody the modern spirit in the way they single out and aestheticize intense personal moments. They share a tendency to contemplate and read rather than act, and both novelists lay emphasis on experiencing and reacting to what one is doing, rather than on the activity itself: physical sensations, and in particular visual perception, take precedence over intellectual knowledge. Mourey even suggests that Proust and Pater share the same objective of portraying homosexuality in their work, by pointing out that their protagonists have intimate friendships with other male characters.[64] Ramon Fernandez (1928) pursued Mourey's comparative study of Proust and Pater in an article entitled 'Note sur l'esthétique de Proust'. Four years earlier, he had published a review of the French translations of *Marius the Epicurean* and *Plato and Platonism*, followed by a postscript on Georges Duthuit's provocative book on Oscar Wilde and Walter Pater, *Le Rose et le noir*. Fernandez had announced his particular view of Pater's prose as being 'like careful wash drawing, and I would even go so far as to say that it is a meticulous cleansing of his impression and his thought. [....] I know few styles which are more analytic than his.'[65] In his later article on Proust's aesthetics, Fernandez expands his discussion to include Pater's theoretical essay 'Style', focusing on its affinity with Proust's reflections on art in the concluding volume of *A la recherche du temps perdu*:

> These pages from *Time Regained* are essentially an essay on style, and another famous essay on style, published in 1888 by Walter Pater, allows us to date it. Both essays, despite the two score years that separate them, belong to the same spiritual era, I mean to say that they mark the same stage in what could be called the conquering of the rights of art. Their difference – and not an insignificant one at that – comes from the fact that Proust's work is based on personal experience, whereas Pater stayed in the sublimated realms of culture and ideology. Proust's venture has greater depth, because it envelops the most fugitive and commonplace details of reality. Pater's is greater in scope and human significance, because the author of *Marius* had a spiritual register which was more flexible and richer.[66]

---

[63] On the same question, see Hafley 1957.

[64] For an extended discussion of how Proust used British art and literature in his representation of homosexuality, see Eells 2002.

[65] 'La phrase de Pater est un lavis scrupuleux, et j'oserai dire un méticuleux nettoiement de son impression et de sa pensée. [...] je connais peu de styles plus analytiques que le sien' (Fernandez 1924, 247).

[66] 'Ces pages du *Temps retrouvé* sont essentiellement un essai sur le style, et un autre et célèbre essai sur le style, publié en 1888 par Walter Pater, nous permet de le dater. Les deux essais, malgré la quarantaine d'années qui les séparent, sont de la même époque spirituelle, je veux dire qu'ils marquent une même étape dans ce qu'on pourrait appeler la conquête des droits de l'art. Leur différence, et elle n'est pas petite, vient de ce que Proust a travaillé à même la vie, tandis que Pater est

Fernandez refrains from asserting that the author of *Le Temps retrouvé* had read 'Style', though he points out that Proust's aesthetic preoccupations – and the terms he uses to express them – are strikingly similar to Pater's. He cites Pater's definition of the writer's aim, which is not to transcribe objective reality, but the sensation and sentiments that the writer has in experiencing the world. Like Pater, Proust denigrates factual description and values the aesthetic expression of subjective impressions. Fernandez makes the point that for both writers, style is the alliance of word and inner image: 'Style is the only means the artist has to render objective and communicable the unique world that he carries in himself.'[67] Several critics have pursued Mourey and Fernandez's pioneering comparative studies of Pater and Proust,[68] but despite the evidence I found in Proust's manuscript material, there is no irrefutable proof that he had read more than 'Denys l'Auxerrois', 'Notre-Dame d'Amiens', 'Vézelay' and 'A Prince of Court Painters'. Nevertheless, there is no doubt that Proust's novel is redolent with elusive remembrances of Pater.

4

The most striking example of Pater's occult – and occluded – influence in France is a long essay about him in Raymond Laurent's volume of *Etudes anglaises*, published by Bernard Grasset in November 1910. Laurent was the first to write an extended, comprehensive, interpretative study of Pater in French, but at the time of its publication, it received almost no coverage apart from a succinct paragraph by Henry-D. Davray in the book review section of the *Mercure de France*. Davray (1910) summarizes the introduction to *Etudes anglaises* and Laurent's 'ingenious' essay, 'backed by a wealth of arguments',[69] which presents Coleridge as the precursor of the Pre-Raphaelite movement, and Pater and Wilde as its literary development. Davray's announcement apparently had no effect, and Laurent's defence of Pater has remained practically unknown in France,[70] and has been all but

---

[67] demeuré dans les régions sublimées de la culture et de l'idéologie. L'expérience de Proust l'emporte en pénétration, puisqu'elle enveloppe les plus fugitifs et les plus mesquins détails de la réalité. Celle de Pater l'emporte en étendue et en signification humaine, parce que l'auteur de *Marius* possédait un registre spirituel plus souple et plus riche' (Fernandez 1928, 272).

[67] 'Le style est le seul moyen dont l'artiste dispose pour rendre objectif et communicable le monde unique qu'il porte en soi' (Fernandez 1928, 273).

[68] In addition to the works already cited, see Baker 1959; Cecil 1955; Fraser 1994, 244–49; Lauro 1995, 79–84; Robert 1976, 30–34.

[69] 'soutenue avec une abondance d'arguments' (Davray 1910, 172–73).

[70] In a joint review of the French translation of *Marius the Epicurean* and Georges Duthuit's *Le Rose et le noir, de Walter Pater à Oscar Wilde*, Edmond Jaloux does however refer to Laurent. After criticizing Duthuit's 'improper' portrait of Pater, he recommends Laurent's superior study, praising his sound knowledge of late nineteenth-century England, and his understanding of Pater's genius, shown by the way he had 'pénétré l'esprit clair et sinueux de Pater' ('penetrated into Pater's clear but sinuous mind', Jaloux 1923, 2). Laurent's work does not figure in Germain d'Hangest's extensive and authoritative bibliography (1961).

neglected abroad.[71] The book hardly circulated: only one copy is catalogued in the nationwide French library network and it belongs to the Maurice Barrès bequest to the Bibliothèque nationale de France.[72] When the volume was brought to me for consultation there, it was immediately evident why Laurent's work has been completely overlooked: most of the pages were uncut, indicating that it had never been read. An obliging librarian quickly rectified that, literally opening up Laurent's five essays on nineteenth-century British art and literature, and in particular his 120 pages on Pater. They form the longest chapter in the book, which traces the Romantic movement from Coleridge to Oscar Wilde, and positions Walter Pater as an informing presence at the centre of the study.

In an introduction to his section on Pater, Laurent states that his purpose is to compensate for the limited attention the French literary world had paid to him, citing de Wyzewa's favourable but restrictive work in the *Revue des deux mondes* and the lack of widespread response to Khnopff's translation of *Imaginary Portraits*.[73] Laurent explains that if the French were 'refractory' or even 'rebellious' in their acknowledgement of Pater's talent, it is because they are more attracted to exceptional literary personalities than to exceptional literary movements (Laurent 1910, 143). Laurent's essay is heavily indebted to Benson's *Walter Pater* (1906). He follows Benson's basic outline, which uses the chronology of Pater's life to structure the exegesis of his work, and even uses many of the same quotations. Laurent underscores the comprehensiveness of Benson's study in his introductory paragraphs on Pater, and occasionally acknowledges him as a source in the course of his discussion. However, the insightful, original points he adds make his essay into more than just a condensed translation of Benson.

Laurent's study is a thorough, penetrating analysis of Pater's writing, which emphasizes the psychological importance of the formative years of childhood, the significance of Pater's knowledge of Greek mythology and the philosophical content of his work. It opens with reflections on aesthetics, and Laurent suggests that if Pater chose criticism as his mode of expression, it was because it enabled him to live his enthusiasms and exaltations through others: Winckelmann's adventures, Michelangelo's sonnets in stone, Botticelli's Holy Families all bring vicarious passion into Pater's secluded existence. According to Laurent, Pater's fascination with Winckelmann reflects a shared desire for an aesthetic ideal and Pater's essays on the Renaissance are a continuation of the German critic's work.

---

[71] Seiler (1980, 6) makes only a passing reference to it and Court (1980, 80–81) summarizes Laurent's long essay into two paragraphs.

[72] According to the 'Worldcat' database, a small number of American libraries possess a copy, but the only listing in COPAC is of the British Library's copy. Their catalogue confuses the author with his homonym, Raymond Laurent, a president of the Parisian town council.

[73] Laurent refers to de Wyzewa's 'article' in the singular, with the vague indication that it was published about 'ten years ago' (Laurent 1910, 143). There is not enough information to assert whether he is referring to one article in particular, or to an amalgamation of them.

Laurent recognizes that the 'Conclusion' to *The Renaissance* is a turning point in the development of ideas in England (Laurent 1910, 148) and summarizes its doctrine as follows:

> existence is made up of different forces which unite, join together and then become untied again. A perpetual state of becoming transforms what appear to be the most stable combinations; analysis shows that even personality, the last refuge of this false equilibrium, is merely made up of fortuitous groupings, which are unstable and unmoved by all suggestions. And yet, reality means for us simply the moment when these contingent forces unite.[74]

Laurent defines Pater's criticism as both 'intuitive', by which he means that Pater strives to capture the very moment when the artistic mind produces the masterpiece, and 'creative', in that the critic often constructs more than he deduces or deconstructs from the artwork. In his section on *Greek Studies*, Laurent draws a parallel between the interpretation of myths and art appreciation, emphasizing how individuals react to legends or artworks according to their subjective tastes and preoccupations, colouring them with personal associations. Laurent summarizes Pater's notion of subjective criticism in the following terms:

> In an untranslatable 'agony of home sickness', we want to know ourselves and to derive pleasure from that self-knowledge; we want to discover or to re-discover ourselves. Henceforth, philosophical formulae themselves cease to be the object of reasoning and understanding, and become the object of vision and sensation. An unknown physical world appears, in which instinct has a voice, where primitive nature uncovers itself with all its force, without having recourse to the emotions of art and myth.[75]

Laurent's analysis of Pater's fictional prose begins with a reading of *Imaginary Portraits*, which he praises as studies of different sensitivities. They vary in tone as if they were written in different musical keys and Laurent recalls how Benson gave them various colour names, like the titles of Whistler's paintings in his series of 'Harmonies' (Laurent 1910, 224). Laurent explains that the first French translation of *Imaginary Portraits* failed to awaken much interest among French readers, firstly because they were unfamiliar with Pater's work generally, and secondly because 'the style wasn't there to shed light on the

---

[74] 'l'existence est faite de forces diverses, qui se joignent, s'assemblent et se dénouent à nouveau. Un perpétuel devenir transforme les combinaisons en apparence les plus stables; l'analyse montre que même la personnalité, dernier refuge de ce faux équilibre, n'est pas composée que de groupements fortuits, instables, dociles à toutes les suggestions. Or, la réalité, c'est pour nous simplement le moment où ces forces contingentes s'unissent' (Laurent 1910, 153).

[75] 'En une intraduisible 'agony of home sickness', nous voulons nous connaître et jouir de cette connaissance, nous trouver, nous retrouver. Désormais, les formules philosophiques elles-mêmes ne sont plus objet de raisonnement et de compréhensions, mais de vision et de sensation. Un monde physique inconnu apparaît, où l'instinct parle, où la nature primitive se manifeste, avec toute sa force, sans recourir aux émotions de l'art et au mythe' (Laurent 1910, 166–67).

discursive passages which were often obscure'.[76] Laurent captures the originality of these prose pieces:

> the mysticity which envelops them and that sort of animation given to silent paintings, to immobile statues, accentuates their purely decorative and musical character. They are like dreams which take form, which make their fantasies take shape. Feelings are born in them like the feelings in dreams – brusque and impetuous.[77]

Laurent recognizes the importance of *Imaginary Portraits* as a fictional representation of Pater's aesthetic and ethical preoccupations:

> Thus these *Imaginary Portraits* are not tales about human beings, with their conflicting passions, but they are tales about superhumans, or rather ideologies, with conflicts of trends of thought, diverse artistic expressions, current dogmas, metaphysical systems which evolve, societies which are undergoing change, civilizations in decline or in renaissance.[78]

He quotes extensively from 'The Child in the House', which is in his opinion 'one of the most beautiful poems ever written',[79] using his own elegant French translation and choosing passages which highlight the importance of the indelible impressions received in childhood.

Laurent continues with an analysis of *Marius the Epicurean*, which develops Pater's study of sensitivity by showing how the 'self' becomes the centre of the universe (Laurent 1910, 179). The heart and the soul reign over the intellect and reason, and Marius is portrayed as an experiencing subject. Laurent could be called a precursory psychoanalytic critic, as he recognizes that *Marius* – like *Imaginary Portraits* – is a study of the unconscious. He makes Pater's novel into a modern, profane 'Bible' of various personal experiences, whose verses apply to everyday existence. Laurent classifies Pater as a nominalist, in keeping with the tradition established by Locke, Berkeley, Hume and Stuart Mill. For all these philosophical writers, 'the apparently simple intellectual elements become a network of sensations and impressions'.[80]

Laurent's section on *Marius the Epicurean* contains an extended comparison between the works of Pater and those of Maurice Barrès, as both writers had in common an exceptional gift for analysis, an elegant prose style and a

---

[76]   'le style n'était pas là pour éclairer des dissertations souvent obscures' (Laurent 1910, 225).

[77]   'la mysticité qui les enveloppe, cette sorte d'animation donnée à des tableaux muets, à des statues immobiles, accentue leur caractère purement décoratif and musical. Ce sont des rêves qui prennent forme, qui réalisent leurs fantaisies. Les sentiments y naissent pareils aux sentiments des songes, brusques, impétueux' (Laurent 1910, 225).

[78]   'Aussi les *Portraits imaginaires* ne sont-ils pas des contes humains, avec des conflits de passions, mais des contes suprahumains, des idéologies pour mieux dire, avec des conflits de courants, d'expressions artistiques diverses, de dogmes en cours, de systèmes métaphysiques qui évoluent, de sociétés qui se transforment, de civilisations à leur déclin ou à leur renaissance' (Laurent 1910, 228).

[79]   'un des plus beaux poèmes qu'on ait jamais écrit' (Laurent 1910, 169).

[80]   'les éléments intellectuels d'apparence simple deviennent un tissu de sensations et d'impressions' (Laurent 1910, 217).

psychological approach concentrating on sensibilities, which they link to the primordial feelings represented by myths. In their writing, a character is not portrayed in relation to external circumstances, but as an individual with his or her own, isolated consciousness. They are not characters of action, so the interest in their representation lies in the accompanying 'philosophical and sociological discourses'.[81] Laurent dismisses *Gaston de Latour* as an inferior repetition of *Marius*: its eponymous hero lacks emotional depth and individuality and the narrative of the eventless action is wanting in clever craftsmanship to redeem it (Laurent 1910, 233).

Laurent justifiably recognizes the importance of Pater's essay on style as a fundamental piece of literary criticism with a self-analytic dimension. Laurent reads Pater's apologia of the art of prose as self-defensive. He underlines how Pater strives to reconcile the apparently conflicting demands of the Flaubertian 'mot juste' and the allusive vagueness of artistic expression exemplifed by Michelangelo's sculpture which owes its intensity to 'a puzzling sort of incompleteness, which suggests rather than realises actual form' (1902, 68). Laurent carries out a detailed analysis of Pater's prose and recognizes hypallage as characteristic of his style, citing such examples as 'One pensive afternoon' and 'The penitential blue of the sky'. He explains that, drawing as it does on both intelligence and sensitivity, Pater's writing is fired with emotion and his style 'laden with heady perfumes'.[82]

Laurent further stresses how form and matter complement each other in Pater's writing: an accumulation of attributes and appositions mirror an association of ideas. Laurent illustrates how Pater gives depth to 'Mona Lisa' by enumerating the various emblematic women she embodies. He is probably quoting from memory: his quotation is truncated and reorders the original elements, naming Leda, Helen of Troy and Saint Anne, before jumbling up partial citations from Pater's description which reads, when translated back into English: 'she has been dead many times, trafficked for strange webs with the East, has learned the secrets of the tomb, known the sound of lyres and flutes; the look in her eye is drowsy and her eyelids are a little weary' (Laurent 1910, 226–27). This quotation exemplifies Laurent's point that:

> just as the words are accompanied by their myriad attributes, so the thought seizes other closely related thoughts, absorbs them and ends up growing, as if it were a real living organism. Hence the complexity of this style, its obscurity: it wants to capture in a sentence the development of an entire page. But on the contrary, it gains in depth. One feels, on reading it several times, that one has not grasped everything: horizons unfold which at first one had not seen. There is where his mystery lies.[83]

---

81   'dissertations philosophiques ou sociologiques' (Laurent 1910, 181). In a footnote, Laurent gives brief bibliographical references. He is citing J. Ernest-Charles (1906) 'La carrière de Maurice Barrès', *Le Censeur* (27 October), 1 no. 4.

82   'ce style "lourd de parfums"' (Laurent 1910, 237). Laurent's quotation marks indicate that he is citing Benson (1906, 215), though he does not name his source.

83   'de même que les mots vont accompagnés de leur mille attributs, de même la pensée saisit d'autres pensées connexes, les englobe et finit par d'agrandir, véritable organisme vivant. De là la complexité de ce style, son obscurité: il veut resserrer en une phrase le développement de toute une page. Mais, en revanche, il

To illustrate this point, Laurent quotes Pater's description of Demeter from *Greek Studies*: 'She is the goddess of dark caves; she gave men the first fig, the first poppy; she is the mother of the vine; [. . .] she knows the magic power of certain plants' (Laurent 1910, 238/Pater 1895, 102). Laurent perceptively points out how Pater can bring all the symbols together and make them stand out by effacing the subject. Thus, in 'Apollo in Picardy', he counts six phrases dependent on one subject in the sentence: 'He had been brought to the monastery as a little child; was bred there; had never yet left it, busy and satisfied through youth and early manhood; was grown almost as necessary a part of the *communauté* [sic] as the stones' (Laurent 1910, 239/Pater, 1895 143). Laurent anticipates how Yeats presents a portion of Pater's ekphrasis of the Mona Lisa as free verse,[84] when he punctuates a quotation from 'The Child in the House' with slashes in order to bring out the cadence in Pater's prose: 'In the house and garden of his dream/ he saw a child moving/ and could feel the main stream and blast of the winds/ that had played on him and study so the first stage/ in that mental journey' (Laurent 1910, 239–40/Pater 1895, 173).

Laurent concludes his chapter on Pater by putting him into the context of the Oxford movement. He portrays Pater as a humanist, highlighting the way he makes man – divested of his social function – the centre of his preoccupations. Laurent ascribes great importance to Pater's achievement, ranking him beside Browning and Meredith, and contending that he constructed the most solid literary edifice in contemporaneous England (Laurent 1910, 258). *Etudes anglaises* ends with a chapter on Oscar Wilde, whom Laurent presents as a disciple of Pater. According to Laurent, Wilde's work is a final, brilliant illumination of Pre-Raphaelitism and what he calls 'Paterism' (Laurent 1910, 258 and 310), although that notion of 'Paterism' made almost no impression on the French intelligentsia.

Laurent's personal history can in part explain why his work on Pater was ignored. Although he did not make a name for himself as a literary critic, Laurent figures prominently in the inaugural issue of *Akadémos*, a journal founded by the Baron Jacques d'Adelswärd-Fersen whose express purpose was to create a forum for 'Greek love', or homosexuality. Its first issue was published in January 1909 and opens with an illustrated article dedicated to the memory of Raymond Laurent.[85] It presents him as a kind of French Oscar Wilde and relates how he staged his own death in Venice, in the early hours of 23 September 1908. Suffering rejection from his male lover and more generally from a sense of exclusion from a society that did not condone same-sex love, the 21-year-old Laurent left his hotel and ordered a gondola to take

---

gagne en profondeur. On sent, à le lire plusieurs fois que l'on n'a pas tout saisi: des horizons se déploient, que d'abord on n'apercevait point. C'est là que gît son mystère' (Laurent 1910, 238).

[84] William Butler Yeats (1936) makes lines from Pater's description of the Mona Lisa into the first poem of his collection *The Oxford Book of Modern Verse, 1892–1935* (Oxford: The Clarendon Press).

[85] 'In Memoriam: Raymond Laurent' was published in *Akadémos* on 15 January 1909, 66–71, signed by 'Sonyeuse', probably a pseudonym for Jacques d'Adelswärd-Fersen.

him across the Grand Canal to the church of Santa Maria della Salute. When the bells in St Mark's Square chimed two in the morning, the young man shot himself and fell dead onto the moonlit marble steps. The only witness present was Oscar Wilde's son, Vyvyan Holland. A few days later, Jean Cocteau – a former classmate of Laurent's at the Lycée Condorcet who was also in Venice at the time[86] – wrote a poem in memory of Laurent entitled 'En manière d'épitaphe' (By way of epitaph), and another poem dedicated to the man who forsook Laurent, thereby triggering his self-destruction.[87] The way in which *Akadémos* made Laurent's suicide into a sacrifice for the homosexual cause compromised any chance of his literary criticism gaining recognition, and his name has become better known in gay studies than it has ever been in Pater studies.[88]

The copy of *Etudes anglaises* in the Barrès collection of the Bibliothèque nationale de France contains evidence that Raymond Laurent's mother instigated its posthumous publication, as well as her discreet attempt to publicize it. She sent the book along with black-bordered letter, signed by 'une mère inconsolable' ('an inconsolable mother'), explaining that she hopes that Barrès will find some interest in the work of her son, who had himself been a great admirer of his. She probably asked Reginald Tiddy of Trinity College, Oxford, to write the introduction in order to give some academic credibility to her son's essay and to counter the disrepute undoubtedly caused by the article in *Akadémos*. Her choice of advocate for her son's work is ironic, as Tiddy had his own eccentricities: he was a founding member of the 'dancing dons' who performed Morris dances in the streets of Oxford, dressed in wide-brim floppy hats and knee-high golden boots.[89] In his introduction, Tiddy indicates that Laurent compares Barrès's work to Pater's, and Barrès's self-interest was revealed when I realized that the only pages he had cut open in his copy of *Etudes anglaises* correspond to that section. Barrès might have refrained from publicizing even the little he knew of Laurent's work in an

---

[86]   André Germain (1953), in his chapter on Cocteau in *Les Clés de Proust* (Paris: Editions Sun), p. 186, hints that homosexuality had motivated this gathering of young men in Venice: 'Un voyage à Venise fut une concession aux imprudences qui commençaient d'être à la mode. Le voyage tourna bientôt au tragique. L'un des compagnons de Cocteau, un jeune écrivain qui s'appelait Raymond Laurent, trop romantique, se tira un coup de revolver sur les marches de la Salute' ('A trip to Venice was a concession to the imprudences which were beginning to be fashionable. The trip quickly had a tragic twist to it. One of Cocteau's companions, an overly romantic young writer named Raymond Laurent, shot himself with a revolver on the steps of the Salute').

[87]   For the texts of these poems, see Jean Cocteau (1999) *Œuvres poétiques complètes*, ed. Michel Décaudin and others (Paris: Gallimard, Bibliothèque de la Pléiade, pp. 1283–84). The lover who rejected Laurent was an American named Langhorn Whistler (I have not managed to ascertain if he was related to the painter with the same surname).

[88]   His name figures in at least two electronic archives of texts on gay studies. See 'Documenti di storia gay' (digilander.iol.it/giovannidallorto/testi/xxindice.html) and 'Histoire de l'Amour au masculin' (membres.lycos.fr/textes.htm).

[89]   See 'The Ancient Men' (http://www.am39.fsnet.co.uk/history.html).

attempt to preserve his own reputation and to thwart any possible link between his name and that of a young man whose homosexuality had become public knowledge shortly after his death. Barrès makes this clear in a comment, recorded by Paul Léautaud, concerning how uneasy he felt that he was connected with *Akadémos*.[90] In addition, Laurent's work obviously did not incite Barrès to further his knowledge of Pater: although he owned *Marius the Epicurean*, he apparently did not read it, and the pages of his copy of *Portraits imaginaires* are still uncut.[91] Yet again Pater's work had failed to find a prominent and promising spokesman to promote it in France. If the enlightening work of this precocious critic had not been overlooked, Pater would probably have been better known in France than he was before the outbreak of the First World War.

5

Firmin Roger-Cornaz's translation of *The Renaissance* was published in 1917 and marks a turning point in the reception of Pater's work in France. It brought in its wake a series of publications which establish a surprising correlation between the aftermath of the First World War and French interest in Pater, as if his erudite Aestheticism could somehow assuage the devastating sense of loss. The French translation of *The Renaissance* appears as if in response to Edmund Gosse's article 'France et Angleterre: l'avenir de leurs relations intellectuelles' ('France and England: the future of their intellectual relationship') which appeared in October 1916 in the *Revue des deux mondes*. It was written as a rallying call to protect the culture of the allies against German hegemony, in reaction to the Manifesto signed by ninety-three German intellectuals in October 1914 declaring their intention to impose their order. Gosse argued that collaboration between France and England was necessary in the literary and artistic spheres as a means of resisting the Germans, though he stresses that each country should maintain its individuality. He pleads in favour of an 'entente intellectuelle' to reflect the Anglo-French alliance and to prolong the well-established rich cultural exchange between the two countries, citing Walter Pater as one example of a British author deeply influenced by French literature (Gosse 1916, 530). Gosse addresses his article to the French, because he sees France as the master builder in the process of reconstruction imposed by the war, which he advocates should recreate the former European civilization on new foundations.

---

[90] Léautaud notes in a diary entry dated 21 January 1909 that Barrès is 'très embêté' ('very embarrassed') that his name is associated with *Akadémos*, 'une revue de pédérastes' ('a periodical for homosexuals') (Paul Léautaud, [1955] *Journal littéraire*, Paris: Mercure de France, 2: 363).

[91] The Barrès bequest to the Bibliothèque nationale de France contains a copy of the second edition of *Marius the Epicurean*, in two volumes, published by Macmillan in 1885. The pages of the first volume are only partially cut, and the only annotation made on them is not in Barrès's hand; the second volume is uncut. The same collection has an uncut copy of the second edition of Georges Khnopff's translation of *Imaginary Portraits*, dated 1899.

Pater's study of how European culture renovated and revived its classical heritage in the Renaissance provides a historical model for the kind of artistic reconstruction Gosse had in mind. Pater's essays on cross-cultural exchange in Renaissance Europe, in particular between Italy and France, therefore constitute an appropriate text to translate at a time when the French and English felt the need to form an informal aesthetic alliance to complement their military alliance. Roger-Cornaz's translation is based on the third edition of *The Renaissance*, published by Macmillan in 1888, though it is possible that he worked from a subsequent reprint. The French volume contains the entire text of the 1888 edition, but not the frontispiece which figures in the English version.

Roger-Cornaz used material from Benson's monograph on Pater in the preface to his translation. He appealed to what might interest his readership by introducing Pater as one of the first to endorse the French aesthetic movement of 'art for art's sake' and by pointing out how indebted Oscar Wilde was to him. Roger-Cornaz presents Pater as the embodiment of the reversible Wildean concept of 'The Artist as Critic', citing his pages on the Mona Lisa as exemplary of how criticism can aspire to the status of art. Pater strove to achieve in English what Gautier and Flaubert had done in French prose, and Roger-Cornaz compares Pater's musical style to Mallarmé's. He recognizes that the inextricable intertwining of matter and manner in Pater's prose makes it particularly challenging to translate, and warns that his own approach gives priority to elegance rather than literality.

The translation of *The Renaissance* succeeded in attracting attention to Pater's works where previous French publications had failed. Paul Souday – one of Proust's early critics – published a lengthy article on *La Renaissance* in the *Le Temps* of 31 January 1918. He begins by quoting from the biographical information in the translator's preface, which claims that Pater thought he was of French origin and a descendant of the eighteenth-century painter and student of Watteau, Jean-Baptiste Pater. Although Pater was 'practically unknown' when he died,[92] Souday explains that his influence has grown noticeably since then. He highlights Pater's love of France and the French language, and his particular interest in French authors. He echoes Roger-Cornaz's appeal to the French public's interest in Oscar Wilde, by relating a conversation the latter had with Pater concerning the relative difficulties of writing prose and verse. He passes the chapters of *The Renaissance* in favourable review, before ending his article with an enticing invitation to read Pater's volume, as it 'evokes enchanting images and subjects to meditate on for days or even weeks'.[93]

In 1924, Madeleine Cazamian praised Roger-Cornaz's translation for its success in conveying 'a bit of the supple, ample and somewhat feline movement of the original'.[94] Her eloquent and insightful article argues that

---

[92]   'presque obscur' (Souday 1918, 3).

[93]   'évoque des images enchanteresses et des sujets de méditation pour des jours et des semaines' (Souday 1918, 3).

[94]   'un peu de l'allure ample, souple, et comme féline de l'original' (Cazamian 1924, 443).

Aestheticism developed in France with 'more simplicity, spontaneity, audacious insouciance'[95] than in Victorian Britain, which explains why Pater had to struggle to reconcile his Aestheticism with other conflicting principles:

> An English heart and mind which have been trained to respect social, religious and moral rules, nourished by the past, enamoured of ancient hierarchies, could not conceive of or adopt the cult of art for art's sake without feeling profoundly the effect of this doctrine on his entire moral life, without anxiously searching for its foundation and its diverse consequences, without vibrating with troubling emotions.[96]

She makes a similar allusion to the link between Aestheticism and eroticism in her explanation of Pater's decision to delete the 'Conclusion' from the 1877 re-edition of *The Renaissance*:

> Still today, the moral danger which his doctrine presents, together with certain equivocal traits in his physiognomy and in his life, as well as the excesses indulged in by an intemperate Aestheticism in England at the end of the nineteenth century, sometimes bring about the curt condemnation of the man and his work.[97]

By pointing out that the decadent and even the reprobate qualities of Pater's work were censured in England, Cazamian was implicitly inviting French readers to pass their own judgement on his work.

Régis Michaud's *Mystiques et réalistes anglo-saxons* (*Anglo-Saxon Mystics and Realists*) was published in 1918 and includes a twenty-page chapter on Walter Pater entitled 'Un païen mystique' ('A Mystic Pagan'). Michaud relates how Pater experienced a crisis of agnosticism, accompanied by extensive reading of Greek philosophy and German metaphysics, which led him to become a mystic pagan. He stresses the autobiographical content of Pater's work, identifying the author with the various characters he creates, beginning with 'The Child in the House' and progressing to a reading of the essay on Winckelmann as a self-portrait of a man for whom art is an all-absorbing activity. Michaud sees Gaston de Latour's initial fascination with ritualism as a projection of Pater's own preoccupations, and the way Marius makes living into an art as a reflection of Pater's Aestheticism. Michaud dubs 'The Conclusion' to *The Renaissance* the 'gospel of the perfect dilettante, the quintessence of agnosticism'.[98] He concludes that Pater has founded a religion

---

[95] 'plus de simplicité, de spontanéité, d'audace insouciante' (Cazamian 1924, 443).

[96] 'Un cœur et un esprit anglais, formés au respect des règles sociales, religieuses et morales, nourris du passé, épris des hiérarchies anciennes, ne pouvaient concevoir, adopter, le culte de l'art pour l'art sans éprouver profondément le retentissement de cette doctrine sur toute la vie morale, sans en rechercher anxieusement le fondement et les conséquences diverses, sans vibrer de troublantes émotions' (Cazamian 1924, 443–44).

[97] 'Aujourd'hui encore, le danger moral que présente sa doctrine, rapproché de certains traits équivoques dans sa physionomie et dans sa vie, et des excès auxquels se porta un esthétisme intempérant en Angleterre à la fin du XIXè siècle, entraîne parfois la condamnation sommaire de l'homme et celle de son œuvre' (Cazamian 1924, 445).

[98] 'l'évangile du parfait dilettante, quintessence d'agnosticisme' (Michaud 1918, 71).

on what he calls 'the will to Beauty, or the desire of the beautiful'.[99] He defines Pater's religion as Aestheticism and his objective as a fusion between two different sensibilities: his work is built on the tensions between the Middle Ages and the Renaissance, the north and the south, British and Latin mentalities, religion and humanism. In his final section, Michaud relates Pater's work to French interests, particularly when he discusses Pater's aesthetic affinity with Huysmans, Renan, Flaubert, Baudelaire, Gustave Moreau and Félicien Rops.

The publication of Emmanuel Coppinger's translation of *Marius the Epicurean* in 1922 marks the end of Pater's 'occult' presence in the French *monde des lettres*. Coppinger's translation was motivated by the conviction that *Marius the Epicurean* would have particular meaning in France at a time of postwar upheaval and a renaissance of paganism. He sounds an almost evangelical note in the 'Avant-Propos' when he invites French readers in search of direction to turn to *Marius the Epicurean*. This translation therefore signals a development from private readings of Pater's work to a public reading agenda: whereas we only have a second-hand report of the Abbé Bremond's recommendation to read *Marius the Epicurean* for spiritual guidance, Coppinger exhorts his readers to see Marius's life as a lesson in Christianity. With the publication of *Marius the Epicurean*, the French were being asked to listen to Pater. That they did so is signalled by the opening statement of Madeleine Cazamian's review article published two years later, in 1924: 'Walter Pater has been eliciting a great deal of interest in France over the past few years.'[100]

---

[99]   'Pater fonde ainsi une religion sur ce qu'il nomme *the will to Beauty*, le désir, la volonté du beau' (Michaud 1918, 72).

[100]   'Walter Pater suscite en France beaucoup d'intérêt depuis quelques années' (Cazamian 1924, 443)

5 'An Untimely Soul'? Pater's Academic Reception in France from the Early 1920s

Bénédicte Coste

1

For a great number of French students Pater remains an unknown writer, a Ruskinian epigone, whom only specialists of Proust and/or the Decadent movement read. The reasons for this deserve consideration, and it is the object of this essay to trace Pater's academic reception in France.[1] Pater's academic fate repeats, with a few decades' delay, his relative disappearance from the English canon in the third quarter of the twentieth century, when only a few specialists still discussed him. Indeed, his French reception follows more or less the vicissitudes of his Anglo-American appreciation, with Pater being viewed more as a stylist or a veiled confessional writer than as a thinker.

The myth of the withdrawn author, playing hide-and-seek in his imaginary portraits including *Marius*, 'the mask without the face' as Henry James (Seiler 1980, 293) cunningly put it, began in Great Britain. One could trace Pater's changing critical reception back to the late 1870s, when the polemical author of *The Renaissance* (whose style in particular had annoyed some reviewers) became the great prose writer. A critical trend praising the stylist at the expense of the thinker (an artificial but long-lasting distinction) was established and continued until the beginning of the twentieth century when, as Anne Henry noticed, international recognition began (Henry 1985b, 45). Yeats's inclusion of the rewritten 'Lady Lisa' portrait in his edition of the *Oxford Book of Modern Poetry* (1936, 1) canonized the 'most consummate prose-writer alive'[2] (Mallarmé) at the expense of the essayist, all the more so as

---

[1] I would like to express my deepest thanks to colleagues who kindly, swiftly and precisely responded to my queries: Germain d'Hangest (Emeritus Professor, Université Paris IV), Anne Henry (Emeritus Professor, Université Montpellier III), Martine Lambert-Charbonnier (Université Paris IV) and Jean-Baptiste Picy (Institut Catholique de Paris). Their comments and reflections on Pater have been both challenging and illuminating. I also wish to thank J. B. Bullen from the University of Reading who, one day in 1995, asked me to read a book called *Studies in the History of the Renaissance*, thus initiating my interest in Pater. Professor B. Salignon (Université Montpellier III) encouraged me to appreciate Pater within the aesthetic field.
[2] 'J'y sais le prosateur ouvragé par excellence de ce temps' (Mallarmé 1897, 373).

Yeats had presented the portrait in *vers libres*. France inherited this implicit distinction between a thinker whose radicalism had disappeared and a writer who epitomized a decadent era focused on stylistic issues, and academics echoed it through the works (essays and doctoral theses) that we shall discuss here.

Along with dissertations and essays we have included translations and their prefaces which, maybe more than the academic studies, bear witness to some predilection for the Paterian style, which is all the more paradoxical as most of his fiction remains untranslated or, when it has been translated, is out of print. We shall not consider the accuracy of these writings but view them in their relation to the dissertations and essays: Robert André published his 'Ecole de Giorgione' in the *Nouvelle revue française* in 1963 as a response to Germain d'Hangest's 1961 dissertation, with an excellent synthesis of Pater's 'Conclusion' and a discussion of its influence on Proust (André 1963; d'Hangest 1961). It is as a specialist of Proust's reception of the nineteenth-century history of ideas that Anne Henry translated large excerpts of Pater's texts (Henry 1985b). Yet there is still no French translation of *Greek Studies*, *Appreciations* or *Miscellaneous Studies*. Only in 1998 did Jean-Baptiste Picy provide an authoritative edition of *Plato and Platonism* (*Platon et le platonisme: Conférences de 1893*, Picy 1998). An absence of translation is also an important symptom of critical reception, since the untranslated texts of Pater are precisely such essays as might serve to correct a one-sided vision. It is also true that the absence of an edition of collected writings in his lifetime in English-speaking countries impacted on his reception in France, a fact which Philippe Neel regretted in 1930 (Neel 1930). It is to be hoped that Picy's previously mentioned translation will give rise to a reassessment of Pater's philosophy, ending the vicious circle according to which the lack of discussion of his essays on art and philosophy stems from their unavailability in French, while the translations of his fiction reinforce the stereotype of the elaborate abstruse writer.

2

In the twentieth century Pater's reception in France can be divided into three periods: the first in the 1930s with Louise Rosenblatt's and Albert Farmer's dissertations, on the doctrine of art for art's sake and the Aesthetic movement respectively; the second with d'Hangest's dissertation in 1961; and the most recent starting in the 1980s, with new translations and theses. The Fellow of Brasenose was seen successively as a participant in a movement which was in the process of being defined, then as a writer *per se*, before attention finally shifted to his poetics. In this respect Pater's academic reception also follows twentieth-century changes in critical attitudes.

Within the French academy, Pater is still essentially seen as a writer, a questionable vision when one considers how the range of his works implies a questioning of the academic disciplines themselves, and to this extent, his reception should also be understood in the context of increasing barriers between the disciplines. Except for the art historian André Chastel, for whom he was one of Ruskin's disciples, Pater is still undiscussed by art critics or philosophers, although Picy confirms that there is evidence that he is known by some.[3] Chastel (1978, 11) acknowledged his own debt to 'Oxford's speculative Aestheticism', which helped him to break free from an excessively literary history of art. But Mikaël Dufrenne's influential essay on the phenomenology of the aesthetic experience (Dufrenne 1953) ignored Pater, an absence we may view partly as the effect of his reduction to a mere stylist, but also as the result of the academic specialization that became stricter at the very period when Pater was writing. His all-embracing vision may not have passed the test of the modern academy. What remains to be seen is whether he is condemned to remain in the 'English Literature' section in France, or whether transdisciplinarity will give Pater a larger dimension.

In 1918, Régis Michaud, a French academic at Princeton University, published *Réalistes et mystiques anglo-saxons* (Realist and mystic Anglo-Saxons), with a chapter on Pater's mystic paganism. Michaud was interested in Montaigne's influence on the American Transcendentalists and on Pater, but he curiously omitted the portrait of Montaigne in *Gaston de Latour*. He saw Pater primarily as an agnostic who reconciles opposites, 'no longer sees religion as anything more than a form of the fine arts',[4] and reflects himself in his creations.

Relying on his fiction and neglecting altogether *Greek Studies*, *Plato and Platonism* and *Appreciations*, Michaud drew an imaginary portrait of Pater whose 'favourite method [. . .] is to see himself reflected in other existences, in accordance with the one of which he dreams',[5] an interpretation that proved long-lasting and was never denied by Pater himself. Mrs Humphry Ward may have started the trend when she read *Marius* as a veiled autobiography justified by the British native resistance to open confession,[6] and, regardless of their theoretical schools, later critics have followed her. It should be stressed that Pater also questioned the possibility of an impersonal discourse in 'Prosper Mérimée': 'Personality versus impersonality in art:— how much or how little of one's self one may put into one's work: whether anything at all of it: whether one can put there anything else:—is clearly a far-reaching and complex question' (Pater 1895, 23). Unfortunately, this text is almost never discussed.

For Michaud, the unity of Pater's writings is achieved through the art of the imaginary portrait which shows him bent on reconciling paganism and Christianity, the Middle Ages and the Renaissance, North and South: a reconciliation that will find its summation in 'Apollo in Picardy' where

---

[3]   Conversation, 10 July 2002.

[4]   'ne regarde plus la religion que comme une forme des beaux-arts' (Michaud 1918, 56).

[5]   'sa méthode favorite [. . .] est de se mirer en d'autres vies conformes à celle qu'il rêve' (Michaud 1918, 57).

[6]   'As a nation we are not fond of direct "confessions". All our autobiographical literature, compared to the French or German, has a touch of dryness and reserve [. . . .] English feeling [. . .] has almost always something elusive in it, something which resents a spectator, and only moves at ease when it has succeeded in interposing some light screen or some obvious mask between it and the public' (Seiler 1980, 131).

'Apollo is the antique soul exiled in the mists of Thule, poorly exorcised by people of the Church, asleep and buried for centuries beneath the secret of the palimpsests, the Hellenic soul that Byron, Keats and Shelley would one day awaken'.[7] Neglecting Heine's gods in exile, a reference he may not have been aware of, Michaud was clearly influenced by Taine's theses of place, race and time.

But Pater is also the 'aesthetic precursor of Oscar Wilde and Des Esseintes',[8] as well as 'one of the harbingers of the artistic cult of the self'[9] promoted by Barrès in the 1880s. Michaud attempts to inscribe Pater within a literary genealogy, an enterprise that had begun during his lifetime. In his style and his '*morbidezza*', Pater is Wilde's spiritual father; in his melancholy he is also the offspring of the British Romantic poets, retaining 'the symptoms of the nostalgia for the South that is in the heart of every Anglo-Saxon'.[10] His unfulfilled quest for the South resulted in him spending his life in the seclusion of Oxford.

As the best illustration of this, *Marius* provides 'the synthesis of Pater's aesthetics and philosophy',[11] predicating Pater's dilettantism and Christianity on an Epicurean basis and turning aesthetics into a religion. It is impossible to decide if Marius dies as a Christian or not, because he is a figure of reconciliation, or, as Michaud wrote, 'the most Christian of sceptics, the most pagan of martyrs',[12] an assertion that can be traced back to Thomas Wright's biography, as he was the first to mention Pater's abortive attempt to enter the Church after he had lost his faith (Wright 1907). The anecdote was to have considerable importance because it raised the issue of Pater's religion, and he would be seen in turn as an Anglican, an agnostic or a reprobate, while *Marius* was read as a self-testimony.

Yet this ethos of reconciliation cannot be separated from the '*morbidezza*' of the culture of nineteenth-century decadence, which favours art and artifice at the expense of existence and reality. Thus Pater seeks 'his embellished self-reflection' in the European museums, which he patronizes like 'psychotherapeutic spas'.[13] Seeing art as the antidote to ontological unrest, and artifice as a precaution against suffering, Michaud is repeating the decadent *credo* without distancing himself from it, and he turns Pater into 'a Des Esseintes of the ideal'[14]: the author of a blazing 'Conclusion', an admirable craftsman of

---

[7]   'Apollyon c'est l'âme antique exilée aux brumes de Thulé, mal exorcisée par les gens d'Eglise et sommeillant depuis des siècles sous le secret des palimpsestes, l'âme hellénique telle que Byron, Keats et Shelley la réveilleront un jour' (Michaud 1918, 63).

[8]   'esthète précurseur d'Oscar Wilde et de Des Esseintes' (Michaud 1918, 60).

[9]   'l'un des annonciateurs du culte artistique du moi' (Michaud 1918, 60).

[10] 'les symptômes de la nostalgie des terres du sud qui tient au cœur de l'Anglo-saxon' (Michaud 1918, 74).

[11] 'la synthèse de l'esthétique et de la philosophie de Pater' (Michaud 1918, 67).

[12] 'le plus chrétiens des sceptiques, le plus païen des martyrs' (Michaud 1918, 70).

[13] 'un reflet embelli de son moi'; 'comme des stations de psychothérapie' (Michaud 1918, 71).

[14] 'un Des Esseintes de l'idéal' (Michaud 1918, 71).

English prose whose Flaubertian style is 'all iridescent with shimmering rays and perfectly diaphanous'.[15]

Michaud synthesized the contemporary readings of Pater as a decadent, mixing them with Tainian analyses. His essay already involves the recurring questions of Paterian studies: the nature of Pater's religion, his attempts to reconcile opposites and the autobiographical nature of his portraits, the latter also involving the concealed question of his sexual orientation.

The French critic Charles Du Bos (educated at Oxford between 1904 and 1906, at a time when memories of Pater were still fresh) had an altogether different view of *Marius*, which he shared at first with André Gide. As Charles G. Hill has demonstrated (1967), their subsequent quarrel focused on *Marius*. Indeed, the reading of *Marius* represented a 'significant event' for Du Bos who, in 1930, published one of the four conversations with Gide that it had inspired: 'Sur *Marius l'Epicurien* et Walter Pater' (Du Bos 1930). *Marius* is for Du Bos 'a book whose reading determined and is still influencing my intimate being'.[16] In this respect he reverses Dowling's 'fatal book' topos (Dowling 1986, 104–74) since the decadents' fatal book becomes his breviary. *Marius* questions the necessity of religion in a post-Renanian context of upheaval, and the eponymous hero has a deeply religious nature to which faith is denied, leaving him only with the solution of self-sacrifice. Like Michaud, Du Bos notices that the question of Marius's conversion is left pending, while his death 'gives all its meaning to a life which was always dedicated',[17] without finding its due reward. Du Bos echoes Mrs Humphry Ward's explanations of the painstaking writing of *Marius*, but he is also responsive to the formal qualities of what is almost an *anti-roman*, just as he responds to Pater's choice of a period when paganism and Christianity coexisted peacefully together to serve his own conciliatory views concerning tolerance and the necessity of religion.

Du Bos's reading belongs to morals and aesthetics, and deserves to be mentioned, since it will be more or less echoed by d'Hangest, and since it underlines the Paterian stance vis-à-vis religion rather than his alleged suffering. Back within the fold of the Catholic church, Du Bos produced an original reading of *Marius* and of a Pater with whom he was religiously at loggerheads. Anne Henry has justifiably suggested that his essay increased Pater's French readership, coming at the end of a period in which the first group of translations had appeared.

In fact, Georges Khnopff had been the first of Pater's French translators, with *Imaginary Portraits* (*Portraits imaginaires*) appearing in 1899 for the newly established Mercure de France publishing house, which specialized in 'modernistic' writings of the 1890s. But French readers had to wait until 1917 for a translation of *The Renaissance* (*La Renaissance*) by Firmin Roger-Cornaz, despite the fact that it was already known to the French decadents. In 1922, Emmanuel Coppinger published *Marius* as *Marius l'Epicurien: un roman*

---

[15] 'tout irisé de rayons chatoyants et d'une diaphanéité parfaite' (Michaud 1918, 73).

[16] 'un livre dont la rencontre orienta et n'a pas fini d'influencer mon être intime' (Du Bos 1930, 41).

[17] 'conférer tout son sens à une vie qui s'est toujours dédiée' (Du Bos 1930, 63).

philosophique. The translation of the full title is maybe more explicit than the original *His Sensations and Ideas*. In 1923 Dr Samuel Jankélévitch published his translation of *Plato and Platonism* (*Platon et le platonisme*), and in 1930 Philippe Neel published his *Imaginary Portraits* (*Portraits imaginaires*), the only translation we have had so far, which was reprinted in 1985 with a foreword by Mario Praz (Neel 1930).

Neel's preface to his translation is interesting, as it provides the reader with a portrait of Pater as he had come to be seen in the late 1920s, at a time when the Decadent era was still alive, albeit as an afterglow. While other critics mainly relied on Wright's biography, Neel invoked Symons to present a portrait of Pater as a 'quiet and shy' child,[18] who should have been educated as a Catholic but became an Anglican when his father decided to break away from the family tradition. Such a decision in his view produced a return of the repressed when Pater developed an almost Catholic devotion to the 'profane divinity'[19] of Art, after discovering the writings of Ruskin at Oxford.

Like Ruskin and Wilde, according to Neel, Pater belonged to Oxford where he developed into 'a voluntary recluse'.[20] A confessional writer whose 'slow and grave dance' moved within a 'circle as narrow as a prison-cell',[21] he sketched heroes closely resembling himself, 'timid, solitary, shying from action, fearing the world and seeking refuge in dreams'.[22] Ignoring texts which did not fit his views, Neel cited in particular 'Winckelmann', *Studies in the History of the Renaissance* and *Marius*, considering *Marius* to be 'the most significant and important of his works'[23] because it showed that 'the aesthetic ideal could be the object of a soul as pure, as exposed as that of any ascetic'.[24] Concentrating on Pater's poetics, Neel drew a parallel between Flaubert and Pater, but underlined that the latter was more of a verbal colourist than the rhythmically inclined Flaubert. Pater also paid attention to the construction of sentences (an echo of Paul Bourget's famous definition of the Decadent style of composition),[25] and to a type of style where the form was dissolved 'in imprecise, fading shades of colour'.[26] Yet Pater's melodious style was also a

---

18   'silencieux et timide' (Neel 1930, x).
19   'divinité profane' (Neel 1930, ix).
20   'reclus volontaire' (Neel 1930, xii).
21   'sa danse lente et grave se meut dans un cercle étroit comme celui d'une prison' (Neel 1930, xii).
22   'un timide, un solitaire qui répugne à l'action, redoute le monde, et se réfugie dans le rêve' (Neel 1930, xvi).
23   'le plus significatif et le plus important de ses ouvrages' (Neel 1930, x).
24   'l'idéal esthétique peut être l'objet d'une âme aussi pure, aussi dépouillée que celle d'aucun ascète' (Neel 1930, x).
25   'A decadent style is one where the unity of the book disintegrates to make way for the independence of the page, where the page disintegrates to make way for the independence of the sentence, and the sentence to make way for the independence of the word' ('Un style de décadence est celui où l'unité du livre se décompose pour laisser place à l'indépendance de la page, où la page se décompose pour laisser place à l'indépendance de la phrase, et la phrase pour laisser place à l'indépendance du mot') (Bourget 1993, 14).
26   'l'imprécision des nuances mourantes' (Neel 1930, xiv).

logical one with its 'quasi-mathematical series of links and deductions',[27] and in this respect Neel echoed Pater's theses in 'Style'.

A more interesting perspective is provided by Neel's views on Pater's art of portraiture as a way of probing into the minds of others, since '[t]o criticize a work [. . .] is to enter the soul of his creator, to divine his intentions, to clarify his unexpressed designs'.[28] This is a quest which is akin to 'divination',[29] as Neel acknowledges, but which also starts from the assumption that what is most interesting in a writer is precisely that which is lacking, whether through being censored or being resistant to expression. For once, here is a critic who does not equate Pater with the writers whom he chose to study. Far from superimposing his self on Wordsworth, Shakespeare and others, Pater withdrew before them, with the unexpected result that he becomes one of those who 'finish by unwittingly erecting to their own glory the monument they dreamt of erecting for others'.[30] Hence he has merited his critical fortune where he stands in the 'highest place because he was the most disinterested'.[31]

Neel's preface reads at times like a pastiche of the 'Conclusion' to *The Renaissance* (something likely to happen when discussing Pater), and it may have contributed to turning Pater into an exponent of art for art's sake, by emphasizing his solitariness in the 'ivory tower'[32] of Oxford, his 'laborious giving birth',[33] the 'lack of recognition by the masses or by society'[34] and the total absence of emotional and sexual relationships. This last point opposed the views of Georges Duthuit, whose *Le Rose et le noir: de Pater à Wilde* (1923) had performed one of the first 'outings' of the century. But as Jean de Palacio (1993) has convincingly argued, Decadence proved long-lasting in France and the 1920s witnessed a spate of 'late-Decadent'[35] novels, which confirmed the existence of a readership for a genre which also included *Imaginary Portraits*. As a general rule, the 1920s and 1930s still seemed interested in Pater. It was only after the Second World War that he almost ceased to feature in discussions.

Louise Rosenblatt took Pater as the pivotal figure for her doctoral dissertation *L'Idée de l'art pour l'art dans la littérature anglaise pendant la période victorienne* (*The Idea of Art for Art's Sake in Victorian English Literature*) in 1931. In this doctoral dissertation in comparative literature, on the literary history of a movement viewed as a general philosophy of life fuelled by art, Pater occupies a particular place as the 'principal' protagonist.[36]

---

27   'une série d'enchaînements et de déductions quasi – mathématiques' (Neel 1930, xv).

28   'Critiquer une œuvre [. . .] c'est pénétrer à sa faveur dans l'âme de son créateur, deviner ses intentions, préciser ses desseins informulés' (Neel 1930, xvii).

29   'divination' (Neel 1930, xvii).

30   'finissent à leur insu par élever à leur propre gloire le monument qu'ils rêvaient d'édifier pour autrui' (Neel 1930, xviii).

31   'à la place la plus haute, parce qu'il fut le plus désintéressé' (Neel 1930, xix).

32   'tour d'ivoire' (Neel 1930, xvi).

33   'parturition laborieuse' (Neel 1930, xiii).

34   '[Pater] ne connut ni l'enthousiasme des foules ni les approbations mondaines' (Neel 1930, xix).

35   'décadences de décadence' (de Palacio 1993, 138).

36   'principal' (Rosenblatt 1931, 169).

For Michaud Pater was a mystic pagan, for Rosenblatt he is a proponent of the 'aesthetic mysticism'[37] whose worship of the Beautiful is undeniable. After four chapters devoted to tracing the Victorian attitude towards literature, presenting the Romantic or Pre-Raphaelite precursors of the art for art's sake movement, and showing Ruskin and Swinburne's influence, Rosenblatt devotes thirty-six pages to turning Pater into the official British exponent of art for art's sake. Her perspective is both diachronic, inscribing Pater within literary history, and synchronic, since he is shown to crystallize the literary and artistic trends of the movement.

Unlike Ruskin's moralizing art criticism and Arnold's absolute poetical types, Pater promoted a lifestyle predicated on contemplation, one that was born of religious disenchantment rather than open rebellion, while being endowed at the same time with an oblique way of subverting current opinions without openly attacking their proponents. Reading his most famous texts but not the whole corpus (she does not seem to have had access to the 1889 edition of *Appreciations* or the 1868 'Poems by William Morris'), she notices that Pater goes from the manifesto of the 'Conclusion' to the 'more marked mysticism of the last ten years of his life, [which] is not the negation of his past attitudes but rather their development and expansion'.[38] There is no rupture in Pater's thought but a continuity, despite the critical reception of *The Renaissance* which she both notes and discusses. Rosenblatt also underlines the point that the young Pater is 'the only important proponent of the idea of art for art's sake to be directly influenced by German aesthetic theory',[39] a fashionable thesis at the time (all the more so as Rosenblatt was supervised by Fernand Baldensperger, Professor of Comparative Literature at the Sorbonne but, more importantly, a distinguished Germanist). This argument has been subsequently qualified by other writers on Pater (Ward 1966; Shuter 1971).

Tracing his direct influences and relying on Wright's biography, Rosenblatt mentions the Pre-Raphaelites and Swinburne: 'it is probably through the direct contact with the Pre-Raphaelites' ideas and more especially those of Swinburne that this attitude [of art for art's sake] crystallized in a conscious theory'.[40] The opposition between the active and the contemplative life and the importance given to form over meaning in 'Leonardo da Vinci' clearly derive from Swinburne's *William Blake: A Critical Essay* of 1868. It was only after 1870 that Pater chose Flaubert as his literary mentor, an influence apparent in 'Style', which was in turn to influence English literature by bringing in 'the ideal of an elaborate, chiselled prose and the image of the prose writer as a real craftsman, serving a long apprenticeship, consciously

---

[37]   'Le Mysticisme esthétique' is the title of Rosenblatt's chapter on Pater.

[38]   'mysticisme plus accusé des dix dernières années de sa vie [qui] n'est pas la négation de ses attitudes antérieures mais plutôt leur développement et leur expansion' (Rosenblatt 1931, 185).

[39]   'le seul partisan important de l'idée de l'art pour l'art qui fut directement influencé par la théorie esthétique allemande' (Rosenblatt 1931, 187).

[40]   'c'est probablement au contact direct des idées des préraphaelites et plus particulièrement de Swinburne que cette attitude [la théorie de l'art pour l'art] se cristallisa en théorie consciente' (Rosenblatt 1931, 193).

applying himself to the "craft of his art"'.[41] At odds with Victorian utilitarianism, his morals allowed him to set down the ideal of the artist-writer as Flaubert had done in France.

Pater appears as a stylist-cum-theorist, but also as a subtle moralist who discriminates between 'good' and 'great' art, subordinating criticism to morals towards the end of his life. Yet this change of tone ('Pater seems to have sided with the enemy', in Rosenblatt's words)[42] is first of all a qualification aimed at dismissing any hint of immorality, which continued long after 1873. In the 1890s Pater focused on 'the interpretation of the value of the aesthetic experience in art and life'[43] and obliquely assessed the Decadent movement in his lectures on Plato. Pater had not fully calculated the consequences of the publication of *The Renaissance*, and had to spend the rest of his life qualifying his theses, an opinion which seems hard to dismiss even if critics still differ on the effect of the reception of *The Renaissance* on the later Pater.

Although she has read *The Renaissance, Marius, Gaston de Latour* and some of the essays, Rosenblatt omits the visual art studies, with the effect of suggesting three particular achievements by Pater: his contributions to art for art's sake literature in Great Britain, his application of aesthetic values to life, and his statement of a doctrine which would soon be adopted by other artists similarly responsive to German idealism. In this she was following André Cassagne, whose dissertation on *La Théorie de l'art pour l'art en France* (*The Theory of Art for Art's Sake in France*, 1906) had portrayed a period in which art was slowly becoming autonomous, symbolized by the figure of the secluded writer bent on applying a monastic devotion to his œuvre. The two essayists still see the worship of beauty as an 'attitude', whereas sociologists tend to read it as the symptom of a societal mutation. Rosenblatt argues that Pater gave the 'aesthetic attitude the first place',[44] leaving the sociological reasons analysed by Pierre Bourdieu (1999) implicit.

3

Pater thus becomes the prophet of the 1890s against his own wishes: the pronouncement will be repeated and popularized. It was also in 1931, in an age of transition which echoed Victorian transitions, that the other great dissertation on the period, Albert Farmer's *Le Mouvement esthétique et 'décadent' en Angleterre, 1873–1900* (*The Aesthetic and 'Decadent' Movement in Great Britain*) was published (Farmer 1931a). This work came with a supplementary dissertation in English, *Walter Pater as a Critic of English Literature: A Study of 'Appreciations'*, on Pater's literary theories, a subject to which scant attention had previously been paid (Farmer 1931b).

---

[41] 'l'idéal d'une prose travaillée, ciselée et l'image de l'écrivain en prose, véritable artisan, faisant un long apprentissage, s'appliquant consciencieusement à la "technique de son art"' (Rosenblatt 1931, 200).

[42] 'Pater semble avoir passé dans le camp ennemi (Rosenblatt 1931, 201).

[43] 'l'interprétation de la valeur de l'expérience esthétique dans l'art et la vie' (Rosenblatt 1931, 200).

[44] 'donné à l'attitude esthétique une place de premier ordre' (Rosenblatt 1931, 205).

This dissertation traces the evolution of the Aesthetic movement in Great Britain, Farmer preferring the term 'aesthetic' to the term 'decadent', which still carried pejorative undertones. Apparently his preference met with some success, as the expression has entered French academic discourse. His purpose was also to replace the portraits and anecdotal essays, through which the late nineteenth century was all too often perceived, with a comprehensive study of Aestheticism. The memoirs of its protagonists had reduced Decadence to a raunchy episode or a gallery of portraits, whereas Farmer aimed at inscribing it in a literary history dominated by paradigmatic characters. This is not too distant from the Paterian aesthetic where literary history is constructed through portraits, but while Pater thinks in terms of figures and types as being exemplified by their style, Farmer thinks in terms of persons and influence.

The period inappropriately called 'Decadence' was a formidable renewal, and Farmer wishes to carry out the 'impartial study of a movement whose importance is now beyond doubt'.[45] This stance may account for the comparatively small place occupied by Pater in his essay. The first chapter traces the origins of the Aesthetic movement in Keats, Rossetti, Morris, Ruskin and Pater, including foreign influences mainly imported by George Moore; the second is devoted to the 'Wilde case', which epitomizes the Decadent movement; and the last chapter discusses the magazines of the Yellow Nineties and their contributors (Beardsley, Johnson and Beerbohm *inter alia*).

The so-called Aesthetic movement is assumed to have begun in 1873 with the publication of *The Renaissance*, 'which defined and concentrated into a coherent doctrine the scattered trends within the atmosphere of the period [...] [and formed] the true starting point of English *Decadentism*'.[46] *The Renaissance* is both the point of origin and the synthesis, while Pater is a humanist, a dutiful educator who will be swept away by a movement he did not control. The worship of the beautiful soon becomes a worship of the artificial, of the morbid, of the *macabre*, so prevalent in *fin-de-siècle* literature and deriving, as Pater had pointed out in his 'Postscript', from Gautier and Baudelaire. Pater can also be credited with having introduced a new type of hero, with his ambiguously beautiful young men heralding Wilde's Dorian Gray.

Farmer's biographical sketch focuses more on Pater's intellectual life than his personal one, as he skims through 'Coleridge's Writings', 'Winckelmann' and *The Renaissance*, arguing that here one can see the birth of Pater's impressionist method, which he understands as the verbalization of the sensations aroused by the work of art. The 'Conclusion' amounts to a 'higher Epicureanism',[47] a spiritual discipline and 'true gospel' for future disciples,

---

[45]   'l'étude impartiale d'un mouvement dont l'importance ne fait plus de doute aujourd'hui' (Farmer 1931a, vi).

[46]   'qui précise et concentre en une doctrine cohérente les tendances dispersées dans l'atmosphère de l'époque [...] le véritable point de départ du *décadentisme* anglais' (Farmer 1931a, 34).

[47]   'épicurisme supérieur' (Farmer 1931a, 41).

despite the negative comments it provoked, such as those in William Hurrell Mallock's *New Republic*.

Describing it as a mediocre novel of action, leading its hero 'onto the threshold of faith',[48] Farmer argues that *Marius* illustrates an elitist doctrine reserved for a scholarly minority; written to qualify *The Renaissance*, it ironically amplifies the Aesthetic movement. The same applies to *Imaginary Portraits*, which belongs to the genre of 'fictionalized criticism',[49] serving to develop *Marius*'s theses. Their heroes' failures just before the point of success raise the issue of an ontological disharmony between the beautiful and the modern world, and can also be read as a counterpart to Pater's enthusiastic pronouncements in 1873. As for the 1896 *Gaston de Latour*, it is the 'confession of a sceptic who cares about matters of faith as a *dilettante* only'[50] [my italics], and who seems more estranged from them than Marius. Confronted with misunderstanding in 1873, Pater never recanted; he simply became more serene with age.

Appreciations is only briefly mentioned here because Farmer will discuss it in his second dissertation, and *Plato and Platonism* is summarized in a single paragraph; it is described as 'a fine essay in imaginative criticism'[51] which modern criticism has surpassed. Acclaimed in 1893, *Plato and Platonism* was dismissed in 1931 since (if we are to believe Farmer) philosophy had ceased to be a method of questioning and had become a matter of erudition. Such a dismissal demonstrates the widening gap between disciplines, which was increasingly evident during this time. From this perspective, Pater ceased to be a lecturer in philosophy, and became instead a prose-writer endowed with a 'musical and sinuous phrase'.[52] The differences in academic background between Farmer and the Fellow of Brasenose may account for the premature burial of Pater's philosophical work, the effect of which was to locate him firmly within the field of English Literature. In more general terms Pater was held to be not one of the best writers, but merely a good writer, because of his obscurity, his excessive technique, his preciosity, his attention to detail and his artificiality – all these being constitutive features of Decadence as they were to be defined by Vladimir Jankélévitch two decades later (1950, 337–89).

As for Pater's sexual 'aberration', Farmer mentions it in veiled terms in a footnote, but he makes it clear that he has a duty to do so at a time when critics were reluctant to link Pater to the Decadent movement.[53] Pater's

---

48 'au seuil de la foi' (Farmer 1931a, 48).

49 'critique romancée' (Farmer 1931a, 60).

50 'confession d'un sceptique qui ne se soucie de la foi qu'en *dilettante*' (Farmer 1931a, 64, my italics).

51 'bel essai de critique imaginative' (Farmer 1931a, 65–66).

52 'phrase onduleuse et musicale' (Farmer 1931a, 66).

53 'at a time when the biographers of Pater refuse to admit any connection between his inspiration and that of the "decadents". While acknowledging the moral concern which never ceased to drive this master, and while paying homage to the scruples which acted on the evolution of his thought, it would be vain to deny the profound analogies which connect him to the writers of the *fin-de-siècle*' ('à l'heure où les biographes de Pater se refusent à admettre un rapport quelconque entre son inspiration et celle des "décadents". Tout en saluant le souci moral qui n'a jamais

homosexuality links him to the Decadents, who are thus reduced to a brotherhood of 'inverts'. One can see the moral reason why Farmer wanted to replace the disparaging term 'decadent' with the more acceptable 'aesthetic', thereby closeting 'abnormal' sexualities. But, sexual preferences apart, what is at stake here is a definition of the literary canon in which Pater has a marginal place. It is also in the light of the hostility between generations that he himself experienced in the late 1920s that Farmer was concerned to discuss and define a movement in which sons rose against their fathers (Pater included). Paradoxically he was aligning his own practice with the rebellious sons by turning Pater into a nice, innocuous stylist in his *Study of Appreciations*.

In *Walter Pater as a Critic of English Literature: A Study of 'Appreciations'*, the second of the two dissertations, Farmer dismisses the validity of any psycho-biographical reading as a means of presenting Pater's method, while also emphasizing that his work involves no major reassessment. Starting with 'Coleridge's Writings', the paradigm of Paterian criticism, he overlooks the essays published in the *Guardian* and, more importantly, 'Aesthetic Poetry'. It might be argued that in this respect he was in fact following the lead of Pater, who had excluded the latter from the 1890 edition of *Appreciations*. But it is more difficult to account for his omission of 'Feuillet's *La Morte*', which replaced it. John Conlon (1981) later paid a justifiable tribute to this text, in which Pater discussed religion extensively in the context of Feuillet's (long-forgotten) novel. 'Prosper Mérimée' underwent the same process of exclusion, with the effect of foreclosing any attention to the central question of literary enunciation as it is raised there, and thus confirming the view of Pater as the creator of a narcissistic literary style, where the portrait is first and foremost a self-portrait and, when its original meaning is lost, a self-reflection.

After a presentation of his Romantic predecessors (Coleridge, Hazlitt, De Quincey), whose criticism he synthesized, Farmer shows Pater's originality as a critic: criticism has no origin but in the critic's relation to the text. Strangely Farmer distinguishes between poets and prose-writers, a distinction Pater himself repudiated, attributing to both the same relationship to language, which determined what he called a 'style'. Farmer then underlines the similarity between the literary and the imaginary portraits, both of which do not involve scholarly criticism but tend to focus on the psychological behaviour manifested by their characters. Pater's works are always contextualized but it is the psychological aspect that is privileged: Coleridge is morbid, Browne is haunted by death and Lamb is modest. These characteristics also apply to Pater himself, who could have echoed Flaubert's famous statement: 'Madame Bovary, c'est moi'. From a perspective according to which literature is the direct translation of a psyche expressed in consciousness, Farmer turns the Paterian method into a mirror for reflecting other souls.

Similarly, in his studies on Shakespeare, Pater sought the psychologist behind the playwright, a stance that accounts for his original remarks on texts

---

cessé d'animer ce maître, et en rendant hommage aux scrupules qui agirent sur l'évolution de sa pensée, il serait vain de nier les analogies profondes qui le rattachent aux écrivains de la fin du siècle', Farmer 1931a, 75).

that specialists have tended to neglect. Yet he overlooked the tragedies in order to underline that the Shakespearean genius lay in the historical plays, and he omitted to consider any text that would invalidate those views. Unfortunately, this typical Paterian strategy does not give rise to any further development, as Farmer, missing a real opportunity, focuses his analysis on the text itself rather than on what it omits.

However, the various portraits are also studied at length in their literary dimensions to show the importance of their rhetoric and form. 'Wordsworth' is praised for its innovative character, by contrast with the facile pronouncements of Matthew Arnold. But the 1880 'Coleridge' puts too much emphasis on the poet's morbid sensuousness, overlooking the more pleasing aspects of his poetry, and his writings on versification. The chapter devoted to 'Style' and the 'Postscript' stresses their polarized structure ('imaginative/unimaginative'; 'soul/mind'; 'great/good art'; 'classical/romantic'), and pays tribute to the modern art of prose, understood as a restrained art of composition practised by Pater which would turn him into the master of a generation.

For Farmer, finally, Pater reconciled ethics and aesthetics while being 'an admirable writer [. . .] a model of perfect prose' (Farmer 1931b, 96). He provided a model for an aristocratic style with long and complex sentences (with a vocabulary more Latin than Saxon) that inspired Joyce, Proust and Valéry. The theses of *Appreciations* have become canonical and are recognized even by the likes of Arthur Symons, J. B. Priestley, J. C. Squire and Bonamy Dobrée, as well as by American humanists such as Babbitt and More – a highly ironical assertion when one considers the role that such critics played in Pater's decline in the United States (Seiler 1980, 40). The image of Pater that one gets from Farmer's essay is thus that of a second-rate narcissistic writer whose works and person have been conflated. No doubt Pater raised the issue of enunciation with too much subtlety to be understood by an audience which confused character and author, and the subjects of the portraits with Pater's own self-reflection. It would take the emergence of Structuralism in the 1960s to clarify that distinction. Nevertheless, *Walter Pater as a Critic of English Literature: A Study of 'Appreciations'* resulted in the eponymous text being put on the syllabus for the *Agrégation* (the national exam to recruit high-school teachers and a reliable thermometer of the English Literature canon in France). It was the first and the last time that Pater was placed on the *Agrégation* syllabus, but it had an immediate impact, as another budding scholar discovered Pater as a result. This was the point at which the newly promoted *agrégé* Germain d'Hangest decided to work on Pater.

4

D'Hangest's doctoral dissertation, *Walter Pater: l'homme et l'œuvre* (*Walter Pater: The Man and his Works*), was eventually published in 1961. Supervised by Farmer, this dissertation was 775 pages long, with appendices that featured for the first time in France all of Pater's publications and a comprehensive bibliography. With the publication of these two volumes, Pater is seen for the first time as a writer deserving a book-length study, following the established academic pattern of 'the man and his works' but also subverting it to some extent by emphasizing Pater's psychology.

D'Hangest starts with 'The Child in the House' and 'An English Poet', and tries to draw a portrait of Pater as a writer whose texts show the hauntings and obsessions of a man hiding 'behind his elevated and subtle writings [. . .] who seems to flee from us and wrap himself in mysteries'.[54] As a child Pater appears both withdrawn and fascinated by the spectacle of pain and beauty, before turning into a lonely young man mocked by his Canterbury schoolfellows. He arrives at Oxford before he discovers the pleasure of reading and loses his faith. D'Hangest insists on Pater's prodigious knowledge and erudition, but also on the discipline to which this supposed dilettante submitted himself. From 1869 to 1873, his social and academic life was highly successful, and all the conditions were in place to carry this dreamer into the world of imagination, a world which sometimes gained the upper hand over the more rigorous criticism of 'Coleridge's Writings' (Pater's response to his religious crisis of the early 1860s), and dissolved both ontology and morals through the use of such recurrent images as weaving, the flame and the vortex.

Pater thus gave form and coherence to a tragic and austere aestheticism that cannot be reduced to an attitude, but partakes of an exclusive and difficult ideal: a higher humanism that ranks life beyond art as long as it is artistic, and takes the Renaissance as representing the full blossoming of humanity's powers. With Pater, meditation on art becomes a meditation on existence that attains a singular wisdom. Like all his texts, *The Renaissance* has consistency and beauty, and yet, inherent in the erudite and highly imaginative critique, there lurks a morbid, unhealthy element that culminates in the portrait of Mona Lisa. Simultaneously the goal of an obsessive search, the *femme fatale* and the literal symbol of the Renaissance, 'Lady Lisa' is 'the apex of a period, the extreme point of a psychological oscillation'[55] between fascination and reason.

However, the reception of *The Renaissance* is a turning point: the heterodox Oxford scholar is criticized by his peers, ridiculed by William Hurrell Mallock in *The New Republic*, and above all rejected by the highly influential Benjamin Jowett. His career is not compromised, but it goes no further. Neither in 1877 nor in 1883 is Pater promoted to a professorship. According to d'Hangest, Pater had not fully calculated the effect of the publication because his seclusion within the small circle of his friends prevented him from knowing his audience. *The Renaissance* earned him a fame that he had to pay for, professionally, personally and intellectually. Yet the more he was ostracized by the academic community, the more some of his students admired him, the best example being Wilde, 'the official sycophant of the new lifestyle',[56] and the person responsible for diffusing the legend whose dubious aura reflected back upon the real Pater. Faced with this reception, Pater took refuge in a total silence, interrupted only by the publication of the 1877 version of *The*

---

[54]   'derrière son œuvre haute et subtile [. . .] qui semble nous fuir et s'envelopper de mystères' (d'Hangest 1961, I: 10).

[55]   'le sommet d'une période, la pointe extrême d'une oscillation psychologique' (d'Hangest 1961, I: 199).

[56]   'thuriféraire officiel du nouvel art de vivre' (d'Hangest 1961, I: 209).

Renaissance and by the essays devoted to literature and mythology in the late 1870s. His friends remained faithful, but the spell was broken: from then on, his writings were to be both apologetic and melancholic, obsessional and slowly invaded by the themes of pain, madness and death as he was 'silently haunted by the flowers of evil, by a kind of black magic of art'.[57] Under their erudite, smooth surface, they testified to all the questions that Pater was incapable of solving.

In *Greek Studies*, Pater was one of the first to depart from the Victorian vision of a naive and happy Greece. He discussed Hellenism, and looked for lessons palatable to his times. But these essays also represent a step in the transition between his criticism and his fiction: 'in a moving attempt to express himself more completely, Pater is trying out new paths',[58] at the same time as his native mysticism returns and his religious attitudes are changing. The paths that he took led him to *Marius*, 'Pater's *masterpiece*'.[59] *Marius* is the story of a person who tries out a number of philosophies, but above all it is a text through which Pater rereads the 'Conclusion' to *The Renaissance,* and tries to dispel any ambiguity: 'his text [. . .] soon becomes a plea for the most personal of causes'.[60] At the same time, it displays 'Pater's inability to go beyond himself and to live'.[61] Like Du Bos, d'Hangest concludes by reviewing Pater's incapacity to believe, and by underlining the psychological problems to which it gave rise.

On the literary level, d'Hangest also places emphasis on Pater's distinctive textual unity and praises his art of the understatement. A 'kind of diary',[62] *Marius* provides an answer to moral, aesthetic, philosophical and literary questions of the *fin de siècle* as well as achieving, through an intense effort, the triumph of a lucid and courageous (but increasingly melancholic) mind. *Marius* enjoyed a favourable reception, but that did not allow its author to escape from academic purgatory. Increasingly he was seen as a guide for the younger Decadent generation, a position he tried to qualify, but not always successfully. His need for recognition was pursued through his search for a wider audience, and through a more diverse production that incorporated the 'imaginary portrait', 'a partial, transposed self-projection'.[63] This genre fitted Pater's own individual experience, with sources dating back to his childhood finding expression in 'The Child in the House'. D'Hangest goes on to examine all the portraits, stressing their morbidity, which reaches its peak in 'Emerald Uthwart'. Pater's characters are 'the sources and the mirrors of desires, combining dream and reality in the embellished self-image that they

---

[57] 'd'une hantise sourde des fleurs du mal, d'une sorte de magie noire de l'art' (d'Hangest 1961, I: 239).

[58] 'dans un effort pathétique pour s'exprimer plus complètement, Pater est en train de se lancer sur des routes nouvelles' (d'Hangest 1961, I: 269).

[59] 'Œuvre *maîtresse* de Pater' (d'Hangest 1961, I: 291).

[60] 'son texte [. . .] devient très vite un plaidoyer pour la plus personnelle des causes' (d'Hangest 1961, I: 300).

[61] 'incapacité de Pater à sortir de soi-même et à vivre' (d'Hangest 1961, I: 300).

[62] '[S]orte de journal intime' (d'Hangest 1961, I: 333).

[63] 'projection partielle et transposée de soi-même' (d'Hangest 1961, II: 56).

reflect'.[64] Again Pater is pleading *pro domo*, and he is qualifying his earlier pronouncements in *The Renaissance*.

However, the balance achieved in *Marius* was still precarious, and the question of evil was to resurface in *Gaston de Latour*, whose writing, according to d'Hangest, mainly took place between 1888 and 1889. He was the first in France to read this work in its entirety, manuscripts included, as he had access to John Sparrow's personal library at Oxford. D'Hangest gives a detailed summary of the unpublished chapters of this novel, which he read as a meditation on the Decadent movement and on the impasse ensuing from an ill-digested Aestheticism. As it remained unfinished, probably as a result of Pater's fatigue, *Gaston de Latour* was a dramatic revelation of the 'terror of imbalance [and] disintegration'[65] that had been concealed in *Imaginary Portraits*.

Appreciations was a less disturbed work because Pater published it for an audience whose tastes he had learned to understand. The book represents the 'crowning event of one of his major activities',[66] and it also expresses the theory that his fiction had put into practice. It displays a rigorous conception of criticism that cannot be reduced to an 'impressionist method' (i.e. a reflex), but seeks the genesis of the creative gesture within the subject, and reflects itself in other writers in order to have a better understanding of them. D'Hangest's explanation (almost an optical model in the manner that Lacan [1966] was developing at the same time) had the merit of being more complex than Farmer's reflex theory, but it likewise relegated the portrait genre in the end to a form of personal confession.

All the same, Pater was haunted by obsessive questions and if *Plato and Platonism* represented 'the achievement of a whole existence',[67] the problem of beauty and evil still remained unsolved. Plato functions for Pater as a model of Aestheticism understood as an ascesis aiming at the reconciliation of beauty and evil, ethics and aesthetics. Yet if this possibility exists for Pater, such was not the case for Plato, whom he overtakes in the real *coup de force* of his analysis. In this 'classical work [. . .] with a visibly pedagogical purpose',[68] Pater is in effect formulating anew the question of evil which runs through all his writings, and leaves it hanging like a gold thread to unify them. In 1893, Pater was on the point of leaving London where, like everywhere else, he had been unable to find a satisfying way of life, and intended to go back to Oxford and revert to art criticism. An untimely death interrupted this career which was dedicated to so demanding a quest. The unfinished 'Pascal' shows that Pater's religious attitudes had never overcome the crisis of the 1860s, even though his doubts had mellowed. In 1894 as in 1885, Pater had not managed to overcome his scruples.

---

[64]   'miroirs et sources de désirs [qui] combinent le rêve et la réalité dans l'image embellie qu'ils lui renvoient de lui-même' (d'Hangest 1961, II: 87).
[65]   'terreur du déséquilibre, de la désintégration' (d'Hangest 1961, II: 114).
[66]   'le couronnement d'une de ses activités majeures' (d'Hangest 1961, II: 138).
[67]   'l'aboutissement d'une existence entière' (d'Hangest 1961, II: 192).
[68]   'œuvre toute classique [. . .] au propos visiblement éducatif' (d'Hangest 1961, II: 227).

Drawing a line between gossip and fact at a period when the life was often used as a pretext to explain the work, d'Hangest's remarkable book conveys a troubled and troublesome Pater, tragically bent on making contact with humanity but finding himself unable to do so. Pater appears as a rigorous and enduring thinker, not devoid of a certain sense of humour, never recanting, and always content to polish his texts again and again, so as to explain his conceptions more effectively through the elaborate style to which d'Hangest devotes the last chapter of his dissertation. Using the *Gaston* and 'Pascal' manuscripts, he shows Pater ceaselessly refining his thought with the help of his vast erudition and detailed research, never hesitating to make minute corrections to the different versions of his publications. The sentence for Pater is 'a magnet around which suggestions flock, correcting or clarifying his first idea'.[69] It is also a musical ghost that he will enrich or animate in stages. What emerges here is the attention devoted to rhythm: even a short Paterian sentence does not stop abruptly but dies out 'on a *legato* which is one of the most original features of his prose'.[70] Pater's style is animated by a tension between Dorian restraint and Ionian excess, while being always in harmony with its intended meaning. His prose may be abstruse but it is never hermetic. Indeed, his rhetoric is all too often complex even though it proceeds by juxtaposition more than by coordination; it is all too often afflicted by the recurrence of certain words or expressions, because Pater is haunted by an obsession that makes his pen falter just as he is approaching a climactic point. Felicitous expressions may be found in Pater but he does not possess the style of a great writer. He sounds as if he is soliloquizing, but he certainly stands alone in spite of the self-proclaimed inheritors against whom d'Hangest, following Farmer, has no words strong enough. Not only are there 'few [who] discern the exact meaning of his message',[71] but one should refrain from comprehending Pater through the 'distorting prism'[72] of the Aesthetic movement, which turned him into an amoral writer despite the fact that he led a blameless life.

5

Pater cannot be accused of being an 'invert', even if he sometimes expressed a certain homophilia in his writings, which was also 'a source of suffering'.[73] It is interesting to read these pages in parallel with the work of Richard Dellamora, for whom Pater is a militant gay (Dellamora 1990). Further research (Inman 1994) has confirmed the rumours which Farmer was unwilling to disseminate, and in the interval the 1970s liberation movement has changed the meaning of 'sexuality'. But we should remember that this dissertation was published in a

---

[69] 'aimant autour duquel s'agrègent des suggestions qui corrigent ou précisent l'idée première' (d'Hangest 1961, II: 263).

[70] 'un *legato* qui est un des caractères les plus originaux de sa prose' (d'Hangest 1961, II: 301).

[71] 'bien peu discernent le sens exact de son message' (d'Hangest 1961, II: 309).

[72] 'prisme déformant' (d'Hangest 1961, II: 309).

[73] 'source de souffrance' (d'Hangest 1961, II: 323).

time when working on the late nineteenth century was itself morally suspect.[74] As de Palacio reminds us: 'The Academy was not open to such a form of literature'.[75] D'Hangest's study confirmed the image of a Pater too discreet to be really brilliant, a vision that seems to echo the judgement of Henry James, who acknowledged Pater's style but denied him the place that he might have rightfully occupied. What is revealed by the scholar's pen is the 'essential melancholy of this soul who [...] was never completely happy',[76] who was always hiding, as if shy of others, obsessed and haunted. But the fact remains that Pater was questioned because he had started the process of questioning. This doctoral dissertation may have reduced the imaginary or literary portrait to a form of mimicry, and oddly the question of genre remained undiscussed. But it certainly established Pater in France as a British writer. More importantly, Professor d'Hangest should be given credit for the dissemination of Pater among his students at the Sorbonne, most of whom became teachers in turn and cited Pater in their lectures on Victorianism. Pater was henceforth perceived as a remote figure, a writer rather than an art historian or a philosopher, but at least his presence could no longer be erased.

D'Hangest would return to the issue of Pater's relation to his Decadent successors in his later essay 'La Place de Walter Pater dans le mouvement esthétique' (1974). Here he underlines the ambiguity of the very term 'aesthetic' insofar as it means both what is apprehended through one's senses and the study of the beautiful. This is the ambiguity that lies at the heart of the Aesthetic movement, of Pater's own writings and of the misunderstanding that affects them both. It is an ambiguity that brought about the tragedy of the *Yellow Nineties* and of Pater himself, who felt misunderstood when the sensuous became the sensual, thus impelling him to reformulate his aesthetics in the 1880s with a 'painfully didactic intent'.[77] This led to the development of a 'redefined and humanized Aestheticism'[78] that would find its best embodiment in 'Style' and 'Prosper Mérimée', which can be read as a critical analysis of Aestheticism. According to d'Hangest, Pater spent his life correcting the misunderstanding of his aesthetics rather than justifying his academic misfortunes.

D'Hangest's dissertation gave rise to several responses, the first of which came from Robert André, who translated 'The School of Giorgione' (1963a) and wrote a study of Pater's influence on Proust (1963b). Discriminating between two kinds of influence, one direct, and the other indirect but deeper, he sees Wilde as an instance of the first and stigmatizes the 'irritating side of

---

[74]   See the testimony of Jean de Palacio, another professor at the Sorbonne at the time: 'one could not chose to study Decadence with impunity [...] at this time, such a design was not only eccentric but vaguely immoral' ('on ne pouvait impunément prendre la Décadence comme objet d'étude [...] un tel dessein était à cette date, non seulement excentrique, mais vaguement immoral', de Palacio 1993, 10).

[75]   (de Palacio 1993, 10).

[76]   'l'essentielle mélancolie de cette âme qui [...] ne fut jamais complètement heureuse' (d'Hangest 1961, II: 310).

[77]   'une volonté douloureusement didactique' (d'Hangest 1974, 166).

[78]   'un esthétisme repensé, un esthétisme humanisé' (d'Hangest 1974, 166).

Aestheticism'.[79] Conversely, Proust is an instance of the second kind, succeeding where Pater failed in discovering the means of dealing with necessarily brief sensations through art. Pater is the exponent of a post-Kantian aesthetics that can only return from sensations to lost memories, whereas Proust was able to experience the transformation of his remembrances into music and landscape. André's analysis is short, but it paves the way for studies that gradually eliminated the tiresome psycho-biographical approach, which was under attack from Structuralism, in order to focus on Pater's thought and sources. Meanwhile, in France, other voices were heard from within the history of ideas, and these also had an impact on his reception.

In 1985 Anne Henry, a specialist on Proust, published a selection of Paterian excerpts inappropriately titled *Essais sur l'art et la Renaissance,* with a very important preface that marked Pater's forays into aesthetics (Henry 1985). Henry, who happened to have read *The Renaissance* in her teens and never forgot it, exemplifies the recent contribution of French Literature or Comparative Literature scholars, most of whom derived their knowledge of Pater through Proust and other late nineteenth-century writers. Among them was de Palacio, who was also urging his students to read Pater in the seminars that he delivered on the French Decadent movement. Henry's selection was published in a collection of texts on aesthetics and appeared after her study, *Marcel Proust: théories pour une esthétique (Marcel Proust: Theories for an Aesthetics),* which deals with the theories that Proust had used in his writings, including Aestheticism (Henry 1983). She achieved for Pater what she had achieved for Proust, re-contextualizing his writings within the history of ideas. Her contention is that Aestheticism derived from Schelling's writings, which were widely read in the nineteenth century and gave birth to many diverse ideas before reaching their conclusion in Structuralism. She argues that Pater is not just a writer but a major proponent of a 'psychological aesthetics'[80] which addresses individuals rather than humanity in general and is predicated on empiricism. Boldly, she only gives a few biographical elements at the end of her preface (although she provides a full list of biographies on which she has relied), and instead she devotes forty solid pages to situating Pater vis-à-vis Transcendental Idealism and the German philosophy of art known through Schopenhauer who, she argues, was the main conduit through which German philosophy seeped into European thought. She attacks the schools of criticism that brand Pater as a cranky Victorian when he attempts to diverge from traditional philosophy. A 'positivist compound',[81] the 'Preface' to *The Renaissance* is also a manifesto which aims to dissolve the differences between art, philosophy and scholarly criticism. By taking the visual arts as the starting point of a liberating reverie, Pater is distancing himself from Ruskin's theory of social art, thus begetting a new mode of writing which would inspire Wilde, Proust, Marcel Schwob and Kenneth Clark. An enthusiastic reader of Karl Otfried Müller (as was Nietzsche), he hid his radical views behind the tame genre of the monograph.

---

[79] 'le côté irritant de l'esthétisme' (André 1963b, 1083).
[80] 'l'esthétique psychologique' (Henry 1985, 16).
[81] 'florilège positiviste' (Henry 1985, 20).

Henry makes explicit the nineteenth-century theories of representation which Farmer had taken for granted, reminding her reader that the theories of *Einfühlung* (empathy), on which *The Renaissance* discreetly relies, transform the imagination into a chain of images, subject to the laws of association and memory, whilst inspiration is seen as an impulse liberating the free flow of images when the artist is 'tickled' by reality. The creative process becomes the projection of the unconscious of the artist. Against this perspective, Pater is to be criticized for attributing the motivation of the creative act to the merely reactive imagination, even though he reintroduced the criterion of pleasure which the Idealists had banished from the philosophy of art. As for the function of 'impressions', it is a matter of apprehending the meaning of art in its strangeness and singularity. As a reader of Schopenhauer, Pater posits an obscure Will struggling to assert itself ('the Schopenhauerian theory of the unconscious Will'),[82] which feeds on an unconscious and infinite source (Schelling's Nature). This finds its embodiment in the bizarre element that indicates both good and evil, as in the ambiguous smile of the Mona Lisa, or the destructive hero of 'Apollo in Picardy'.

Pater was also influenced by the Arts and Crafts movement, and praised Greek craftsmen in his *Greek Studies*, emphasizing the fascination of the artist with the material with which he has to contend. His atrophied Victorian conception of the body did not prevent him from being interested in the 'emergence of corporeality',[83] or from having 'an aptitude for exteriorizing the feeling of life in purely sensory terms'.[84] As for 'Style', Henry reads it both as Pater's *ars poetica* and as the forerunner of Formalism. Like d'Hangest, she notices that Pater turned Plato into 'the precursor of his own theory of art for art's sake'.[85]

Even though he is not a real philosopher, this discreet academic is for Henry 'a subtle rebel'[86] who introduces a dissenting tone into the various fields that he explored, disguising new interpretations behind well-established genres, and not hesitating to engage in skilful pastiches. His art criticism relies on new modes of presentation and seeks to display not the constancy of his obsessions but those of the artists he presents: those who, like Leonardo, are able 'to crystallize within a single image humanity's elusive aspirations'.[87] When he is given his place within the history of ideas, what appears is a Pater freed from the narcissistic stigma that was (and still is) his bane. Indeed, Pater's style is referred to as 'elegant prose with a mellow yet quite small stock of vocabulary', while his syntax 'is not exempt from affected and compressed turns of phrase in the manner of Tacitus'.[88] One needs to have translated Pater

---

[82]   'la théorie schopenhauerienne du Vouloir inconscient' (Henry 1985, 34).

[83]   'surgissement de la corporéité' (Henry 1985, 28).

[84]   'aptitude à extérioriser en termes purement sensibles le sentiment de la vie' (Henry 1985, 28).

[85]   'le précurseur de sa propre théorie de l'art pour l'art' (Henry 1985, 42).

[86]   'un rebelle subtil' (Henry 1985, 1).

[87]   'cristalliser en une seule image les aspirations diffuses de l'humanité' (Henry 1985, 39).

[88]   'prose élégante au lexique moelleux mais assez étroit pendant que la syntaxe n'est pas exempte de raccourcis précieux à la Tacite' (Henry 1985, 41).

to take the full measure of such an appreciation, which is openly at odds with the double-edged praise heaped on him for more than a century. For Henry, Pater is first and foremost an art critic, and his lack of theoretical and conceptual power may account for the unobtrusive place that he occupies within the aesthetics whose 'points of no return'[89] he explored.

If Henry's selection evidenced the change in Pater's critical reception, the English literature specialists did not openly respond to the publication of her translations. Given that she inscribed Pater in the field of aesthetics, it is remarkable that this achievement should come from a critic who occupies a certain place within Proustian studies, as if the study of Pater demanded a certain academic marginality. But the point also demonstrates the important part being played in reception by translations. As we noted before, the issue of translation is a vexed one as translators have generally hovered between Pater's fictional writings and *The Renaissance*, ignoring his essays on art, literature and philosophy. One cannot but notice that the range of translations is still narrow, self-repeating and liable to reinforce the stereotype of the Decadent dilettante. More often than not Pater is conflated with William Hurrell Mallock's Mr Rose, the proponent of a mock Aestheticism which seems to have had a much better fate than the original in France. All of Pater's essays still await a much needed translation. *Gaston de Latour*, which might dispel the distorted vision of Pater, is still unread because it is untranslated, though Théodore de Wyzewa reviewed it in the *Revue des deux mondes* as early as 1896. The text of this work may raise editorial questions, particularly in the last chapters. However, Gerald Monsman (1995) has proved that an edition of Pater's unpublished manuscripts is still feasible.

6

A few more recent translations remain to be mentioned. In 1992, Hélène Bokanowski translated the 'Preface' and the 'Conclusion' to *The Renaissance*, with an introduction in which she praised Pater as a radical thinker of modest origins struggling against the Oxford elitism dominated by Ruskin's ideas (Bokanowski 1992). Bokanowski reads 'Diaphaneitè' as Pater's *fons et origo*, an assertion with which few would care to disagree if they could have access to this still untranslated text. However, her introduction contains a number of general mistakes, as it draws on Wright's biography. It is not properly speaking an academic text, even though it aims at presenting Pater to the well-educated readership of José Corti's publishing house.

1992 was also the year when Guillaume de Villeneuve published a new translation of *Marius l'épicurien*, whose short and condensed introduction pays tribute to Pater's erudition, linking him to the French Decadence and to the Hellenic Revival in Great Britain. Villeneuve derives his compassionate portrait of Pater from Michael Levey (1978), seeing him not as a bourgeois ('nothing more erroneous than the myth of Pater as a bourgeois'[90]) but as an

---

89   'les points de non-retour' (Henry 1985, 16).

90   'rien de plus faux que le mythe qui fait de Pater un grand bourgeois' (Villeneuve 1992, 12).

ostracized graduate and dangerous teacher. According to him, Pater can be seen as 'the adult tainted by the Socratic suspicion of corrupting youth, which is too beautiful', forced to cope with 'the calumny which will deprive him of all the posts to which he had a claim'.[91] Pater's struggle is intensified by his constant 'obsession with mortality'.[92]

The *tour de force* of this preface consists in presenting Pater as a homosexual without mentioning the term. But even if he claims to 'speak about Marius as [he] would about Pater',[93] Villeneuve's reading deserves attention as it stresses that Pater weighs Epicureanism, Stoicism and Christianity against one another as Marius progresses through them in a Platonic fashion. Marius dies a Christian after having experienced the main doctrines of Antiquity. Read alongside Carolyn Williams's fine analysis of the typological structure of *Marius* (1990), this interpretation is one of the most fruitful ways of approaching a text which is always on the verge of dissolving into a series of vignettes and portraits.

Strangely enough, it took an entire century to translate four of Pater's most characteristic imaginary portraits, although the translator was none other than Pierre Leyris (*L'Enfant dans la maison*, 1992), who also provided a sympathetic introduction emphasizing the parallel between Pater and Proust. Both write as they feel, imposing that peculiar form of slow reading through which one can experience one's mortality. Pater has the knack of delineating the future within the present, or of turning it into a remembered past by anticipation, through the poetics of a layered temporality. As far as we can see, Leyris was one of the first French-speaking essayists to mention the issue of time in Pater, an interest possibly aroused by a study of the Proustian relationship to time or by the perusal of Williams's account of this major Paterian theme.

A different Pater emerged with Jean-Baptiste Picy who, in 1998, published a fine annotated translation of *Plato and Platonism* (partly to replace Jankélévitch's, about which he expresses some reservations) thereby giving evidence to Pater's return into the philosophical field from which he had been excluded for too long (Picy 1998). Vrin, a distinguished publishing house specializing in philosophical works, was responsive towards the project of this translation, since its editor already knew the text. Indeed, in his introduction Picy stresses how Pater is still unknown, save for a few students of English literature, and how any student in philosophy would benefit from a reading of Pater's 'primer' on Plato. Far from being 'a dusty historical document from Queen Victoria's last decades',[94] a self-justification against the accusations of the Victorians or a narcissistic tract, *Plato and Platonism* comes from a specialist in ancient philosophy. Picy's views are therefore at loggerheads with Farmer's dismissive approach.

---

[91] 'l'adulte entaché du soupçon socratique de corrompre une jeunesse trop belle [...] la diffamation qui le privera de tous les postes auxquels il pouvait prétendre' (Villeneuve 1992, 11–12).

[92] 'l'obsession de la mortalité' (Villeneuve 1992, 12).

[93] 'je parle de Marius comme de Pater' (Villeneuve 1992, 12).

[94] 'un document historique et poussiéreux des dernières décennies du règne de Victoria' (Picy 1998, 13).

Picy explains that the writing of *Plato and Platonism* derived from three motives: the Victorian revival of Antiquity through German philosophy, Pater's predilection for the essay which he held as the favourite genre of modernity, and his concern for relative judgements. He argues that Pater was 'the master of a generation',[95] and that he heralded Constructivism but also bears a relevance to our own times. *The Renaissance* may have been 'a thematic collection whose scope proves to be remarkable',[96] but in 1883, when the heyday of Aestheticism had come to a close, Pater had not yet written half of his works. He had still to qualify his vision of Christianity in *Marius* and to show the 'tragic experiences of art and its relative value'[97] in *Imaginary Portraits*. In the 1890s Pater 'becomes an indistinct figure [. . .] transfixed into a kind of meticulous, definitively Victorian "highbrow" aesthete or, even worse, a "hazy Decadent", all things that the post–1945 generations had almost no chance to appreciate'.[98] Far from hagiography or Decadent martyrology, Picy's aim is to present a relevant, objective and serious study of Plato while being aware of the distortions brought about by the Pater myth transmitted by the academy, according to which Pater's ideas are conflated with his style or his person, both being seen as obscure, abstruse and outmoded.

Reviewing his translation for *Etudes anglaises* in 2000, d'Hangest praised this short comprehensive introduction, the helpful comments and the clear and precise translation that followed Pater's thought and rhythm (d'Hangest 2000, 224). Bent on widening Pater's readership, Picy has subsequently given papers on Pater's imagery at different symposiums and used his texts in his translation classes. Indeed, the 1990s were the decade of the academic return of the Fellow of Brasenose, who had finally shed the garb of a stereotyped Decadent. This is further illustrated by Martine Lambert's 1999 doctoral thesis, 'Miroirs de la culture et images de soi: du portrait au portrait imaginaire chez Walter Pater' ('Mirrors of Culture and Self-images: From the Portrait to the Self-Portrait in Walter Pater', Lambert 1999). Lambert was introduced to Pater by Jean de Palacio, who supervised her Master's dissertation on Oscar Wilde. In Lambert's view Pater is more a writer than a thinker, who invites his audience to ponder on the nature of culture, art and writing, through portraits which are all imaginary, in the sense of not being mimetic, and give a discredited genre its rightful place in art. Her study is focused on the genre of the portrait as the means to inscribe Pater within culture, and she sees Pater's portraits both as the extension of his critical activity and as a veiled confession: 'they enable him at the same time to present a history of culture and to reveal himself, in a veiled manner'.[99]

After a thorough analysis of the portrait as a literary and painterly genre (a much needed clarification), Lambert embarks on a detailed analysis of all of

---

[95] 'le maître d'une génération' (Picy 1998, 13).

[96] 'un recueil thématique dont la portée s'avère remarquable' (Picy 1998, 9).

[97] 'des expériences tragiques de l'art et de sa valeur relative' (Picy 1998, 9).

[98] 'Pater s'efface [. . .] figé en une sorte d'esthète "high brow", méticuleux, définitivement victorien, ou pire encore, en tant que "décadent fumeux", toutes choses que les générations d'après 1945 n'ont guère de chance d'apprécier' (Picy 1998, 11).

[99] 'ils lui permettent à la fois de présenter une histoire de la culture et de se révéler, de manière voilée' (Lambert 1999, 8).

Pater's portraits, discriminating between 'shorter' and 'longer' ones, the first placing emphasis on the final effect, the second on the 'infinite course of a development [which is] both cultural and aesthetic'.[100] We no longer find a chronological or psycho-biographical study here but a study of Pater as a well-known and distinguished author, whose existence is supposed to be already known to the reader. Dissolving the vexed issue of Pater's belonging to Decadence or Aestheticism, Lambert focuses on a thematic study, even if she joins d'Hangest in claiming that Pater's views have been misrepresented by his alleged inheritors. Indeed, she discusses him for his own sake, as a scholar and a teacher from whom anyone can derive a lesson, provided one lets oneself be captivated by the charm that permeates his works. All the same, Pater was foremost an educator, and attention should be paid to his precise vocabulary (etymology included) which is dominated by the opposition between 'mind' and 'soul', and 'confirms the tension between the image and the line perceptible in the paradoxical expression of the "imaginary portrait"'.[101] Pater drew his inspiration from the *ekphrasis* in his alliance between word and image, but he also made the two patterns of tragedy and romance coexist. He may portray characters or dwellings, but they are in the first place the means to assert the permanence of an ever-returning past as well as permanent genius. At the time of writing, Lambert is preparing a book on Pater, due to be published by l'Harmattan, another sign that Pater is being revived in the French academy. Pater's academic reception in France has followed the major critical changes of the twentieth century, focused in turn on the study of a movement, a man and a genre. The most significant contributions have come from disciplines outside literature, or from translators who are English literature specialists, who were able to draw on extensive reading of English criticism, but may have been barred by academic specialization from discussing Pater's philosophical or aesthetic essays as such. It is not particularly easy to discuss art and philosophy outside institutionalized, legitimate circles. It is even harder to get a hearing or at least, to be read. The specialization imposed on scholars and doctoral candidates has foreclosed the opportunity of paying tribute to Pater's all-encompassing thought, pigeonholing him in the field of English literature, which has annexed him as a writer while rejecting him as a thinker. It has been decades since Pater was on the syllabus of the *Agrégation*, thus cutting off any interest in his writings in the case of those who do not already know him. As Picy pointed out, a dissertation on Pater's beautiful, rich and complex imagery still remains to be done.

7

Indeed, Pater's writings continue to raise the issue of an academy which, in spite of recurrent calls for more interdisciplinarity, still rigidly categorizes disciplines, authors and works, and resists what could be described as Pater's

---

[100]   'le parcours infini d'un développement à la fois culturel et esthétique' (Lambert 1999, 18).

[101]   'recoupe la tension entre l'image et le trait perceptible dans l'expression paradoxale de "portrait imaginaire"' (Lambert 1999, 13).

wager on style, or indeed his use of mainstream Victorian discourse to frame thoughts that subvert that very discourse. As opposed to Freud who, almost at the same time, broke free from the discourse of psychology and philosophy to found psychoanalysis as a distinct field, Pater would remain the prisoner of a discourse that would lose sight of him, or closet him within the nineteenth-century theories of representation. Commentators invariably and rightly emphasize his timidity and his reluctance to engage in public debate. The point remains that Pater was never free enough to assert his radical views and thus might appear to have failed in his intellectual ambitions. Or is it that those ambitions have been misrepresented, and all his critics are victims of a suspension of disbelief, in taking him at his own valuation? Pater may or may not be a good writer – a debate that postmodernity has tended to dissolve – but he remains a thinker, a dimension that virtually no one will notice as long as he is categorized as a stylist. Indeed, Pater lost his wager when his style became conflated with Decadent hermeticism in the first half of the twentieth century, and again it was overtaken by the development of the discourses of social sciences in the second half. What kind of theory or discourse can restore his well-merited radicalism? A possible critique might be inclined to take up with him (and not against him) two central notions in his writings – the notion of time and the notion of the subject – as they are articulated in his portraits. Indeed, as Martine Lambert has consistently shown, the Paterian portrait is a genre in need of redefinition, whose meaning we should try to retrieve in spite of the epistemological gap that separates modern readers from the Victorians.

What discipline can there be for the Paterian subject that cannot be reduced to gender or identity, that cannot be accounted for by a purely socio-historical determinism, but demands that we focus our attention on the notion of the subject conceived in terms of a tension between being and time, rather than on an object defined according to these categories? This was the question that Pater had highlighted through the composition of *The Renaissance*. Far from being a naive attempt at historiography, *The Renaissance* is a tightly structured work with a 'Preface' and a 'Conclusion', in which Pater gives a precise and thorough definition both of the subject and of aesthetics that is still worth our attention, and should be borne in mind when looking at all the portraits that he wrote subsequently. Moreover, this definition should not seen in isolation from the portraits that it frames: their arrangement supplies a temporal dimension, thus reinscribing the subject in history. Carolyn Williams's work has dwelt brilliantly on this 'aesthetic historicism' , but it may be argued that the main emphasis should be placed on the purely aesthetic dimension in his writings. Pater's definition of the subject should be located and studied in the area of ontology, however unpalatable such an approach might appear in our relativistic times.

Pater's place is the place of an untimely soul, one that is deprived of its true time. If it is to have a time, this will have to be the time of his reception, and not that of an umpteenth first-class burial. His place is that of a thinker who questioned the very meaning of what we mean by thinking. It is through his reception that he may cease to be an untimely soul.

6 A German View of Walter Pater

Wolfgang Iser

At the threshold of the twentieth century, Walter Pater enjoyed an extraordinary reputation in England among intellectuals from different walks of life. The critic Logan Pearsall Smith took Pater's writings for 'the discovery of a gospel, of a new way of living' (Smith 1936, 67). The poet William Butler Yeats maintained for himself and his friends that 'we looked consciously to Pater for our philosophy'.[1]

The Anglican clergyman J. A. Hutton contended: 'There is a stage, and in our day amongst educated people it has come to be almost a necessary stage, at which the writings of Pater are able to define our troubles to ourselves, and, in a way, to deal with them as no writer whom I know can with equal discernment' (Hutton 1906, 66–67).

After a very short time these voices had fallen silent, and increasing distance made Pater's standing shrink, as pinpointed by T. S. Eliot, who wrote: 'The right practice of "art for art's sake" was the devotion of Flaubert or Henry James; Pater is not with these men' (Eliot 1953, 443).

Pater did not initially make any comparable impact on German letters, nor was he later disparaged for what he had done. Instead, he was highly respected, frequently invoked in order to endorse or validate literary and scholarly statements, but seldom influential. Hence his work is assessed rather than actually received: the appraisal turns out to be the dominant form of Pater's 'reception' in German literature and academia.

It was the Austrian poet and playwright Hugo von Hofmannsthal (1874–1929) who, towards the end of the nineteenth century, alerted German literati to the importance of Pater. This is significant insofar as aestheticism was a dominant feature in Austrian letters, whereas in Germany there were not 'even decadents [...] in the sense of Aubrey Beardsley and Baudelaire', as Rudolf Borchardt (Borchardt 1987, 35–36) – the only German writer to have been directly influenced by Pater – remarked explicitly. This may indeed be one of the reasons why Pater's work fell on barren ground in Germany.

Hofmannsthal also set the tone for Pater's appreciation by German writers. He contended that Pater 'was enamoured of the artist, just as the latter was of life' (Hofmannsthal 1956, 202) as evinced by *The Renaissance*, which portrayed the interpenetration of art and life in an unparalleled manner. He likens Pater's

---

[1] Quoted in Edmund Wilson (1961) *Axel's Castle: A Study in the Imaginative Literature of 1870–1930*, London: Collins, 3.

extraordinary sensibility to a divining rod, allowing him to trace the dazzling attractiveness of unearthed treasures of art (Hofmannsthal 1956, 202). Hofmannsthal took the *Imaginary Portraits* to be the closest approach to perfection in art, because in his opinion Pater had succeeded in revealing the extent to which the art of the past made 'the life of the soul' of bygone ages virtually tangible (Hofmannsthal 1956, 204). Moreover, the several portraits epitomize the ideal aesthete, whose devotion to a life in fantasy is compellingly evocative (Hofmannsthal 1956, 204). Hofmannsthal, however, had certain reservations about *Marius the Epicurean*, which also reverberate in appraisals of the novel by German writers. 'The third book, "Marius the Epicurean" shows a basic inadequacy whenever one tries to build one's whole life on the aesthetic view of the world. The book is immensely clever, but its effect is arid, without greatness, and without humanity' (Hofmannsthal 1956, 204).[2]

Rudolf Kassner (1873–1959), though born in Moravia, and educated in Vienna, lived for more than three decades of his productive life in Switzerland, and was by no means as closely embedded in Austrian culture as Hofmannsthal was.[3] So we might well consider him a German writer, which Hofmannsthal himself had sensed very early on, when writing in 1904 that Kassner 'is potentially the most eminent "literary man" that Germany has ever had'.[4]

Owing to their common Viennese background, it was through Hofmannsthal that Kassner became acquainted with Pater, 'the aesthete and essayist' (Kassner 1957, 307), and he seems to have taken to him immediately. A few years after Pater's death he even travelled to Oxford, where he met Benjamin Jowett, who was instrumental in promoting a widespread interest in Plato, and who had certainly inspired Pater's devotion to Plato (Kassner 1957, 696). Kassner also talked frequently to the great man's former students, who seemed like a living embodiment of Pater's teaching by exemplifying the delicate balance of body and mind, which he had intended his students to acquire (Kassner 1949, 323–24). Kassner had an unbounded admiration for Pater's style, calling him 'the pre-Raphaelite of English prose' (Kassner 1969, 214), and trying to emulate him in his first book (Kassner 1984, 620).

It was Pater the critic, however, who fascinated Kassner most. He ranked him side by side with Friedrich Schlegel, Sainte-Beuve, Taine, Ruskin and Herman Grimm (Kassner 1969, 12), but was fairly unspecific as to what distinguished Pater from his peers. He merely commented that Pater had the keenest insight into the nature of art, and approved of the fact that he took Schiller for 'an adventurer' in German culture (Kassner 1976, 609).

What also intrigued Kassner was Pater's clear distinction between Gothic elements in Greek sculpture and Doric proportions in Gothic art (Kassner 1969, 735) in an age in which the mixture of styles tended to cancel out historical differences. It is Kassner's early work *Die Mystik, die Künstler und das*

---

[2] For further details see Stamm 1997.

[3] On Hofmannsthal's deep roots in Austrian literature and culture see Breuer 1995, 217–20.

[4] Quoted in Baumann 1961, 23.

Leben (1900) which is imbued with the spirit of Pater and the English poets of the latter half of the nineteenth century (Kassner 1976, 744), and it is worth noting that Hofmannsthal – who initially introduced Kassner to Pater and English aestheticism – wrote to him six months before his death in November 1928: 'I still remember the enormous impression which your first book on English poets and artists made on me. The book offered a whole philosophy of the imagination. I sensed a blueprint of an "edifice", an edifice which you now have built.'[5]

Although there are no traces of Pater in this 'edifice' any more, what Kassner shared with him was a certain intellectual affinity. Just like Pater, he was totally averse to any kind of systematic thinking. 'I have no system', he writes, 'and hence not even the language that a system would require' (Kassner 1992, 348). Therefore, he preferred the essay as the most flexible form to highlight the harmonization of the heterogeneous. It is not actually Pater's 'antinomianism' (Pater 1919, 24) that Kassner sets out to portray in the essay, but rather the unity between 'soul and language', as he phrased it (Kassner 1992, 355).

There is a faint echo of Hofmannsthal's reservation concerning *Marius* in Kassner's later writings. In 1942 Kassner wrote to Pellegrini, who had compared Kassner's *Julian* to Pater's *Marius*: 'There is a big difference between my *Julian* and *Marius the Epicurean*. Pater's eloquence lacks resonance; at least, I find that the blank surface has no musical reverberation' (Kassner 1982, 561). Such a statement reflects a certain detachment from what Kassner had enthusiastically embraced in his younger days. But in spite of his great admiration for Pater, he was not really influenced by him, though he shared Pater's basic intellectual disposition as a 'scholar-artist', to quote Lord David Cecil (1955).

There was more enthusiasm from the other prominent German writer, Rudolf Borchardt (1877–1945), who was intimately acquainted with Pater's work. In 1939 Borchardt wrote a lengthy essay entitled 'Walter Pater zu seinem Hundertsten Geburtstag' (Borchardt 1960, 402–22), which offers by far the greatest praise ever bestowed on Pater in German letters. Borchardt's panegyric highlights first and foremost Pater's aesthetic world view, summarizing the German translation of the 'Conclusion' at great length (Borchardt 1960, 407–11). He senses a close affinity to his own aesthetic leanings, which no one could have expressed better than Pater.[6]

'Der hohe Engländer', as Borchardt called Pater (Borchardt 1960, 421), was for him the last monumental critic to intervene in the history of his epoch in a manner which otherwise only great poets were able to achieve (Borchardt 1960, 402). What struck him as being even more important was Pater's impact

---

[5]   Quoted in Baumann 1961, 21.

[6]   Pater had always been closely associated with aestheticism in German scholarly writings. Obenauer (1933, 380) writes, 'Walter Pater was an aesthete, a man who lived by enjoying and recreating beauty'. Mattenklott (1987, 236) maintains that Pater, though leading an inconspicuous life, nevertheless indulged in an extravagant form of self-staging', which he contrasts with the 'aesthetic provincialism' prevailing in Germany at the time (247).

on Hofmannsthal, which led to a revitalization of poetic prose in German literature (Borchardt 1960, 420). Consequently, it was through Pater that 'unserem formflüchtigen Volk die Form wieder zu einer Ordnung des Inneren geworden ist' ('for our form-shy people, form has again become an order for things internal', Borchardt 1960, 421). What enabled Pater to perform such a Herculean task was his capacity for mastering dualities. He defended the clarity of concepts against threatening obfuscations of fantasy; and though basically a sceptic, he was simultaneously a 'mystical mathematician', which made him into 'an athlete of pure prose' (Borchardt 1960, 406) – Borchardt's way of describing Pater's latinate diction.

Moreover, as Borchardt writes, Pater was steeped in German thought, and promoted a cultural exchange between Germany and England on a scale hardly ever achieved before. He was at home in German philosophy and literature, and yet refrained from plunging himself into the German 'Traum- und Zaubersphäre' (sphere of dream and magic), as some of his contemporaries did (Borchardt 1960, 420). For Borchardt Pater channelled German thinking into English letters by simultaneously transforming its systematic intent into practical guidance.

Finally, in view of the late romantic degeneration of the historical novel as exemplified by Victor Hugo, Pater developed – according to Borchardt – a different approach to history. This is not purely factual, nor is it a narrative sequence. Instead, it can only be imaginatively conceived, which implies that fantasy organizes the factual events without ever eclipsing them (Borchardt 1960, 416). Striking such a balance reveals how the 'scholar-artist' inscribes himself into his imaginative history (Borchardt 1960, 416). This interfusion of historical facts with a hidden self-portrayal is the salient feature of *Marius the Epicurean*, which epitomizes what the historical novel was able to achieve (Borchardt 1960, 419).

Extracting the main points of Borchardt's essay on Pater's centenary does not really give an idea of the vein in which this piece is written. The broader context for its publication will be discussed at length in the essay by Martina Lauster in this volume. In itself, however, it is a Paterian 'purple patch', and when one reads it, the impression of Pater's 'Mona Lisa' looms large. Pater is enshrouded in a mood that builds itself up through a succession of new associations into which his intellectual accomplishments are unfolded. One feels as if one is in a hazy dream, in which expressions of intensity accumulate to such a degree that Borchardt's unbounded admiration at times drifts towards unintelligibility.

Pater's decisive influence, however, was on Borchardt's translation of Plato's *Lysis*. The latter is modelled on Pater's conception of Plato, whom Borchardt also took to be a poet (Hummel 1987, 172). Thus for him, Plato had no system of thought, but was continually mediating between empirical reality and the realm of ideas. Mind and matter permeate one another, making the lofty universals gradually slide into corporeal shapes without removing the ontological difference; such an interweaving of the invisible and the visible makes Platonic ideas tangible, brings them to life, and allows perception of the imperceptible (Hummel 1987, 171–73). Thus it was Pater's sensuously conceived image of Plato that guided Borchardt's rendering of *Lysis*.

While translating, Borchardt avowed that Pater's *Greek Studies* were 'constantly open by my side' (Borchardt 1987, 48–49), and he was particularly taken by the essay 'The Age of Athletic Prizemen', which he quotes at great length in his essay 'On Form' that introduces the translation. What appeared to have fascinated Borchardt most was Pater's detailed exposition of the 'Discobulus at Rest', 'the veritable prince of that world of antique bronze and marble'. Borchardt ends this quotation with the sentence: 'He merited Revelation, something which should solace his heart in the inevitable fading of that visible world', and adds that he might use this 'simple and emotionally charged word' as a motto for 'my *Lysis*' (Borchardt 1987, 48–49). There is a plaintive note ringing in Pater's sentence, bemoaning the transience of artistic achievement, and this is exactly what Borchardt shared with him. This mutuality arose out of their common intention to resuscitate a sensuously conceived antiquity in order to reinvigorate the present.

Reference to Pater in German academic and scholarly writing is just as scanty as in German literature. He was barely mentioned in the syllabus of English studies in German universities, except occasionally in connection with Oscar Wilde, who eclipsed him. When scholars did refer to him, they reproduced his main tenets much as poets and writers are summed up in histories of literature. Friedrich Brie's early study *Ästhetische Weltanschauung in der Literatur des XIX. Jahrhunderts* (1921) is a case in point. Pater gets a couple of pages, which reproduce the 'Conclusion' and his view of art and literature, which is likened to that of the Goncourts and contrasted with that of Ruskin (Brie 1921, 67–69). In providing information for students or educated readers, the study is representative of most scholarly publications, and such informative presentations are not forms of reception.

This holds equally true for Hans Hecht's 'Walter Pater: eine Würdigung' (1927), written as a contribution to a journal, in an issue devoted to Renaissance studies. Although Hecht had translated *Plato and Platonism* into German and consulted Kassner (Kassner 1957, 1074) over certain difficulties, the piece is at best a paraphrase of Pater's work (Hecht 1927, 550–82). The very fact that a professor of English offers nothing but a rewording of Pater's writing is indicative of how little Pater was known in German academia. Thus information about him was something new which, if taken for an assessment of Pater, either reflects a scholarly backwardness, or an aloofness towards him that must have prevailed at the time.

The situation is somewhat different when Pater is invoked in order to authenticate scholarly statements. Ernst Robert Curtius, who developed the idea of an unbroken continuity of art and literature from antiquity to the Middle Ages in his *Europäische Literatur und Lateinisches Mittelalter* (1948) took Pater as the main witness for his thesis, which he characterized as follows: 'We do not need a storehouse of traditions, but a house in which we can breathe – a "House Beautiful which the creative minds of all generations are always building together" as Walter Pater has said', and then Curtius ends up by quoting the same line in English again (Curtius 1948, 400). Thus Pater is made to endorse Curtius' conception of continuity, which, however, means that the canon is not just augmented, but is also continuously reshuffled by the new work of art added to it. To such a conception, Pater's idea of the 'House Beautiful' bears eloquent witness. Furthermore, Pater appeared to have put his idea of assembling the great human accomplishments into practice by marshalling, in *Marius the Epicurean*, Stoic philosophy, Cyrenaicism and 'The Golden Book' of Amor and Psyche into a conflicting order, thus turning his own creative writing into a paradigm for the tension operative in canonicity (Curtius 1948, 403).[7]

Another instance of invoking Pater to confirm scholarly insight is Hugo Friedrich's conception of the 'essay' in his book on *Montaigne* (1949). Friedrich details the form of the essay as follows: 'The essay is the medium for a mode of writing that seeks to be not a result but a process, just like thinking, which here unfolds itself through writing. The special character of this particular type of thinking – scepticism – has found its ideal vehicle in the essay [. . .]. As scepticism replaces an overall view with the vision of the individual, the flexible essay opens itself up to the sensual and inner vision; it describes, narrates, articulates, and thus testifies to its capability of articulating truth more adequately and less imposingly than any discursive analysis is able to achieve' (Friedrich 1949, 430). In order to corroborate such a description, Pater's exposition of the essay in *Plato and Platonism* is quoted at length (Friedrich 1949, 443), with the claim that Pater was absolutely in harmony with Montaigne's attitude and manner of writing.[8] Little wonder since Montaigne was Pater's 'patron saint' of his intellectual activities!

What Friedrich and Curtius allow us to perceive is the authority Pater enjoyed in scholarly circles after the Second World War in Germany. The authentication he was meant to provide is all the more remarkable as both Friedrich and Curtius were professors of Romance philology and did not have to concern themselves with him at all. This would have been the province of professors of English.

The intellectual climate in postwar Germany was dominated by existentialism, which had repercussions on the study of literature. Literary criticism served to translate a past into terms of a present, and so it was inevitable that present interests should govern and indeed condition the framework of interpretation. The mid 1950s saw the decline of the life-and-letters and history-of-ideas approaches as guidelines for criticism, and witnessed in their wake the flourishing of New Criticism with its devotion to close reading, which was as widespread then as Deconstruction is now.

In the 1950s a monograph on an author's complete works entailed using the classic form of scholarly positivism in order to bring out one's own intention by shattering the conventions of the genre. Instead of an accumulation of

---

[7]   An early indication of Curtius' assessment of Pater is to be found in a letter which he wrote to Georg Lukács on 11 November 1912 after having received Lukács's book *Die Seele und die Formen*. He criticizes Lukács for his dogmatism and continues by saying 'Pater does not fit into your schema', which identifies the essayist with the critic, not least as Lukács – according to Curtius – seems to consider the essay as a prefiguration of metaphysics (Lukács 1982, 302).

[8]   Burdorf (2001, 310–19) gives a detailed account of Pater's conception of form: Pater has set the guidelines for developing a cultural criticism in essayistic form in Germany (310). His *Renaissance* was a highly sophisticated attempt to grasp the world through artistic form, and this made a lasting impact on a 'vitalistic approach to form in Germany' (318).

factual data – more often than not compiled for their own sake – and a record of the history and environment of an author and his sources, the focus shifted to the aesthetic dimension of the work. If the latter came under scrutiny, then inevitably the interpretation veered towards a New Critical approach, which sought to strip the work of all the extraneous factors and grasp it as an autonomous object.

Caught between this Scylla and Charybdis of literary criticism, I found myself attracted to the figure of Walter Pater (Iser 1960/1987).[9] An analysis of his work seemed to promise experience of what it meant to make Art the ultimate value of finite existence. Such an experience would bring to light the problems that New Criticism could not cope with, since it was no longer concerned with the consequences of the autonomous object. Pater dealt precisely with these problems, because for him Art was an ultimate value, enabling human beings to forget the pressure of finite human existence. Autonomous Art and real life joined hands, as it were, under the table – a relationship that could only be anathema to the basic principles of New Criticism. And so, by analysing Pater's work, I hoped to uncover what had been glossed over by New Criticism, and had thus ultimately caused its demise as a paradigm of interpretation.

Anyone whose life is devoted to Art lives aesthetically. Therefore, Pater's work can be read almost as a blueprint for the aesthetic existence, which he attempts to illuminate. I borrowed the necessary heuristics from Kierkegaard, especially *Either/Or* – that penetrating analysis of all romanticism – though with the reservation that the aesthetic existence was not to be viewed as a sign or even as a preliminary stage of any other form of existence. In order to give shape to the constituent elements of aesthetic life, I tried to interpret Pater through Pater by applying his own hermeneutic principle of the 'spiritual form' to himself. 'Spiritual form' is a kind of Aristotelian *morphe* that Pater seeks to detect in every phenomenon, thus allowing him to grasp the perceivable aspects as a manifestation of this concealed form. It is a principle that he practises with great virtuosity, and by applying it to Pater himself I hoped to lay bare the 'spiritual form' of his own writings. This proved to be the aesthetic moment – the basic constituent of the aesthetic existence, which he so incessantly propagated and which, being the root of all his work, was something that he could not pull to the surface himself, for a transcendental stance towards oneself would mean transcending the aesthetic existence.

If with hindsight I can now say that my approach sometimes seems rather intrinsic, this is because I was striving not to impose a systematic and hence alien frame of reference on an unsystematic and richly faceted body of work. To have done so would have eliminated the vast range of nuances produced by the Paterian brand of repetition. The aesthetic existence, narcissistically turned upon itself and yet unable to sustain this fixation, seems to require viewing from standpoints outside itself, but to do this would have meant blotting out all inherent problems – especially if one were to use the Kierkegaardian reference of the ethical decision or the religious renunciation

---

9   The fact that I had written a monograph on Pater was the reason I was asked by the editor of the volume, Professor Stephen Bann, to write this account.

of the self, not to mention the condemnation the aesthetic existence would have suffered if viewed from a sociological angle. Thus my focal point was the aesthetic moment, and as a result I perhaps unjustifiably neglected those elements of the work that might be taken as pointers to the cultural situation of Pater's time.

In historical terms, then, my monograph may be taken to reflect the problems of literary criticism in the 1950s. On the one hand, I was trying to free literature from being taken as evidence for anything other than itself, so that I could focus on its own specific qualities; on the other, I wanted to show, through Pater's work, what was entailed in the concept of autonomous art. Today these aspects have faded into the background, and what was at the time not of prime significance for me now seems to link my study (which is over forty years old) with a problem whose importance is far greater than I had envisaged – namely, the idea of legitimation. Pater's urgent need to legitimize autonomous art sprang from the instability of the aesthetic existence, which he was eager to underpin. Even though the aesthetic existence is nowadays identified with aestheticism – the final fling of a now all but defunct bourgeois culture – the idea of legitimation is still a burning issue. For Pater, legitimation was still not abstract but concrete, since he believed that history and myth were guidelines that give solid foundation to the enhanced moment. His very search for such legitimation shows that he had anticipated a problem that was to become crucial for the twentieth century, with its crisis of legitimation spreading further and further afield, and plaguing social and ideological orders as well as the arts. Pater's concern, though, was to remove instability, and to this end he mobilized the entire past. His invocation of history and myth sought to elevate the intensified moment into a lifeline for the aesthetic existence, thus indicating a change in the function of legitimation. In the past, world pictures had provided orientation, whereas Pater set out to justify both the transitoriness and the in-between state of the aesthetic existence by making the totality of the human past subservient to this end, thus inverting the idea of legitimation. Instead of providing a framework under which cultural and social activities had to be subsumed, legitimation now applied itself to private longings. It is this aspect of Pater's work rather than his elucidation of the aesthetic existence that makes him more interesting for us today. What haunted twentieth-century thought – a search for an all-embracing legitimation bearing out the diversified intellectual commitments, social requirements and multiple ideologies – Pater had anticipated in his own way, and to this extent he is a figure of transition in a sense quite different from that which I had discerned some forty years ago.

Equally important was Pater's attempt to use literary fiction in order to overcome difficulties that had proved to be insurmountable for literary criticism. Criticism is hedged in by reference to which its statements are connected, whereas literary fiction crosses the boundaries marked by these frames. The boundary-crossing potential of fiction is actualised when referential writing runs up against its inherent limitations. This is borne out in Pater's writings: whenever he reaches an impasse regarding history and myth as sanctions for his ideas, fiction continues the thread, exploring the reasons for failure by imagining situations in which an aesthetic life might – but never does – achieve the longed-for unity with itself. Where cognitive criticism comes to an end, literature begins, for fiction alone can stage that which is inaccessible to referential discourse.

Although Pater remains deeply rooted in the nineteenth century, and so is usually classified as a Late Romantic, there can be no doubt that his work prefigured the problems that have become dominant in our time. Our interest no longer lies in what he represented so much as in what he might have anticipated. Did he throw light – and if so, how much – on issues that are now current? If the human mind's relation to truth is dependent on the form of discourse chosen, as detailed in *Plato and Platonism*, then he did indeed open up an issue that has become prominent in our time – namely, what actually happens in interpretation (Iser 1995, 42–60). Pater provided, almost in a nutshell, an anatomy of interpretation and, even more importantly, he fed his insights back into his own writings, thus splitting them up into a diversity of differently operating discourses. Each interpretation translates something into a different register or, as Pater has phrased it: 'Well! all language involves translation from inward to outward' (Pater 1920a, 34). If that is so, then a space opens up when something is translated into something else. As each act of interpretation creates such a space, its intent will realize itself in the way in which this space is negotiated. If interpretation is primarily a form of translation, clearly it is dependent on what is translated, and Pater was well aware of this when he stated, 'methods of writing are [...] determined directly by matter' (Pater 1920b, 175). How Pater practised interpretation as modes of translatability is revealed by his different 'methods of writing'. What makes him exemplary for current concerns is his rejection of axioms and definitions as starting points of interpretation. Instead, he prefers to measure the distance caused by any transposition of something into something else, and by incorporating that distance into his own interpretations, he developed modalities of handling this space that anticipated modern forms of interpretation, ranging from the hermeneutic circle to the cybernetic loop. Thus Pater emerges from the shadows to which his aesthetic label has so long confined him.

Pater's role in German letters and scholarly writings was marginal. Appreciating him required not only a classical education, but also a commitment to Greek and Roman culture in one's own writings. Hence it was the scholar-artist who related to Pater. This relationship is marked by two tendencies: (1) It was the sensuously conceived antiquity that appealed to German writers, who modelled their understanding, especially that of Plato, in terms set by Pater. (2) It was a reawakening of a distant but glorious past in order to reinvigorate the present that made Pater into a point of reference for German writers. These tendencies were basically anti-modernistic as proclaimed by Borchardt's 'kreative Restauration' (creative restoration).[10]

Pater's erudition and its artistic presentation did not concern German scholars to any considerable extent, and at best he figured as an authority if one needed corroborative evidence for one's own ideas. This, however, shows that Pater, the scholar, provided multiple answers to a heterogeneous set of problems, and these answers have not become obsolete over time. His

---

[10]   For details see Breuer 1995, 153–54, and Schmidt 2003, 39–43.

aestheticism was never considered as paradigmatic. His reticence, discipline and fastidiousness were not exactly in keeping with the notoriety and flamboyance of the aesthetic attitude, which is why in German circles Oscar Wilde eclipsed him. Finally, as reception is always context-bound, it is revealing that Pater's writings appear to illuminate important issues even when contexts change.

7 'Time Flowing and Time Suspended': Hofmannsthal's Variations on a Paterian Theme

Ulrike Stamm

Hugo von Hofmannsthal's work is characterized by intensive reading and by his attempt to come to terms with the long tradition of literature. In the process of discovering himself as an 'heir' of European culture,[1] he absorbed texts from all European literatures in his work and assimilated them into his own mode of writing, spurred by his own imaginative impetus.[2] Michael Hamburger describes this receptive process in the following way: 'Hofmannsthal was one of those poets who, in a roundabout way, come back to themselves, armed with means which have become their own organs: the works of other people which Hofmannsthal experienced through reading were part of these detours, and Hofmannsthal made them part of his work, as with everything that he had experienced'.[3] Accordingly his work is full of reminiscences on and influences from different European authors.

Walter Pater constitutes one of the major sources that played a part in the formation of his work and thought. After Shakespeare he is probably Hofmannsthal's most important counterpart among English authors.[4] Yet for a long time Pater's influence on Hofmannsthal was seen purely in connection

---

[1] The famous poem 'Lebenslied' ('Song of Life'), which starts with the equally famous line 'Den Erben lasst verschwenden' ('The heir may freely spend'), can be read as an illustration of this position (Hofmannsthal 1961, 17; trans. Arthur Davidson).

[2] For a discussion of this subject see Hamburger 1961.

[3] 'Hofmannsthal war einer dieser Dichter, die auf Umwegen zu sich selber zurückkehren, mit Mitteln bewaffnet, die ihre Organe geworden sind: zu den Umwegen gehörten die Werke anderer Menschen, die Hofmannsthal lesend erlebte, darum auch wie alles Erlebte in das eigene Werk aufnahm' (Hamburger 1961, 76).

[4] Even though the number of quotations should not be overestimated, and even though Richard Exner's *Index Nominum* could not take into account the great quantity of Hofmannsthal's unpublished works, the number of quotations that he gives for individual authors still acts as a useful indication of Hofmannsthal's interest in a writer and are therefore repeated here: Rossetti 5, Ruskin 6, Wilde 7, Browning 8, Keats 8, Shelley 10, Swinburne 10, Pater 11 (Exner 1976).

with the latter's interest in and discussion of Aestheticism; it was assumed that Hofmannsthal had read Pater only in his early years, and that Pater's ideas played no further role in Hofmannsthal's later works. But when one looks at the reading dates recorded in the surviving works by Pater in Hofmannsthal's library, and the Pater quotations throughout the huge bulk of his unpublished works, one discovers that Pater's work in fact represented a significant source of intellectual exchange over the different periods of Hofmannsthal's writing.[5]

In the essay that follows, I want to pursue the main strand of the relationship between these two writers. I take 'influence' not as a tangible gift that is handed over from one writer to the other, but as something more like a pervasive connection that tends to act as a reinforcement of the receiving writer's ideas, and thus depends very much on a correspondence or affinity between the two writers. As a consequence, influence in this sense does not lead a writer to use different ideas or images after reading a certain work. In the case of Hofmannsthal and Pater there is indeed a general 'congeniality of temperament' (Weiss 1973, 162), so that influence should be seen as more like a mirroring whereby one author finds an incentive in the work of another to discuss similar questions and ideas, and as a consequence moves towards a deeper understanding of his own impetus and motivation.

Concentrating on the main points of reference that one discovers in the quotations, it becomes clear that Hofmannsthal was especially interested in Pater's representation of and questions surrounding time, his notion of subjectivity[6] and his theoretical ideas on aesthetics. In this essay I want to focus on the subject of time and its importance to both authors. I will start by briefly summarizing the different works by Pater that Hofmannsthal read, continue with a presentation of Pater's 'Conclusion' to *The Renaissance*, and conclude by following up the echoes of this text in Hofmannsthal's work.

---

[5]   Two contemporaries of Hofmannsthal already saw Pater's influence as a decisive one, providing evidence of Pater's wider influence on modern literature. One is Rudolf Borchardt, one of the most enthusiastic readers of Pater in Germany and also a close friend of Hofmannsthal. In 1939 he wrote in an article commemorating Pater's hundredth birthday: 'Der Wiederaufbau der deutschen Prosa durch Hofmannsthal ist ohne ihn [Pater] nicht denkbar; seit den letzten Jahren des Jahrhunderts zieht in den Jugendschriften diese richtende Spur' (Borchardt 1960, 421). The second critic who pointed out a more general correspondence between Hofmannsthal and Pater was Charles Du Bos, who in a letter to Hofmannsthal in 1925 sees Pater as the ideal critic to analyse the work of Hofmannsthal: 'I still bathe [...] in the atmosphere which is yours, but it would have required Pater – my model, my friend, my "assistant" for all time – in order to evoke it truly ('Je baigne encore [...] dans l'atmosphère qui est vôtre, mais dont il aurait fallu Pater – mon modèle, mon ami, mon "assistant" de toujours – pour la pouvoir vraiment évoquer' (1929, 303).

[6]   On this topic see Stamm 1997b.

1

Hofmannsthal read Pater for the first time in the spring of 1894, though he was probably already acquainted with Pater's work through the writings of Oscar Wilde.[7] The first works by Pater that he read in 1894 were *The Renaissance, Imaginary Portraits* and *Marius the Epicurean*, as demonstrated by the essay 'Walter Pater' which he wrote for *Die Zeit*, a journal owned by his friend Hermann Bahr. Unfortunately the notes on reading dates in Hofmannsthal's library only start after 1902, which is after he had married and moved to Rodaun. Nevertheless, they indicate that he subsequently read nearly all of Pater's works, and some of them several times, for example *Greek Studies* in 1904 and 1911, in connection with his work on the drama *Pentheus*. He didn't own *Imaginary Portraits* (though by 1894 he had clearly read the book), *Gaston de Latour* or *Essays from the Guardian*. The copy of *The Renaissance* from 1904 contains no reading dates or underlinings, which shows that this work was not so important for him after the turn of the century. Obviously he had also possessed a copy of *Marius the Epicurean*, which he had lent to Leopold von Andrian during the 1890s and wanted back in 1919 in order to work on a text concerning the 'Verschwörung des Catilina' ('Conspiracy of Catiline', Hofmannsthal 1968, 304).

He must have read part of Pater's *Miscellaneous Studies* not later than 1902, as he refers to Pater's concept of 'Diaphaneitè', which became very important to him. In 1906 he read 'The Child in the House' from *Miscellaneous Studies*. In 1905 he read Pater's *Appreciations* while working on his essay 'Shakespeares Könige und große Herren' ('Shakespeare's Kings and Noblemen'). Besides this repeated but intermittent reading of texts by Pater, Hofmannsthal's interest in, and reflection on, Paterian ideas is also demonstrated by the thirty or so Paterian quotations to be found in his work. These facts have only come to light in the context of research on the whole corpus of material, which is still in the process of publication as part of the critical edition of Hofmannsthal's work.[8]

2

From the late nineteenth century onwards literature and thought are characterized by the fact that the notion of time had become problematic. This was partly due to the loss of the notion of a metaphysical order, that in former times had offered an eternal timelessness as a solution to the problem of the transience of being, but was now no longer accessible to most writers. Of equal importance was the view that the linearity of time and its irreversible orientation towards a goal had been lost to a large extent (Wendorff 1980). This implied that the dimension of the present had lost its clear position on the

---

[7]   For the precise dates of Hofmannsthal's reading and the connection these readings had with his various plans see Stamm 1997a, 12.

[8]   Exner's *Index Nominum zu Hugo von Hofmannsthals Gesammelten Werken* refers only to the edition of Hofmannsthal's work by Hugo Steiner, and was written without access to the many unpublished notes. See Stamm 1997a, 1–17.

line between a past that was definitely over and a future that was still to come, which in turn meant that the present became an unreliable concept and could not provide a clear direction in relation to the other dimensions of time. It also entailed the loss of the notion of a calculable continuity of time binding together past, present and future as elements in one temporal chain, and acting as an antidote to time's transitoriness. The different dimensions of time became isolated and interchangeable (Kohlschmidt 1965).

All these factors thus contributed to an increased consciousness of the transitoriness of time, accompanied by a disorientation with regard to time's different dimensions. As a result of the loss of continuity, greater importance was placed on the moment itself, insofar as it offered the last concrete access to reality. But at the same time the moment was apt to dissolve into the dimension of the past which – beginning with Romanticism – had become the dimension that gained most attention.

With the loss of continuity and the subsequent isolation of the different dimensions of time, the concept of simultaneity of time became prominent in philosophy and literature. Thus Henri Bergson criticized the supposed objectivity of time measured mathematically, and as an answer he developed, under the heading of 'la durée' (duration), a concept of time that retains the past and preserves time's different dimensions. Time for Bergson is a complex layering, in which the dimensions of time and space cannot be neatly separated, but are united by a movement that not only creates space but also forms the basis of temporal succession. So time as succession is not transitoriness, but 'the successive construction of a quality within a presence, in which even though results happen, no concept of earlier or later can be discerned. This succession is at the same time transformed into simultaneity'.[9] The concept of 'la durée' implies a successive building up of a quality within a present. It is crucial that simultaneity in this context is not thought of as a stasis or 'standstill', but as a sort of moving spatial entity that is ideally realized in a new concept of the work of art.

I have given this short outline of modern thought about time as a background for my analysis of how Pater and Hofmannsthal approached the matter, since to a large extent their works reflect this critical notion of time. Pater's 'Conclusion' to *The Renaissance* is a radical analysis of modern thought that points inevitably to an increased consciousness of the transitoriness of object and subject alike – an analysis that he took up again and revised in his novel *Marius the Epicurean*. And Hofmannsthal's reflections on time span his whole career, from his first drama with the suggestive title 'Gestern' ('Yesterday') right up to his late autobiographical notes 'Ad me Ipsum', in which he says: 'Two antinomies had to be solved: the one between time flowing and duration'.[10] In order to be able to analyse Hofmannsthal's reaction

---

[9]   'sukzessives Aufbauen einer Qualität innerhalb einer Präsenz, in der zwar Folgen statthaben, aber kein Früher oder Später unterscheidbar ist. Diese Sukzession ist zugleich aufgehoben in eine Simultaneität'(Kümmel 1962, 17).

[10]   'zwei Antinomien waren zu lösen: die der vergehenden zeit und der Dauer' (Hofmannsthal 1980, 613). On the importance of the transitoriness of being for Hofmannsthal's work see Fülleborn 1992, 170.

towards Pater's argumentation in 'The Conclusion', I intend first to summarize Pater's main ideas as they are presented in this key text of Modernism.

3

Pater's 'Conclusion' is concerned with the analysis of the effects that the passage of time, demonstrated by modern science to be the primary fact of life, has on cognition and action. In the first two paragraphs Pater writes from the perspective of modern science 'staging "the passage and dissolution" of mind, body, soul, self, and text' (Williams 1989, 13). In the ensuing paragraphs, which are based on these premises, he draws his conclusion on the subject, and devises a kind of aesthetic attitude in response to the challenges of modern thought.

According to Pater, modern science has increased the feeling of transitoriness by presenting outward life as a continual combination of elements and forces that leaves no room for any notion of stability, whether it be the stability of an individual body or the stability of clear outlines. These are revealed to be 'but an image of ours [. . .] a design in a web, the actual threads of which pass out beyond it' (Pater 1902, 234). As science presents subject and object as only provisional configurations in an endless movement, everything is dominated by the passage of time. In paragraphs three to five, where Pater addresses the assumptions of modern science, he does not deny the effects of the passage of time, that is to say, the loss of all coherence of form and the fragmentation of the subject. As an answer, he proposes an ethics of attention in which aesthetic form is always realized for the moment only: 'Every moment some form grows perfect in hand or face' (Pater 1902, 236). Being attentive to these moments of focus means being mobile, always moving with the shifting focus; on the other hand, it also means being concentrated and intense, thus enabling the subject to expand the moment: 'For our one chance lies in expanding that interval, in getting as many pulsations as possible into the given time' (Pater 1902, 238).

Pater therefore propounds a kind of programme for dealing with the passage of time, which he also illustrates by working with different key images. The images of the stream and of the flame are the prominent figures for representing movement. Pater talks about the flame-like quality of our life, seeing in 'the inward world of thought and feeling [. . .] the flame more eager and devouring' (Pater 1902, 234), and referring to the 'impressions which burn and are extinguished' (Pater 1902, 235). The second image for the passage of time, the image of water, is introduced at the beginning of his analysis of physical life. He starts in a situation of recoil from the watery flood; this image is continually repeated, in expressions such as 'elements and currents', 'whirlpool', 'race of the midstream', 'flood of external objects', and other general images of passage. However – and this is important – in a seemingly contradictory way Pater has a third dominant metaphor, which tends to represent the spatial aspect, namely the 'web' or the 'weaving'. This different notion of time's workings is first alluded to in the assumption that 'that clear, perpetual outline is [. . .] but a design in a web, the actual threads of which pass out beyond it' (Pater 1902, 234). Here time is not the stream that runs on continually and dissolves everything, but an endless structure that – even though we glimpse the outline only for a moment before it dissolves again – remains intact. The configuration and the focus inside the structure change, but the net represents a stable and continuous reality, containing everything within its already completed space.

These more spatial aspects of time are also alluded to in the final words of the second paragraph, where Pater talks about 'that strange, perpetual weaving and unweaving of ourselves' (Pater 1902, 236). Here the passage of time, the temporal, is combined with a spatial figure expressing the way in which the working of time produces a kind of structure. In this case, then, the passage of time is not represented as transitoriness but as a construction, one that is nonetheless followed by a deconstruction, implying yet another construction that involves new configurations of elements and forces.

So time is presented in two complementary ways: on the one hand, we find the stream of time dissolving outward objects but also loosening the inner reality into a group of unrelated impressions; on the other hand, time is presented as a kind of moving structure that lies replete with all possible configurations, and assembles experience into a greater whole. The three images or metaphors that depict the action of time in Pater's 'Conclusion' illustrate completely opposite concepts of temporality. Whereas the first two stand for the movement of time and the continual process, the third points to the constructive work of time, building larger and larger structures and offering simultaneity instead of development.

However, the opposition of these two notions of time is not the final point of Pater's argument. His essay finally connects those two strands: temporal versus spatial concepts of time and process versus structure. In the famous appeal '[t]o burn always with this hard gem-like flame, to maintain this ecstasy' (Pater 1902, 236), which is, as Carolyn Williams states, 'the culminating moment in Pater's transvaluation of "modern thought"' (1989, 29), Pater creates a picture that combines both stasis and movement. The question of how man should react to the passage of time is answered by this paradoxical figure. Pater calls for a kind of existence that connects adjustment to the passage of time with an intensification of experience. Whereas the inconsistency and instability of the flame represent the mobility of character, the opposite aspects of the unchanging, almost eternal stability of the jewel stand for the intensification and concentration of experience. With this image Pater seems to suggest that intensity can come close to a kind of congealment: his image implies that the formerly fragmented experience is on the brink of materializing into something hard and solid like a jewel, not an object of transitoriness but, on the contrary, an emblem of stability.

The ethical method that Pater selects as a reaction to the passage of time calls then for a combination of the opposed aspects of time, namely process and structure. Carolyn Williams has stated that this dichotomy of process and structure, and 'the effort to forge a dynamic interaction – and a philosophically coherent interaction – between these two aspects' (Williams 1997, 147), is a fundamental aspect of Pater's whole work. In accordance with this interpretation, it is the thesis of this essay that both Pater and Hofmannsthal, in a seemingly contradictory way, present time as process and also as structure, and that it is their goal to combine these two contradictory views. The image of the 'hard, gem-like flame' is, in its modernity – its uniting of opposites in one central vision – one of Pater's main figures for the interaction of spatial and temporal aspects. But in this case we do not have 'a philosophically coherent interaction' as in other texts by Pater, but a paradoxical expression, where he steps out of the frame of rational argumentation and replaces it with a visual image.

Finally, I want to look at the status of the subject in this constellation. Pater makes it clear that the subject realizing this ecstasy does not gain solidity and stability, but remains in the process of ever new formations and configurations. The aesthetic subject that Pater proposes is thus characterized by its self-division. By continually changing its focus the self remains always outside its former selves, in a position from which it can regard itself in retrospect. In this position, as Williams makes clear (1989, 29), it also breaks free from the spatial figure of the prison that Pater evoked in his famous description of 'each mind keeping as a solitary prisoner its own dream of a world' (Pater 1902, 235). Mobility and self-division imply that the self gains only a temporary coherence in the moment of retrospection. In this way Pater modernizes and temporalizes the romantic figure of self-division.

Because the self can regain its wholeness temporarily in connection with a position of retrospection, the past becomes the main dimension for the art critic and the aesthetic subject. This is one of the points where Pater's analysis supports the modern concept of time. Other aspects of his reflections on time also coincide with the modern concept of time, in particular those involving the loss of temporal continuity (which, in the 'Conclusion', is dissolved by time's rapidity), the exceptional significance of the single moment, and the effort to think of time as simultaneity. But the important difference in Pater's writings – and the one that marks the greatest point of divergence from Bergson – lies in his creation of a kind of programme to accommodate the passage of time, and at the same time to achieve at least a temporary coherence in the moments of aesthetic experience.

4

Hofmannsthal definitely read Pater's 'Conclusion' in 1894, and this reading marked his first encounter with the author. Echoes of this text and of its arguments can be found in a number of his works. The first echo is in his famous three poems 'Terzinen'('Stanzas in Terza Rima'), written between 25 and 30 July 1894, precisely when Hofmannsthal started reading Pater. The fact that in the handwritten draft the first poem has the quotation from Heraclitus cited in Pater's 'Conclusion' as a heading is further proof that Pater's text was on his mind while he was writing these poems. I shall therefore interpret them as a transcription of, and a response to, Pater's 'Conclusion'.

The title and subject of the first poem is the transitory nature of life on which Hofmannsthal reflects from different perspectives. The poem starts with the evocation 'Noch spür ich ihren Atem auf den Wangen' ('Still on my cheek I feel their warm breath fall', Hofmannsthal 1961, 29),[11] which invokes

---

[11]   'Noch spür ich ihren Atem auf den Wangen' (Hofmannsthal 1984, 45).

a kind of bodily remembrance. Against the flow of time, memory keeps experience alive without being able to stop this flow. But this ability of memory to contain a bodily 'relic' of the past experience is only short-lived, and the movement of the poem in the next verse leads towards a re-enforcement of the notion of transitoriness, condensed in the last line of the second verse which states: 'That all flows by us, leaving us behind' (Hofmannsthal 1961, 29).[12] In the third verse the perspective turns again toward the lyrical subject, complaining about its own transitoriness and the ensuing estrangement of the 'self' from its own former versions: 'And that unhindered my own self could flow/Out of a little child whom now I find/Remote as a dumb dog, and scarcely know' (Hofmannsthal 1961, 29).[13] Here we find the same figure of self-division that was so important for Pater's aesthetic solution to the problems of modern thought, but now the self is divided over longer periods of time, and the difference opens up between the child and the grown-up self. From the perspective of the grown-up self the child is compared to the dog, introduced here as a symbol of strangeness and muteness. The development from child to adult is understood not as a process of growth but actually as a loss, leading to a complete difference between former and later selves. Retrospection does not lead to a temporary constitution of the self, but to a feeling of complete estrangement. Here again the passage of time and its transitoriness loosens all feeling of continuity, so that the self can only see its different versions as unconnected fragments.

In an astonishing way the fourth verse turns the whole argument around, thereby producing a change which most commentators have ignored. Whereas the movement of time up to this point encompassed everything, the focus of complaint now is the unchanging continuity of elements that leads to a close affinity of the self with its past: 'that in lives a century old I share/And kinsmen laid in coffins long ago/Are yet as close to me as my own hair' (Hofmannsthal 1961, 29).[14] One wonders why the passage of time suddenly seems to have collapsed and become static, leaving everything intact. Now time is seemingly suspended, so that there is no movement, no development but only an everlasting reality. In the last line the poem reinforces this notion of continuity, transforming it even into an all-encompassing unity: 'Are no less one with me than my own hair' (Hofmannsthal 1961, 29).[15] This presupposes a 'standstill' of time. Both notions of time – the passage of time and the frozen standstill of time – are bemoaned as being 'far too terrifying for lament' (Hofmannsthal 1961, 29),[16] indicating that this poem does not arrive at a positive answer to the transitoriness of life.

---

[12] 'Daß alles gleitet und vorrüberrinnt' (Hofmannsthal 1984, 45).

[13] 'Und daß mein eignes Ich, durch nichts gehemmt/Herüberglitt aus einem kleinen Kind/Mir wie ein Hund unheimlich stumm und fremd' (Hofmannsthal 1984, 45).

[14] 'daß ich auch vor hundert Jahren war/Und meine Ahnen, die im Totenhemd,/Mit mir verwandt sind wie mein eignes Haar' (Hofmannsthal 1984, 45).

[15] 'So eins mit mir als wie mein eignes Haar' (Hofmannsthal 1984, 45).

[16] 'viel zu grauenvoll, als daß man klage' (Hofmannsthal 1984, 45).

One of Hofmannsthal's notes might help us to understand the change between the third and the fourth verse: 'we are neither more closely nor more directly one with our "self" of ten years ago than we are with the body of our mother. Eternal physical continuity. To see clearly: we are one with everything that exists and has ever existed, nothing secondary, nothing excluded.'[17] This sounds like a radicalized version, or a development, of the Paterian concept of inextricable interrelation illustrated in the following passage: 'Far out on every side of us those elements are broadcast, driven in many currents, and birth and gesture and death and the springing of violets from the grave are but a few out of ten thousand resultant combinations' (Pater 1902, 234). The fact that Hofmannsthal refers to eternal physical continuity clearly shows that he is thinking in terms of material elements and forces, rather than in terms of idealistic interrelations.

Reading Hofmannsthal's note against the background of Pater's 'Conclusion' provides insights into the movement of his poem. If the subject is assumed to be a process resulting from a permanent combination of elements, then an interrelation exists between everything. Consequently the self is no more nor less identical with its former 'self' than with its mother. In contrast to Pater, Hofmannsthal places a greater emphasis on the fact that this play of combinations forms a principle of unity.

But the point of comparison that Hofmannsthal chooses in order to demonstrate the great gap between the self and its former selves is highly ambivalent: it appears natural that a mother should be nearer to a person than other, more unrelated objects. So, in this example, Hofmannsthal weakens his own argument for an all-encompassing unity and leaves open the question of how near or far the affinity is that he wants to demonstrate. As a result the

---

17   'wir sind mit unserm Ich von Vor-10-Jahren nicht näher unmittelbarer eins als mit dem Leib unserer Mutter. Ewige physische Continuität. Den Gedanken scharf fassen: wir sind eins mit allem was ist und was je war, kein Nebending, von nichts ausgeschlossen' (Hofmannsthal 1984, 230). This note is very similar to a note written under the influence of Ernst Mach in 1891: 'We have no consciousness besides the moment because each of our souls only lives for one moment. Memory belongs only to the body: it seems to reproduce the past, that means it produces something similarly new in the mood. My "self" of *yesterday* concerns me as little as the "self" of Goethe or Napoleon.' ('Wir haben kein Bewusstsein über den Augenblick hinaus, weil jede unsrer Seelen nur einen Augenblick lebt. Das Gedächtnis gehört nur dem Körper: er reproduziert scheinbar das Vergangene, d.h. er erzeugt ein ähnliches Neues in der Stimmung: Mein Ich von *gestern* geht mich so wenig an wie das Ich Napoleons oder Goethes' (Hofmannsthal 1980, 333). This note makes clear that the notion of time devouring reality was very prominent around the turn of the century, and Pater's 'Conclusion' could easily be understood as a similar statement. The difference between those two quotations refers to Hofmannsthal's break with literary impressionism, which was characteristic of his early works. It is possible that this development was provoked by the argument in Pater's 'Conclusion', which enabled Hofmannsthal to see the movement of time as a process forming ever new combinations, which are all interconnected and therefore lead to a new form of unity.

status of similarity or difference cannot actually be decided upon, as it is in a state of permanent oscillation.

The same ambivalence characterizes the comparisons in the poem, and the assessment of time as transitoriness or as stasis depends on the interpretation of these comparisons. They are also built on a play between similarity and difference: the dog is referred to as an example of estrangement, whereas the hair is used as an example of proximity and affinity. But both examples are ambivalent: the dog is the animal closest to man and calls, as Renate Böschenstein has argued, 'for a totally different, "befriended" relationship between the Outer Self and this fundamental principle'.[18] The hair also calls for a different interpretation, because as a symbol of sexuality it refers to the energy of life; it is not necessarily something strange, but on the contrary something very near. With their openness and non-distinguishable nature, these comparisons stand in stark contrast both to the relentless passage of time as well as to its equally menacing stasis.

Compared to Pater's 'Conclusion', Hofmannsthal's poem does not express movement, even though the passage of time is continually a focus of complaint. The transition from time moving to time standing still seems like the sudden turn of a switch. This impression is heightened by the static character of the points of comparison that encompass just three different positions: that of the child, of the ancestors and of the self. The more or less static juxtaposition, and opposition, of the three positions in time is emphasized in the last line, evoking the stasis of a complete unity, so that the poem ends with an image of the total stasis of time. Only the different successive comparisons bring a kind of oscillation and openness into the poem.

The second poem of the three 'Terzinen' also deals with transitoriness, but now with reference to young girls who feel that their lives are flowing out of their limbs into the surrounding trees and grass. This situation repeats the Paterian passage about the concurrence of forces, and illustrates again the inextricable interrelation of everything. But now it is transposed into the subdued atmosphere of the *fin de siècle* with its quiet, pale and smiling girls.

The third poem, 'Wir sind aus solchem Zeug wie das zu Träumen' ('We are such stuff as dreams are made on', Hofmannsthal 1961, 3; trans. Michael Hamburger)[19] deals more intensively with the relationship between change and unity. But now it is in the sphere of the dream that these questions are dealt with. Here, in contrast to the other two poems of 'Terzinen', movement is interpreted as a beginning, not as an end, and the dream in particular is characterized by means of various textual strategies as a form of beginning, introducing novelty: 'Our dreams as suddenly open wide their eyes/As little children under cherry-trees' (Hofmannsthal 1961, 31).[20] In accordance with this world of beginning, the quietly gliding motion of the moon that dominates the first three verses, and creates the magical atmosphere of the

---

[18] 'zu einem ganz andern, "befreundeten" Verhältnis zwischen dem Mantel-Ich und diesem fundamentalen Prinzip' (Böschenstein 1990, 88).

[19] 'Wir sind aus solchem Zeug wie das zu Träumen' (Hofmannsthal 1984, 47).

[20] 'Und Träume schlagen so die Augen auf/Wie kleine Kinder unter Kirschenbäumen' (Hofmannsthal 1984, 47).

poem, stands in stark contrast to the passage of time interpreted as transitoriness in the former poems. The flux of time has been transformed into the movement of the dream, leading into a new world.

The fourth verse seems like a concentration of Paterian formulations from the 'Conclusion'. The picture of 'each mind keeping as a solitary prisoner its own dream of a world' (Pater 1902, 235) is transformed into the description of the self harbouring the dreams in its innermost being: 'Our inmost life is open to their weaving;/Like ghostly hands in a locked room they teem/Within us, always living and conceiving' (Hofmannsthal 1961, 31).[21] In both formulations the dream is at the core of the human being, which appears as a room closed off from the outer world, whereas the subject is constituted by the 'Weben' (weaving), echoing Pater's formulation of 'that strange, perpetual weaving and unweaving of ourselves' (Pater 1902, 236). But again Hofmannsthal transforms the Paterian image, so that in the poem – contrary to Pater's 'Conclusion' – the dreams become the subject of the whole poem and the human being is the room in which these dreams appear and weave. Furthermore the word 'dream' has changed its meaning: whereas for Pater the 'dream' carries the danger of solipsism and unreality, it becomes a positive key-term in Hofmannsthal's poem, being understood as a possibility for realizing a new beginning.

Here we see a decisive difference between Pater and Hofmannsthal: Pater's assertion that 'what we have to do is to be forever curiously testing new opinions and courting new impressions' (Pater 1902, 237) calls for novelty as a means to expand the moment, whereas Hofmannsthal abstains from this call for novelty and delegates this engine of renewal to the dream, thereby surrendering to the dream's unreality.

It is important to notice that although the dreams here are connected with a new beginning, they are also connected with the past. As Steven Sondrup has convincingly shown, the term 'Geisterhände' ('ghostly hands') must be understood as 'agents of the continuing presence of the past' (Sondrup 1989, 198). Therefore the past is also contained in the sphere of dreams, not as dead memory but as a source of beginnings, as Hofmannsthal makes clear with the formulation 'und haben immer Leben' ('always living and conceiving', Hofmannsthal 1984, 47; Hofmannsthal 1961, 31). In the illogical sphere of dreams open to all forms of unreal combinations, a simultaneity of past and present is reached.

Hofmannsthal's representation of the self also shares affinities with Pater's, especially in its paradoxical aspects. In the logic of the poem the innermost room of the subject is open, whereas the subject in its outer regions is a closed room. The self in both texts is characterized by the ambivalence between being open and being closed. Whereas in Pater's text it was the intense experience of the aesthetic moment that was able to set 'the spirit free for a moment', in Hofmannsthal's poem it is the dream that brings about an openness inside an always closed room. In Hofmannsthal's poem, Pater's version seems to become radicalized, the subject appearing as a hollow room

---

[21]   'Das Innerste ist offen ihrem Weben;/Wie Geisterhände in versperrtem Raum/ Sind sie in uns und haben immer Leben' (Hofmannsthal 1984, 47).

closed off from the outer world and only open for the dream. The Austrian poet combines the images of the weaving and of the closed room, thereby creating another figure representing an interaction of structure and process, of spatial and temporary aspects. But – and this is decisive – in the poem the fixed motionless space is the dominating figure that encompasses the process of the weaving of the subject. So the dichotomy of stasis versus process is not solved and the whole argument is drawn towards a standstill.

This tendency towards closure is emphasized by the last line of the poem: 'And three are one: a man, a thing, a dream' (Hofmannsthal 1961, 31).[22] On the one hand, with this assumption of unity all processes have stopped and a kind of fulfilment and standstill has been reached. On the other hand, this shows that the condition of the dream-like passage does not imply solipsism but reaches out to the object. This again can be read as a commentary on Pater's 'Conclusion'. Whereas in Pater's text each mind keeps 'its own dream of a world' (Pater 1902, 235), Hofmannsthal gives the dream a more concrete content, namely 'ein Ding'('an object'), which has a high value in German. If the self, constituted by the dreams, is identical with the 'Ding', it already has an inner knowledge of and a relationship to the outer world without having to open the wall surrounding itself. In the poem, world and self have collapsed into the dream. So Hofmannsthal's transformation of the suggestive Paterian image foreshadows the poetics of the dream, which was later to become a potent element of twentieth-century literature.

In the sphere of the dream another order of time emerges in which aspects of process and aspects of structure come together. The first are realized as the dream places everything in the horizon of a beginning; the second are realized as the past, invoked as 'Geisterhände' ('ghostly hands'), forms a completed structure inside the closed room of the subject.

5

There are many other passages in Hofmannsthal's works where he tries to represent time as an interaction of structure and process, not always directly influenced by Pater but in keeping with his main ideas. One term Hofmannsthal uses to come to grips with this interaction is 'gleiten' ('to glide'), and this is of special significance to him. The concept appears as a variation on Pater's call for mobility of character, which is formulated most clearly in *Marius the Epicurean*: 'It was as if, recognising in perpetual motion the law of nature, Marius identified his own way of life cordially with it, "throwing himself into the stream", so to speak. He too must maintain a harmony with that soul of motion in things, by constantly renewed mobility of character' (Pater 1914, 139). Again, Pater calls for an adjustment to the constant motion of things by being ready for new experiences and constant change, but now he characterizes the passage of time as something positive and poetical by talking about 'the soul of motion in things'. This more poetical view may have been especially suggestive for Hofmannsthal's concept of 'gleiten'.

---

[22] 'Und drei sind Eins: ein Mensch, ein Ding, ein Traum' (Hofmannsthal 1984, 47).

The term 'gleiten', which also often occurs in the French formulation 'Il faut glisser la vie' ('One has to glide life', Stoupy 1989), appears especially frequently in the year 1894. This might suggest that through reading Pater Hofmannsthal was inspired to renewed reflections on the transitoriness of time. The word 'gleiten' could well be a translation of the key-term 'pass' in Pater's suggestive question 'how shall we pass most swiftly from point to point' (Pater 1902, 236). The term 'gleiten' is in itself already suggestive: 'gleiten' is a gentle form of motion, in which the person who is gliding, for example a skater on the ice, partly loses gravity because the moving body touches a different point of the medium at every moment during the process of passing. Consequently the concept of 'gleiten' is bound to the moment. To float with the moment means to have no secure standpoint but to affirm the passage of time: 'But the essence of our era is polyvalence and indeterminateness. It can only rest on things passing, and knows that what other generations believed to be stable is actually a form of passing.'[23] So, similar to Pater's 'Conclusion', Hofmannsthal devises a programme of mobility that calls for adaptation to the passage of time. A part of this programme is that – as he makes clear in the following note – one can neither search for anything stable nor try to detain the flow of time: 'Those who want to separate clearly the present from the past endanger terribly the life of the soul: they want to hold on to one point! One has to glide.'[24]

But the programme of 'gleiten' encompasses not only an adaptation to flowing time, but also envisions a fullness of time overcoming transitoriness, as Hofmannsthal makes clear in a letter from 1895:

> because time is something completely relative, a mere form of visual perception, one can put infinite content into one moment, and I am convinced that I sometimes experience more while travelling on the tram than another person on a journey. I can imagine that one can be liberated from the concept of time flying as easily as one can from the concept of insignificance, and that this is also meant by the strange saying: one has to glide in life and not press on it.[25]

The proposal to fill the moment with 'unending content' echoes Pater's appeal to expand the moment, which Hofmannsthal – like Pater – combines with a call for mobility. But the concept of 'gliding' is also similar to Pater's

---

23   'Aber das Wesen unserer Epoche ist Vieldeutigkeit und Unbestimmheit. Sie kann nur auf Gleitendem ausruhen und ist sich bewußt, daß es Gleitendes ist, wo andere Generationen an das Feste glaubten' (Hofmannsthal 1979, 60).

24   'Furchtbar gefährden das Seelenleben alle welche streng Gegenwart von Vergangenheit sondern wollen: sie wollen einen Punkt festhalten! Il faut glisser' (unpublished note, quoted from Stoupy 1989, 26).

25   'da Zeit etwas höchst Relatives, eine bloße Anschauungsform unseres Geistes ist, so kann man wirklich in einen Augenblick unendlichen Inhalt legen, und ich bin der festen Überzeugung, daß ich tatsächlich manchmal bei einer Fahrt mit der Tramway mehr erlebe als ein anderer auf einer Reise. Ich kann mir vorstellen, daß man den Begriff des Enteilenden fast ebenso loswerden kann wie den Begriff des Unbedeutenden, und das liegt auch in dem merkwürdigen Wort: il faut glisser la vie, ne pas l'appuyer' (Hofmannsthal 1935, 148).

representation of time, because it connects figures of a devouring time with figures of a near standstill of time, as becomes especially clear in the title of an unpublished note, 'Geist auf Gleitendem zu ruhen' ('The spirit rests on gliding', Hofmannsthal 1980, 465). The adaptation to the flowing of time enables the mind to attain a sort of calmness, that stands in stark contrast to the rapidity of time described in the note itself:

> And yet all greatness is of a terrible rapidity. Napoleon's activity like a transition of the eagle-like tension on his young face to the almost feminine smile of his death-mask. The blossoming of Athens as rapid as a fever. Goethe only well for 24 hours.
>
> All deeds are waste: the aspiration is everything.[26]

Here the passage of time has become so rapid that long developments through time are condensed into an extremely short span. The devouring quality of time now seems so rapid that not even the work of art, product and outcome of a longer development, can have any permanence in the sense that it retains 'life'. It seems astonishing that – considering the rapidity of time's flow – the mind can reach a status of calm by adapting to the passage of time. But it is precisely by giving itself over to the rapidity of time that the self can reach a state of calm. In so doing it becomes detached from the individual developments, and through this distancing gains a broader picture over a long time-span, allowing the whole to be perceived as a completed structure. So here again we have a connection of time seen as a process – even as an extremely quick process – and time seen as a finished structure. This interaction of different aspects of time is realized only by the subject viewing these developments; therefore this interaction cannot be materialized within the work of art which, in itself and in its material reality, is simply the waste product of these ongoing processes.

In reaction to this, and as an answer to this 'dead' status of the completed work of art, Hofmannsthal devises a method of perception that will enable the viewer to see in the object the process of its emergence: 'The idea that no beautiful thing could be dead or get lost. The idea: one must glide not press. Life and dream (the work of art) measured against each other. A tendency: to follow each creature back into the time when it was alive: while looking at the amber, to consider how it trickled from the green tree as resin.'[27]

The connection between the first two sentences makes clear that 'gleiten' is a way to preserve beauty. Therefore a method is devised not only for the sphere of natural objects but also for the sphere of art. In this example it

---

[26] 'Und doch ist alles Große von entsetzlicher Rapidität. Das Tun Napoleons wie ein Übergang von der Adler-Spannung auf seinem jungen Gesicht zu dem fast weiblichen Lächeln der Totenmaske. Die Blüte Athens von der Rapidität eines Fiebers. Goethe nur 24 Stunden wohl.

     Alle 'Werke' sind Abfälle: das Streben ist alles' (Hofmannsthal 1980, 465).

[27] 'Die Idee, daß nichts Schönes tot sein und verloren gehen könne. Die Idee: il faut glisser ne pas appuyer. Leben und Traum (Kunstwerk) gegeneinander abgewogen. Eine Tendenz: jedes Geschöpf in die Zeit zurückverfolgen, wo es lebendig war: beim Bernstein zu bedenken, wie er als Harz von einem grünenden Baum geträufelt ist' (Hofmannsthal 1980, 392).

becomes clear how this preservation is brought about. Hofmannsthal devises a method of perception that is capable of seeing a process in a static object: just as the spectator perceives in the piece of amber the different phases of its development, so he can see a long time-span in a concentrated form. The object that presents itself as a completed structure can also be seen as a summary of time that can be unfolded once again, and seen as a process, in this way gaining the 'life' of a new beginning. The fact that Hofmannsthal mentions amber here, as a special form of jewel with its origin in a kind of motion, can be read as a further commentary on the Paterian image of the 'hard, gem-like flame', exemplifying the point that Hofmannsthal, like Pater, related this image to questions of time. The amber becomes a figure for the structural simultaneity of time, here presented not as transitoriness but as an interaction of process and completed structure that gathers the different stages of its development into a whole. It is decisive that it is the spectator who – with a right method of perception – is able to 'realize' this interaction and so resuscitate the 'life-energy' inherent in the object.

There are many other images in Hofmannsthal's work that represent this relation of process and structure, of time flowing and time standing, such as the image of the whirlpool, which is of central importance in the 'Chandos Letter'. I want to focus on just one more of Hofmannsthal's central images because it illustrates a particular direction of thought and reflection. It is contained in a passage from Hofmannsthal's essay 'Englischer Stil' ('English Style'), written in 1896, at a time when he was intensively involved with Pater's works:

> Whoever searches for the rigid and the given will always grasp at emptiness. Everything is in continuous motion, everything has as little reality as the suspended stream of the fountain, where myriads of drops fall incessantly and myriads of new drops rise incessantly. With those eyes, which lie to us about the fountain, we must perceive the lives of human beings: for the beauty of their gestures and their actions is nothing else than the combination of myriads of vibrations in one moment.[28]

Hofmannsthal here transfers the Paterian dichotomy of atomism and inextricable interrelation to the image of the fountain, comprising the constant unification and separation of elements. The myriads of vibrations coming together correspond to Pater's 'elements [. . .] driven in many currents' (Pater 1902, 234), and the fountain is the 'focus' where the vibrations unite for a moment only to part again. An important difference from Pater's 'Conclusion' lies in the transition from 'elements' to 'vibrations'. Vibrations imply a general mobility of the elements; they are less material and refer to a subject tuned – like a sounding board – to their reception.

---

[28] 'Wer das Starre sucht und das Gegebene, wird immer ins Leere greifen. Alles ist in fortwährender Bewegung, ja alles ist so wenig wirklich als der bleibende Strahl des Springbrunnens, dem Myriaden Tropfen unaufhörlich entsinken, Myriaden neuer unaufhörlich zuströmen. Mit den Augen, die uns den Springbrunnen vorlügen, müssen wir das Leben der Menschen anschauen: denn die Schönheit ihrer Gebärden und ihrer Taten ist nichts anderes als das Zusammenkommen von Myriaden Schwingungen in einem Augenblick (Hofmannsthal 1979, 572).

Furthermore, vibrations belong more to a poetical atmosphere, and less to the world of the 'Conclusion', in which the natural sciences play a large role as a background to the argument.

Nevertheless, in keeping with Pater's ideas in the 'Conclusion', the image of the fountain is an especially convincing illustration of a seemingly static form that is actually full of motion. Here the interaction of process and structure becomes an apparent unity whilst the whole is still perceived as a static and closed structure. So Hofmannsthal once more proposes a method of perception that detects the unending processes which constitute what appear to be solid objects.

However, it also becomes clear that Hofmannsthal's outline of an interaction of time flowing and time suspended is directed towards a vision that is more or less harmonious and closed. The image of the fountain is a well-known literary symbol for beauty and harmony, and this meaning of the image is emphasized by the fact that the movement of the water flows back, so that the fountain presents a closed cycle. A comparison with the Paterian figure of the 'hard, gem-like flame' shows the difference between Pater's paradoxical and radical image of process and structure – designed to explode concepts of rationally understandable order – and Hofmannsthal's more conservative, harmonizing tendency.

The question of how the interaction between 'Sein und Werden' (being and becoming), between structure and process, could be achieved remains an important topic of Hofmannsthal's work. He approaches this question in the character of the adventurer, a prominent figure in his dramatic works. A further example is to be found in his drama *Der Schwierige* (*The Difficult Man*) where the two main characters, Hans-Karl (the eponymous difficult man), and Helene, his future bride, share a similar outlook on time: both perceive occurrences from a detached position, enabling them to see actual processes as a completed structure.[29]

One can summarize by saying that both writers agree on the attempt to formulate an interaction between process and structure as a response to the passage of time. Their aim to gain a broader view of the completed structure certainly has to do with the feeling of belatedness that is distinctive of their understanding of their position in history. At the same time, both endeavour to accept their modern position, and work with the aim of linking the present

---

[29] For instance, Helene says: 'For me the moment does not exist, I am standing here and see the lamps burning, and inside myself I see them as already gone out' ('Für mich ist ja der Moment gar nicht da, ich stehe da und sehe die Lampen dort brennen, und in mir sehe ich sie schon ausgelöscht', Hofmannsthal 1993, 60). And later Hans-Karl describes his feeling that there is nothing new: 'That everything already exists somewhere, finished a long time ago, and it only becomes visible all of a sudden. Do you know how in autumn, when the water was let out of the pond at Hohenbühl, one suddenly saw the carp and the tails of the stone Tritons, which one hadn't seen before?' ('Daß alles schon längst irgendwo fertig dasteht und nur auf einmal erst sichtbar wird. Weißt du, wie im Hohenbühler Teich, wenn man im Herbst das Wasser abgelassen hat, auf einmal die Karpfen und die Schweife von den steinernen Tritonen da waren, die man früher kaum gesehen hat?', Hofmannsthal 1993, 60).

with an overwhelming past. In this way, Pater and Hofmansthal find suggestive images and representations for the kind of moving structure that becomes characteristic of the notion of time in the twentieth century. Furthermore, the two writers coincide in not seeking a dialectical synthesis of the contradictory aspects of time. In this context Ulrich Fülleborn refers to Hofmannsthal as someone 'who does not resolve opposites in accordance with the logic of either/or, but who leaves them remaining beside each other'.[30]

However, I still maintain that there are important differences in the way that these opposing aspects of time are presented and transferred into images. Pater aims more at a paradoxical interaction, whereas Hofmannsthal – in his imagery, in his recourse to the poetical sphere of the dream and in his concept of 'gleiten' – seeks to achieve a harmonious balance and thus to dissolve the harsh contrast between the opposing notions of process and structure.

---

[30] 'der die Gegensätze nicht im Sinne einer Logik von Entweder-Oder auflöst, sondern nebeneinander bestehen läßt' (Fülleborn 1992, 170).

8 The Critic's Critic: Rudolf Borchardt's Centenary Essay 'Walter Pater' (1939)

Martina Lauster

Published in the Sunday supplement of the *Basler Nachrichten* on 13 August 1939, Rudolf Borchardt's article commemorating the English critic's hundredth birthday (Borchardt 1960, 402–22)[1] pre-dates the beginning of the Second World War by just over two weeks. An ultra-conservative, Jewish-German man of letters (philologist, critic,[2] public speaker, translator[3] and poet) who had been opposed to the system of the Weimar Republic and initially supportive of National Socialism, Borchardt had hopes that the plebeian Hitler would turn into a kind of statesman–dictator, or that Nazi rule would prove to be merely a temporary stage on Germany's way to cultural regeneration. These were soon dashed (Bernauer 2001, 142). From 1934 Borchardt therefore pinned his hopes on war, believing that it would be the only way to achieve this aim (Ott 2001, 150). However, his speech given in Bremen in 1931, entitled 'Führung' ('Leadership'), had already stressed the military qualities required of a German 'leader'. Borchardt saw the Germans as a nation lacking a unified will to be led and consequently in need of the application of force. Seen in this context, the Pater essay of August 1939 documents Borchardt's determination to support the cause of cultural rebirth by military pressure, the determination of an intellectual who believed in artistic discipline as a paradigm for politics. The aesthete and ascetic Pater is invoked as a quasi-military model, who has taught educated young Germans to 'steel' themselves. Anyone studying the writings of the 'sublime Englishman', Borchardt argues, will be able to appreciate how much they have helped 'to tighten and purify us, to unify us, to fire us and, it is certain,

---

[1] All page references to Borchardt's essay in the notes refer to this edition.
[2] Borchardt also published two other essays on English writers: 'Rossetti' (1928) and 'Vernon Lee' (1935); those unpublished during his lifetime include an obituary of Swinburne (1909) and an unfinished postscript for the translation of Landor's dialogues (1923).
[3] Borchardt's translations from the English include Swinburne's poetry (*Swinburne, Deutsch*, 1919), a selection from Landor's *Imaginary Conversations* (*Imaginäre Unterhaltungen*, 1923) and an anthology of nineteenth-century English poetry (*Englische Dichter*, 1936).

also to compel us'.[4] To prove the relevance of the almost forgotten Victorian scholar, Borchardt obviously finds it necessary to end his essay on this martial note.

This problematic political context may well be the reason why the essay has hitherto not been subjected to a thorough interpretation, despite the remarkable recent interest in Borchardt and in the art criticism of the *fin de siècle*, which is evident from the bibliography. Another reason may be its forty-year distance from the heyday of Pater's influence in the German-speaking world; yet another may be the sheer effort it requires of the reader to follow complex and idiosyncratic lines of thought. The reference to collective 'self-hardening', through vocabulary such as 'purify, unify, fire, compel', points to the core of the essay's concerns, which transcend the political context. These words include some key terms denoting the creative process as it has been conceived within the Platonic tradition, and they are carefully chosen by a writer of enormous erudition. Aesthetic form arises from sublimated passion; the more ardent the passion, the more challenging the task of mastering it in form, and the harder, purer and more durable this form will be (Lauster 1993). An advocate of 'Schöpferische Restauration' ('Creative Restoration') – which is the title of a notorious speech given by him at Munich University in 1927 (Borchardt 1955, 230–53) – he postulates a revival of this ethic of creation rather than a break with tradition as the basis of modern form. Pater, whose passion was 'ennobled' by 'renunciation',[5] is a model for his cultural conservatism not only because the English critic is an eminent representative of this ethic, but also because the influence of Pater's writings had itself been instrumental in establishing a *tradition* in modern German literature, of which Borchardt's own work forms part. Although he makes no explicit reference to himself, he implies his own involvement in launching this tradition around the turn of the century, when German writers were striving 'to return to principles, however hard they might be; to the narrow and confining space of formal mastery; to the innermost structural cell of the order that is the unity between our lived and our formed existence'.[6]

The author whom Borchardt regards as the head of this generation, and as the master of modern style in the sense of 'Creative Restoration', is Hugo von Hofmannsthal. His 'reconstruction of German prose', he argues, would have been 'unthinkable' without Pater.[7] This judgement is applied mainly to Hofmannsthal's essays, and particularly to the famous so-called 'Chandos-Brief' ('Chandos Letter'), published in 1902 as 'Ein Brief' ('The Letter'). In

---

4   'wie viel der hohe Engländer dazu beigetragen hat, uns zu spannen, uns zu reinigen, zu vereinheitlichen, zu erglühen und allerdings auch zu zwingen' (Borchardt 1960, 422).

5   'die im Verzichte sich adelnde Leidenschaft des reinen, stillen Mannes' (Borchardt 1960, 421).

6   'als er [der Deutsche] um die Jahrhundertwende [. . .] in Prinzipien heimzukehren trachtete, wenn auch harten, in den schmalen und zwingenden Raum der Meisterschaft, in die innerste Ordnungszelle der Einheit des gelebten und gestalteten Daseins' (Borchardt 1960, 421).

7   'Der Wiederaufbau der deutschen Prosa durch Hofmannsthal ist ohne ihn nicht denkbar' (Borchardt 1960, 421).

this imaginary correspondence of Philip Lord Chandos with Francis Bacon, the writer describes and analyses his own linguistic crisis, ending with the hope that he will one day be capable of expressing himself in a new language, the words of which are yet unknown. The essay is now famous for its diagnosis of language as having lost its signifying power, its hint of an unheard-of language of mute objects (both classic modernist qualities) and its own perfection as a piece of prose that already represents a new level of linguistic expressiveness. Borchardt recognizes the significance of the 'Chandos letter' as a 'sacred piece of our classic literature', which owes its status to an intense reception of its English model: 'as a literary form', he argues, it 'would never have existed' without Pater's *Imaginary Portraits*, just as it would 'never have existed as an act of self-judgement without the model of his [Pater's] entire life's work'.[8] In other words, without Pater, Hofmannsthal might not have turned the right way at the 'crossroads' which led him out of the crisis and towards a new identity of content and style.

The young Hofmannsthal, who was keenly interested in contemporary English art and literature and wrote a number of journal contributions on the subject, had discovered the English critic at the age of twenty (Stamm 1997; Eilert 1999). In his article 'Über moderne englische Malerei' ('On Modern English Painting', 1894a), he translated some sections from the 'Gioconda' passage of the 'Leonardo da Vinci' essay in *The Renaissance*, and he published his article 'Walter Pater' later in the same year, apparently unaware of the death of his celebrated author a few months earlier (1894b). As has been indicated, he was by no means the only German-speaking writer ready to absorb Pater's influence, even if others only got to know the English critic through him. Rudolf Kassner, inspired by Hofmannsthal's essays of the 1890s which familiarized him with Swinburne, Pater and the Pre-Raphaelites, published a collection of essays in 1900 which dealt with English artists and poets, entitled *Die Mystik, die Künstler und das Leben* (*Mysticism, Artists and Life*). Its first essay, 'Dichter und Platoniker' ('The Poet and the Platonist'), and its last one, 'Stil' ('Style'), are clear responses to Pater's *Plato and Platonism* and 'Style'. 'Stil', written in the form of a dialogue, presents a character called Walter with whom Kassner empathizes. The significance of English nineteenth-century art and literature and of Pater's criticism as the link between Hofmannsthal and Kassner has been explored by Stephen Rizza (1997). It is certain that such a link also exists between Hofmannsthal and Borchardt. In their development of an intense (and intensely Platonic) friendship, the ideal of the English gentleman, thought to be embodied, for example, in the admired Oxford critic, provided the role model (Lauster 1992, 135–6). The combination of art and life, or 'lived and formed existence', which Borchardt refers to as something young Germans learnt from Pater around 1900, manifests itself in the art of conversation cultivated by Hofmannsthal (who made his villa at Rodaun near Vienna a centre of

---

8   'die Erinnerung daran, daß ein Heiligtum unserer klassischen Literatur [...] – Philip Chandos' Brief an Bacon – als Form ohne die "Imaginären Porträts", als Selbstgericht ohne dies ganze Lebenswerk nie gewesen wäre' (Borchardt 1960, 422).

intellectual sociability). It finds its main creative outlet in the imaginative writing of discursive prose, often in the form of dialogues or letters and often on English subjects or with imaginary English characters. This particular Anglo-Saxon variant of the dialogical essay offered these writers a creative alternative to traditional German scholarly discourse (Burdorf 1999; Eilert 1999; Lauster 1992). When Borchardt first visited Hofmannsthal in 1902 (the year in which the art publisher Diederichs brought out a seminal German translation of *The Renaissance*; Vilain 2000, 70),[9] he had completed an essay in dialogue form, entitled 'Das Gespräch über Formen' ('The Conversation About Forms'). A few detailed comments will be made on this dialogue before the interpretation of Borchardt's centenary essay on Pater is resumed.

'Das Gespräch über Formen' ('The Conversation About Forms')

This essay was written in 1901–02 and finally published in 1905 as an introduction to Borchardt's own translation of Plato's 'Lysis'. It therefore enacts in a modern form, i.e. in witty and serious, erotically tinged and intellectually high-powered contemporary dialogue, the Platonic dialogue Borchardt translates from the Greek. The *subject* of the conversation between two modern young men is translation (sparked by the work of the slightly older of the two, Arnold, on a translation of 'Lysis'), and their very dialogue 'translates' Plato's original; not its words, but the intellectual and libidinous energy inspiring its *form*, which the receiving subject recognizes and recreates (Lönker 1997, 215). Capturing the 'form spirit' of the classical text as a translator counts as paramount for Arnold/Borchardt, who deplores the decline of classical education in Germany after 1870. It has produced academic renderings of Greek texts lacking any sense of the unity between form and content which their originals possess. Borchardt's 'Gespräch' presents just that: a formal realization of what is reflected upon. This self-reflexivity of 'spirit' and 'form' reaches its peak when Arnold mentions the great mediator of this dialectic:

> And here I turn to Walter Pater whose book I keep open and next to me as usual. It's his *Greek Studies*. On the subject concerning us he'll always have something more valuable to say to you than German antiquarians with their numb illusions, who think of themselves as ever so Greek when they state that Phidias was a βάναυσος unable to produce hexameters. The man who wrote the essay on Lionardo [sic] and the one on Botticelli, the 'Postscript' to *Appreciations* and the magnificent 'Conclusion' to the 'Renaissance'; – that man embraced life and knew its meaning. He concludes his essay, *The age of the athletic pricemen* [sic] with the following words about the Discobolus in the Vatican: 'You have pure humanity there, with a glowing yet restrained joy and delight in itself: and it is pure. There is nothing

---

9   This was followed, in 1904, by a translation of *Plato and Platonism*. Rilke wrote an enthusiastic review of Wilhelm Schölermann's translation of *The Renaissance* in the *Bremer Tageblatt* on 27 July 1902 (Rilke 1902).

certainly supersensual in that fair round head, any more than in these long agile limbs, but also no impediment whatever, natural or acquired.'[10]

Borchardt quotes the concluding passage of 'The Age of Athletic Prizemen' from *Greek Studies*, which discusses the sculpture of the *Discobolus at Rest*, at full length and in the English original. Pater's language is deliberately not translated because it already 'translates' ancient Greek sculpture into 'glowing yet restrained' modern prose. As Hildegard Hummel (1987) has shown, Pater's innovative interpretation, adopted by Borchardt, consisted in drawing analogies between Plato's text and the plastic qualities of Greek sculpture. The stylistic and spiritual model of Borchardt's own prose, fusing form and content so that content becomes form and vice versa, is allowed to speak for itself. Arnold's reading aloud of Pater's text then elicits an interpretative response from the younger man, Harry, who emphasizes the evocative power and the atmospheric suggestiveness of Pater's prose, while also stressing what he sees as an affinity of Oxford's (and, by extension, England's) humanism with the ancient Greek world:

> The whole of Oxford is present, Brasenose, the old quadrangle with its ivy as thick as fur, the chapel with its baroque of stone, and Pater's own green-panelled rooms. And everything he says about a Greek statue is so uniquely in agreement with his own being and that of his people. The sound of his words evokes all the unforgettable beauty, the strong and the slender bodies, the masculine simplicity of those upright, chivalrous souls [....] And between all this and his own nation's past, coloured by the Celtic tradition and resplendent of that of the Renaissance, there is no rupture.[11]

What is expressed between the lines suggests that the bond between ancient Greece, Oxford and the English past is one of sublimated male homosexual passion; the crucial intertext which Borchardt leaves unmentioned here is Pater's lectures in *Plato and Platonism*. This sublimation forms the bond between Pater, the 'forms' which constitute the subject of Harry and Arnold's conversation, and the interlocutors themselves, as has already been indicated.

---

[10] 'Hier liegt Walter Pater wie immer aufgeschlagen neben mir; es sind die *Greek Studies*. Er wird Ihnen immer Wertvolleres über alles Hierhergehörige mitzuteilen haben als deutsche Antiquare, deren stumpfer Wahn sich wunders wie griechisch dünkt, wenn er feststellt, daß Phidias ein βάναυσος gewesen sei, der keinen Hexameter habe machen können. Er, der den Essay über Lionardo [sic] und den über Botticelli, das Postskript zu den *Appreciations* und die grandiose Konklusion zur "Renaissance" geschrieben hat, er hatte das Leben und kannte seinen Sinn. Er schließt den Essay: *The age of the athletic pricemen* [sic] mit diesen Worten über den vatikanischen Diskobol: [...].' (Borchardt 1957, 362–3).

[11] 'Ganz Oxford spricht mit, Brasenose, das alte Quadrangel mit dem Efeu, der so dick ist wie Pelz, das steinerne Barock der Kapelle, seine eigenen grüngetäfelten Zimmer. Und welche beispiellose Einigkeit von allem dem, was er da über eine griechische Statue gesagt hat, mit seinem eigenen Wesen und dem seines Volkes. Alle unvergeßliche Schönheit kommt mit dem Klang seiner Worte herauf, die starken und die schlanken Leiber, männliche Einfalt der geraden, ritterlichen Seelen [....] Und zwischen diesem allem und der nationalen Vergangenheit, der keltisch gefärbten und der renaissancehaft glänzenden, kein Bruch' (Borchardt 1957, 363).

Their English-sounding names, the aura of the English man of the world with which Arnold surrounds himself, as well as the very form of the 'imaginary conversation' used for the essay, underline Borchardt's elective affinity as an anti-academic German scholar with what he perceives as English culture and learning. For him, absorbing the model of Pater's 'glowing yet restrained' scholarly personality, objectified in essayistic prose, points the way out of Germany's cultural decline since the foundation of Bismarck's empire. Retrospectively, in 1939, he talks of Pater as having been not 'imitated', but 'assimilated' by the young writers of the turn of the century: 'We thought we found ourselves again when we found him', a process to which Borchardt will assign national relevance: 'in this way, he [Pater] has also become part of the history of German intellectual formation'.[12]

This emphasis on the rediscovery of the (national) self seems to obliterate the fact that, around 1900, the Austrian/German reception of Englishness in general and of Pater's writings in particular meant a personal assimilation of 'German' selves to the imagined cultural environment and to the intellectual physiognomy of the 'English' other. The imaginary young Germans Arnold and Harry, conversing about their scholarly subject not with the pedantry of German academics, but with the ease of English men of letters, have an immediate predecessor in Hofmannthal's gentlemanly 'English' alter ego, 'Archibald O'Hagan, B.A.', whose address is given as 'Old Rookery, Herfordshire [sic]'; this is how the Viennese author had signed his essay on Pater (1894b). Yet even in his centenary essay forty-five years later, Borchardt expressly acknowledges cross-cultural assimilation as a precondition for the formation of identity. However, to write about his subject, he no longer invests his prose with an aura of Englishness. The imagined other is inherent in the text in more complex ways, just as the image emerging of Pater in 1939 is a great deal more complex than that of a contemporary who unites an uninterrupted national tradition with the spirit of ancient Greece.

Pater's European synthesis

By the time of Pater's hundredth birthday, the Victorians have faded from cultural memory both in England and Germany, so much so that Borchardt sees his task as that of a literary archaeologist extracting his subject's 'golden name' from the 'rubble' of the nineteenth century.[13] Under the impact of the First World War, even England has suffered consequences which, in Borchardt's/Harry's eulogy half a century before, it had always been spared:

> For the first time in English history the thread of continuity has been torn. [. . . .] [T]he fragments of the crushed generation that returned home found

---

[12] 'Ja, wir haben uns selber wieder zu finden geglaubt, als wir ihn fanden; er ist nicht nachgeahmt worden, sondern assimiliert; und er ist dadurch zu einem Teile der deutschen Bildungsgeschichte geworden' (Borchardt 1960, 421).

[13] 'So ist das späte und mittlere England des 19. Jahrhunderts [. . .] zu der unbesuchten Ruine zerfallen [. . . .] Unter ihrem Schutt liegt weit mehr als nur Walter Paters goldener Name' (Borchardt 1960, 403).

that the bond was severed, and that a defiant people was resolved to [. . .] remake itself naively on the basis of what remained. The national mould was to be neither retrieved nor adopted, but to be improvised.[14]

In this context, Borchardt's celebration of Pater thirty years after his fall into oblivion must also be seen as an attempt to remind potential English readers of their 'national mould', which was thrown away after the First World War, exactly at a time, ironically, when prominent members of the German and Austrian *fin-de-siècle* generation had completed their turn towards nationalism (Petzinna 2001). Borchardt implies that, even if tradition has failed to provide the 'hidden elastic band' that could pull the present-day English back to their national heritage, they ought at least to discover their affinity with someone like Pater. This Victorian anticipates the age following him, but not, as Borchardt stresses, through his undeniable belief in something absolute, which is a faith he shares with contemporaries as different as Swinburne, Meredith, Ruskin, Carlyle, Browning, Froude, Darwin and John Stuart Mill. What points forward in Pater is the power of his criticism, the 'microscopizing anatomy' and the 'sparkling finesse' of his 'critical tools'.[15] This quasi-medical scepticism constitutes a link between him and the generation living under the aegis of George Bernard Shaw, those 'grandsons' for whom 'anything absolute' has 'crumbled to nothing'.[16] The interpretation of Pater as the critical anatomist cutting through 'the walls of Victorian orthodoxy or of Victorian euphemism'[17] could scarcely contrast more with Borchardt's early appreciation of the English critic as the epitome of cultural 'unity'. That said, the centenary essay portrays Pater as the master of cross-cultural synthesis, and it seeks to draw its persuasive power precisely from acknowledging instability, disunity and scepticism as the preconditions of such a synthesis.

The place where, in Borchardt's view, the momentous intellectual shifts and transitions of the nineteenth century could be felt most acutely, especially 'by the divining nerves of the most delicate connoisseurship which is at home there',[18] is Oxford. Rather than characterizing it as the centre of a lively Greek spirit, which was the case in 'Das Gespräch über Formen' ('The Conversation about Forms'), Borchardt now describes it as the hub of the previous century's intellectual cross-currents. A scientific mind like Pater's, working in almost monastic seclusion, was able to receive, register the impact and calculate the

---

[14] 'Zum erstenmal in der englischen Geschichte ist die Kontinuität gesprengt worden. [. . . .] [S]o fanden die heimkehrenden Trümmer der zerschlagenen Generation dies Band gerissen und das Volk trotzig dazu entschlossen, [. . .] sich von dem verbleibenden Reste aus naiv neu anzusetzen, die nationale Form weder zurückzugewinnen noch zu übernehmen, sondern zu improvisieren' (Borchardt 1960, 402–3).

[15] 'mit der mikroskopierenden Anatomie des von Feinheit funkelnden kritischen Werkzeugkastens' (Borchardt 1960, 405).

[16] 'dem Enkel, dem alles Absolute an sich in Nichts zerfallen ist' (Borchardt 1960, 404).

[17] 'Auswege durch die Wand der victorianischen Orthodoxie oder des victorianischen Euphemismus' (Borchardt 1960, 404).

[18] 'mit den divinierenden Nerven der dort heimischen allerheikelsten Kennerschaft' (Borchardt 1960, 405).

long-term effects of all these European developments. The small body of his published work therefore reflects every aspect of continental influence in its interaction with English culture, but Pater's main achievement, as Borchardt seems to indicate, is the considered way in which he makes his own cross-culturalism 'universal'. Borchardt traces Pater's development from his first two essays, the one on Coleridge and the one on Winckelmann, published in the *Westminster Review* in 1866 and 1867 respectively, via *Studies in the History of the Renaissance* and *Marius the Epicurean* to *Imaginary Portraits*, with brief or oblique references to various essays published individually and to the 'Postscript' of *Appreciations*. Pater's development as a critic is paradigmatic for Borchardt's cultural conservatism as it combines the legacies of German, French and English Romanticism; in other words, of periods that intensely looked back on the European cultural heritage, with a tendency towards an apotheosis of western culture. This universalism or encyclopedism is finally portrayed as the original characteristic of German culture which needs to be reappropriated by the Germans themselves.

Through his two earliest published essays, his first works to be published, Pater establishes himself within the powerful, but gradually receding, current of German influence on nineteenth-century Britain:

> When the young lecturer, still almost a student, began to publish, in small articles or drop by drop, as they say (but filtered, golden drops), the whole intellectual world of England still found itself under the slowly declining German star; German Idealism of the speculative and of the critical kind, historical criticism, the new, systematic foundations of all those branches of knowledge emerging from the decay of late Romanticism, revolutionary theology and scientific radicalism – all these had immigrated, complete with their terminologies and, above all, with their antinomic pairs, still unknown in English circles, which had only been assimilated with great reluctance. The German theological battles of the century were increasingly stirring the Oxford air, and the critical scrutiny of old formulae as well as the thinking through of new ones also filled cognate disciplines with unprecedented excitement.[19]

The reader is invited to see the 'golden drops' produced by Pater in this climate as the condensation of air vibrating with German critical ideas. Borchardt admits that the essay on Coleridge received its philosophical dimensions only much later, but stresses the fact that Pater is concerned with

---

[19]   'Als der junge Dozent, fast noch Student, zu publizieren begann, in Aufsätzchen, tropfenweise, wie man sagt, aber gefilterten goldenen Tropfen, stand das ganze geistige England noch unter dem langsam niedergehenden deutschen Gestirn; der deutsche spekulative und der kritische Idealismus, die historische Kritik, die neue Systematik aller aus der zerfallenen Spätromantik entstandenen Wissenschaften, die revolutionäre Theologie, der naturwissenschaftliche Radikalismus waren mit ihrer gesamten Terminologie und vor allem ihren, für das englische Ohr noch unerhörten Antinomien-Paaren eingewandert und sehr widerstrebend assimiliert worden; von den deutschen theologischen Kämpfen des Jahrhunderts zitterte die Oxforder Luft immer stärker mit, und die kritische Prüfung der alten Formeln, das Durchdenken der neuen, versetzte auch die Nachbargebiete in eine noch nie erlebte Spannung' (Borchardt 1960, 405).

Coleridge as 'the poetic messenger of German revelations' right from the start.[20] However, the young scholar's rise to the rank of a 'character in English literature' is due to his essay on Winckelmann, which is Pater's very own 'contribution to the Anglo-German cultural give-and-take of the nineteenth century'.[21] In it he already proves himself a master of style, strictly and patiently restraining his pen, 'this quill touched by pinions'.[22] It is as a stylist, Borchardt argues, that Pater, the descendant of French forebears, comes into his own and at the same time turns to French culture. However, an external reason for Pater's interest in France is also mentioned: his encounter with Rossetti. The essay on Rossetti's poetry, which was conceived long before being published in 1883, is seen by Borchardt as evidence of a fundamental reorganization of Pater's mental map, along 'the old historical semicircle, Italy-France-England, 1450 to 1650'.[23] Pater's ambition is now to give substance to a historical idea which originated in France, that of the 'Renaissance'. Drawing on French sources (which Borchardt does not identify), Pater produces his 'glorious studies' on an 'Italian subject, framed above and below by French themes'[24] – a book which is as inspired by Rossetti's notion of beauty as it is remote from Jacob Burckhardt's nearly contemporaneous work, published in 1859, which also uses the French term in its title: *Die Cultur der Renaissance in Italien* (*The Civilization of the Renaissance in Italy*). While Burckhardt, the historian, does not recognize anything as an *a priori* absolute, let alone as a magical one, Pater, the critic, illuminates his notion of the 'magical absolute', beauty, in an imaginative way and from all kinds of different angles by studying Renaissance artists, works and lives.

The intensity with which the Pre-Raphaelite revival of the Middle Ages and of the Renaissance expresses itself through Pater's criticism prompts Borchardt to speak of England in 1860 as the country 'in which that mighty European movement' of Romanticism was finally, 'after seventy years of moving from country to country', experiencing 'its historic day of triumph'.[25] Germany, its country of origin in his view, had defined Romanticism as a *critical* movement through the fragments of Novalis and Friedrich Schlegel, without producing the criticism to put the programme into practice. In France, then, the influence of German Romanticism hit the hard frame of the

---

[20] 'den dichterischen Botschafter der deutschen Offenbarungen' (Borchardt 1960, 406).

[21] 'zu einem Charakter der englischen Literatur [. . .] Paters wirklicher Beitrag zu dem englisch-deutschen Kulturausgleich des 19. Jahrhunderts' (Borchardt 1960, 406).

[22] 'dieser von Fittichen angerührten, aber mit strenger Geduld an den Schritt gehaltenen Feder' (Borchardt 1960, 406).

[23] 'des alten geschichtlichen Halbbogens Italien-Frankreich-England, 1450 bis 1650' (Borchardt 1960, 407).

[24] 'die herrlichen Studien [. . .] das Buch, das diese sechs Aufsätze italienischen Themas oben und unten durch französische Themata einrahmt' (Borchardt 1960, 407).

[25] 'im England von 1860, in dem diese mächtige europäische Bewegung nun endlich, nach siebzig Jahren des Zugs von Land zu Land, ihren geschichtlichen Triumphtag erlebte' (Borchardt 1960, 414).

classicist tradition and smashed itself to bits, 'degenerating' into the 'grimaces, cruelty, psychology and mere pose' of French Romanticism.[26] Only the England of 1860 was able to follow the original precepts of Romanticism, which, as Borchardt stresses, had precisely *not* been confined to art and literature, but had theoretically united the spheres of art (conceived as the realm of the 'imagination') and life (conceived as the realm of 'passion'). Pre-Raphaelitism, led by 'the poet, painter, organizer, charmer and magic transformer Dante Gabriel Rossetti, that practical figure',[27] makes the theoretical unity between art and life real. Borchardt mentions the Gothic revival as well as Pre-Raphaelite painting and poetry, arguing that the latter moulds 'physiognomies of passion' and real-life 'women and men' after its own image, thus achieving a 'primacy of art over life'.[28] If Rossetti is the 'centre of power' of Romanticism during its heyday, Pater is an important 'planet', fulfilling Romanticism's original mission, that of criticism. Nowhere would Pater's stature as a Romantic critic become more evident than in the 'Conclusion' to his *Studies in the History of the Renaissance*, with its emphasis on the primacy of passion and of the imagination. However, this 'German' legacy within Pater would never have been sufficient to create the impact of the 'Conclusion'. Another essential element is the heritage of French Romanticism, i.e. the scepticism of *la décadence*, and yet another is that of English and German 'Hellenism'.

Borchardt devotes a total of more than five pages to the 'Conclusion', including his own extensive translation of Pater's text into German.[29] In his eyes, this piece of writing marks the triumph of French positivism (Comte) over the older influence of German Idealism and *Religionskritik* (the left Hegelians). Fused with English aestheticism and sensualism (Rossetti), this scepticism produces 'as revolutionary a declaration as ever emerged from the quiet room in which the thoughts of a moral Platonist are hatched'.[30] The 'anatomist' in Pater, who dissects the world and the self into an infinite sequence of fleeting physical sensations, clearly responds sympathetically to the

---

26   'in dem gleichzeitigen Frankreich, in dem sich am aufrechten Rahmenwerk der harten klassischen Tradition die Romantik schon beim Einströmen zerschlagen, aufgespalten und zu Fratze, Grausamkeit, Psychologie und Pose denaturiert hatte' (Borchardt 1960, 413–14).

27   'im England des Dichters, Malers, Organisators, Beschwörers und Verzauberers Dante Gabriel Rossetti, der praktischen Figur' (Borchardt 1960, 414).

28   'wo sie [diese mächtige Bewegung] die Mienen der Leidenschaft, Frauen und Männer, sich nachgemodelt hatte, und den Primat der Kunst über das Leben [...] erzwungen' (Borchardt 1960, 414).

29   Borchardt translates the following sections of Pater's essay: from '[t]hat clear, perpetual outline' to 'parting sooner or later on their ways' (Borchardt 1960, 408); the entire passage, with a few cuts, from the quotation of Novalis: '*Philosophiren* [...] *ist dephlegmatisiren vivificiren*' to 'has no real claim upon us' (Borchardt 1960, 409–10); and the concluding passage from the quotation of Victor Hugo, '*les hommes sont tous condamnés à mort*' to 'simply for those moments' sake' (Borchardt 1960, 410–11).

30   'eine so revolutionäre Ansage, wie sie nur je aus dem stillen Gedankenzimmer eines sittlichen Platonikers hervorgegangen ist' (Borchardt 1960, 408).

analytical, physiological, psychological, completely anti-metaphysical approaches of the French school, and he also subscribes to the anti-moralism of *l'art pour l'art*. On the other hand, it is the humanism, the valuing of life for its own sake, in other words, the 'Hellenism' of Oxford which Borchardt adulated in his 'Das Gespräch über Formen' ('Conversation About Forms'), that makes Pater resilient to the sombre mood of contemporary French thought. As a 'moral Platonist', he is able to summon all his passion in defence of the human experience of a moment's happiness, the indivisible atom in a world of constant transition. Significantly, this is where Borchardt detects the lingering (and thoroughly absorbed) influence of German culture, notably of Goethe. Referring to the poem 'Dauer im Wechsel' ('Permanence in Change'), he points to Goethe's concept of human freedom as the liberty of the will to contract moments of experience which are inalienably human into one moment, discarding everything lying in between. In other words, the continual change which makes and unmakes the world of objects and the self is acknowledged and shut out at the same time by the will, which gives 'permanence' to the moment. Borchardt quotes from the poem's last stanza: 'Then let the beginning and the end contract into a single point, and let yourself speed by even more swiftly than these objects!' (Goethe 1964, 196).[31] This 'Goethean' or 'Hellenic' power of wrenching durability, the durability of the 'Heraclitean moment', from eternal transition, is what Borchardt admires most in Pater, someone who can, of course, no longer rely even on Goethe's transcendental notions of 'spirit' and 'form'. Nevertheless, Borchardt emphasizes Pater's distance from positivism, however much it may provide the modern scientific basis of his considerations. The very fact that the 'Conclusion' shifts the focus of its observation from physical change to the dynamic of mental processes shows 'with how much energy it [Pater's thought] is able to leap off the coarse springboard of positivist commonplace':

> The entire empirical world, as the sphere of experience, and the world of the senses, as the sphere of appearances, are excluded as a reality, in order to be raised to a different sphere in which they are nothing but a passive object, subjected to the individual's consciousness and, more extremely, to his will, so that they will be shaped into a limitless sculpture.[32]

The core of Pater's analytical empiricism is described in terms of an ethic of sculpting. Here the 1939 essay clearly takes up the main interest of 'Das Gespräch über Formen'. Pater is presented as the master of sculpted prose, encapsulating experienced moments, as well as moments and movements of

---

[31] Goethe's lines in Borchardt's quotation: 'Laß den Anfang mit dem Ende Sich in eins zusammenziehn, Schneller als die Gegenstände Dich dir selbst vorüberfliehn' (Borchardt 1960, 409).

[32] 'Aber der Übergang der Betrachtung von dem physischen auf den geistigen Vorgang zeigt, mit welcher Spannkraft sie sich von dem groben Sprungbrette des positivistischen Gemeinplatzes fortzuschwingen vermag. Die ganze Welt der Empirie, als Erfahrung – der Sinne, als Erscheinung –, wird als eine Realität ausgeschränkt, um gleichzeitig, in eine neue Sphäre gehoben, als passives Objekt dem Bewußtsein des Individuums, in schärfster Ausprägung seinem Willen, zu einer grenzenlosen Plastik unterworfen zu werden' (Borchardt 1960, 408).

thought, with restrained Platonic passion. The text of the 'Conclusion' is therefore timeless, despite its strong period flavour. Having translated the whole of its concluding passage, Borchardt senses that the major part of his archaeological task has been fulfilled. With the 'dust of decades blown away' from 'these glowing and cool lines',[33] it is now evident that the sense of an era reaching its end, which expresses itself in Pater's text, is not at all that matters. What matters is the appeal to England's young generation, residing in this 'programme of the twenty-nine year old', a programme which, 'though it might, with one step, have led the way to the artistic pessimism of post-Romantic France, at the same time led out of it with a thousand steps'.[34] The revolutionary aspect of this programme was not its scepticism as such, but its revival of Romantic sensuality on the basis of scepticism. Puritanical Oxford, Borchardt indicates, was not slow to realize the appeal of Pater's text to young men, and the poisonous backlash (the kind of public response that was to kill a Rossetti, but not a Swinburne) forced Pater to be cautious. The 'Conclusion' contains an appeal, not just in the famous lines, '[t]o burn always with this hard, gem-like flame, to maintain this ecstasy' (Pater 1925, 250), but also in the admonition to the reader: 'Only be sure it is passion – that it does yield you this fruit of a quickened, multiplied consciousness' (252). This appeal must, in Borchardt's understanding, be as valid to twentieth-century moderns who have lost any belief in absolute values as it was to late nineteenth-century sceptics. Before pointing to himself and to his own generation as living proof of Pater's relevance, Borchardt deals with the formal and stylistic achievements of the English critic, which, to him, are possibly even more important than the subjects of Pater's criticism.

Pater's critical prose as a model

In *Marius the Epicurean* and *Imaginary Portraits*, Borchardt sees Romantic criticism reach its perfection. The latter work is Pater's genuinely creative, formal translation of the ideas expressed in his 'Conclusion'. The swift movement of time, and the transitoriness of the world and of human experience, are preconditions of the creative act, in this case, of the writing of historical portraits. Transitoriness determines the very texture of the work which outlasts its creator and its time. The 'easel' of these portraits, an image with which Borchardt alludes to Goethe's *Faust*, is the 'humming loom of time', and their 'canvas is literally the "web" from the "Conclusion" of the *Renaissance*, the portrait being breathed onto rather than brushed on those threads, "which pass out infinitely beyond it"'.[35] Although Pater's portraits

---

33   'Jedem der heut den Staub der Jahrzehnte von diesen glühenden und kühlen Zeilen fortbläst' (Borchardt 1960, 408).

34   'daß dies Programm des Neunundzwanzigjährigen, der Jugend Englands, zwar mit einem Schritte in den artistischen Pessimismus des nachromantischen Frankreich hineinführen mochte, aber mit tausend Schritten wieder aus ihm heraus' (Borchardt 1960, 411–12).

35   'Die Staffelei ist der "sausende Webstuhl der Zeit", die Leinwand wirklich das Gewebe aus der "*Conclusion*" der "Renaissance", das Bildnis nur auf die Fäden

present imagined characters in the manner of a historical novel, they lack precisely the 'thread' leading from picture to picture; in other words, the narrative links of a story. In a passage which anticipates today's debates about history as a narrative construct, Borchardt judges Pater's essayistic approach to the writing of history to be superior to that of a historical novelist. Pater presumes historical narrative to be something late nineteenth-century readers will be more than familiar with, and thus he is free to depict each of his characters like a figure from a novel where 'the actual book has been lost'.[36] The freedom of these historical portraits from fictional contexts means that they leave behind 'the uncertain ground of any narrated history that claims to convince'.[37] This ground is uncertain because historical fiction needs to disguise the fact that it is an imaginative construct; the less conspicuous its creator, the more convincing its claim to truth. The imaginary portrait, by contrast, admits the fact that its 'ground' is purely imagined or even imaginary. The portraitist, himself not imaginary, is thus always present in the portrait. This emancipation of the historical portrait from the two genres that make up the 'hybrid' form of the historical novel, fiction on the one hand, historiography on the other, marks the culmination of Romantic criticism. It asserts itself as an art form in its own right,[38] at liberty to engage in 'play with history as much as with narrative and with criticism',[39] and it also becomes a special cognitive form in which the knowledge of the *century of history* is both presumed and stored. Pater, who in Borchardt's view does not possess a self-conscious understanding of the critical essence of Romanticism, nevertheless acts as the 'Romantic who concludes Romanticism'.[40] Taking stock of the vast amount of 'material, knowledge and pain' accumulated in 'the European mind' over 'two generations', he refrains from Romantic fancy and irony as well as from poetic self-expression in the controlled medium of his prose.[41] The personal model of the critic and poet Borchardt imposing on himself the ethic of form is to be found in Pater:

---

gehaucht, "die jenseits von ihm unendlich weiter verlaufen"' (Borchardt 1960, 417). The corresponding passage in the 'Conclusion' reads: 'That clear, perpetual outline of face and limb is but an image of ours [...] – a design in a web, the actual threads of which pass out beyond it' (Pater 1925, 247).

[36] 'als wäre von einem historischen Roman [...] das eigentliche Buch überhaupt verloren' (Borchardt 1960, 417).

[37] 'der unsichere Grund aller mit Anspruch auf Überzeugung erzählten Historie' (Borchardt 1960, 418).

[38] See also Borchardt's reference to Pater, at the beginning of his essay, as the 'last great European critic, who had the privilege of leaving his mark on the face of the epoch as distinctively as otherwise only a great poet would' ('Der Name des letzten großen europäischen Kritikers, der sich in das Gesicht der Epoche noch so einschneidend, wie sonst nur der große Dichter, hat verzeichnen dürfen', Borchardt 1960, 402).

[39] 'ein Spiel mit der Geschichte, wie mit der Erzählung, wie mit der Kritik' (Borchardt 1960, 418).

[40] 'der abschließende Romantiker' (Borchardt 1960, 416).

[41] 'Der Stoff, das Wissen und die Schmerzen des europäischen Geistes sind in zwei Generationen so ungeheuerlich in den Raum gewachsen, daß für Purzelbäume an ihrer Seite keine Gelegenheit mehr ist' (Borchardt 1960, 417).

[a]rtist, historian, critic and the master of a type of prose which is ruled by the imagination and yet has rid itself of the imagination, [someone] who must never silence the poet in himself and never allow the poet in himself to break through to the surface.[42]

Pater's Romantic nostalgia for distant epochs has been condensed into prose, written

by a lover of the period who hides his profound knowledge [and] banishes his longing for all those nooks, crannies and crossings in which the moods of the epoch can be traced, into nothing but the tone vibrating between his evocative sentences.[43]

The criticism thus produced is not 'exact' or 'scientific' as it is born out of the passion of an amateur or 'eclectic collector', an expression Borchardt applies to another English essayist, Walter Savage Landor, whose *Imaginary Conversations* he sees as a forerunner of Pater's *Marius* and *Imaginary Portraits* (Borchardt 1960, 355 and 363). What this type of criticism does produce is a subjective universe of European culture, a universe in which the collecting subject and the collected substance of historical objects are assimilated to each other through the old humanist 'ethos bound in form' (Borchardt 1960, 363). In Borchardt's 'Gespräch über Formen' ('Conversation About Forms'), the Germans Arnold and Harry are assimilated, mainly by the form of their dialogue, to the 'English' as well as to the 'Greek' other (the spirit of Oxford; the art of sublimating the erotic impulse in dialogue). In Pater's *Imaginary Portraits*, the other is not an image of a 'real' sitter, but a projection of the painter's/critic's imagination: a character or a life as they could have existed in a period which the historical connoisseur has at his fingertips. Through pictorially and atmospherically evocative prose, the critic who is longing for the moods of distant epochs absorbs his passion in the image created by his own critical imagination. This is why Borchardt describes the six characters drawn in *Imaginary Portraits* as 'adventures of this man's soul even more than they are adventures of his mind'.[44] The object of criticism, however 'real', will always be a reflection of the critic's mind, and by creating an imaginary object as the sum total of his own knowledge and longing, the critic expresses the essence of criticism (and, by implication, the essence of Romanticism, which is that of criticism).

Borchardt sees *Marius the Epicurean* as Pater's chief imaginary portrait, i.e. as a self-portrait of the yearning, discerning and collecting spirit. As such, *Marius* only has a single forerunner: Coleridge's *Biographia Literaria*. Since Borchardt is

---

[42] 'Künstler, Historiker, Kritiker und der Meister einer von der Phantasie beherrschten und der Phantasie wieder ledig gewordenen Prosa, der den Dichter in sich nie zum Schweigen bringen und nie zum Durchbruch kommen lassen darf' (Borchardt 1960, 416).

[43] 'von einem Liebhaber des Zeitalters, der seine tiefe Kennerschaft verbirgt, seine Sehnsucht nach den Winkeln und Kreuzungen aller Stimmungen der Epoche nur in den Ton verbannt, der zwischen den heraufbeschwörenden Sätzen vibriert' (Borchardt 1960, 418).

[44] 'die sechs Gestalten sind sechs Abenteuer mehr noch dieser Seele als dieses Geistes' (Borchardt 1960, 419).

determined to represent Pater as the critic who sums up Romanticism, he suggests that, apart from the *Biographia*, there is a symbolic line of ancestors of which *Marius* forms the last descendant. His 'pedigree could be proved' if Romanticism had produced intellectual autobiographies, or more precisely, portraits of self-formation through reading: the kind of work suggested by Wieland's *Agathon*, which Friedrich Schlegel and Novalis merely sketched out but never created in full.[45] Borchardt thus regards Pater's veiled intellectual autobiography as the epitome of a Romantic genre that was waiting to be developed, a genre which is also prone to weaknesses because of the enormity of its task. Thus, *Marius*, the result of a five-year labour, is an Unding (monster), one of those Romantic attempts to achieve the impossible by 'surpassing oneself in a giant project'.[46] Its strength lies in the scope and intensity with which a nineteenth-century critic accounts to himself for his own indebtedness to the European cultural heritage. In a hyperbolical passage, linking economic with spiritual metaphors, Borchardt betrays how much he sees himself as someone in the same vein:

> [T]he author [. . .] makes an attempt never made before, which is to declare his whole intellectual debt to the past, and at the same time to clear himself of his debt by taking it upon his own soul, thus transforming the world history of the spirit into his own inner biography. In its conception as well as in its formal realization, as a product of weakness and of strength, as a universal poem of the human spirit in the forms of critical biography, and in its urge to redeem, to illuminate all ages through one another and with a view to the goal of humanity, the highest aim which makes all ages equal – in all these respects, this is the final work of Romanticism in Europe.[47]

Even if the idealistic notion of a 'goal of humanity' has not transcended the age of Romanticism, Pater's critical universalism, contracted into an 'inner biography', is seen by Borchardt as a personal and as a national model in the post-Romantic age. The extent to which he identified with Pater's art of autobiography, which fuses together the history of his personal learning and a kind of biography of the European intellect, can be seen in the fact that Borchardt published part of his own autobiography, *Kindheit und Jugend*

---

[45] 'Sein Stammbaum wäre aufweisbar, wenn die Romantik den von Wielands Agathon übernommenen Rahmen je wirklich mit solchen Werken gefüllt hätte, wie Friedrich Schlegel sie nur sich selber entwarf, und Novalis kaum als angedeutete Untermalung hinterließ' (Borchardt 1960, 419).

[46] 'als romantischer Versuch, in einem Riesenunternehmen sich selber zu übertreffen, als eine Geburt aus jenem Willen zum Unmöglichen' (Borchardt 1960, 419).

[47] '[D]er Autor [. . .] unternimmt den nie vorher unternommenen Versuch, sich seiner gesamten geistigen Schuld an die Vorzeit gleichzeitig schuldig zu bekennen und zu entledigen, indem er die Weltgeschichte des Geistes auf die eigene Seele übernimmt und in seine innere Biographie verwandelt. Sie ist als Entwurf wie als Lösung, als ein Werk der Schwäche und der Stärke, als ein Weltgedicht des Geistes in den Formen kritischer Biographie, und sie ist in ihrem Erlösungs- drange, alle Zeiten durcheinander zu beleuchten, auf das Ziel der Menschheit hin, vor dem sie alle gleich sind, das Schlußwerk der Romantik in Europa' (Borchardt 1960, 420).

(*Childhood and Youth*) under the title 'Das Kind im Hause' ('The Child in the House').This work can be found in the second volume of his *Schriften*, which appeared as a privately printed edition in 1935 (Borchardt 1966, 101). In order to achieve such power of concentration, Pater, according to Borchardt's 1939 essay, had to learn from French Romanticism (i.e. from the various movements cultivating beauty and form in the 1850s and 1860s) ways in which to fight 'the passionate struggle of the worker for the perfection of a formal miniature in form'.[48] This learning process first became paradigmatic for the English (in an anachronistically Romantic fashion, Borchardt, as usual, equates the cultural elite with 'the nation'), in that the excesses of the imagination, fostered by the dream and fairytale world of German Romanticism, were curbed in favour of form and style. Then the Germans – in other words Borchardt's own generation of writers who were, in their youth, 'fed up to death with themselves'[49] – learnt from the masters of contemporary English and French prose and verse, particularly from Pater. The Germans can still feel 'a sense of pride' in this learning process, which was tantamount to 'claiming back' their own nation's 'substantial historical credit' around 1900.[50] This logic only makes sense if one bears in mind that Borchardt defines Romanticism as a critical movement which originated in Germany. By assimilating Pater, the epitome of Romanticism, Germans found their cultural identity again, which had been lost since the decline of Romanticism in their own country. Borchardt also stresses that the specific circumstances of German intellectual history always favoured a universalist, even encyclopedic outlook, and therefore Germans would respond 'magnetically' to any examples of formal perfection that contained a 'grand structure'; in other words, to the European synthesis of Pater's prose.[51] Therefore the inner cultural universe of the English critic has itself become part of the history of German intellectual self-formation; Pater has been absorbed 'like Montesquieu and Rousseau'.[52] The debt of gratitude Germany owes to the Englishman is paid off, as it were, through Hofmannsthal's 'Chandos Letter', the foundation document of German literary Modernism in the sense of 'Creative Restoration', which Borchardt, at the end of his article, figuratively dedicates to Pater as 'the garland of German poetry' woven 'into the ivy of the quadrangle of Brasenose'.[53]

---

[48]   'der leidenschaftliche Arbeitskampf um Vervollkommnung des Förmchens in der Form' (Borchardt 1960, 420).

[49]   'seiner selbst zum Tode satt' (Borchardt 1960, 421).

[50]   'Es ist ein stolzes Gefühl für den Deutschen, daß er auch große geschichtliche Guthaben einzog' (Borchardt 1960, 421).

[51]   'Aber die alten Fügungen unserer geistigen Geschichte mußten freilich dazu führen, daß überall, wo die dichterische und literarische Reformation das universale, ja das enzyklopädische Postulat wieder aufnahm, das uns eignet, die große Struktur, mit der Walter Pater einen scheinbar kleinen Auftrag an die Ewigkeit abgeliefert hat, vor allem für uns magnetisch wurde' (Borchardt 1960, 421).

[52]   'er [Pater] ist dadurch zu einem Teile der deutschen Bildungsgeschichte geworden, wie Montesquieu und wie Rousseau' (Borchardt 1960, 421).

[53]   'der Kranz der deutschen Poesie in den Epheu des *Quadrangle's* von Brasenose' (Borchardt 1960, 422).

The implicit message of Borchardt's centenary essay, suggested at the beginning of my contribution, is that the cultural renewal of 1900 under the imperative of form must be repeated under a martial imperative. Its nationalism and its decidedly European perspective do not constitute the only paradox of this essay. The other major one is brilliantly expressed by Adorno's dictum about Borchardt: 'The same man who opted for the collective notion of German nationhood remained a man of privately published books throughout his life.'[54] Borchardt's adamantly esoteric style as an essayist certainly did not appeal to a wide public, quite apart from the fact that, as a writer of Jewish descent, he was unable to live or publish in Nazi Germany (in fact he had already settled in Tuscany in 1906). It is difficult to imagine at what kind of readership the Pater essay, published in a Swiss newspaper, was aimed. Given the fact that the figureheads of Borchardt's literary generation, Hofmannsthal, Rilke and George, were dead, the essay reads like the retrospective of a lonely survivor from the era of the Romantic revival. If being the last representative of Romantic criticism is the precondition of Pater's significance, Borchardt may well see himself as similarly significant, as a result of his being the last great critic of a period still touched by Pater's influence in German letters. The difference between himself and Pater, however, is precisely that there is no enthusiastic audience of young men to carry forward the Platonic ethos of Oxford or of Vienna, and the surveying eye of the critic taking in the one hundred years since Pater's birth is that of a lonesome eagle.[55] The critical discourse is monological, despite its spirited and inspiring embrace of the critic Pater. Whatever the undeniable merits of Borchardt's essay are, with regard to making connections between European developments in the nineteenth century and to exploring the nature and importance of criticism, it is *Borchardt's* language speaking through Pater as his alter ego. In his translation of the final paragraphs from the 'Conclusion', Borchardt makes some significant changes in the context of Pater's reference to Novalis's definition of philosophy. Pater quotes it in the original German: '*Philosophiren*, says Novalis, *ist dephlegmatisiren vivificiren*' (Pater 1925, 249). Pater's following sentence is as much an explanation of Novalis's foreign-language words as it is an explanation of a 'foreign' concept of philosophy as 'speculative culture':

> The service of philosophy, of speculative culture, towards the human spirit, is to rouse, to startle it to a life of constant and eager observation. (Pater 1925, 249)

Borchardt translates this as follows:

> Der Dienst der Philosophie am menschlichen Geiste besteht darin, ihn aufzurühren, ihn zu scharfer und dringender Wahrnehmung zu empören. (Borchardt 1960, 409)

---

[54] 'Der für Volkheit optierte, war sein Leben lang ein Mann des Privatdrucks' (Borchardt 1968, 20).

[55] 'Der Geist [. . .] möchte sich im Bogen des Adlers [. . .] aufheben [. . . .] Wenige Gefährten nur würden sich durch einsam gewordenen Himmel an seinen fernen Gesichtspunkt versammeln' (Borchardt 1960, 402).

While Pater feels it necessary to define 'philosophy' as 'speculative culture', Borchardt thus takes this definition, which he sees as a sign of the German influence on Pater, for granted. Omitting the apposition from his translation makes Borchardt's rendering considerably more apodictic. Moreover, the verbs 'to rouse' and 'to startle' are given a sense of revolutionary uprising ('aufrühren', 'empören'), an implication which is definitely absent from the original. Translating the adjectives 'constant and eager' as 'scharf' (sharp, keen) and 'dringend' (urgent; with an implication of 'durchdringend' [penetrating], since the reference is to 'observation') is an outright distortion of Pater's text. Borchardt then omits Pater's gentle lines in which the objects of 'constant and eager' observation are described: 'Every moment some form grows perfect in hand or face' (Pater 1925, 249). The German reader is invited to interpret Pater's lines as a bellicose appeal to the young generation. The Englishman has literally been assimilated to his German critic who, at another point in the essay, refers to criticism as an 'intellectual overpowering, by means of recruitment, seizure, evocation or destruction'.[56]

---

[56] 'Kritik ist geistige Überwältigung mit den Mitteln der Werbung, der Besitzergreifung, der Evokation oder der Zerstörung' (Borchardt 1960, 415).

9 Pater in Hungary

Mihály Szegedy–Maszák

To indicate paradigm shifts in the Hungarian reception of the works of Walter Pater is far from easy. A narrative based on written documents may be not only discontinuous but even misleading. Some of Pater's works may have been known to some Hungarian intellectuals before 1900. In 1888, during his stay in Paris, the prose writer Zsigmond Justh (1863–94) received substantial information from a minor British painter about the Pre-Raphaelites and their associates (Justh 1941, 59). There is good reason to believe that some members of the Nagybánya and Gödöllő colonies (founded in 1896 and 1902, respectively), artists who turned to British and French culture to oppose the hegemony of the German-speaking countries, were familiar with some of Pater's essays. Hungarian *Jugendstil* (Art Nouveau) artists turned to British sources for inspiration, but for them Ruskin, Morris and Walter Crane seem to have been more important than Pater. While Ruskin's *The Stones of Venice*, *Unto this Last* and *Sesame and Lilies* were published in Hungarian in 1896–98, 1904 and 1911, respectively, a much smaller public read Pater in the original or in German. In 1895 five hundred works by Crane were exhibited in the Art Hall of Budapest. In July 1904, a special issue of the journal *Magyar Iparművészet* was published in his honour with a title page designed by Crane himself. Between 10 October and 5 November Crane visited Hungary and made drawings of Hungarian peasant costumes in Transylvania. In the same year the artist Aladár Körösfői Kriesch (1863–1920) gave lectures on Ruskin, Morris, and the Pre-Raphaelites. When published, the four lectures were supplemented by illustrations of works by Dante Gabriel Rossetti, Morris, Holman Hunt, Burne-Jones and Ford Maddox Brown, as well as by translations of texts by Ruskin, Morris, Dante Gabriel Rossetti, and Swinburne. Körösfői Kriesch, one of the founders of the Gödöllő colony, was a painter who also cultivated the applied arts. It would have been difficult for Kriesch – the admirer of both the Italian Renaissance and the Pre-Raphaelite painters and the alert reader of Rossetti, Swinburne and Morris – not to have been familiar with *Studies in the History of the Renaissance*. If he did not mention Pater by name, it was because the cult of art for art's sake attributed to the British essayist was incompatible with the Hungarian artist's functionalist view of art. Hungarian artists took a more serious interest in the more explicitly moral connotations of Ruskin's approach and sometimes even in the socialism of Morris and Crane than in the Aesthetic movement. As an art historian noted about the Hungarian representatives of *Jugendstil*: 'From the two paths of aestheticism they follow that of the romanticism of John Ruskin which propagated the social usefulness of art, versus Walter Pater who was closer to the French "l'art pour l'art'" (Gellér 1990, 162).

The earliest essays that Hungarian authors published on Walter Pater focused on his interpretation of Classical Antiquity. The author of the first of these articles, Sándor Hevesi (1873–1939), was a leading figure in the theatrical life of Budapest. As translator and director he made numerous works by G. B. Shaw accessible to the Hungarian public. At the time his long essay on Pater appeared, he had just started his activity as the theoretician and director of Thália Company, a group known for theatrical experimentation. Retrospectively, Hevesi's interpretation of Pater seems a strange mixture of amateurish statements and perceptive observations. By way of introduction, he summarized the impact of Greek culture on Renaissance and Classicist literature. The assertion that 'Shakespeare [...] is free of the influence of Classical Antiquity'[1] is followed by a sensitive characterization of the art of Corneille, Racine, Dryden, Goethe and Schiller. The rest of the article is based on *Griechische Studien*, translated by Wilhelm Dobbe and published by Eugen Dieterichs in Leipzig in 1904.

In Hevesi's view the chief merit of Pater's book is the critique of the misconception that ancient Greece had a homogeneous religion. Speaking of regional differences, Hevesi summarizes Pater's analysis of the cults of Dionysus, Demeter and Persephone. Inspired by Pater's essays, Hevesi regards Greek literature and art as a legacy that can be a source of artistic innovations. The range of works he discusses is wide; it includes those paintings of Böcklin which are marked by the allegorical use of mythology and the plays of Hofmannsthal.

The German translation used by Hevesi was analysed in detail by Mihály Latkóczy (1857–1906), who studied classical philology in Budapest and Slavic languages in Vienna, and published scholarly works as well as translations of Euripides, Tibullus and others. He started his review by comparing the German with the English text as published by Macmillan in 1901. Having made some critical remarks about the translation, he praised Pater's prose but also pointed to two shortcomings: he referred to 'the excesses of poetic style' and argued that the British author 'relies on highly sophisticated concepts that are incompatible with anthropology and folklore'.[2] The second of these charges is rather serious; what Latkóczy implies is that Pater's approach is in contradiction with the basic principles of historiography. The reviewer refers to Pater's 'perceptive observations on the Doric and Ionic elements in Greek art' but has strong reservations about his scholarship: 'the adherents of a strictly philological method will regret that sources are not considered'.[3]

---

1   'Shakespeare [...] ment maradt minden antik hatástól' (Hevesi 1904, 539).

2   'a poétikus elemek túltengése [...] hyperkulturált képzeteket és fogalmakat terel vissza a szerző olyan korokba és időkbe, amelyek csakis primitív anthropológia és folklore szempóntjából magyarázhatók' (Latkóczy 1906, 147).

3   'finom megfigyelésekre, melyekben a szerző a hellén művészet dór és ión elemeit világítja meg. [...] A szigorú philológiai módszer barátja sajnálatal nélkülözi a forrásokra való hivatkozást' (Latkóczy 1906, 149).

Hungary had a strong tradition of positivistic classical philology. At the same time, the Hungarian reading public was deeply moved by the fate of Oscar Wilde. Pater was appreciated as a fine stylist and as the teacher of the author of *The Critic as Artist*. 'Sebastian van Storck' was translated by Piroska Reichard (1884–1943), a minor poet whose work was strongly influenced by the British *fin de siècle* (Pater 1912). Shortly before the appearance of this translation, Reichard published a longer essay on Pater, arguing that the characteristics of a scholar and a poet were combined in the activity of this author. The imaginary portrait was described as a product of this combination. Having described this genre, Reichard gave an analysis of Pater's style, with special emphasis on the influence of Flaubert. Reichard's piece is itself a portrait in the tradition of Macaulay. The introductory section is biographical and contains quotations from 'The Child in the House' and a letter addressed to Vernon Lee. The much longer second part is a detailed summary of all the works, including those published posthumously. Although the essay is full of praise, the concluding section refers to passages in Pater's works that are 'artificial' and 'mannered' (Reichard 1912, 423). Such a reservation reflected a consensus among Hungarian writers.

One year before the outbreak of the First World War Pater's book on the Renaissance appeared in Hungarian. Its translator Károly Sebestyén (1872–1945) studied in Budapest, Leipzig and Berlin, published works on Greek and Roman culture, and was known as a left-wing critic, a regular contributor to *Pesther Lloyd*, a German newspaper published in Budapest, and a professor of the Academy of Theatre. His translation appeared in a prestigious series called *Világkönyvtár* (Pater 1913) and had a second edition in 1919. In his preface Sebestyén discussed not the essays on the Renaissance but Pater's activity as a whole. What he underlined was the wide gap between the German philological tradition and Pater's approach to his topics. Hungary had been under German influence for such a long time that it was high time for the country to learn about other modes of thinking. This polemical argument was in tune not only with the ideas of the Liberal and Radical politicians but also with those of numerous writers and artists in the Hungary of the prewar years.

After an entirely favourable short notice ('Pater Walter: A Renaissance', 1913), the same scholarly journal published a devastating attack on Sebestyén's translation (Kőszegi 1914). Its author, a secondary-school teacher who later translated another book by Pater, took the description of the Mona Lisa as a starting point to prove that the Hungarian text contradicted the art works described and that the translator had used Schölermann's German text, published by Diederichs, instead of translating from the original. All the corrections made by the reviewer suggest that he was a far more sophisticated interpreter of Pater's work than Sebestyén.

One year after the publication of the Hungarian version of *The Renaissance*, *Greek Studies* appeared in the translation of László Kőszegi. His work was checked by Piroska Reichard and brought out by the Hungarian Academy of Sciences. It reflects the perspective of an instructor who takes a serious interest in teaching how to draw. Accordingly, in the introduction he spoke of Ruskin's influence on Pater and Pater's impact on the Pre-Raphaelites. His critical remarks echo those of Latkóczy: 'Although Walter Pater's essays are rich in ideas, they are works of art rather than analyses'.[4] Commenting on 'Style', the first essay in Pater's *Appreciations*, Kőszegi drew a parallel between Pater and Flaubert, claiming that these two writers succeeded in combining poetry and prose. He drew attention to artistic weaknesses, commenting for example on the loose structure of *Marius*, and provided a short but pertinent analysis of imagery, inversion, fragmentation and elaboration in Pater's works.

In sharp contrast to Sebestyén's translation, Kőszegi's version of *Greek Studies* was received extremely well. Marianne Czeke made some stylistic suggestions, but these referred to nuances rather than to serious differences in interpretation. 'The translation is faithful and the Hungarian text has a beauty that is comparable to the music of the original', she wrote.[5] Her only objection was that 'the occasionally excessive artificiality of Walter Pater's style exerted some influence on the translator'.[6]

It goes without saying that Pater's influence played some role in the evolution of Hungarian literature in the early twentieth century. In 1922 Gyula Szini (1987–1932) published a series of essays. Szini was a short-story writer associated with the Hungarian equivalent of *Jugendstil*. By 1922 this trend had become outmoded; the essay collection is a retrospective, somewhat nostalgic discussion of the works of those writers who served as models for the generation ousted by the Hungarian avant-garde that started around 1915, when its first journal appeared. Pater was one of the twelve authors Szini regarded as canonical for his generation, the others being Anatole France, Baudelaire, Verlaine, Dostoyevsky, Strindberg, Gerhard Hauptmann, Maeterlinck, Wilde, Dante Gabriel Rossetti, Prosper Mérimée and Ernest la Jeunesse. All the portraits are written in such a turgid style that they will not stand close analysis. Their interest is purely historical in the sense that they reflect the taste of a generation that is forgotten today. In sharp contrast to the scholarly perspective of Latkóczy or Kőrösi, the focus is on the imaginary portraits.

For Szini, as for Reichard, Pater was a creative writer representative of the spiritual climate of the late nineteenth century. These minor authors regarded Pater's style as the epitome of subjectivity. From the late nineteenth century a strong reaction set in against positivistic philology, and numerous writers associated with *Nyugat* (West), the periodical started at the beginning of 1908, tended to regard the author of *The Renaissance* as a representative of an alternative tradition. The author of the standard monograph on Mihály Babits (1883–1941), one of the major poets in the circle of *Nyugat*, argued that Pater exerted a decisive influence on the early verse of Babits: 'He borrowed the concept of the lyrical portrait from Walter Pater, who had given an analysis of Browning's treatment of characters presented in dramatic

---

4   'De minden eszmei gazdagságuk mellett is W. Pater tanulmányai nem annyira elemzések, mint inkább műalkotások' (Pater 1914, 9).

5   'A fordítás hű is, szép is, csodálatosan simul a szerző belső nyelvezetéhez' (Czeke 1915, 747).

6   'Walter Pater stílusának néha túlzott keresettsége a fordítóra is hatott' (Czeke 1915, 751).

situations'.[7] The argument may be somewhat far-fetched in so far as no clear definition of such a concept can be found in Pater's works, but it is quite possible that the Hungarian poet drew inspiration from the comments on Browning's 'poetry of situations', in the essay on Winckelmann. There may be an echo of these comments in the essay on Browning that Babits published in *Nyugat* in 1912 (Babits 1978b, 1: 286–9) and in the lectures Babits delivered at Pázmány Péter University in 1919, especially in the remarks on objectivity in the lyric (Babits 1978b, 1: 620). It is also worth remarking that some of the poems published in the Hungarian poet's first two collections, *Levelek Irisz koszorújából* (*Leaves from Iris' Wreath*, 1909) and *Herceg, hátha megjön a tél is!* (*Prince, What if Winter Comes?*, 1911) seem to correspond to the description Pater gave in 'The School of Giorgione' of the 'highest form of dramatic poetry' that 'presents us with a kind of profoundly significant and animated instants, a mere gesture, a look, a smile, perhaps – some brief and wholly concrete moment – into which, however, all the motives, all the interests and effects of a long history, have condensed themselves, and which seem to absorb past and future in an intense consciousness of the present'.

Late in his career Babits referred to Pater's significance in the following manner in his monumental work entitled *Az európai irodalom története* (*A History of European Literature*): 'Style had become of crucial importance. The opponents of Naturalism focused on what they regarded as artistic. In Oxford a circle of the spokesmen of *l'art pour l'art* was formed around Walter Pater, the author of the collection known as *The Renaissance*'.[8] The fact that this passage is supplemented by a more detailed characterization somewhat later in the book suggests that Babits saw Pater as one of the authors who played a decisive role in the literature of the late nineteenth century: 'The most sophisticated literary trends of the end of the century represented an extreme form of the artistic. In Oxford the combination of different styles reached a high degree. The Greek and Renaissance studies of Walter Pater were far from original in content, but their syntax was truly remarkable. His style was complex yet flexible, rich in ornaments and music. Art itself became the topic of these works of art. In the *Imaginary Portraits* even this topic was sometimes deconstructed in the sense that the narrative focused on an artist who was the product of Pater's imagination. The subject became subordinated to the demands of style and colouring'.[9]

---

[7] 'Magát a lírai festmény fogalmát, sőt browningi fölfogásának mintáját Walter Patertől merítette. Ő mutatja meg, Browning a megismerés milyen költői lehetőségére bukkant, amikor verseinek egy-egy hősét drámai helyzetbe juttatta' (Rába 1981, 124).

[8] 'A stílus általában rendkívül fontossá kezdett lenni. A naturálizmus ellenségei artisztikumra törekedtek. Oxfordban egész kis *l'art pour l'art* kör kezdett kialakulni Walter Pater körül, aki a *Renaissance* című könyvet írta' (Babits 1935, 644).

[9] 'A századvég legmagasabb irodalmi törekvései egyáltalában a túlhajtott művésziesség tobzódását jelentették. Az oxfordi csoport végletekbe vitte a stílus ötvözését. Walter Pater görög és reneszánsz tanulmányai tartalmilag alig mondtak újat, de stílusuk szinte mondatról mondatra remekmű. Sűrű és puha stílus ez, bársony és brokát, gazdag ornamenseel, s minden ízében zenei. E műveknek már

Having published his history of European literature, Babits and the critic Gábor Halász (1901–45) made a plan for a textbook that could serve as a supplement to it. This project was never completed but the fragment published posthumously indicates that it would have contained the translation of an extract from *The Renaissance* (Babits 1978a, 237). Accordingly, when after the poet's death Halász compiled an anthology of English literature, he asked the philosopher József Szigeti to prepare a new translation of the description of *La Gioconda*, and also included an extract from 'A Prince of Court Painters' in the translation of Piroska Reichard (Pater 1941a and b).

Although the philosopher György Lukács (1885–1971) cannot be regarded as a member of the inner circle of *Nyugat*, he discussed Pater's activity in an article published in the first year of the periodical. For him Rudolf Kassner seemed the most important essayist of modern times, but his respect for Pater, Ruskin and Taine was no less unqualified. In his 1908 article on the German critic he praised these four essayists for their success in subordinating biography to the discussion of works of art. In Lukács's view the essayist has to disappear behind his topic. 'A Prince of Court Painters' is taken as a perfect example of such impersonality: 'Watteau emerges as a highly impressive character in the diary of the young girl whose presence is hardly perceptible'.[10] In the somewhat later self-reflective text called 'Levél a "kísérlet"-ről' ('A Letter on the "Essay"'), published in the collection *A lélek és a formák* (*Soul and Form*, 1910), Pater is mentioned together with Kierkegaard, Nietzsche, Hofmannsthal and Kassner as one of the most important masters of the genre invented by Montaigne, and *Marius the Epicurean* is described as the masterpiece of its author (Lukács 1977, 320).

Lukács had a much better command of German than of English, but he had a reading knowledge of English from the age of fourteen (Bendl 1994, 35). In the so-called *Heidelberg Aesthetics*, a work that its author left in manuscript in a safe in Heidelberg in 1917 (Bendl 1994, 207), the well-known declaration 'All art constantly aspires towards the condition of music' is cited from a 1913 edition of *The Renaissance*, published by Macmillan. Lukács had no talent for music. In secondary school his singing earned him very bad marks, but before writing his early aesthetics he was exposed to some music, since his sister studied with the celebrated cellist Dávid Popper and the young composer Béla Bartók (Bendl 1994, 22–23). At any rate, he used Pater's statement as a starting point for meditations on 'pure form' as the condition of music in the *Heidelberg Aesthetics*, written during the First World War but not published during the author's lifetime (Lukács 1975, 109).

For Antal Szerb (1901–45), the most popular among the literary essayists of the interwar period, Pater's legacy became a source of constant inspiration. It seems likely that he read *The Renaissance* at the age of nineteen. On 21 July 1920 he mentioned Pico and Leonardo in his diary (Szerb 2001, 73), and on

---

témájuks is csak a művészet: a művészetek művészete ez. Sőt a *Képzelt arcképekben* az író már a tanulmány tárgyát is elveti: tanulmányt ír például egy művészről, aki sohasem létezett!' (Babits 1935, 662–3).

10   'Watteau egy leány naplóján keresztül van ábrázolva, és ködbe foszlik a naplóíró lány alakja' (Lukács 1977, 152).

December 26 of the same year he declared that his goal was 'to burn always . . . ' (Szerb 2001, 83). The three words quoted from the 'Conclusion' of *The Renaissance* are followed by a summary of the concluding section of Pater's work. Six years later, Szerb came to use the same fragment (this time in Hungarian translation) as a starting-point for the characterization of Stefan George's *Weltbild* (Szerb 1971, 87). He continued to identify himself with Pater's aestheticism. In his short book on Castiglione, *Az udvari ember* (*The Courtier*, 1927) he relied on Pater's definition of the Renaissance (Szerb 1971, 154) and in his provocative work on conservatism and modernism in novel-writing, *Hétköznapok és csodák* (*Weekdays and Miracles*, 1935) he argued that the overlap of the outside world and the psyche is a common feature of the art of Pater and Proust (Szerb 1971, 517). By insisting on continuity between Aestheticism and the innovations of the early twentieth century he anticipated Harold Bloom's view that Pater was a 'chief precursor' of Modernism.

All in all, it is safe to assume that between the two world wars Pater was a canonical author in Hungary. In the most popular literary encyclopedia published in the period, he was characterized as 'one of the greatest stylists and most perceptive critics in English literature'. *Studies in the History of the Renaissance* and *Marius the Epicurean* were mentioned as his most important works, but *Imaginary Portraits*, *Appreciations*, *Plato and Platonism* and *Greek Studies* were also briefly described. The author of the article referred to the influence of Ruskin, Arnold, Carlyle and some representatives of German aesthetics, and defined Pater's position in relation to the cult of art for art's sake and Christianity (Rózsa 1927, 925).

During the two decades following the Second World War Hungarian culture was dominated by a version of Marxist ideology that condemned all authors who spoke of art for art's sake. Pater was not even mentioned in the two big volumes of Lukács's second aesthetics, published first in German (*Die Eigenart des Ästhetischen*, *The uniqueness of the Aesthetic*, 1963) and later in a Hungarian translation by the philosopher's young associate István Eörsi (Lukács 1965).

Not much more attention was devoted to Pater's works in the last two decades of East European Communism, when most of the innovative Hungarian scholars worked under the influence of Russian Formalism, Czech and French Structuralism, phenomenology, and New Criticism. In 1967 Európa, the state-owned firm responsible for making world literature accessible to the Hungarian public, published a representative selection of English essays. For this volume the poet István Jánosy was asked to make a new translation of the unabridged text of 'Leonardo da Vinci' (Pater 1967). Except for this anthology not much interest was taken in Pater's works in the last three decades of the twentieth century.

It was not until poststructuralist reader-response criticism had made its influence felt that Hungarian scholars reassessed the British author's legacy. In 1999 Aladár Sarbu (b. 1940), Professor of English at Eötvös Loránd University (Budapest), the author of *Szocialista realista törekvések a modern angol regényben* (*Socialist Realist Trends in Modern English Fiction*, 1967), *Henry James és a lélektani regény* (*Henry James and the Psychological Novel*, 1981) and the novel *Töredék: Egy pártember emlékirataiból* (*A fragment from the Memoirs of a Party Member*, 1983), published an essay as 'part of an intended longer study which purports

to review the whole extent of Pater's contribution to English Modernism'
(Sarbu 1999, 91). Sarbu is planning to write a book that has 'the tentative title
Walter Pater Among the Modernists'.[11] From the chapters he has kindly sent me
before publication it seems that his work in progress has relatively few Marxist
reminiscences, in sharp contrast to his earlier works. Following the lead of J.
Hillis Miller, Harold Bloom and Perry Meisel, Sarbu regards Pater as a
precursor of Modernism. The passages selected to prove the influence of
Pater's mythopoetic experiments (his 'imaginary portraits' and the description
of the Mona Lisa) on other writers include the description of Bronzino's
portrait of Lucrezia Panciatichi in *The Wings of the Dove*, Stephen Dedalus's
theorizing about aesthetic pleasure in *The Portrait of the Artist as a Young Man*,
and Yeats's remarks on the concept of 'Unity of Being' in *A Vision*. The
evidence he provides for his discussion of Pater's influence on Yeats is well
known and satisfactory. It is possible to debate his claim that Pater's works
served as a source of inspiration for Henry James and Virginia Woolf. While
the focus on a link between the Aesthetic movement and these two writers
might be legitimate, simplifications cannot be avoided if the differences are
not highlighted. Although James owned a copy of the 1873 edition of *The
Renaissance*, his treatment of the 'Classical ideal' can hardly be taken as a
decisive proof, especially where the analysis is not restricted to English
literature. Sarbu mentions that Adeline Tintner detects the influence of
Mérimée's 'La Vénus d'Ille', but he seems to be unaware that James translated
this novella, and at the beginning of 1874, the time of the first appearance of
The Last of the Valerii, he published a review of the French writer's last tales, in
which he called *La Vénus d'Ille* 'a version of the old legend of a love-pledge
between a mortal and an effigy of the goddess' (James 1957, 171). In view of
this, it is possible to argue that James relied on Mérimée rather than on Pater
when elaborating on the relations between life and art, a feature also
characteristic of many other works by the American-born writer.

Sarbu gives a detailed analysis of critical studies suggesting that Pater's
theory of aesthetic perception anticipates Stephen's in *Stephen Hero* and *The
Portrait of the Artist as a Young Man*. The claim that Joyce's essay 'James
Clarence Mangan' (1902) merely reiterates an article of faith – first expressed
in the 'Conclusion' of *The Renaissance* – of Modernism: that experience is
inward and its quality depends on the sensibility of the artist may be
exaggerated, since it fails to take into consideration the impact of such authors
as Novalis and Flaubert on Pater. There is also some trace of Sarbu's earlier
Marxism in the thesis that Pater was working within the terms of symbolism
whereas Joyce had moved into psychological realism. A similar reservation can
be made about the comparison with T. S. Eliot. The later work of the two
authors may share a fear of anarchy and a desire for an authoritarian and
hierarchical society, but such a purely ideological parallel may also be drawn
between Eliot and several other writers. Pater's own debt to German
Romanticism and such French writers as Stendhal, Mérimée and Flaubert

---

[11]   'A projektum, amelynek végállomása egy könyv lesz, Walter Pater among the
Modernists címet viseli' (Sarbu 2002).

should be taken into account when he is characterized as a precursor of Modernism.

Sarbu places a high priority on the analysis of the epistemological aspects of Pater's book *Plato and Platonism*, but pays little attention to the international implications of nineteenth-century British literature. That implies that the force of his interpretation is limited to English studies. The revival of interest in Pater in our own time is inseparable from such poststructuralist tendencies as Deconstruction and reader-response criticism. In 2001 the essay as a genre was chosen for the topic of the annual conference of Hungarian critics held in Debrecen. Discussion centred on the conflict between impressionistic essay writing and scholarly studies. Some participants regarded this conflict as a legacy that has had a damaging influence on Hungarian intellectual life. In the past Pater's name was often cited by those who insisted that criticism and poetry were indistinguishable. The 'appreciative' method that such essayists advocated was intended to mime the emotional effect of a work of art through the cadences of the interpreter's prose. For them, Pater's example served as an excuse for a certain looseness in the handling of concepts, and for the use of a vocabulary employing imprecise language, being heavily dependent on figures and on the interplay between images. One of the two keynote speakers of the Debrecen conference tried to correct earlier Hungarian interpretations of Pater by drawing attention to a passage in the essay on Sir Thomas Browne that could be taken as a warning against the temptations of subjectivism for essay writing: 'The faults of such literature are what we all recognize in it: unevenness, alike in thought and style, lack of design, and caprice' (Szegedy-Maszák 2002, 25–6).

In the early twentieth century the influence of Pater's writing played an important role in the formation of the style of those Hungarian essayists who reacted against positivistic scholarship. The current revival of interest in his activity suggests that his example continues to attract scholars working in studies involving comparison between the arts and reader-response criticism. In the past his books were discussed mainly by Classical philologists. Today they are taught in departments of aesthetics, comparative literature and English literature.

10 Pater in Czech Culture: Miloš Marten's Essay on *Marius the Epicurean* (1911)

Martin Procházka

Walter Pater's work became influential in the Czech culture in the first decade of the twentieth century, thanks to the writers of the second wave of the Czech Decadence. *Imaginary Portraits*, part of which appeared in a Czech translation in 1907 as *Imaginární portraity* (Pater 1907) could well have influenced the essays by Artur Breiský (1885–1910) (Stříbrný 1987, 2:566) that appeared in the literary and critical periodical *Moderní revue* (*Modern Review*, 1894–1925)[1] between 1907 and 1910. Breiský, known for his practical jokes and literary hoaxes,[2] may have received from Pater the stimuli for the gestures of self-stylization in his essays on Tiberius, Nero, Byron, Watteau, Baudelaire and Wilde.[3]

A few years later, Pater's reflections in *The Renaissance* had a considerable impact on writers, critics, painters and sculptors in and around the Mánes

---

[1] Founded, edited and published by Arnošt Procházka (1869–1925), a leading Czech Decadent, *Moderní revue* played a key role in the Czech culture at the turn of the century as a platform for Art Nouveau in literature and the visual arts. It was the most important mediator of French, German, Scandinavian, Italian, Russian, English and Spanish Symbolism, Decadence and Expressionism, and other nonconformist cultural trends (for instance, a special issue on Oscar Wilde published in 1895 dealt openly with problems of homosexuality).

[2] Breiský, who from 1904 worked as a customs officer at Teplice and Děčín (close to the northern frontier of the Austro-Hungarian Empire with Germany), used to appear in Prague and Dresden disguised as a rich aristocratic connoisseur of art. His tricks and posing caused some later critics to believe that he had not died in New York (where he worked, reduced to extreme poverty, as a liftboy) in 1910 but that his literary career continued under the new pen-name of Bruno Traven (this pseudonym is most frequently attributed to the German writer Albert Otto Max Feige, 1882/90–1969). When Breiský translated *The Suicide Club* (1882) by Robert Louis Stevenson (*Klub sebevrahů*, 1909), he incorporated two of his texts, 'Báseň v próze' ('A Poem in Prose') and 'Zpověď grafomanova' ('Confession of a Manic Scribbler'), in his translation as Stevenson's own works (Forst 1985, 298).

[3] Breiský's essays were published posthumously as *Střepy zrcadel* (*Fragments of Mirrors*, 1928) by Arthur Novák, an owner of the eponymous press aimed at bibliophiles and known for print collections, artistic binding or rare books. From 1916 to 1934 Novák was publishing books of Czech symbolists, decadents, and Catholic poets.

Association of Visual Artists (Spolek výtvarných umělců Mánes). Two translations of this work into Czech appeared in 1911 and 1913.[4] Similarly *The Renaissance* could well have exercised a formative influence on the essays of a pioneering English literature scholar in the Czech lands, František Chudoba (1878–1941),[5] who, after becoming Reader of English Literature at Charles University in 1913, established English literature studies at the newly founded Masaryk University in Brno in 1922.

All these openings would undoubtedly deserve detailed examination, but their relevance for the Czech reception of Pater's work is difficult to prove without relying a good deal on speculation. This cannot be said, however, about the most important text documenting Pater's reception in the Czech culture, Miloš Marten's (1883–1917)[6] afterword to the Czech translation of Pater's novel *Marius the Epicurean* (Pater 1911, 269–78).[7] This rather short essay written by an important representative of the Czech Decadence demonstrates the complexity of the cultural circumstances where Pater's work was received.

---

[4] Founded in 1887, Mánes Association of Visual Artists promoted the art nouveau, and later also avant-garde trends in art, including cubism and surrealism. Its journal *Volné směry (Free Trends)*, founded in 1896, created a broad platform for artists, writers and critics. The publishing activity of the association was soon extended into book trade. From 1905, several series of books on visual arts, music, literature, history and politics were published. Mánes Association published Pater's *Renaissance* in the translation of Dr J. Reichmann in 1913 as *Renaissance. Studie o výtvarném umění a poesii* in the series Dráhy a cíle (Trajectories and Objectives). This was better than the first Czech translation by Máša Dvořáková, published in 1911 by Kamilla Neumannová as *Renaissanční duchové: studie o umění a poesii*.

[5] Many essays in Chudoba's books are not primarily based on biographical data and close reading but rather on imaginative visions of the work or attitudes of individual authors. This is especially true of his 'Habilitationsschrift' *Wordsworth: pokus o třídění (Wordsworth: An Attempt at Classification*, 1911), and his essays on Shelley, Ruskin, Dante Gabriel Rosetti and other English authors in *Básníci, věštci a a bojovníci (Poets, Augurs and Fighters*, 1915). Both books had an important influence on F. X. Šalda (1868–1947), a leading critic of the time and on the representatives of Modernism, such as the novelist and dramatist Karel Čapek (1890–1938).

[6] Marten is a phonetic transcription of the French surname Martin, which was the maiden name of the author's mother. She was a descendant of a French aristocratic family, which emigrated to Austria after the breakup of the French Revolution.

[7] The translation was published in Prague in 1911 by Kamilla Neumannová (1874–1956), the ex-wife of a Czech Anarchist, later Communist, poet Stanislav Kostka Neumann (1875–1947). When Neumann left Kamilla in 1904, she had to provide for herself and their two children. Therefore she started publishing a series called The Books of Good Authors (Knihy dobrých autorů) including Czech translations from French, English, Russian, Polish, Italian, Norwegian, Spanish, Dutch, German, Finnish, Flemish, Portuguese and Ukrainian literatures. Launched with the help of a major Czech Anarchist poet František (Fráňa) Šrámek (1877–1952), the series (a volume a month with the usual print run of one thousand copies) was supported by subscriptions until 1914. The series editor was Arnošt Procházka until his death in 1925. Afterwards, the series ran until 1931.

Born to an upper-class family in Brno (his father was a high-ranking official in the regional administration), Miloš Marten studied law in Prague and graduated in 1906. At that time he became a close friend with the painter Zdeňka Braunerová (1858–1934) who illustrated and designed his books. She had also stimulated his interest in French culture, which resulted in several long visits to Paris, where he met the painter Emile Bernard and was influenced by the neoclassically oriented group of artists around the review *Rénovation esthétique*, who sought their inspiration in the ancient Roman culture and Catholic art of the Romance countries. After his return from France, where he had fallen ill with typhoid fever, Marten started a correspondence with Paul Claudel, who became a close friend during his period as French consul in Prague in 1909–10. In 1912 Marten married Anna (At'a) Kopalová (1894–1974), the daughter of a miller and factory owner. In 1912–14 he was a clerk at the Prague City Hall. After his mobilization in 1915 he was sent to the Russian front, where he was seriously injured. In 1916 he was again ordered to the Eastern front, but soon sent back because of a serious heart disease, which resulted in his death in July 1917 at the age of thirty-four.

Marten's works include collections of essays on writers and painters, especially *Kniha silných* (*The Book of the Strong*, 1909, revised and enlarged 1910). This was a collection of essays on recent and contemporary French writers and artists, which contrasted the revolt of *poètes maudits*, especially of Baudelaire, with the rebirth of Catholic spirituality in the works of Paul Claudel, and the restoration of related forms of order, such as the revival of neoclassicism in the novels of Elémir Bourges (Marten's friend and the brother-in-law of Zdeňka Braunerová), the synthesis of mysticism and Aestheticism in the essays and poetry of André Suarès, and the search for transpersonal, metaphysical values in the art of Emile Bernard. The theme of the conflict between modern chaos and traditional order also dominates in *Nad městem* (*Above the City*, 1917), an essay in the form of a dialogue between a self-confident citizen of a Catholic Romance-language-speaking country and a Czech riven with inner contradictions. Another important volume of essays, *Akord* (*The Chord*, 1916) traces the continuity of Czech Romanticism, Neoromanticism and Symbolism, linking together three writers: Karel Hynek Mácha (1810–36), Julius Zeyer (1841–1901) and Otokar Březina (1868–1929). Marten's novellas and short stories, for instance *Cyklus rozkoše a smrti* (*The Cycle of Erotic Pleasure and Death*, 1907) or *Dvě novelly* (*Two Novellas*, 1927), are influenced by late romantic French and English authors (Barbey d'Aurevilly, Oscar Wilde). He also published poems, translations (Claudel, Bourges, Baudelaire) and essays and reviews on contemporary painting (Edvard Munch, Paul Gauguin and others).

Since the age of seventeen Marten had been contributing to the *Moderní revue* and by 1911 was one of its important authors. It is most likely that Arnošt Procházka, the editor of the review, asked him to write the afterword to Pater's novel. Marten's interest in *Marius the Epicurean* might indeed have been kindled by Procházka's reflections on 'the Renaissance of paganism' ('renesance pohanství').

This would explain the attention given in his essay to the existence of 'pagan sadness'[8] in Italian Renaissance painting, especially in the works of Sandro Botticelli. Interestingly enough, Marten misquotes Pater's essay on Botticelli in *The Renaissance*, where only 'the sadness with which he [Botticelli] has conceived the goddess of pleasure' is mentioned, and interprets Pater's argument that 'you will find this quaint design of Botticelli's a more direct inlet into the Greek temper than the works of the Greeks themselves' (Pater 1910, 58–60) as a straightforward statement of Botticelli's 'paganism'. Evidently, Pater's approach to the complex emotional implications of Botticelli's paintings is much more sophisticated, stressing the displacement of Christian spirituality but refusing to identify it with the revival of paganism:

> the story [of Botticelli as a commentator on Dante and a disciple of Savonarola] interprets much of the peculiar sentiment with which he infuses his profane and sacred persons, comely, and in a certain sense like angels, but with a sense of displacement or loss about them – the wistfulness of exiles, conscious of a passion and energy greater than any known issue of them explains, which runs through all his varied work with a sentiment of ineffable melancholy. (Pater 1910, 55)

Discussing Pater's approach to the past and its cultures, Marten values 'a strong element of poetic and imaginative potency' more than 'the empirical exactitude and scientific rigor at the base of Pater's essays'.[9] Pater's imaginative gesture is understood as a supreme creative act resulting from 'long and complex inward processes' and 'projecting a certain tension of his spirit, while concealing its innumerable different states and possibilities'.[10] Only when the imagination is disciplined and directed by 'the power of vivid and clear knowledge of the human soul' may it become, as Pater's imagination did, the symbol of 'a creative spirit or a cultural type'.[11]

This symbolic tendency is seen in Pater's *Imaginary Portraits*. On the one hand, Marten sees Pater chiselling out historical details 'with a great love of a connoisseur'; on the other hand, he claims that Pater's imagination breathes 'a soft changeable haze' over them, creating an effect of 'historical chiaroscuro'.[12] Pater's 'pensive, melancholy portraits' are placed against 'clear and calm horizons of a distinctly characterised past'.[13] As a result, they can transcend historical objectivity in a playful yet intense emotional effect, blurring the boundaries between dreams, creations of art and the knowledge of its history:

---

8 'pohanské tesknoty' (Pater 1911, 270).
9 'silný živel básnické obrazotvorné potence [...] empirické přesnosti, tvrdého vědeckého základu essaí Paterových' (Pater 1911, 270).
10 'dlouhými a složitými vnitřními ději [...] promítá určité napětí ducha, jehož nesčíslné jiné stavy a možnosti utajuje' (Pater 1911, 270).
11 'silou živé, jasné znalosti duše lidské [...] tvůrčího ducha nebo kulturního typu'(Pater 1911, 270).
12 's velkou láskou znalcovou [...] měkkou náladovou mlhou [...] historické chiaroscuro' (Pater 1911, 271).
13 'zamyšlené, těžkomyslné podobizny [...]v klidných jasných horizontech minulosti, určitě charakterizované' (Pater 1911, 271).

at other times their airy drawing resembles light but nonetheless intense art of sanguine, dear to the eighteenth century [...] Are they mere dreams, or reminiscences, brought alive, of a certain figure from an old French tapestry, faces from van Steen's painting, or a profile from a Rococo miniature? Be that as it may, they condense and suggest a mood, an atmosphere, an internal tension of ages evoked by them.[14]

A typical feature of this effect is 'a certain fatal link of beauty and sadness, dreaming and feebleness, desire and hesitation [...] toning down the colours of whole ages, producing a harmonious yet fatigued *gris en gris*'.[15]

In Marten's view, Pater's vision of history is harmonious and tolerant: in taming its dynamic and dramatic elements, it can grasp life as 'a vast, undulating infinity of movement, light, emergence, change, as an ocean of hues, all of which deserve the thinker's attention and kindle a joy of his knowledge'.[16] Marten seems to indicate that Pater understands history as a heterogeneity of life, which cannot be adequately grasped either as a Hegelian struggle of contradicitions, or as an outcome of Nietzsche's will to power, but as 'a many-sided yet hesitant awareness of truth', that is mentioned in his study of *Plato and Platonism*.

In *Marius the Epicurean* Pater follows the same path as in *Imaginary Portraits*: the protagonist is both an invented and a real character, being no specific historical person, but 'a precise and faithful sum of emotional tendencies, elements of thought and all the inner life of the age'.[17] The 'imaginary portrait' of the hero merges with 'a sequence of aesthetic and philosophical analyses' characterising his thought and the ways he experiences inherent tensions and problems of his time: above all the transformation of paganism into Christianity, which according to Marten, is 'the greatest, most important event recorded in history'.[18] The result is nothing like nineteenth-century historical novels, the 'clamorous, empty canvasses of Wallaces and Sienkiewiczs', nor even the subtle techniques of the contemporary historical 'novel of ideas',[19] represented by Dmitri Sergeyevich Merezhkovsky (1865–1941). 'Historical atmosphere is condensed into a series of images, connecting

---

14   'jejichž vzdušná kresba někdy zase připomíná lehké a přece intensivní umění sanguiny, drahé XVIII. století [...] jsou pouhými sny, oživšími reminiscencemi kterési postavy ze starofrancouzského čalounu, tváře z obrazu van Steenova nebo profilu z rokokové miniatury? Buď 'jak buď', zhušťují a suggerují ovzduší, náladu, vnitřní napětí dob, jež evokují' (Pater 1911, 271).
15   'jakési fatalné sepětí krásy a smutku, snivosti a malátnosti, touhy a váhavosti [...] tlumí barvy celých věků v harmonické, trochu však znavené *gris en gris*' (Pater 1911, 271).
16   'velkou vlnící se nekonečnost pohybu, světla, vznikání, změny, moře odstínů, jež všechny zasluhují pozornosti myslitele a vzněcují rozkoš poznání' (Pater 1911, 271).
17   'shrnuje přesně a věrně citové proudy, myšlenkové prvky, všecek vnitřní život doby' (Pater 1911, 272).
18   'sled estetických a filosofických analys [...] největší, nejvýznamnější vývojový děj, zaznamenaný dějinami' (Pater 1911, 272).
19   'hlučných, prázdných pláten Wallaceův a Sienkiewiczův [...] ideového románu historického' (Pater 1911, 272).

every outer detail with inner causes explaining it.' Marten sees these images as the hero's meditations on the works of Apuleius, Heraclitus, Aristippus or Marcus Aurelius; meditations, whose sequence 'gradually analyses and assesses the pagan and Christian wisdom of life, thus almost unnoticeably transforming the old ethos into a new one'.[20] Such meditations are taken as representing the continuity of the history of ideas.

Significantly, this continuity is produced by the 'uninterrupted flow' or 'crystallization' of history and not by the dialectical clash of contradictions, caused by 'the antagonism of the new and the old'.[21] Here Marten invokes the Latin sentence *Natura nihil facit per saltum*, printed on the first page of Pater's book on Plato. Within this framework, Christianity is initially perceived by Marius as 'a realisation of the pagan ideal of harmony'.[22]

Despite Marten's refusal of the dialectic, his interpretation preserves some features of a dialectical approach. Marius' Epicureanism is seen to harbour 'forces driving him beyond and above Antiquity, which they have philosophically exhausted'.[23] Dialectic seems to be also implied by Marten's concentration on the 'incessant change' that 'seemed to indicate only a more subtle, all-penetrating motion – the inexhaustible energy of divine will'.[24] However, the principal features of the hero's Epicureanism do not imply a dialectical approach to history. A clear and immediate feeling conveys 'a fullness of life' and leads to 'a powerful vision' able to grasp life as a multiplicity of '*every heroic, passionate, ideal form*'.[25]

It is important that this conclusion articulates the concept of freedom not as a denial or renunciation of truth or beauty, but as their active acceptance. In this respect, Marten's interpretations seem to echo the positive, anti-metaphysical tendencies of Nietzsche's philosophy, accentuated later by Foucault and Deleuze. Nonetheless this anticipatory aspect is counterbalanced by the emphasis on the continuity of the history of ideas, which appears to enclose the endless multiplicity of events within the limits of individual mind, enabling it to experience 'the pleasure of the imaginary presence, of the mystical now'.[26]

In spite of this desire for experience, Marius is very much aware of the lapse of time ('*the headlong fall of everything into the past*'[27]). Therefore, he finds the answers to his questions not in Epicureanism but in the reflections on Stoicism of Marcus Aurelius, where he discovers, according to Marten, 'the divergence

---

[20]   'Dějinné ovzduší se zhušťuje v sled obrazů, spojujících každou zevní podrobnost s příčinami, jež ji vysvětlují. [. . .] zkoumajících a hodnotících postupně pohanskou a křesťanskou životní moudrost a převádějících téměř neznatelně staré ethos v nové' (Pater 1911, 272–3).

[21]   'splynulý tok, krystallizaci [. . .] protikladem nového a starého' (Pater 1911, 273).

[22]   'realisovaného pohanského ideálu harmonie' (Pater 1911, 273).

[23]   'síly, které pudí mimo a nad antiku, již filosoficky vyčerpávají' (Pater 1911, 273).

[24]   'ustavičná změna [. . .] naznačovala pouze jemnější, vším pronikající pohyb – nevyčerpatelnou energii božské vůle' (Pater 1911, 274).

[25]   'plnost života [. . .] mocný pohled [. . .] *každá hrdinná, vášnivá, ideálná forma života*' (Pater 1911, 274).

[26]   'rozkoš pomyslné přítomnosti, mystického ted' (Pater 1911, 274).

[27]   '*střemhlavého klesání všeho v minulost*' (Pater 1911, 274).

between his desire for the "fullness of life" and the inherent possibilities of antiquity'.[28] The speech of Marcus Aurelius is 'a remarkable stylisation of a spiritual *fin de siècle*', where the mask of harmony and joy falls, revealing 'an awful sadness, a feeling of emptiness, a suppressed horror of transitoriness, a fear whose forms are both the *contemptus mundi* of the wise Aurelius and the faint pleasantry of Lucius Verus'.[29] Only the strong will and firm moral criteria of Marius' friend Cornelius and the influence of Caecilia can help the hero to overcome this crisis and find an antipode to pagan sadness in 'Chrisitian joy'.[30] Marten argues that for the hero paganism

> no longer means the highest degree of joyful view of life. The aesthetic charm of the Catholic church, its power to develop everything that expresses the better part of human mind, its elevating notion of the human essence: all what centuries later will be expressed by Dante, Giotto, the builders of cathedrals, or great ritualists like Saint Gregory, all this we can vaguely see anticipated in these magic times at the end of the second century.[31]

It is evident that Marten's essay articulates a strong desire to recognize the aesthetic potential of Catholicism as a power that could overcome the erosive tendencies of the *fin de siècle*. This attitude, which significantly differs from contemporary attitudes of Czech Decadent artists, especially from the paganism of Procházka or Karel Hlaváček's (1874–98), is fully in keeping with Marten's spiritual affiliation to Claudel, Paul Bourget, Emile Bernard and the circle of the *Rénovation esthétique*. Though he is open to the subtle versatility of Pater's art and thought, Marten does not seem to be strong enough to assert his openness in ideological terms. His final comparison of *Marius the Epicurean* with 'the energetic apologias of Chesterton'[32] is misleading. Nonetheless, by interpreting the hero not as an actor, whose heart experiences the transformation of the world, but as a spectator, whose mind mirrors changes similar to those contemplated by many *fin-de-siècle* artists and thinkers, Marten is enabled to identify himself with some of the features of Marius' vision, and to project his own views of history, morals and religion onto them.

---

[28] 'divergenci své touhy po "plnosti života" a vnitřních možností antiky' (Pater 1911, 275).

[29] 'podivuhodnou stylizací duchovního *fin de siècle* [...] strašlivý smutek, cit prázdna, potlačovaný děs pomíjivosti, jehož jsou jen různými útvary *contemptus mundi* moudrého Aurelia aubledlé rozkošnictví Lucia Vera' (Pater 1911, 275).

[30] 'křest'anská radost' (Pater 1911, 276).

[31] 'neznamenalo již nejvyššího stupně radostného pojetí života. Estetický půvab katolické církve, její síla vyvíjeti všecko, co v lepším smýšlení člověkově je výmluvného a výrazného, její povznášející přesvědčení o bytosti lidské: to vše, co tak plně realisovali o století později Dante, Giotto, stavitelé katedrál, velcí ritualisté jako sv. Řehoř – zříme nejasnou anticipací již v kouzelných dobách na sklonku druhého století' (Pater 1911, 276).

[32] 'energické apologetiky Chestertonovy' (Pater 1911, 278).

11 'Our "I" and History': The Polish Reception of Walter Pater

Piotr Juszkiewicz

The title quotation from Stanisław Brzozowski points to several aspects of the Polish reception of Pater (Brzozowski 1990). First, it suggests that the period when the works of the author of *The Renaissance* were translated into Polish and discussed by reviewers was that of the so-called 'Young Poland' of which the work of Brzozowski was a highly significant achievement. Second, it suggests that the reasons for the interest, neglect or disapproval of Pater's writings were related to variously defined concepts of the 'I', individuality or soul, which, regardless of the differences, remained most valid for the 'Young Poland' writers and critics searching for the fundamental meaning of the works of art and literature. Third, the term 'history' implies that neither the ways of reading Pater, nor the concepts of the 'I', individuality or soul were unchanging. Within about two decades, 'Young Poland' as a cultural formation, and particularly the metaphysical foundations of its most outstanding artists and writers' *Weltanschauung* became subject to criticism. With time, the attitude to Pater was changing, too – the accusations of sterile aestheticism or positivistic pedantry gave way to the encomia on the stylistic quality of his texts and the psychological accuracy of the *Imaginary Portraits*.

The epoch of 'Young Poland', perhaps one of the most fruitful periods in the history of Polish culture, has generally been located by scholars between the late 1890s and 1918. Since on the one hand 'Young Poland' borders on the past dominated by positivism, and on the other hand on the interwar decades marked by regained political independence and aesthetic revolutions, it appears to have been the era of various interrelated ideas, simultaneity of different worldviews, and quick changes of dominant intellectual orientations. In general, the brief but fertile period of 'Young Poland' opens with a critique of the positivistic model of the universe, stemming from the sense of the collapse of values founded on the crumbling authority of science, and suffused with melancholy scepticism. The search for answers that could no longer be provided by scientists led towards metaphysical speculations combined with a budding ideology of activism inspiring the Polish independence movement coming of age in the context of emerging social antagonisms. The era began with a turn towards metaphysics and mysticism under the auspices of Schopenhauer, while its progress was fuelled by the ideas of Nietzsche and Bergson. As regards art,

'Young Poland' meant a shift from realism to symbolism, and – later – to early expressionism.[1]

A significant element of 'Young Poland's' programmes was a distinctly articulated question of the autonomous value of art, pursued in a particularly radical way by the critic and poet Zenon Przesmycki, editor of *Chimera* (Przesmycki 1973), as well as by Stanisław Przybyszewski, for whom art, defined as a means of reaching the absolute, was free of any non-artistic obligations (Przybyszewski 1973). Most likely, that last postulate was closely related to the influence of foreign literature and art on Polish writers and artists, which at that time achieved an unprecedented intensity. The belief in the intrinsic value of art which, although it could occasionally play a patriotic role, should not be reduced to its social functions, contributed to thinking about art and literature in terms of universal ideas, changing in the course of their progress through 'various walks of the nation's life' under the 'specific impact of the environment' (Krajewska 1972, 8). The openness to literature and art produced in other European countries manifested itself also in many translations and comments on foreign authors. Traditionally, the most attractive was French culture, but there was also much interest in the works of Scandinavians. According to Wanda Krajewska, English literature was for the most part considered conservative by Polish authors, yet with time more and more information became available not only on the English writers of the past, but also on the literary present. Particularly at the apex of 'Young Poland' which came, in Krajewska's estimation, between 1887 and 1908, English literature gained in importance and its appeal could be compared to that of the French (Krajewska 1972, 11–12).

Information concerning English literature, writes Krajewska, was available to the Polish reader in the press – both in newspapers and in literary and other periodicals – and in books.[2] Published translations, reviews, and comments included and referred to poetry, fiction, drama, literary and art criticism, high-brow and popular literature, authors of the past and those who were still alive and active. Some dailies, such as *Życie* (*Life*) in Warsaw and *Świat* (*The World*) in Cracow, had their regular foreign correspondents who more or less competently discussed recent publications. Among translated authors of the past there were Byron, Coleridge, Shelley and Keats, while a group of translated and reviewed contemporaries included Yeats, Swinburne, Rossetti, Ruskin, Morris, Pater, Wilde, Tennyson and Robert Browning, as well as J. K. Jerome, Conan Doyle and celebrities for a season, such as Grant Allen and Rider Haggard.

Next to the knowledge of the editors, critics and translators, the choice of the English authors whose works were translated and reviewed was determined by French criticism. Once some British author had been 'discovered' for good in Paris, his name was usually soon to appear in the Polish press. What counted as well was the scholarly authority of Taine and his *Histoire de la littérature anglaise*, occasionally supported by other French studies translated into Polish, such as *Ruskin et la religion de la Beauté* (*Ruskin and the*

---

[1]   On the periodization of that era in Polish art, cf. Juszczak 1965.
[2]   Complete bibliography in Krajewska 1972.

Cult of Beauty, 1897) by Robert de la Sizeranne, translated by the eminent critic Antoni Potocki. In use were also studies on English literature by German critics and scholars.[3]

Polish commentators and translators of English literature were particularly interested in the authors of the Aesthetic movement: Ruskin, the Pre-Raphaelites, Swinburne, Morris, Wilde and Pater. The most popular of them all were no doubt Ruskin and Wilde. In 1900 the first translation of the selected works of the former was published, including fragments of the *Seven Lamps of Architecture* and *The Stones of Venice*, to be followed by other translations: *The Ethics of the Dust*, *The Crown of Wild Olive*, *Sesame and Lilies* and *The Queen of the Air*.[4] The foreign works on Ruskin translated into Polish included the study by de la Sizeranne, and a German monograph by S. Saenger, *Ruskin, His Life and Work*. Polish books on the subject included *John Ruskin* by M. Buyno-Arctowa (1901) and *Ku światłu* (*Towards Light*) by Z. Hartingh (1911). Krajewska emphasizes that the reception of Ruskin was filtered through French criticism, which resulted in recognizing the author of *The Stones of Venice* primarily as an aesthetician focusing on the external form of works of art (Krajewska 1972, 78). Though Polish critics revealed his spiritual affinities with Polish poets, and the quality of his prose was readily acknowledged, in contemporary opinion he exerted little influence on the artistic ideas in Poland.

Apparently, Ruskin's popularity with the Polish readers was surpassed by that of Oscar Wilde. According to Krajewska, he was perceived as the main protagonist, and even founder of the 'school of aestheticism' with its central idea of 'art for art's sake'. Since 1897 translations of Wilde's writings were published in the Cracow *Życie* (*Life*), while the programmatic texts of 'Young Poland' reflected his concept of the critic as an artist. Among the translated works were *The Nightingale and the Rose* and other poetic fables (1902), *Salome* (1904), *The Picture of Dorian Gray*, *The Soul of Man Under Socialism*, *Lord Arthur Saville's Crime* and *Poems in Prose*. Critical studies of Wilde included *Poglądy na sztukę i krytykę Oskara Wilde'a* (*Oscar Wilde's Views on Art and Criticism*) by S. Jabłonowski (1905) and an Introduction to *Dialogues* by Adolf Nowaczyński (1905). Wilde was considered an outstanding individualist, a refined aesthete, and a great aesthetician and artist who throughout his whole life opposed the conservative public opinion.

In comparison to the reception of other representatives of the Aesthetic movement, Pater's works were relatively less influential in Poland. Acknowledged later and translated only after 1909, they may have seemed less attractive than those of Ruskin and Wilde who were considered the main champions of aesthetic subjectivism and autonomy of artistic impressions as the proper background of critical activity. Moreover, Pater's texts did not contain one specific motif which particularly appealed to Polish authors. The leftist *Prawda* (*The Truth*) or – even more to the left – *Głos* (*The Voice*) stressed the social

---

[3] This is what Krajewska claims with reference to works on English literature by Feliks Jezierski. Also Cezary Jellenta read Pater for the first time in the German translation.

[4] Complete bibliography in Krajewska 1972, 264.

aspect of Ruskin's and Morris's opinions. In such a context, Pater, classified as a critical impressionist, appeared to be a sensitive connoisseur of beauty, yet much less radical in his aestheticism than Wilde, and much less socially progressive than Ruskin or Morris.

Information and opinions on Pater appeared in the Polish press for the first time in the 1890s. In 1894 Mścisław Edgar Nekanda-Trepka contributed a note on Pater's death to *Biblioteka Warszawska* (*The Warsaw Library*). Three years later, Leon Winiarski – a sociologist and socialist interested primarily in the social aspects of art and literature, residing permanently in France – published a mini-series of sketches on the achievement of the author of *The Renaissance* in *Prawda* of which he was a foreign correspondent (Krajewska 1972, 37–8). His social bias already became quite apparent in the first essay of the first issue of *Prawda* in 1897, where he showed Pater as a melancholy, subtle daydreamer, an artist pursuing ideal beauty, a loner living virtually like a monk. For Winiarski, such an attitude was unacceptable. In his opinion, Pater was 'consistently evading responsibility, action, and direct duty. He preached and practised the gospel of sophisticated intellectual and artistic cynicism, the religion of beauty. It is obvious that there was something abnormal about it. One might say, degenerate. [. . .] Pater was a decadent. [. . .] No doubt, those who believe in science and progress will condemn him. [. . .] He lived only to give a name and expression to a certain state of mind' (Winiarski 1896/97, 9). Winiarski considered *Marius the Epicurean* to be Pater's most outstanding work, identifying in the next number of *Prawda* (where he summarized the book) Marius' spiritual vacillation between Stoicism and Christianity with the ambivalence of the author himself.

Two years later Winiarski returned to Pater – at that time to the *Imaginary Portraits* which he chose to call 'imaginable' – in order to modify his previous judgement. In no. 38 of *Prawda* in 1899, he summarized *Denys l'Auxerrois*, and in no. 40 *Carl von Rosenmold*. On that occasion, *Marius* was referred to by Winiarski as a less significant achievement. What gained importance was the impressionistic critical method which enabled Pater to create 'imaginable portraits' – poems rather than studies – the true 'jewels of criticism'. Winiarski considered as most important Pater's unique ability to describe a given personality as an embodiment of major elements of a historical breakthrough. In 1901 he wrote about Pater one last time, presenting *Sebastian van Storck* in no. 33 of *Prawda*, and combining the two lines of his reasoning about the English critic. On the one hand, *Imaginary Portraits* were a kind of reflection of the universal psychology of a specific place and moment in time ('So far in Sebastian Pater has been showing us the artistic psychology of Holland'), on the other, they reflected the mind of Pater himself – its various aspects were revealed in the successive portraits. According to Winiarski, Denys was an artist who proved able to lead the masses, Rosenmold was a daydreamer, while Storck was a thinker. Consequently, for the Polish critic Pater was not so much an expert on the Renaissance, but a writer focusing on his own subjectivity, who applied the introspective method to a more general objective – probing into the souls of the heroes of his imaginary portraits in order to reach to the characteristics of a more universal psychology of a given time and place.

As late as eight years after the last essay by Winiarski, Pater's achievement again found its way to the Polish cultural scene. In 1909 the first – and until recently (Pater 1998) the only – Polish translations of Pater's works came out in Lvov and Warsaw which then belonged, respectively, to Austria and Russia: in Lvov the selection of Pater's essays was translated by Stanisław Lack (Pater 1909a), while in Warsaw three extracts from *The Renaissance*, translated by Maria Rakowska, were published in 1909 and 1910 in the journals *Literatura i Sztuka* and *Sfinks* (Pater 1909b, 1909c, 1910).

Lack's translation was published by Księgarnia Polska B. Połonieckiego, a press founded in 1872. In 1889 it was taken over by Bernard Połoniecki who turned it into a more ambitious enterprise. Apart from the press, he opened a public library and academic reading-room (50,000 volumes), publishing mainly Polish romantic literature, foreign classics such as Shakespeare and Molière, and works (often first editions) of contemporary Polish authors. In the relatively liberal Austro-Hungarian empire, Lvov was at that time, beside Cracow, a major cultural centre of the province of Galicia. At the turn of the twentieth century, the city had many literary periodicals, an opera house and a theatre specializing in contemporary drama, a university, learned societies, and a large group of 'Young Poland' writers and critics, such as Jan Kasprowicz, Stanisław and Wincenty Korab-Brzozowski, Ostap Ortwin, Józef Ruffer, Maryla Wolska and Leopold Staff. In 1905 the literary critic Ostap Ortwin (Oskar Katzenellenbogen), who had initiated a series called 'Symposion', became head of the literary department of Księgarnia Polska. Lack's selection and translation of Pater's essays was published as volume IV of the series, edited since 1890 by Leopold Staff, an outstanding poet and himself a prolific translator. According to the cultural programme of 'Young Poland', the proper objective of the series was to present to the Polish reader a variety of works by eminent foreign authors, yet not so much the most recent publications, as some fundamental texts of European culture – 'essential excerpts from the timeless masterpieces of antiquity, Renaissance, the age of humanism, the Enlightenment, and early modern times' in 'artistic translation'. The editors wrote in the general introduction: 'The Symposion Library is intended to familiarize the contemporary Polish reader in his mother tongue with the views which shaped the mindset of whole generations, leaving a permanent imprint on their moral pursuits; which today constitute the universal cultural heritage, the most valuable depository of practical wisdom and mature knowledge of man.'

It should be added that the publisher wished to choose texts which 'appeal both to the heart and to intellect', since he did not mean to promote only intellectual interest, pure proliferation of knowledge and 'burdening the reader's memory'. Apparently, then, the writings of Pater seemed to the editors nearly classic – a significant part of the canon of European literature. The preceding volumes were Plato's *Symposium*, *Selections* from Montaigne and *Moral Maxims and Remarks* by Vauvenargues, while the following ones contained the texts of Diderot, Leopardi, La Rochefoucauld, Goethe, La Bruyère, Fichte, Voltaire, Hebbel, Kierkegaard and Newman. The translators were Polish writers and poets, such as Staff and Kasprowicz, as well as critics Stanisław Brzozowski, Antoni Potocki and Stefan Frycz. They belonged – at least some of them – to a group of young literati who held meetings in the

Academic Reading Room, an association of the students of Lvov University. There Staff, editor-in-chief of the series, met Ortwin and Stanisław Brzozowski. It was thanks to them that the literary discussion group of the Reading Room became more active, organizing a series of lectures on Polish and foreign literature. Its members discussed the works of Hamsun, Strindberg, Poe, Longfellow, Coleridge, Wilde, d'Annunzio, Baudelaire, Verlaine, Rimbaud, Leconte de Lisle, Maeterlinck, Rodenbach, Verhaeren, Barbey d'Aurevilly, France, Nietzsche, and – last but not least – Pater (Maciejewska 1965).

It is difficult to establish beyond any doubt who came out with the idea of including a selection from Pater's writings in the series. Staff must have heard of him when he attended the Academic Reading Room, but we do not know how familiar he was with Pater's works. On the one hand, it is known that he started learning English intensively only in 1911,[5] on the other, he wrote to the critic Wilhelm Feldman in 1908:

> It seems to me that from Pater we ought to translate his masterpiece, the culmination of his achievements, *Marius the Epicurean*. Among his other works, the only one that matches *Marius* is the essay on the blooming of dew and fire from the *Greek Studies* [...] Ostensibly nothing but a scholarly trifle, but in fact an ingenious attempt to put under a common denominator the ritual aspect of Greek enthusiasm and the religious affinity of modern soul and nature. How suggestive it is, how it may impress the reader! Not a word of didacticism, no unnecessary wrestling with problems. (Staff 1966, 398–9)

Perhaps Staff read *Marius* and *Greek Studies* in the French translation resulting from the interest in Pater's works in France, reported in 1903 by Antoni Potocki, the Paris correspondent of *Kurier Warszawski* (Staff 1966, 61). The above fragment of Staff's letter indicates that the final decision concerning the selection of Pater's texts was left to the Polish translator.

Stanisław Lack (1879–1909) actually did not belong to the Lvov intellectual circles, but he maintained close ties with them. Born and educated in Cracow, Lack studied in the School of Law and Administration of the Jagiellonian University, but eventually chose to become a literary and art critic, remembered in the history of Polish culture primarily due to his interpretations of the major playwright, painter and poet Stanisław Wyspiański. His selection of Pater's writings proved quite wide-ranging: the opening text 'Platon' ('Plato') was a fragment of *Plato and Platonism* (1893), then came two texts from *Greek Studies* (1895): 'Studyum o Dyonizosie' ('A Study of Dionysus') and 'Epoka atletów' ('The Age of Athletes'), *Imaginary Portraits* were represented by 'Denys l'Auxerrois', while two essays from *The Renaissance* (1873), 'Winckelmann' and 'Konkluzya' ('Conclusion'), closed the volume. The translation is mostly quite accurate, some fragments, however, were not properly corrected probably because of Lack's serious illness which grew more acute in 1908 and finally brought about his premature death on 20

---

5   Staff in a letter of 1911: 'Next year I would like to improve my command of English and start transplanting new herbs onto our ground' (Maciejewska 1965, 61).

January 1909 in Vienna, where he made a stop on his way back to Poland after an unsuccessful treatment in Italy. Some brief passages were left out (e.g., on p. 136, 'possessing an inexhaustible gift of suggestion'), others simplified, and at times the meaning was misconstrued (in 'Winckelmann' the expression 'free of master library' was translated as if it meant 'having the master's library at hand'). Lack's illness may have also been the reason why, in contrast to other volumes, the Pater volume of the 'Symposion' series does not contain an introduction with a general overview of the author's achievement.

Maria Rakowska (1864–1940) was a writer and translator from several languages: French, German and English (from the English she translated, for instance, in 1909 *Dr Jekyll and Mr Hyde* by Stevenson). She also wrote essays on English literature – in *Literatura i Sztuka* (*Literature and Art*) she published a text on Swinburne, and in 1911 her *Zarys literatury angielskiej* (*Outline of English Literature*) came out as a popular book founded predominantly on the ideas of Taine. Rakowska's translations of Pater were limited to his studies on the Renaissance: in 1909 *Literatura i Sztuka* published what was probably her rendering of 'Leonardo da Vinci',[6] in the same year *Sfinks* printed her translation of 'Luca della Robbia', and a year later the same journal published 'Pico della Mirandola'. Unfortunately, nothing is known of the interest of the publisher of *Sfinks* in Pater, though it is known that he – i.e. Władysław Bukowiński (1871–1927), a poet and admirer of Słowacki, Asnyk and Konopnicka – trying to continue the key role of Przesmycki's journal *Chimera* in the 'Young Poland' culture, often published translations and articles on foreign literature. The 1909 translations by Lack and Rakowska were accompanied in *Literatura i Sztuka* (published in Poznań, under Prussian rule, as a weekly literary supplement to the daily *Dziennik Poznański*) by two short texts on Pater signed with the initials C. J. (C. J. 1909a; 1909b). Their author was most probably Cezary Jellenta (1861–1935), a writer and outstanding critic who wrote studies on Polish and European romanticism. His notes were actually summaries of some chapters of *The Renaissance* which Jellenta might have read in the German translation by Wilhelm Schölermann, published in Leipzig and Jena by Diederichs in 1902 and 1906 (Pater 1906). The chapters devoted to the times before the Renaissance were interpreted by the Polish critic as Pater's effort to grasp the characteristic features of the human spirit, appearing for the first time in the Middle Ages, then in France, and eventually flourishing in Italy to persist until the eighteenth century. The most impressive for Jellenta was the story of Amis and Amil from 'Two Early French Stories' which he summarized in some detail. The other text he published in *Literatura i Sztuka* was a summary of 'Winckelmann'.

The period of 1909–10/11, marked by so far the most intensive interest in Pater's works, did not bring any systematic account of his achievement. This could have been written if it were not for the premature death of the most

---

[6] Krajewska suggests that the author of this translation was Rakowska and that it was published in *Literatura i Sztuka* (Poznań), no. 12 (1909), p. 1. In fact, there was a sequence of four extracts from 'Leonardo' and the first one appeared in no. 9: Pater (1909c) of *Literatura i Sztuka*. Therefore, in no. 12 only the last part was printed. Additionally, the name of translator does not appear in any of these publications.

outstanding critic of 'Young Poland', Stanisław Brzozowski, who was phenomenally well read and independent-thinking. Before, however, turning to the reasons why Brzozowski paid some attention to Pater's writings, and, by the same token, why the writers and critics of 'Young Poland' decided to offer them to the Polish audience, one more publication should be noted, which – focusing directly on Pater – concluded, as it were, the most direct, if not the only, phase of the reception of his works in Poland. It was a book-length study by Zbigniew Grabowski, *Walter Pater: życie – dzieło – styl* (*Walter Pater: Life – Work – Style*), published in 1929 in Poznań by the Poznań Society of the Friends of Arts and Sciences, and developed from a doctoral dissertation written under the supervision of Roman Dyboski, a distinguished historian of English literature and professor of Jagiellonian University. Grabowski's book summarizes in detail Pater's works and attempts to locate them against the background of the Victorian era, the author's biography, and the writings of other members of the Aesthetic movement. As an academic study, it also indicates the moment when Pater was excluded from the immediate context of Polish literary tradition and situated in the domain of literary history and the history of criticism.

Walter Pater has been often referred to as a critical impressionist. Such a classification definitely provided enough ground for positivistic critics to repudiate his writings, which was exemplified by the first text of Winiarski. Still, it is not enough to explain the interest in Pater shown by those Polish writers who were critical of the positivistic paradigm, particularly with reference to art, instead stressing the problem of experience, the autonomy of aesthetic emotion, the role of individuality and the power of self-expression. What's more, the writers of 'Young Poland', even though they emphasized the problem of aesthetic experience and the subjectivity of the artist and critic, distanced themselves from the impressionistic method in criticism when it meant nothing but pure, chaotic flux of impressions. That's why, in trying to understand the motivation of the 'Young Poland' writers which might have determined either their interest in Pater's writings, or their rejection of them, we must take a somewhat closer look at the critical method of Pater himself.

For Pater, significant criticism meant aesthetic criticism – an activity which was evidently different both from positivistic pedantry and from metaphysical speculation. Its objective was to reveal the specific identity of the aesthetic object through the analysis of the subject's reaction, that is, answering the question which elements of the work of art exert the strongest and most unique influence on the recipient. The intensity of that influence was rooted in its relationship to the key elements of the creative process: first, with the personality of the artist (reconstructed on the basis of the subject's feelings), which focuses the spiritual energy of the age (history and its understanding appear in an act of the work's comprehension, during reading that makes it the subject's property), and second, with the artistic decisions made, as it were, through the prism of that personality in the context of the tradition defined not as a certain static state of affairs, but as increasing emphasis on the fidelity to the medium. In this respect, aesthetic criticism differs for Pater from academic criticism, which is concerned with biography, attribution and facts, since it aims at the experience of personality and the revelation of the autonomous character of the work's medium.

Besides the problem of history, the question of the medium was of the greatest importance for Pater. In his view, the work of art cannot be reduced just to ideas conveyed in various manners. The sensual value of each medium cannot be translated into another one, which is significant because the work does not appeal to pure sensibility, but to the imaginative intellect which operates on the level of images, while some sensual arousal is necessary to facilitate the perception of the work's other aspects. In these circumstances, the work of art is analogous to the imaginative intellect which is suffused with emotion just as the content of the work is suffused with its form. The quality of the medium's application is important for the meaning and efficacy of the work. In painting the essential question is how the artist deals with the pictorial matter and how he proves capable of choosing Lessing's 'fruitful moment'. Besides, even though every medium is unique in its own right, the common tendency of all the types of art is towards the condition of music, an ideal example of the coexistence of content and form. One might say that the medium and history are combined together in a Hegelian model of the interrelated development of different forms of consciousness and types of art.

The alleged reduction of Pater's critical method to impressionism – writing down personal, highly volatile impressions of the sensitive 'I' – is contradicted also by his idea of the speaking subject, the medium for words. This subject is rarely rendered concrete by means of personal pronouns, and those rare moments are most often signals that history, which unfolds under our eyes as objective, is a reconstruction. The way the text is delivered oscillates, just like our knowledge of Pater's heroes in the imaginary portraits, between the self-presenting objective presence and the momentary flashes of intuition brought about by the power of empathy.

According to Peter Dale, the construction of the image of history through the analysis of subjective data released by an emotional and sensual impulse owes its specific form, characteristic of Pater, to a cluster of both positivistic and anti–positivistic ideas derived from Mill as well as Hegel, Goethe, Heine, Ruskin, Gautier and Winckelmann (Dale 1977, 175). It was founded not only on the negation of the mechanistic concept of man and reality, discarded in favour of a belief in the relative quality of all human knowledge, but also on detachment from metaphysical speculation. In particular, Pater's thought reveals a trace of the debates concerning the possibility of acquiring by the human mind objective knowledge beyond subjective existence. Pater's stress on subjective experience, reinforced by a statement from 'Conclusion' that 'not the fruit of experience, but experience itself is the end', pushed him close to the extreme of solipsism. Dale claims that what actually saved Pater from solipsism was his effort to develop an idea of history founded on the belief in ties and communication between individuals. He describes Pater's understanding of that purpose, i.e. 'interpreting the "mystery" of the mind of the past', by means of Dilthey's idea of history. Both in the case of Dilthey and of Pater, the vision of history as universal consciousness conditions the necessity of its emphatic reconsideration in the search for the meaning of the past. This is made possible, writes Dale, by treating the traces of the past as products of past minds, mental experience of their relations, and the projection of our knowledge of customs, traditions, political circumstances and religious processes on those traces. All this means, Pater seems to think, that there is no essential discontinuity between our minds and the minds of the past. Even though we will never confront the past face to face, there are 'threads' of the past minds which run across time and appear in the minds of the present. In this sense, the study of history is a process of intense retrospection. Thus, in the case of Pater, there is a combination of an intensive effort to express individual impressions in contact with the work, defined as a contact with the artist's unique personality, and the search not so much for the spirit of history, but for its major spiritual powers. It is a mixture, writes Dale, of self-expression and a kind of *Kulturgeschichte* which provides a framework allowing for the transformation of those spiritual powers into the aesthetic dimension of the work of art.

Expression and empathy are two main categories of the 'Young Poland' criticism. Michał Głowiński, the author of brilliant studies on the literary criticism of the period, highlights as its basic assumption a claim that 'the literary work cannot be separated from its author so that the artist's subjectivity is never a factor external to the text; approaching the work, we also naturally take into account its author, for there is nothing that can question such a relationship' (Głowiński 1997, 28). As a result of blurring the boundary between the work and its author, the object of the critic's interest is the artist's mind, even though, on the other hand, psychologism was programmatically opposed to mere biographism. The critic's task was to search in the depth of the work for the author's subjectivity and grasp the authorial experience. Such empathy – the lived experience of the work – did not mean identification with the author of flesh and blood, but rather with the subject created by the author in the work.

To be precise, the meaning of artistic expression and the task of empathy were understood in at least three different ways. The first can be defined as modified naturalism. It was founded on a belief that the only possible basis for the theory of art is not a metaphysical idea of beauty, but psychology. According to Stanisław Witkiewicz, psychology, supported by the physical nature of physiological phenomena, should allow for the formulation of scientific laws of art related to practical artistic knowledge (Witkiewicz 1891). Its modification consisted in acknowledging the role of the artist's personality, which by definition subjectifies the presented world picture and, by the same token, determines the domain of aesthetic analysis able to reveal the character of individual transformations of the objective world picture, which cannot be explained just by the analysis of external factors. The basis of criticism defined in that particular way was subjective sensitivity to beauty, exemplified by the impressionistic studies of France and Lemaître. A subjective critical judgement, understood, as in the case of the critic Ignacy Matuszewski, in terms of sincere confession of individual impressions produced by the work, did not quite exclude objectivism, i.e. references to 'other categories of social phenomena' (Matuszewski 1897).

Another way of defining expression and empathy was related to thinking in metaphysical terms. Placed in such a perspective, the work was supposed to focus all the critical attention which was supposed to ignore its social context. In that case, though, what was repudiated was not only the approach advocated by Taine, but also naive impressionism. The point was to reveal in the work its absolute element, and not just to experience aesthetic pleasure. This does not mean, however, that emotions did not count at all. On the contrary, the absolute was approached in an emotional way, while the process of response was modelled in terms of 'communion' of the artist's and critic's souls. Such a manner of thinking, close to Aurier's theory of symbolism, was characteristic of Przesmycki and the programme of his *Chimera* (Podraza-Kwiatkowska 1985). Stanisław Przybyszewski represented an interesting blend of positivistic science and the categories of metaphysics. His key interpretative category, 'naked soul', implied a shift from the dualism of matter and spirit to that of consciousness and the unconscious dominated by 'chuć' (Przybyszewski's idiosyncratic term corresponding to the Freudian libido). The true reality revealed through an artistic symbol, a flash of the absolute, was for Przybyszewski the moment of the revelation of 'naked soul' (Boniecki 1993).

For naturalists the writings of Pater must have been difficult to accept, since they were liable to be regarded as examples of impressionism. Stanisław Witkiewicz accepted the prose of Ruskin only as literature; as an achievement of a specific individual uniquely and persuasively formulating his judgements on the works of art. Hence, he recognized the author of the *Stones of Venice* only as a master of verbal art, and not as a critic. On the other hand, to the metaphysicians Pater probably seemed little more than a relic of the positivistic past. Przybyszewski wrote in one of his letters: 'Writing about all those petrified mammoths – the Wordsworths, Arnolds, Kellers, Mörikes, Paters – thank God, it is finally coming to an end!' (Krajewska 1972, 68).

The third way of understanding empathy and expression, characteristic of the generation and the circle of Pater's translators, was related both to their distance from positivism, and to the critique of metaphysical rapture. Particularly striking was the evolution of Stanisław Lack – from a manifesto of the impressionistic criticism of the kind represented by Lemaître and France, as well as Ruskin (which meant resistance against the debasement of the individual self by the universalist theories of beauty) through metaphysical longings[7] to a concept of criticism as 'tracing literary ideas and their fates over centuries' (Lack 1977c, 314). The task of the critic, formulated in the above quoted text of 1905, was for Lack '[t]o acknowledge the progress and continuity of ideas and various manners of expressing them. An outstanding token of progress may be consciousness which expresses itself through the construction of events, that is, of a new work.' Then Lack added that a critic

---

[7] 'New criticism is symbolic, one, and by that it becomes an offshoot of art, also symbolic. It will be neither subjective, nor objective, for we have seen how easily these concepts may be misinterpreted. It is self-evident, however, that criticism will be individual, since it is practised by the artist who condenses and concentrates the changeable and, above all, perishable phenomena and makes durable statues of stone; immortal, moving with their own specific, separate, and only rhythm. He creates the synthesis of the individual identity of the 'artist under discussion', and connects him with the universal being – first of all, with its eternal type. The artist, just like religion (and art is a religion) connects an individual human being with its eternal type which is called God or Nature, it does not matter' (Lack 197b, 477–8).

who 'manages to suppress his desire to psychologize on the mysteries of the soul may logically trace the course of an idea and follow its life in the minutest details of construction' (Lack 1977c, 321) This, however, did not mean abandoning an individual perspective and denying the emotional value of the work, but only a shift of interest towards history which manifests itself in it.

Stanisław Brzozowski, perhaps the most astute and profound mind of 'Young Poland', included among the tasks of literary and art criticism shaping the future of both art and non-artistic matters, which was, in his view, impossible without the understanding of the present and the past. A key role in the process of understanding was played by the recognition of human subjectivity and the position of the 'I' against the background of history. To Brzozowski, Pater's detachment from the positivistic kind of objectivism, resulting in the appreciation of the personal perception of the world, was quite obvious. The Polish critic supplemented the critical lesson of Kant with a Marxian analysis − such a combination allowed him to approach reality as a human product subject to continuous transformation. That, in turn, brought Brzozowski to a specific understanding of culture, produced in connection with the process of human labour directed at external reality ('From this point of view, every culture is a system of the instruments of self-preservation'), which, contrary to fact, undergoes continuous mythologization. The essence of that mythologization is artificial separation of culture from its genesis − the autonomization, and, finally, ritualization of its achievements. In this sense, mythologization means universalization of the historical − our metaphysics, Brzozowski claimed, is always nothing but our social mythology. Mythologization pertains also to the 'I' which is not something primary, but an outcome and product of history. 'Our "I"', he wrote, 'does not stand outside history, but it is history itself. There is no way to free oneself of history, for there is nothing in the "I" which does [not − P. J.] belong to it.' This idea, even though it reached beyond the horizon of the Paterian reconstruction of history inscribed in his works, implied that Brzozowski was likewise interested in penetrating the creative personality through which, as through all of us, 'flows the river of history'. Of course, that did not mean the endorsement of criticism championed by Lemaître or France, referred to by Brzozowski as a set of accidental remarks made with no sense of responsibility. What mattered was the understanding of the human soul in connection with its historically conditioned world − the analysis of the latter gives us a chance to reach to the creative depths.

Consequently, criticism was for Brzozowski a form of social self-consciousness, an effort to answer the question of human identity. His line of reasoning, pervaded with the atmosphere of social revolt, marked with anticipation of action, seems very distant from Pater's serene silence. Yet for the Polish critic the silence of Pater's texts was only ostensible − he sensed in them enormous emotional tension. Brzozowski called Pater's style 'malarious', full of subdued passion and feverish.[8] That specific emotional aspect stemmed

---

8   'Pater's style is so malarious, that one can sense in it thrills, hypodermic fever, blissful desire, disturbing, suffocating joy − in other words, all this is just apparently and only apparently thought; in depth, it is a world that is ill, feverish, cruel, and

from the blend of 'high emotional culture' and tremendous intellectual effort which penetrates deeply into 'moral longings, nostalgias and the cognitive values of truth', most likely causing the oscillation between strong emotions and the endeavour to keep them under control in the process of understanding. Perhaps this explains other references by Brzozowski to the works of Pater – all of them happen to connote the same heavy atmosphere, sultriness and strained standstill. Yet the most significant element of Pater's intellectual achievement, highly appreciated by his Polish reader, was related to the problem of history – a specific introspective interpretation developed in search for the historical meaning inherent in the reconstructed artistic personality. In a late essay included in his posthumously published collection, 'Głosy wśród nocy' ('Voices at Night'), Brzozowski wrote, asking a question about the chances to reveal the secret of the growth of artistic soul:

> When will come a man able to reveal, show and impose on people an understanding of the growth of artistic soul? Each artist has such a secret within himself [. . .] Pater, a master, ought to be born again in Polish letters, since much power is needed to acknowledge the existence of those inner realities and stop at that, as we know that whoever does not see them in the work, will not notice them when helped by the critic, either. (Brzozowski 1990b, 1064)

For Brzozowski as well criticism was essentially an act of judgement that one soul passed on another, except that the Polish critic, standing on the threshold of the twentieth century and appreciating the power of Pater's empathy, wanted the critic to embody the moral consciousness of a given epoch, to make it clear that man should attempt to control the historical forces which determine him. Of course, this is not the Paterian history of the inner development of a spiritual community, close in its concreteness to the Hegelian spirit of history, and besides, the aesthetic bliss evaporates from it, too. Instead, what we have is distance from the practice of quietist individual aestheticism.[9] History becomes a task, and the artistic or critical activity a way to its fulfilment, though a key to its understanding still remains in the artist's 'I', manifesting itself in an act of expression and accessible through empathy.

---

evil. To me, there is no doubt about it. Berenson and probably Shadwell could not appreciate the portrait of Watteau, they did not want to understand it. It is almost Dostoyevskian [. . .] A strange kind of sadism which consists in bleaching the blood and emotion out of the writing subject. Then Sebastian Storck [. . .] When Pater writes about curiosity which multiplies the content of the world, he means also that content which is usually considered something more profound than curiosity – when there is a change in this respect, there is neither time, nor strength to think in psychic terms; this is something new as a fact, as knowledge, because it is not only that knowledge changes, but the knowing subject as well. Yet Pater wanted to live, let's say, in the Baudelairean sense, and wearing Spinoza's cassock' (Brzozowski 1913, 57).

[9]   'As a matter of fact, the type of modern "cultured" mind is represented by such people as Remy de Gourmont, Anatole France, Oscar Wilde, Pater, Georg Simmel, etc. They all have one feature in common: taking advantage of historical experience for their own individual purposes [. . .]' (Brzozowski 1990a, 699).

12 Fernando Pessoa and the Reception of Pater in Portugal★

Maria Teresa Malafaia and
Jorge Miguel Bastos da Silva

1

Issues concerning the canon and the reception of authors have been brought into the academic arena in a decisive way over the past two decades. They have become a characteristic area of debate between scholars, and it was with this background in mind that we accepted what, at first sight, appeared to be the considerable challenge of investigating the reception of Walter Pater in Portugal.

As our research method we decided to begin our quest by looking at the catalogues of the main Portuguese libraries, i.e. the National Library (Lisbon) and the Library of the University of Coimbra, the Libraries of the Faculties of Letters (Lisbon, Oporto, Coimbra and Évora), the English and Portuguese departmental libraries, as well as a few others, such as the Oporto City Library.

Originally, we believed that this method would produce good results. Yet we rapidly came to understand that the results would be almost nil. Indeed, when consulting the catalogues of these libraries, the most significant record of Portuguese translations throughout history, only one single reference to Walter Pater was found.[1] A short excerpt from the chapter 'Leonardo da Vinci' in *The Renaissance* was translated by no less a person than Fernando Pessoa, the most prominent literary figure of Portuguese Modernism and probably of the twentieth century in Portugal as a whole.

After further research, this dearth of bibliographical information on Pater's works, both those published during his lifetime and the posthumous ones, was

---

★ We would like to express our gratitude to Dr Maria Aliete Galhoz and to Professor João Almeida Flor from the Faculty of Letters (University of Lisbon) and to Professor Arnaldo Saraiva from the Faculty of Letters (University of Oporto) for their advice, especially as regards matters related to Fernando Pessoa.

[1] See Rodrigues, A. Gonçalves, *A tradução em Portugal: tentativa de resenha cronológica das traduções em língua portuguesa excluindo o Brasil de 1495 a 1950*. Lisbon: Imp. Nacional-Casa da Moeda, 1992. vol. 1, 1495–1834; vol. 2, 1835–50. Inst. de Cultura e Língua Portuguesa, 1992; vol. 3, 1851–70; vol. 4, 1871–1900; vol. 5 1901–30, Inst. Sup. de Línguas e Administração, 1999.

confirmed. We did not easily admit the fact that translations of Pater's works were next to non-existent. But we realized nonetheless that the situation could be explained by the extent of French influence on Portuguese culture and society at the time. Although the period between 1871 and 1900 did correspond to a marked expansion in publishing coinciding with ideological conflicts, the influence of French culture was throughout the period dominant in Portugal. Exceptions to this trend that we were able to trace amounted to no more than a few translations into Portuguese of English poets and writers: Elizabeth Barrett Browning, Percy Bysshe Shelley, Robert Southey, Tennyson, Dickens, Charles Darwin and Herbert Spencer.

Throughout Pater's life, and even afterwards, the influence of French culture was thus of prime importance, and the penetration of English writers quite limited. But even nowadays, when the above-mentioned influence no longer persists, Pater is still viewed in Portugal as a non-canonical writer and is not usually included in current university syllabuses.

After the investigation of the main Portuguese libraries, we visited Pessoa's home (Casa Pessoa, Rua Coelho da Rocha, 16, Lisboa) where the on-line catalogues simply confirmed what we had found out in the other libraries where we had begun our research.

In the Casa Pessoa, where a part of the written remnants of the poet's literary legacy is kept, we were able to confirm the poet's activity as a translator of Pater, among others. Teresa Rita Lopes, who is the editor of several works on Pessoa, states in *Pessoa inédito* (*Unpublished Pessoa*, 1993) that the poet translated in all twenty-six texts, poetry and prose. Moreover, one of the prose translations among them is from 'an aesthetic essay by Walter Pater' (77). As we shall see, the *Athena* magazine that Pessoa edited with Ruy Vaz published a translation entitled 'La Gioconda' by Fernando Pessoa (*Athena: Revista de Arte [Lisbon]*, 1.2, November 1924, 58).

It is within the cultural framework of this work as an editor and translator that many notes by Pessoa make sense. The same can be said of the publishing projects that he envisaged in relation to Olisipo, the firm that he set up in 1920. The list of works that he then had in mind to publish confirms his intention to cover the whole text of *The Renaissance*. (See Lopes 1993, 78–80.)

2

Thus, as far as it has been possible to establish through our research, the only translation of a work by Pater is that of these two paragraphs from the essay on 'Leonardo da Vinci' published by Pessoa in 1924. Meagre as the excerpt may appear, we believe that it can be proved relevant in the context of Pessoa's writing (the idea of Pessoa's writing as a *whole*, it must be said, being itself a highly problematic concept).

The paragraphs in question are those in which Pater states that '*La Gioconda* is, in the truest sense, Leonardo's masterpiece, the revealing instance of his mode of thought and work' and that 'The presence that rose thus so strangely beside the waters, is expressive of what in the ways of a thousand years men had come to desire.'[2] Leonardo's painting bridges the ancient and the modern sensibility. It can even be seen to transcend the Greek realization of the ideal.

The translated passage is included in *Athena*, a short-lived magazine of literature and art (no less, compare the subtitle to Pater's book), published in Lisbon, in whose pages Pessoa figures very prominently – albeit very much in disguise. Not only is he co-editor of the magazine (the other editor, Ruy Vaz, it would appear, not having any responsibility for the literary section), but he also writes the editorial (of which more to come later) and contributes translations of Poe and O. Henry. But this is not all. It is in *Athena* that we see the first publication of poems by Ricardo Reis and Alberto Caeiro, as well as an important literary manifesto by Álvaro de Campos. Although the public was not aware of it at the time, these literary figures are none other than *heteronyms* of Pessoa himself, that is, distinct identities of his creative personality, fictions of himself expressed in terms of different writers. From Pessoa's point of view, if not that of his co-editor, the magazine may well have been conceived as a stage where the heteronyms could come into the open (as suggested by Teresa Sousa de Almeida 1983, ix).

It is important to note that Pessoa had already been making plans (and quite possibly kept on doing so) for the translation of works by Pater. Surveying his literary remains, a veritable maze which still defies the capacities of scholars (two separate critical editions are in the course of publication), the critic Arnaldo Saraiva has identified plans made by Pessoa at several stages for translating pieces of literature, philosophy, essays and such like. One such list, undated but written in the back of a publication of 1923, includes 'Leonardo da Vinci' and the epilogue to *The Renaissance* (Saraiva 1996, 33). Another list, also undated, again involves the latter text (36). With regard to the unpublished translations among Pessoa's papers, Saraiva surmises that 'those translations, or attempts, or drafts, may sometimes result from the appeal of circumstance, but on the whole they are in harmony with Pessoa's literary taste and constitute a coherent plan of cultural intervention, bearing in mind the community of the Portuguese language'.[3] The point can of course be extended from these unpublished drafts to the whole of Pessoa's project as a translator of literature.

What then is the significance of Pessoa's interest in Pater? The point is surely that the magazine *Athena* was pervaded with a specific meaning involving the culture of ancient Greece, and that this meaning can be related directly to Pater's aesthetic criticism. Indeed, there is also undoubtedly a theoretical argument of a similar kind involved in the contributions signed with the names of Reis, Caeiro and Campos. This argument entails a radical

---

2   Pater 1990b, 79–80. It may be interesting to note that in a letter in English, dated 31 October 1924, Pessoa states that 'we, the editors of *Athena*, have found it to be treated by the local press with even more silence than we had legitimately expected' (Lopes 1993, 317). *Athena*, therefore, was not able to make Pater known to the Portuguese public at large.

3   'essas traduções, ou tentativas, ou esboços de traduções podem por vezes dever-se a apelos circunstanciais, mas, no seu conjunto, correspondem a gostos pessoais e a um plano coerente de intervenção cultural, tendo sobretudo em conta o horizonte da comunidade de língua portuguesa' (Saraiva 1996, 31).

revaluation of Paganism – a topic congenial to Pessoa, and one central to his intentions of intervening in the cultural scene at large. In the editorial of the first number of *Athena*, Pessoa states that civilized men owe their spirit to ancient Greece (see no. 1, October 1924, 5). His heteronym Reis is a poet of classical style and temperament, who adopts an attitude of non-commitment towards the realities of life. Caeiro, on the other hand, creates poetry unthinkingly, not only with spontaneity but seemingly with no intervention whatsoever of the powers of reflection and abstraction (not, at least, in the poems reputed to be the best – by the other heteronyms, that is). Finally, in 'Apontamentos para uma esthetica não-Aristotélica' ('Notes Towards a Non-Aristotelian Aesthetics'), Campos presents the Greeks of Antiquity as aesthetes, a qualification that echoes an important essay published under Pessoa's own name some two years before:

> Beauty, harmony, and proportion were for the Greeks not intellectual concepts, but rather intimate dispositions of their sensibility. That is why they were a *people of aesthetes*, seeking, demanding beauty *every single one of them, in everything, always*. That is why they have with such violence projected their sensibility over the world of the future, so much so that we are still subjects of its oppression.[4]

To all of this, which amounts to a sustained interest in Pater on the part of Pessoa, at least in the 1920s, there must be added his most explicit statement regarding Pater's significance: his emphatic commendation of Pater as 'the greatest of European aesthetes'.[5] The epithet occurs in an essay on the poetry of António Botto, which appeared in another literary review, *Contemporanea* (no. 3), in July 1922.

The essay 'António Botto e o ideal estético em Portugal' ('António Botto and the Aesthetic Ideal in Portugal') is a critical appraisal of Botto's poetry, which brings in Pater along the way. Botto's book *Canções* (*Songs*, first edition 1921, an enlarged edition published in May 1922 by Olisipo) had met with a ferociously unfavourable reaction on the part of some conservative groups. His poetry provoked scandal as a result of the overtly homoerotic sensibility that it conveyed. Some writers claimed that society needed to be purified in the light of its alleged turpitude and degradation. The public outrage reached such a pitch that the book was eventually banned by the authorities in May 1923.

Pessoa's essay purports to be a defence of this major collection of poetry by Botto, as a unique work of art, and so exempt from such charges of immorality. It actually turns out to be, in the main, a dissertation around the concept of the *aesthete* and its relevance to (literary) culture. Pessoa states right at the outset that

---

[4] 'A belleza, a harmonia, a proporção não eram para os gregos conceitos da sua intelligencia, mas disposições intimas da sua sensibilidade. É por isso que elles eram um *povo de esthetas*, procurando, exigindo a belleza *todos, em tudo, sempre*. É por isso que com tal violencia emittiram a sua sensibilidade sobre o mundo futuro que ainda vivemos subditos da oppressão d'ella' (*Athena* no. 4, January 1925, 159).

[5] 'o maior dos estetas europeus' (Pessoa 2000, 179).

António Botto is the only Portuguese, among those who nowadays write for the public, to whom the name of aesthete can be adequately applied. With perfect instinct, he follows the ideal which has been called aesthetic and which is a form, though a minor one, of the Hellenic ideal. He follows it, however, with a perfect intelligence along with his instinct, because Greek ideals, as they are intellectual, cannot be followed unconsciously.[6]

This is highly provocative. In the first place, because it excludes from the particular category of *aesthete* all Portuguese writers except Botto: a judgement which hints at the (lack of) merit of all writers thus excluded and might also imply that they are out of tune with modernity. Secondly, because Botto's being exceptional as the only one such writer among all those who write 'for the public' leaves open the possibility of there being others – heteronymic aspects of Pessoa himself, for instance – who are waiting to come to the fore. This interpretation would amount to reading the essay as an attempt at aesthetic self-definition, and prospective self-canonization, on the part of its author. The third cause for provocation is that there is a stated dissociation of Portuguese literature and art from one of the fundamental roots of European culture, the legacy of Greece.

Finally, there is the point that Pessoa's review emphasizes the importance of combining feeling with intellect – Portuguese literature in general being overly sentimental. This, too, reflects back on Pessoa himself, whose writing is very much defined by the adoption of an intellectual approach to emotional response. It also reflects on Botto. While seeking to define the distinctive quality of the book (and of Botto's sensibility), later in the essay, Pessoa underlines the technical accomplishment of Botto's poetic art and points out: 'the lack of emotional spontaneity which manifests itself in every line. Everything is thought out, everything is critical and conscious'.[7] The tone is frankly apologetic – indeed, on the face of what we know of Pessoa's own writing, it mirrors his own concerns.

To this extent, Pessoa's intention of standing up for his misjudged fellow-poet provided an opportunity for something broader and deeper. This does not mean that Pessoa was insincere in his avowed admiration for Botto's poems. He went so far as to translate a number of the *Canções* into English. Yet Botto's vindication had proceeded by way of an aesthetic-theoretical argument which, short though the essay may be, amounted to a description *in nuce* of the identity of European culture, and beyond – one which could be considered instrumental in the revaluation of Paganism within the context of Pessoa's own thinking. Pater plays a crucial role in the argument, both as a

---

6   'António Botto é o único português, dos que hoje conhecidamente escrevem, a quem a designação de esteta se pode aplicar sem dissonância. Com um perfeito instinto ele segue o ideal a que se tem chamado estético, e que é uma das formas, se bem que ínfima, do ideal helénico. Segue-o, porém, a par de com o instinto, com uma perfeita inteligência, porque os ideais gregos, como são intelectuais, não podem ser seguidos inconscientemente' (2000, 173).

7   'a falta de espontaneidade emotiva que em cada verso se manifesta. Tudo é pensado, tudo é crítico e consciente' (2000, 180).

prime representative instance of a particular ideal and also, one may imagine, as an inspiring source for some of the ideas themselves.

In developing his concepts, Pessoa recalls Hegel in establishing a fundamental opposition between the 'Hellenic' ideal, on the one hand, and the 'Indian' and 'Christian' ideals, on the other, the former being immanent whilst the latter two are transcendental in character.[8] All these ideals stem from a feeling of imperfection, though that feeling is of a different kind in each case. The Hellenic ideal has to do with the feeling that reality is inherently defective in that it fails fully to realize its own nature. This is a legacy from ancient Greece. The transcendental ideals that Pessoa associates both with Christian culture, and with Hindu and Buddhist spirituality on the other hand, rest on the conviction that there is a beyond which is fundamentally real and true, the consciousness of which conflicts with the consciousness of finitude. 'Only God, and the soul which he has created and resembles him, are perfection and true life'.[9]

This line of argument leads one back to aesthetic considerations. While the Christian and the Indian are 'metaphysically happy',[10] because they contemplate the divine perfection – the whole or the absolute – the Hellenic ideal offers an opportunity not just of contemplating, but of contributing to, the full realization of its own sphere, which is the world of nature.

> The man of Hellenic ideal has a different kind of spiritual life. He perceives life to be imperfect because it is imperfect; still, he does not reject life, because it is on it that his eyes are fixed. Even if he sees the supreme beauty he longs for in the world of the gods, he longs for that same beauty in men. 'The race of gods and of men is one and the same', Pindar said; what belongs to the one ought to belong to the other. Thus, of the three idealist types, the Hellenic is the one which cannot reject the life he calls imperfect. Therefore, his ideal is humanly the most tragic and profound.[11]

---

[8] The essay's point of origin explains Pessoa's care in defining the concepts on which his argument is founded. It is clear that he is stepping onto dangerous ground, and he knows it. This is not only because of the polemics around Botto. It is apparent in the way he distances himself from Decadence, and in the way he deals with the topic of homoeroticism itself. He detaches it from life, he aestheticizes it, he even makes an existential necessity out of it (for some temperaments, those which he nevertheless terms pathological). This is another way in which Pater comes in as well.

[9] 'Só Deus, e a alma, que ele criou e se lhe assemelha, são a perfeição e a verdadeira vida' (2000, 175).

[10] 'metafisicamente feliz' (2000, 176).

[11] 'Outra é a vida espiritual do homem de ideal helénico. Esse vê que a vida é imperfeita, porque é imperfeita; porém não rejeita a vida, porque é na mesma vida que tem postos os olhos. Mesmo que veja no mundo dos deuses aquela beleza suprema, pela qual anseia, anseia também por essa beleza nos homens. "A raça dos deuses e dos homens é uma só", disse Píndaro; a uns deve pertencer o que aos outros pertence. Por isso, dos três idealistas, é o heleno o único que não pode rejeitar aquela vida a que chama imperfeita. O seu ideal é, portanto, humanamente o mais trágico e profundo' (2000, 176–7).

His is, in a word, the path of artistic intervention, the deployment of artistic creativity in the interests of the fullest possible aesthetic realization of nature. His way lies not in stepping outside life in the direction of the beyond, but in infusing life with a special (aesthetic) quality. Deprived of the spiritual consolation of religion, the man of the Hellenic ideal seeks consolation in life itself, 'perfecting life, so that its imperfection pains him the less. And how does he perfect it? It cannot be objectively, because human action on the universe is extremely limited. It is therefore only subjectively that he can perfect it, by perfecting his concept and his feeling of it.'[12] In other words, the Hellenic sensibility strives to achieve the 'absolute aesthetic ideal', and 'Art is the subjective perfecting of life'.[13] Clearly, the formative presence of the Conclusion to *The Renaissance* can be felt at this point.

Appealing to Pater explicitly, Pessoa's vindication of Botto then turns to presenting the paradox of an amorality infused with high existential consequence:

> The first characteristic of an aesthete's art is therefore the absence of metaphysical and moral elements in the substance of his invention. As, however, all Hellenic ideals proceed from a directly critical application of intelligence to life, and of sensibility to the content of life, the absence of metaphysics is not an absence of metaphysical ideas, just as the absence of morals is not an absence of moral ideas. There is an idea which, without being metaphysical or moral, stands for moral and metaphysical ideas in the work of the aesthete. He substitutes the idea of beauty for the ideas of truth and of good. For that very same reason, he nevertheless gives to that idea of beauty a metaphysical and moral consequence. The famous 'Conclusion' of *The Renaissance*, by Pater, the greatest of European aesthetes, is the culminating instance of this attitude.[14]

Along with Pater, Pessoa will go on to mention Winckelmann, 'the founder of aestheticism in Europe',[15] an author whose words he, in fact, quotes from Pater, not from the original (see 181–2). He describes Winckelmann and Pater (perhaps excessively) as almost, in truth, the only two exact types of the

---

12   'Aperfeiçoando a vida, para que a sua imperfeição lhes doa menos. Aperfei-çoando–a como? Objectivamente não pode ser, porque a acção humana sobre o universo é menos que limitadíssima. É portanto só subjectivamente que se pode aperfeiçoá-la, aperfeiçoando o conceito e o sentimento dela' (2000, 177).

13   'o ideal estético absoluto', 'A arte é, com efeito, o aperfeiçoamento subjectivo da vida' (2000, 177).

14   'O primeiro característico da arte do esteta é pois a ausência de elementos metafísicos e morais na substância da sua ideação. Como, porém, os ideais helénicos procedem todos de uma aplicação directamente crítica da inteligência à vida, e da sensibilidade ao conteúdo dela, essa ausência de metafísica não será uma ausência de ideias metafísicas, nem essa ausência de moral uma ausência de ideias morais. Há uma ideia que, sem ser metafísica nem moral, faz, na obra do esteta, as vezes das ideias morais e metafísicas. O esteta substitui a ideia de beleza à ideia de verdade e à ideia de bem, porém dá, por isso mesmo, a essa ideia de beleza um alcance metafísico e moral. A célebre "Conclusão" da *Renascença* de Pater, o maior dos estetas europeus, é o exemplo culminante desta atitude' (2000, 179).

15   'fundador do estetismo na Europa' (2000, 181).

aesthete which European civilization can boast of'[16] – just as Botto is the only aesthete in Portuguese literature. One might even say that Pessoa's insistence on the uniqueness of Botto among Portuguese writers is, in itself, an explanation for the almost complete absence of Pater as a point of reference in Portuguese literature, philosophy and art. It would appear that (in Pessoa's terms) the predominance of 'moral' concerns, 'metaphysics' and sentimentality in Portuguese literature precluded him from becoming a reference of any consequence there.

Indeed, it is very interesting to note that, in a reply to Pessoa's essay published in the following issue of *Contemporanea* (no. 4, October 1922), the journalist Álvaro Maia does not even mention Pater, crucial though he may be to Pessoa's argument. Adopting a stance of moral conservatism, Maia explicitly condemns art for art's sake, the moral indifference of which he believes to be a form of cultural and social irresponsibility leading to national degeneracy. That this is as much an invective against Botto as against Pessoa's defence is significant in view of our hint that Pessoa's discussion of 'the aesthetic ideal in Portugal' had everything to do with his own artistic agenda.[17]

What very much displeased readers like Maia was that, having detached art and the artistic life from truth and conventional morality, Pessoa presented the appreciation of physical beauty and of pleasure as an alternative ethics. As the most perfect body is the male body, which combines grace and strength, achieving the highest possible degree of perfection at a sub-divine level, that is what the poet has to write about.

Sexuality is an animal type of ethics, the first and most instinctive of ethics. However, as the aesthete sings beauty without ethical preoccupations, it

---

[16] 'quase, em verdade, os únicos tipos exactos do esteta que a civilização europeia pode apresentar' (2000, 184). It is interesting to notice that, throughout the essay, Pessoa consistently applies the word *aesthete* to creative writers. The only essayists qualified as *aesthetes* are Pater and Winckelmann.

It is also interesting to note Pessoa's care in distancing the aesthetes from the 'minor Satanist' ('o satânico menor'), the rebellious Christian, the wilful sinner, the blasphemer (cf. 2000, 179). In other words, from 'the decadent bad Christian, like Baudelaire or Wilde' ('do mau cristão decadente, como Baudelaire ou Wilde', 180). Unlike Decadence, Aestheticism is a positive, not a negative, ideal.

[17] Maia's title paraphrases Pessoa's while bringing to the fore the moral issue, which constituted anathema: 'Literature of Sodom: Mr Fernando Pessoa and the Aesthetic Ideal in Portugal' ('Literatura de Sodoma. O Sr. Fernando Pessoa e o ideal estético em Portugal'). Maia sees the nineteenth century as an era of mental and moral anarchy. The 'literature of Sodom' would then be a mere sequel to nineteenth-century 'putrescence' (his style can be as violent as this, and more). He denies that Botto is endowed with true feeling for beauty. Not even among the Greeks, he says, had there been homage paid to male beauty, for even then there had been sexual degradation and aberration. That homage required 'absolute purity of instinct and ideas' ('absoluta pureza de instinto e de ideias', Fernandes 1989, 60). Also, that purity would not exclude female beauty.

The fact that Pater is not mentioned in the chain of texts that followed the scandal of *Canções* is symptomatic. (The texts have been collected and annotated by Aníbal Fernandes.)

follows that he will sing it where he most finds it, not where suggestions external to aesthetics, like sexual suggestion, would make him search for it. As he thus follows only beauty, the aesthete sings preferably the male body, as it is the human body which can accumulate the most elements of beauty, of the few which are possible.[18]

Detached from the sexual impulse, Botto's homoeroticism is thus aesthetically justified.

As has been suggested, it may not be going too far to suggest that, for Pessoa, the point at issue is less how to deal with the poetry of Botto than how to formulate the essentials of a truly modern sensibility. His own attempts involved both translating Pater and writing practical criticism along Paterian lines. This relationship with Pater is more specifically relevant in the larger context of Pessoa's ambition of being a *creator of civilization*. A project for a revolution of conscience which would provide both spiritual and intellectual fulfilment through a revival of Paganism is present in the plans for *Athena* from the very start, and is the cornerstone of the work of Pessoa's heteronym António Mora. It is also, as we have seen, present in Pessoa's contributions (under several names) to the magazine. Finally, it involved, on occasions, the discussion of Pater's aestheticism in writings which remained unpublished during Pessoa's lifetime.[19]

3

Besides the 'La Gioconda' translation by Pessoa in *Athena* there are about twenty further relevant items in Portuguese libraries, which comprise both English editions of the main works, and French and Spanish translations of Walter Pater's *The Renaissance: Studies in Art and Poetry*, together with a small number of other published works that are listed in the bibliography.

There are also two dissertations on Walter Pater, from 1985 and 1997, that testify to his recent reputation in academic circles, and will be briefly summarized here.

---

[18]   'A sexualidade é uma ética animal, a primeira e a mais instintiva das éticas. Como, porém, o esteta canta a beleza sem preocupação ética, segue que a cantará onde mais a encontre, e não onde sugestões externas à estética, como a sugestão sexual, o façam procurá-la. Como se guia, pois, só pela beleza, o esteta canta de preferência o corpo masculino, por ser o corpo humano que mais elementos de beleza, dos poucos que há, pode acumular' (2000, 181).

[19]   See especially Lopes 1990, vol. I: 197–213; vol. II: 283–5 and 380–5; Pessoa 1966, 176, 233–4, 248–9, 286–7, 352. References to Pater in notes presumably written in 1916–17 are not quite as approving as the 1922 essay. For instance: 'Among the attempts at Paganism that the last century produced there is not one that does not suffer from being Christian. Even Walter Pater, who had both a perfect understanding of Paganism and a perfect desire of being a Pagan, was no better than a sick Christian with a craving for Paganism' ('Das tentativas de paganismo, que o século passado produziu, não há uma que não sofra de ser cristã. Mesmo Walter Pater, que unia a um perfeito entendimento do paganismo, um perfeito desejo de ser pagão, não passou de um cristão doente com ânsias de paganismo' – Pessoa 1966, 352).

In her MA thesis on 'Walter Pater: Aesthetic Relativism and the Role of the Critic' ('Walter Pater: o relativismo estético e a função do crítico', Faculty of Letters, University of Lisbon, 1985), Maria Teresa Malafaia begins her study by signalling Walter Pater's discovery of the world through the feminine perspective as well as his intellectual development and his love of literature. The biographical part is marked by meticulous documentation of Pater's studies at Brasenose College and his youth in Oxford.

The confluence of the phenomenological projects as they appeared in Pater's essays 'Coleridge's Writings' (1865), 'Winckelmann' (1866), and the Conclusion to 'Poems by William Morris' (1868) is suggested as being Pater's way of achieving conceptual unity and thus the basis of Aestheticism. The importance of the British empirical tradition, and the influence of the development of psychological studies in the formulation of Aestheticism, are also incorporated in this study. When the formulation of Aestheticism is considered, the path from fragmentation to conceptual unity is viewed in terms of a dynamic interdependence in which solipsism and collective experience are intertwined. The unique position of the artist in relation with the universe justifies not only the aesthetic relativism that Pater derives from scientific analysis but also the role given to the expression of the aesthetic assumptions, with their special bias towards relativism, within the framework of Paterian poetics.

After Part I, in which the formulation of Aestheticism is analysed, Part II deals with the evaluation of poetic experience. Here the nature of art, and the relativism of beauty, are studied in conjunction with the definition of the scope of the critic. Aesthetic criticism and its double aim – formal and psychological – come into consideration, and Teresa Malafaia makes reference to both the critic's and the artist's roles. Her special interest is also apparent in her description of Impressionism as the fundamental element in aesthetic criticism, and in her explicit acknowledgement of the relativism of judgement. A last aspect of the coherence of the Paterian method needs finally to be addressed, and that is its defence of subjectivism within the framework of the unique relationship between the individual and the art object. Two further articles by Malafaia, on *Marius* and on the echoes of Pater in Edward Said, are listed in the bibliography (Malafaia 1987 and 1993).

In his dissertation 'Walter Pater and Kant' ('Walter Pater e Kant', Ponta Delgada / Universidade dos Açores, 1997, 2 vols.), E. J. Moreira da Silva seeks to explore Pater's relationship to German idealist philosophy.[20] Reminding the reader that Pater taught philosophy at Oxford for many years, he analyses the relevance of the work of Kant, Schiller, Fichte, Schelling and Hegel to Pater's own thinking. His starting point is the essay 'Coleridge's Writings' (*The Westminster Review*, 1866), which is not taken primarily to be a statement on Coleridge, but is valued rather for the fact that it contains Pater's most significant and explicit references to Kant and Schelling. Pater's treatment of Coleridge thus becomes a touchstone for the understanding of the author's relationship to German idealism. Furthermore, this is taken to be a definitive relationship, whose repercussions are traceable

---

[20]   Moreira da Silva has also organized a *Concordance* to Pater's works.

in later works such as *The Renaissance, Marius the Epicurean, Imaginary Portraits* and *Plato and Platonism*.

Taken as a whole, this study amounts to an investigation of the philosophical background of Pater's conception of the nature and function of art and, indeed, of his interpretation of the historical development of Western culture. According to Moreira da Silva, Pater's thinking revolves around the problem of the dissociation of the two spheres of human experience: that of the speculative and the spiritual from that of the concrete and the sensory. The author terms this 'the modern problem', and argues that it was a dissociation of which Pater strongly disapproved. Pater wished to establish (in fact, to re-establish) a dual outlook. The equilibrium of that dual sphere had been a feature of Classical Greek civilization, but it had collapsed under the stress of the Christian proneness to asceticism and disregard for sensation. The Renaissance had partly restored the balance between abstraction and the concrete (which explains Pater's special interest in the artistic productions of the period) but the Enlightenment, in its empiricist as well as in its rationalistic tendencies, did not help matters. More recently, Romantic conceptions of the substantiality of subjectivity (with Schelling as the epitome), could be seen to move very much along the same lines, with regard to this problem. Contemporary culture thus made it necessary to reject any form of supernaturalism that did not envisage the necessity of compromising with the natural, the sensory and the concrete.

The existence and perceptions of the Greeks, on the other hand, were not affected by such a dualism, being essentially sympathetic. They stood for the combination of the positive and the spiritual in a perfect wholeness of experience, in which patent reality was unproblematically linked to the realm of religious experience and to art. Predictably, Pater's solution to 'the modern problem' depends on a reversal of the process of dissociation, and relies on Kant's epoch-making philosophy, as Pater himself interpreted it (consider the opening paragraph of 'Prosper Mérimée'). To recover the holistic perfection of the Greek outlook, which created an impeccable balance of mind and sensation, is his aim, and it is something which has to do not only with vision or perception (and art), but also with a certain dignity and poise in facing up to the human predicament.

Moreira da Silva suggests that the way advocated by Pater relies on elements taken from Kant's aesthetics in the *Kritik der Urteilskraft*. Kant's imposition of limits on the knowability of ultimate reality need not confine us 'into the narrow chamber of the individual mind' (in the words of *The Renaissance*, 151) as a chamber with no way out. Rather, it can be used as a cornerstone in the process of restoring an integrity of outlook that has been lost over the course of Western intellectual history.

The value of Kant's philosophy had to do with its having a systematic character – it could be taken as the great synthesis of post-Enlightenment thought – whilst it also successfully avoided the pitfall (as several of his Romantic followers did not) of identifying spirit and reality. On the other hand, for Pater philosophy and art have similar functions,

> for, given the limits to human knowledge imposed by Kant, any kind of order the mind may impose on the chaos of empirical diversity [...] is

inevitably the result either of 'the artifice and the invention of the understanding' [a phrase from 'Coleridge's Writings'] or of the artifice of aesthetic ideas: the lack of discrimination of thought and sensation (form and matter, unity and diversity) through which the aesthetic imagination tries to objectify the empirical totality presupposed by the synthetic unity of rational ideas.[21]

Accordingly, the solution to 'the modern problem' is for Pater 'the transformation of the diversity and chaos of *modern* life into subjective unity and order artistically constructed'.[22] The grounds for advocating aesthetic contemplation as an end in itself are to be found in the definition of aesthetic perception presupposed in the *Kritik der Urteilskraft*. From this comes Pater's project for the aestheticization of existence, his ambition to live for the enjoyment of self-sufficient artistic experience, that is to say, for the fulfilment of one's humanity. 'For art comes to you proposing frankly to give nothing but the highest quality to your moments as they pass, and simply for those moments' sake' (153). So reads the final passage of *The Renaissance*, and that can be seen as one possible theoretical consequence both of Kant's idealism and of his conception of the disinterestedness of the work of art.

4

Just as Pessoa is one of the very few true anglophiles in Portuguese literary history,[23] so the impact of *The Renaissance* on his writing stands out as the only significant instance of a productive encounter between Portuguese culture and Pater's thought. This may eventually read as too definitive a judgement, since it is always possible that new data may be identified. But it is the only judgement validated by the data that are at present available.

In the period following Pessoa, the Pater connection in Portuguese culture appears to have remained confined to the universities, and indeed exclusively to English departments. No dissertations have yet been produced bearing specifically on the significance of Pater's work in the fields of aesthetics or art.

---

[21] 'porque, dadas as limitações impostas ao conhecimento humano por Kant, toda e qualquer ordem que a mente possa impor ao caos da diversidade empírica [...] resulta, por força, ou do "artifício e invenção do entendimento" ou do artifício das ideias estéticas: a indistinção entre pensamento e sensação (forma e matéria, unidade e diversidade) com que a imaginação estética tenta objectivar a totalidade empírica pressuposta pela unidade sintética das ideias racionais' (II: 421).

[22] 'a transformação da diversidade e do caos da vida *moderna* na unidade e na ordem subjectivas construídas artisticamente' (II: 424).

[23] Another example, from the Romantic period, would be the great anglophile poet Almeida Garret.

13 War and Peace – Pater's Part: Translations of Walter Pater in 1930s and 1940s Spain

Jacqueline A. Hurtley

1

Translations of Walter Pater in Spain have largely been produced in Barcelona and have focused on three of his texts: *The Renaissance* (Catalan, 1938; Castilian, 1945, 1982, 1999), *Imaginary Portraits* (Castilian, 1942) and *Marius the Epicurean* (Castilian, 1944). His *Plato and Platonism* was first published in Buenos Aires (Castilian, 1946), but here I shall be limiting myself to a consideration of the translations published in war-stricken Barcelona and in the postwar period. It is not surprising that the Pater translations should be produced in Barcelona over the 1930s and into the 1940s, as so many translations were; and this, as has been widely acknowledged (Fuster 1980; Pericay and Toutain 1996; Medina 2000), was a fundamental part of the cultural construction and consolidation of a national identity for a Catalonia with international ambitions. But in order to understand why Pater in particular, the tenets of *noucentisme*[1] need to be considered since the translations of Pater's texts were promoted or produced by Catalan intellectuals who had been influenced to a greater or lesser degree by the principles pronounced by Eugeni d'Ors i Rovira (1881–1954), prime mover of the early twentieth-century doctrine.

Noucentisme has been defined as 'a desire to be and a desire for power'[2] on the part of a Catalan bourgeoisie eager for its own national identity, in control of its political power, its economy and culture. The early twentieth century was a promising period for Catalonia in this connection with the founding of the *Mancomunicat de Catalunya* (Commonwealth of Catalonia) in 1914, an administrative institution presided over by Enric Prat de la Riba i Sarrà (1870–1917), which brought together the four Catalan county councils of Barcelona, Girona, Lleida and Tarragona and would do much to promote a sense of Catalan national identity, as well as focusing hopes for an independent

---

[1] 'A cultural-political movement in Catalonia at the beginning of the XIXth [sic] century' is the definition of *noucentisme* provided in Oliva and Buxton (1986). Nineteenth, instead of twentieth, century is erroneous. Parcerisas (1997, 59) defines it as a '[c]ultural and political movement in Catalonia at the turn of the century'.

[2] 'voluntat de ser i voluntat de poder' (Comadira 1999, 109).

Catalonia, through a variety of bodies, such as the Institute of Catalan Studies (L'Institut d'Estudis Catalans), the Library of Catalonia (La Biblioteca de Catalunya) and the School of Librarians (L'Escola de Bibliotecàries),[3] until General Primo de Rivera's coup in 1923. Eugeni d'Ors was appointed Director of the School of Librarians and also occupied other posts of prominence before his fall from grace in 1920, in the wake of the latter's death in 1917, and his subsequent defenestration under Prat de la Riba's successor, the 'uncompromising and ill-tempered'[4] Josep Puig i Cadafalch (1867–1957). An important component in the creation of a distinct sense of nation would be the language and in the year before the founding of the *Mancomunitat*, the eminent grammarian and lexicographer Pompeu Fabra i Poch (1868–1948), at the head of the Philological Section of the Institute of Catalan Studies since 1911, would produce the *Normes ortogràfiques*, published by the Institute in January 1913, which prescribed rules for the correct writing of Catalan. D'Ors was a member of the committee set up at the Institute to come to an agreement as to the norms to be established, although he had been influential in creating a style through the column he had been publishing in the conservative Catalan daily *La Veu de Catalunya* (*The Voice of Catalonia*) since 1906 (Pericay and Toutain 1996, 93). D'Ors's aesthetic project has been connected to Jean Moréas's Romanism in *fin-de-siècle* France (Vallcorba 1994; Pericay and Toutain 1996) and although it claimed to embrace modernity, d'Ors looked back to European humanism and the eighteenth century as providing a model for the present (Pericay and Toutain 1996, 93), a present which aspired to consolidate an enlightened bourgeois order characterized by voluntarism, refined manners, a sense of balance and a concern to create quality,[5] all expressed in a style which sought an urban sophistication and was prone to artificiality.

In an article published in his column in *La Veu de Catalunya* (*The Voice of Catalonia*) in 1908, Eugeni d'Ors mentions Walter Pater in passing, claiming that he would place 'something'[6] of the English author in an ideal library, which would include the chosen in terms of concision [sic]. It would fall to a second generation *noucentista*, Carles Riba i Bracons (1893–1959), a 'faithful disciple and leading apologist'[7] of d'Ors, to find a translator for Pater's *The Renaissance*. He himself would polish the translation, which was published in 1938 under the auspices of the Institution of Catalan Letters (Institució de les Lletres Catalanes), a body created in autumn 1937 and of which Riba was to become Vice-President as well as jointly heading the Publications Section

---

[3]   The translation of *mancomunitat* as commonwealth is provided by Oliva and Buxton (1986). See the entry under *Mancomunitat de Catalunya* in the *Gran Enciclopèdia Catalana* (1981). The *Mancomunitat de Catalunya* signified a degree of home rule and constituted the roots of what would become the Home Rule Statute (Estatut d'Autonomia de Catalunya, 1932) in the wake of the founding of the Second Spanish Republic (Segunda República Española, 1931).

[4]   'intransigent i colèric' (Castellanos 1987, 37).

[5]   'voluntarisme, civilitat, mesura', "Obra Ben Feta"' (Jardí 1967, 52–3, 59, 116; Santaeulàlia 1999, 120).

[6]   'alguna cosa' (d'Ors 1950, 897).

[7]   'un fidel seguidor i un destacat apologista' (Pericay and Toutain 1996, 13).

(Campillo 2003, 10, 11–12; Medina 2000, 10). The translator Riba chose was Marià Manent i Cisa (1898–1988), a poet and translator like himself (Riba had produced a prologue for Manent's translation of Rupert Brooke's poems into Catalan in 1931), as well as someone who had shared his political sympathies, i.e. those expressed by Catalan Action (Acció Catalana), initially a breakaway group from the conservative Regionalist League (Lliga Regionalista) party, whose negotiating with the Spanish central government was not supported by the more radically nationalist young (Baras 1984). Jordi Malé has claimed that Carles Riba's *noucentista* identity went beyond the bounds of d'Ors's doctrine to embrace both Prat de la Riba and Pompeu Fabra's thought. He speaks of Riba's 'strong and sincere conviction as regards what *noucentisme* signified in terms of a collective task, one of construction and organization of the country (Catalonia), to which he contributed, as an intellectual and man of letters, by means of his activities in the realm of culture'.[8] Undoubtedly, Riba's cultural impact in Catalonia, both before the Civil War and following it, cannot be ignored. Like Manent, he published as a poet at the end of the First World War (Riba 1919), but his contribution as a translator of the classics – Plutarch, Plato, Sophocles, Aristotle, Euripides and Homer, amongst others – in the years following the First World War, as well as after 1922 when he occupied a Chair set up for him at the Bernat Metge Foundation (Fundació Bernat Metge), financed by the Regionalist League (Lliga Regionalista) parlamentarian Francesc Cambó i Batlle (1876–1947), has been regarded as a fundamental contribution to Catalonia's cultural reconstruction. Indeed, as Malé has pointed out, Riba's translating, producing of manuals and teaching were all a consequence of a profound conviction as regards 'his "duty" in relation to that great task, concerned with educating a people and public who were just coming into being, in a political, linguistic and cultural sense'.[9] Moreover, Malé asserts that Riba always used the concept of 'duty' with Socrates in mind: 'This conviction, this "*noucentista* spirit" of his, was with him throughout his life'.[10]

If, as has been claimed, by incorporating the texts of classical authors into Catalan culture, Riba was bringing the values of classical culture into the language (Medina 1987, 93), then the values of English culture might be made part of Catalan too. Moreover, if the English authors were upholding classical values, they would perfectly fit the *noucentista* requirement. Thus, it might be said that Walter Pater, looking back to classical times, recreating the Renaissance, and expressing himself in a style which lacked spontaneity, was tailored to the task.

---

[8]   'la seva convicció ferma i sincera en el que significava l'obra col.lectiva que fou el noucentisme, obra de construcció i de redreçament del país, en la qual ell va contribuir, com a intel·lectual i home de lletres que era, per mitjà de les seves realitzacions en l'àmbit de la cultura' (Malé 1999, 158).

[9]   'el seu "deure" envers aquella vasta obra, dirigida a educar una gent i un públic que just llavors es desvetllava, tant políticament com lingüísticament i culturalment' (Malé 1999, 158).

[10]   'Aquesta convicció, aquest seu "esperit noucentista", no el va abandonar al llarg de tota la seva vida' (Malé 1999, 158).

2

I have had a long conversation with Carles Riba. He says that the present government and his group of intellectual friends who are working for 'the restoration of the culture and spirit of Catalonia' represent counter-revolution.[11]

In his diary entry for 21 December 1937, Manent records having spoken at length with Riba on one of his visits to Barcelona. He spent the greater part of the Spanish Civil War period in the village of Viladrau, north of Barcelona, in the municipality of Osona, in accommodation made available to him by a personal friend, a student of Carles Riba's and translator of Greek poetry, Jaume Bofill i Ferro (1893–1968). Manent's *El Vel de Maia* (The Veil of Maia) is a diary covering the time spent there (January 1937 – February 1939), where he speaks of his daily activities, including translation, which provided a source of income.[12] He refers to reading a variety of authors and journals, a number of them English – the *New Statesman and Nation*, the *London Mercury*; Llewelyn Powys on Dr Johnson, W. H. Auden on Pope, Rebecca West on 'Mrs Montagu', T. S. Eliot on Byron, G. K. Chesterton on Victorian literature, Edwin Muir's biography of Walter Scott, Joan Bennett, Herbert Read's *The Meaning of Art* – as well as to translating a variety of poets and prose writers. Names which evoke the Georgians and First World War poets are mentioned, for example, Harold Munro, Wilfred Owen and Isaac Rosenberg, though canonical authors of the seventeenth and eighteenth centuries are present (Shakespeare, Donne, Fletcher, Herrick, Pope) as well as the Romantics (Wordsworth and Blake) and the contemporary Cecil Day-Lewis and Mary Webb. There are occasional mentions of visits to Barcelona, on some of which he would meet his English friend John Langdon-Davies, a friend since the early 1920s when Langdon-Davies and his family settled in Ripoll, and who would organize food parcels to relieve the hunger of a number of Catalan writers during the war.[13] It was on one of Manent's visits to the city, on 9 November 1937, that he would meet Carles Riba, who would inform Manent that he would be asked to produce 'the translation of the essays by Walter Pater on the Renaissance'.[14] Manent appears to have been familiar with Pater's work already, since he refers to rereading *Plato and Platonism* once he had completed his translation of *The Renaissance* (Manent 1975, 178). On 19 January 1938, Barcelona suffered 'one of the most terrible

---

[11] 'He parlat llargament amb en Carles Riba. Diu que el govern actual i el grup d'intellectuals amics seus que treballen per "la restauració de la cultura i l'esperit de Catalunya" representen la contrarevolució' (Manent 1975, 142).

[12] In his diary entry for 27 August 1938, Manent refers to having completed the translation of W. P. Ker's *Form and Style in Poetry*, for which he would be paid 1,994 *pessetes*. The translation was lost with the disappearance of the Institution of Catalan Letters (Institució de les Lletres Catalanes) in 1939 (Manent 1975, 196).

[13] For information on John Langdon-Davies's relationship with Catalonia, see Berga 1987 and 1991.

[14] 'la traducció dels assalgs de Walter Pater sobre el Renaixement' (Manent 1975, 130).

air raids'[15] since the outbreak of the war and on 26 January, the sound of three raids ruptured the calm of Manent's 'mountain oasis'.[16] Nevertheless, on 14 February 1938, the translator began his task, managing to render fourteen pages of *The Renaissance* into Catalan in four hours (Manent 1975, 162). On 9 and 11 March, he refers to continuing his work on the translation and remarks on the 11th that he is producing ten or twelve pages a day (Manent 1975, 166). After five weeks' work, he finishes the translation, on 3 April, having chalked up '450 sheets'.[17] Two days later, with time on his hands, having completed the translation, he will be reading Charles Du Bos and T. S. Eliot on Pater and will refer to the former's 'admirable interpretation of Pater's [*Marius the Epicurean*]'[18] in his 'Preliminary Note'[19] to *El Renaixement: estudis d'art i poesia* (*The Renaissance*). In the latter part of July 1938, Manent refers to going through the galley proofs of his translation, which incorporated corrections made by Riba (Manent 1975, 191), and within the week he had completed his introductory piece, where, he noted: 'I try to situate [Pater's] philosophy and summarize recent critical comment on it'.[20]

El Renaixement (*The Renaissance*) came off the press in Barcelona in November 1938, just two months before General Franco's troops occupied the city. The Institution of Catalan Letters (Institució de les Lletres Catalanes) had been publishing a variety of series: 'The Autonomous Catalan Government's Literary Prizes' (Premis Literaris de la Generalitat de Catalunya), 'Catalan Authors' (Col·lecció d'Autors Catalans) and 'Foreign Authors' (Col·lecció d'Autors Estrangers), of which *El Renaixement* appears to have been the first volume.[21] There were plans to translate Christopher Marlowe's *Edward II*, *Dr Faustus* and *Hero and Leander* as well as 'works' by Coleridge, De Foe [sic] and Sterne[22] but the arrival of General Franco's troops would play havoc with such forward planning: the translator of Marlowe's texts, C. A. Jordana, would subsequently be in exile and Manent's translation of Coleridge's Shakespeare criticism, together with a selection of his own poetry to be published in the 'Catalan Authors' series, would be lost, as Manent himself explains in a footnote to his diary entry for 24 May 1938: 'These two original manuscripts (of which I didn't make copies) disappeared following the entry of the conquerors into Barcelona'.[23] Fifty special copies of

---

15   'un dels bombardeigs més terribles' (Manent 1975, 154).

16   'oasi muntanyenc' (Manent 1975, 157).

17   '450 quartilles' (Manent 1995, 174).

18   'interpretació admirable de la novel·la de Pater' (Manent 1938b, 11).

19   'Nota Preliminar' (Manent 1938b, 9–18).

20   'intento de situar la seva filosofia [de Pater] i de resumir-ne els comentaris crítics recents' (Manent 1975, 191).

21   I say 'appears' as the published volume states on the front cover that the text belongs to the Foreign Authors (Autors Estrangers) series and that it is number II. However, on the inside flap, *El Renaixement* figures as the only volume which has appeared.

22   See the inside flap of *El Renaixement* (Pater 1938), where the names and texts mentioned figure below a heading 'Under preparation' (En preparació).

23   'Aquests dos originals (dels quals no vaig fer còpia) van desaparèixer després de l'entrada dels vencedors a Barcelona' (Manent 1975, 183). See also note 12 above.

El Renaixement were produced: twenty-five numbered from I to XXV in rag paper and not for sale, another twenty-five numbered from 1 to 25, in paper of the same quality, and 1,500 copies in paper of a more common quality. *El Renaixement* went on sale at fourteen pessetes.[24] The inside back flap of the volume carried reference to Manent's own poetic work starting with *La Branca* (*The Branch*, 1918), as well as to his volume of criticism *Notes sobre literature estrangera* (*Notes on Foreign Literature*, 1934), in which he published pieces on a wide range of authors and critics, from John Donne to Walter de la Mare and W. P. Ker, passing through Virginia Woolf and D. H. Lawrence, amongst others, in English literature, together with the Romanian poet Ilarie Voronca and the American Gertrude Stein.

The inside back flap of *El Renaixement* also listed Manent's translations, not only of English literature, but there are seven English texts in the list of ten: Keats, Kipling, Chesterton, Brooke, Rackham, J. M. Barrie and his *Versions de l'anglès* (*Renderings from the English*, 1938a), a selection of English poetry from the sixteenth up until the twentieth century. Manent had published Keats's *Sonets i odes* (*Sonets and Odes*, 1919), handsomely prologued by Eugeni d'Ors, almost twenty years before the appearance of his Pater translation. His first letter to John Langdon-Davies in the early 1920s was in French (Berga 1991, 46) and a French translation of *The Renaissance* by F. Roger-Cornaz had been published in Paris in 1917 (Pater 1917), but by the late 1930s Manent was a proven translator from English and the title page of *El Renaixement* stated that the translation was from the English. Given Manent's competence in English by this time, the accuracy of the translation into Catalan is not problematic. There are occasions, however, when Manent renders a concept less precisely or makes an omission. For instance, at the end of the essay on Pico della Mirandola, Pater refers to an oracle beside which living men and women 'have hushed their voices' (Pater 1998, 32), whilst Manent uses the Catalan verb 'to silence' ('apagar', Pater 1938, 55) where he might have used 'apaivagar' more appropriately and, in the final paragraph of the Conclusion, where Pater lists ways in which people may spend the 'interval' between life and death, he refers to some spending it 'in high passions' (Pater 1998, 153), Manent omits the adjective, producing the starker 'en passions' (Pater 1938, 207). In this same paragraph, in speaking of passion and its intensity, Pater twice uses the adjective 'quickened' (Pater 1998, 153), which is first translated by Manent as 'excitat' (excited) and five lines on as 'amatent' (prompt, quick, hasty, Pater 1938, 207). Neither of Manent's options convey what in the original expresses intensity and, therefore, might have been more effectively rendered into Catalan by 'aquest sentit de la vida més intens' and 'una consciència més intens i multiplicada', respectively. It also strikes me that the use of the conjunction 'i' (and) in this latter example in Catalan, to join the adjectives 'intense' and 'multiplied', achieves a more concentrated effect than the use of the comma as in the original English, the effect of which, in Catalan, is to interrupt the flow. However, the concentrated impact is there in

---

[24]   As in note 12 above, I have used the Catalan term for the Spanish currency. The price was announced on the back cover of the volume: 'Preu: 14 ptes.' (Price: 14 *pessetes*).

English through the play of stress on the first syllable of the disyllabic and trisyllabic adjectives in sequence, qualifying the trisyllabic noun, also stressed on the first syllable, all of which creates a sensual rhythm. Nevertheless, as I have stated, such inaccuracies, omissions or stylistic weaknesses are incidental to the whole. Therefore, I will now turn to considering Manent's introductory note to his translation and the significance of the publishing of Pater's text in war-ravaged Barcelona.

Manent's introductory essay follows the original February 1873 dedication to Charles Lancelot Shadwell, 'C.L.S.', and the epigraph to the text from the Book of Psalms, chapter 68, verse 13, which respects the English edition of 1893 (Hill 1980, 207). Pater's 1873, 1877, 1888, 1893 Preface is also included and follows Manent's introduction, preceding the nine essays and Conclusion which made up *The Renaissance* (1893). The introductory essay is composed of four paragraphs, which cover almost four pages and are divided into two blocks of two paragraphs each. I would say that the piece reflects Manent's difficulty in dealing with the content of *The Renaissance* given the number of other writers and critics he refers to in the relatively short space, that is, fifteen (W. B. Yeats, Maurice Barrès, André Gide, Shakespeare, Rabelais, Montaigne, Seán O'Faoláin, Oscar Wilde, Charles Du Bos, Ruskin, St Augustine, Alphonse Daudet, Renan, Rilke and Coleridge), and because he limits himself to referring to Pater's controversial Conclusion, in the first block, and alluding to another of Pater's texts, *Marius the Epicurean*, in the second. The introductory essay, then, cannot be said to be enlightening with regard to what follows; rather, it reflects Manent's diligent reading of other nineteenth- and twentieth-century critics and authors, both on Pater and in general. Thus, Manent can begin by situating *The Renaissance* and commenting on its outstanding impact for *fin-de-siècle* English letters: '*The Renaissance* has been one of the most influential books for English letters at the end of the century'.[25] Having completed this initial pronouncement, he will turn to the Conclusion, referring to it as inspiring an ideal for a whole generation of prose writers and poets, of whom, he declares, Yeats is the most distinguished. Following a pertinent quote from Yeats, he will go on to ponder 'the message'[26] contained in the Conclusion, which will lead him to the subject of life lived in intensity and to introduce pertinent quotes from Gide's *Les nourritures terrestres* (*Fruits of the Earth*[27]) and Barrès. His second paragraph of this first part of the introductory essay will consider Pater's failure to come to terms with the cruder dimension of life and a pertinent quote from O'Faolàin [sic] will confirm this claim and lead Manent to assert that Pater's message was a contemplative one, that of an aesthete, a message which will subsequently be distorted by Pater's disciples into an isolationist doctrine, one which would justify an ivory tower remoteness. Thus, Manent will recognize that a whole period of English literature had been misled by exaggeration with regard to the Victorian author's thought and, in this connection, will refer again to

---

[25]   '*El Renaixement* és un dels llibres que més ha influït en les lletres angleses de fi de segle' (Manent 1938b, 9).

[26]   'el missatge'.

[27]   As translated by Dorothy Bussy and published by Penguin Books in 1970.

Yeats's interpreting art as a refuge against life and will quote from Wilde too on this subject, both of whom, he claims, failed to appreciate Pater's recognition of a positive relationship between art and life. The final block of the introductory essay will be concerned to show that Pater is not a pure aesthete 'in the narrow Wildean sense', nor 'a mere hedonist', but concerned to convey 'higher realities to which those who are not "children of this world" can consecrate their multiplied consciousness'.[28] This will lead Manent to *Marius the Epicurean* and to focus on the protagonist's path to perfection. However, he will finally situate Pater 'in an ambiguous place between epicureanism and faith',[29] concluding with Pater's own words on lack and longing.

El Renaixement: estudis d'art i poesia, based on the fourth edition of *The Renaissance: Studies in Art and Poetry* (1893), covers pages 13 to 207 of a volume measuring 19 and a half centimetres wide and 13 centimetres long, which includes Pater's 1873 'Preface' and the 'Conclusion', originally the last quarter of Pater's review 'Poems by William Morris' in the *Westminster Review* for October, 1868 (Hill 1980, 443). The index to the volume appears at the end, as was customary in books published in Spain, and indicates that apart from Manent's introductory essay and Pater's Preface and Conclusion, it carries the nine essays which make up *The Renaissance* (in the editions produced after the first in 1873), all of them individually dated: 'Dues velles històries franceses' ('Two Early French Stories', 1872); 'Pico della Mirandola' (1871); 'Sandro Botticelli' (1870); 'Luca della Robbia' (1872); 'La poesia de Miquel Àngel' ('The Poetry of Michelangelo', 1871); Leonardo da Vinci (1869); 'L'escola del Giorgione' ('The School of Giorgione', 1877); 'Joachim du Bellay' (1872) and 'Winckelmann' (1867).

3

> In the texts which Riba published [in the Bernat Metge Foundation], he was conscious of 'influencing our language through the values contained in classical culture. That is to say, to do what in other nations was done at the time of the Renaissance.'[30]

In 'Towards Humanism' ('Vers l'humanisme'), one of his articles in *La Veu de Catalunya* (*The Voice of Catalonia*) in 1906, d'Ors recalled that Catalonia had not benefited, as other European nations had, from that rebirth of culture from the late fifteenth into seventeenth century Europe in the wake of the rediscovery of Greek texts of antiquity. Catalan culture was eclipsed in the wake of the victory of the Catholic Kings, Ferdinand and Isabel, giving way to

---

[28] 'en l'estret sentit de Wilde'; 'un mer hedonista'; 'unes realitats més altes a les quals poden consagrar llur consciència multiplicada els qui no són "fills d'aquest món"' (Manent 1938b, 11).

[29] 'en un lloc imprecís entre l'epicureisme i la fe' (Manent 1938b, 12).

[30] 'En les obres que [...] Riba [...] publicà [a la Fundació Bernat Metge] era conscient d' "influir la nostra llengua per mitjà dels valors de la cultura clásica. És a dir, fer allò que els altres pobles va ésser fet al Renaixement' (Medina 1987, 93).

'black days', as d'Ors qualified the period. He went on to affirm: 'The Renaissance in Europe coincided with our downfall'.[31] Therefore, as Catalonia was regaining a new sense of national vigour in the early twentieth century, it was important, essential as d'Ors saw it, to go back and recover what had been forcefully forfeited. The rising led by General Franco in July 1936 interrupted another opportunity afforded Catalonia during the Second Spanish Republic (1931–9), with the Catalan Home Rule Statute (Estatut d'Autonomia de Catalunya) of 1932, to develop her national difference. During the Civil War years (1936–9), Catalonia experienced Anarchist collectivization as well as Communist infiltration but the Institute of Catalan Studies (Institut d'Estudis Catalans) continued to function and to this was added the Institution of Catalan Letters (Institució de les Lletres Catalanes). By the time Manent's translation was coming off the press (November 1938), with eleven countries having granted the 'Nationalists', led by General Franco, *de jure*, and thirteen *de facto*, recognition, among the latter the United Kingdom (Edwards 1979, 193), the country might well have a sense of an ending and those concerned with rebirth in Catalonia after the war might profitably look back to the European humanist movement as inspirational once again.

Of the nine essays contained in *El Renaixement*, I would highlight five, where ideas are expressed which might be considered as particularly pertinent by those concerned to regenerate Catalonia with humanist values. Moreover, they carry ideas of particular importance to a class anxious to restore or reinforce its sense of nation as expressed through its religion and its language, yet no less anxiously pursuing restraint, suspicious of theory, and aspiring to form part of Europe. Therefore, Pater's exaltation of ancient Greece in such comments as: 'the [...] perfect sweetness in the Hellenic world' (Pater 1998, 2); 'the charm of the Hellenic spirit' (Pater 1998, 114); 'Hellenism, which is the principle pre-eminently of intellectual light' (Pater, 1998, 122); 'Hellenism is not merely an absorbed element in our intellectual life; it is a conscious tradition in it' (Pater 1998, 128), 'Hellenic generality or breadth [...] is a law of restraint' (Pater 1998, 139); 'Hellenism [...] its transparency, its rationality, its desire of beauty' (Pater 1998, 146) would be sympathetic to those of a *noucentista* persuasion. Then the reconciling of Greek antiquity with Christianity, referred to by Pater in his essay on Pico della Mirandola, would be perfectly compatible with Catalonia's Catholicism (Pater 1998, 20, 29), as would Winckelmann's conversion to Catholicism, noted by Pater in his essay on the eighteenth-century scholar, alongside 'his life-long struggle to attain the Greek spirit' (Pater 1998, xxxiii). Indeed, Pico, 'a true humanist' (Pater 1998, 32), and Winckelmann, 'in sympathy with the humanists of a previous century [...] the last fruit of the Renaissance' (Pater 1998, xxxiii), would be inspirational for *noucentista* sympathizers harried by Communist intrigue, agitated by Anarchist aspirations, in 1930s Catalonia.

In his essay on Joachim Du Bellay, Pater refers to 'a little tract' (Pater 1998, 102) written by the 24-year-old Du Bellay, *La Deffense et illustration de la langue*

---

[31]   'negres dies'; 'El Renaixement de l'Europa coincidí amb la nostra caiguda' (d'Ors 1950, 18).

Françoyse, and highlights its core concern: 'how to illustrate or ennoble the French language, to give it lustre' (Pater 1998, 102), a fundamental preoccupation of *noucentisme* with regard to Catalan. Pater's quote from Du Bellay's tract would aptly communicate what would constitute a challenge and contribute to a consciousness-raising in Catalonia with regard to the language: 'Languages [. . .] are not born like plants and trees, some naturally feeble and sickly, others healthy and strong and apter to bear the weight of men's conceptions, but all their virtue is generated in the world of choice and men's freewill concerning them' (Pater 1998, 103). Furthermore, Pater's assessment of Du Bellay's struggle in favour of the language was Catalonia's own: 'In this effort to ennoble the French language [. . .] what Du Bellay is really pleading for is his mother-tongue, the language, that is, in which one will have the utmost degree of what is moving and passionate. [. . .] and in pleading for the cultivation of the French language, he is pleading for no merely scholastic interest, but for freedom, impulse, reality, not in literature only, but in daily communication of speech' (Pater 1998, 104).

Pater also registers in *The Renaissance* a note of deprecation with regard to theory, an attitude which would also appeal to *noucentista* pundits and their pupils, subjected to political theories during the Civil War which were totally antagonistic to their pursuits and who privileged individual genius, the artist possessed by inspiration or vision. Thus, in the essay on Winckelmann, Pater asserts:

> The impression which Winckelmann's literary life conveyed to those about him, was that of excitement, intuition, inspiration, rather than the contemplative evolution of general principles. The quick, susceptible enthusiast [. . .] apprehended the subtlest principles of the Hellenic manner, not through the understanding, but by instinct or touch. (Pater 1998, 124)[32]

And in the penultimate paragraph of Pater's notorious 'Conclusion', the sense of disdain towards theory is reasserted and the value of individual perception exalted:

> To burn always with this hard, gem-like flame, to maintain this ecstasy, is success in life. [. . .] With this sense of the splendour of our experience and of its awful brevity, gathering all we are into one desperate effort to see and touch, we shall hardly have time to make theories about the things we see and touch. [. . .] The theory or idea or system which requires of us the sacrifice of any part of this experience [. . .] has no real claim upon us. (Pater 1998, 152, 153)

Finally, the idea of a European cultural identity, expressed by Pater in the essay on Winckelmann and the notion of a continuity between Pagan and Christian art would appeal to Catalonia's European ambition and complement d'Ors's counter-revolutionary principle of Blessed Continuation (Santa Continuació), contained in a *Veu de Catalunya* (*Voice of Catalonia*) article in 1910 (d'Ors 1950, 1346):

---

[32] However, as Maria Campillo has pointed out, Riba did recognize a historical function (una funció històrica) in relation to literary creativity (1999, 201–2).

The history of art has suffered as much as any history by trenchant and absolute divisions. Pagan and Christian art are sometimes harshly opposed, and the Renaissance is represented as a fashion which set in at a definite period. That is the superficial view: the deeper view is that which preserves the identity of European culture. The two are really continuous [. . .] (Pater 1998, 145)

This sense of continuity between the Christian present and pagan past may be juxtaposed to Pater's rejection of the complexity of his times, which he presents as distracting from his ideal:

Breadth, centrality, with blitheness and repose, are the marks of Hellenic culture. Is such culture a lost art? [. . .] Certainly, for us in the modern world, with its conflicting claims, its entangled interests, distracted by so many sorrows, with many preoccupations, so bewildering an experience, the problem of unity with ourselves, in blitheness and repose, is far harder than it was for the Greek within the simple terms of antique life. Yet, not less than ever, the intellect demands completeness, centrality. (Pater 1998, 146)

Carles Riba and others of like mind were set on satisfying the intellectual requirement outlined by Pater at the end of the above-quoted extract. In Riba's absence following the end of the Civil War, his disciples would continue the translating task.

4

[Thomas Woodrow] Wilson created a concern with small nationalities, and this doctrine so poisoned European souls that certain Catalans, certain Basques [. . .] and other separatist fauna, found encouragement there and it kindled their aspirations.[33]

In the wake of the victory of General Franco and his troops, finally achieved with the occupation of Madrid on 1 April 1939, the Spanish Civil War was brought to a close and a new state created which was determined to re-Castilianize Catalonia (Benet 1979). The censorship of books became obligatory (Abellán 1980, 15–19) and, thus, a procedure was established whereby publishers were obliged to present an application to the Vice-Secretary's Department for the Education of the People (Vice-Secretaría de Educación Popular), with a copy of the text for which the application was being made. The texts were farmed out to readers who reported on the appropriateness of a given text within the ideological confines established by the new regime. Of the three publishers who brought out Pater's *Imaginary Portraits* (1942), *Marius the Epicurean* (1944) and *The Renaissance* (1945), perforce in Castilian translation, one had already established himself as a publisher in Castilian in the 1920s, one had been a publisher in Catalan during

---

[33] 'Wilson nos trajo la preocupación de las pequeñas nacionalidades, y tanto envenenó esta doctrina las almas europeas, que en ella encontraron alientos y pujos hasta ciertos catalanes, ciertos vascos [. . .] y demás fauna separatista' (Aznar 1940, 1).

the years of the Second Republic, and one now set up as a publisher for the first time.

Jaume Aymà i Ayala (1882–1964), a teacher of Catalan during the years of the Republic, refashioned as Jaime Aymá in the postwar period, founded the publishing house Aymá with his son, Jaume Aymà i Mayol (1911–89), in Barcelona in 1944; but, already in 1939, he had begun publishing under the name of Editorial Alcides (Manent 1989). In 1942 he brought out the Castilian translation of Pater's *Imaginary Portraits*, *Retratos imaginarios*, by J. Farrán y Mayoral, that is, Josep Farran i Mayoral, his forename reduced to the initial letter so that he would not have to exhibit the Castilian version of his name: José, and the Catalan conjunction 'i' linking the two surnames, now in Castilian: 'y'. (There would still be a sense of Catalan identity in the presence of the conjunction, albeit in its Castilian form, as the use of the conjunction between the two surnames would not be common practice in Castilian.) This relaunch of Pater in postwar Spain by an heir of the eminent linguist Pompeu Fabra, Aymà i Ayala (Manent 1989), facilitated by a follower of the spirit and taste of d'Ors, Farran i Mayoral,[34] would create a symbolic connection with the cultural project initiated in Catalonia in the early years of the century, interrupted by Primo de Rivera's dictatorship, and undertaken with renewed vigour over the Republican years. Moreover, bibliophile editions would be produced: five copies on Haesbeek Holland paper marked A, B, C, D, E, with boxwood illustrations illuminated by hand, the work of the artist Manuel Benet,[35] and twenty copies in a linen-based paper numbered in Roman numerals I to XX. The latter copies[36] consisted of a hard back measuring 26 by 19 centimetres, fastened with two sets of ribbons inserted in the hard-back binding to maintain ten quires in place, which carried the text, awarding the volume a fifteenth-century stamp.[37] These were followed by the four boxwood illustrations which introduce each story, now crossed out by the engraver's burin, and a further quire with the sixteen paintings or engravings which appear over the text of the four portraits: four paintings by Watteau in 'Un príncipe de pintores cortesanos' ('A Prince of Court Painters'); an engraving of the façade of Auxerre Cathedral, a fifteenth-century engraving entitled 'The Sermon of the Demented' and two details from the vault in the choir of Auxerre Cathedral in 'Dionisio el Auxerrés' ('Denys l'Auxerrois'); a 'Winter Landscape' by Isaac van Ostade, a 'View of Delft' by Vermeer, a 'Young Girl Watering Flowers' by G. Dou and W. van der Velde's 'Fleet' in 'Sebastián van Storck'. Finally, Dürer's 'Apollo and Diana' and his 'The Knight, Death and the Devil', together with G. von Kaulbach's 'Goethe skating' and Hans Wechtlin's 'Orpheus', were inserted in 'El Duque Carlos

---

[34]   See the *Gran Enciclopedia Catalana* entry under Farran i Mayoral, Josep.
[35]   I have been unable to come up with any information on Manuel Benet.
[36]   I have not managed to see any of the five copies produced on Haesbeek Holland paper. The National Library of Catalonia (Biblioteca de Catalunya) in Barcelona possesses no copy of *Retratos imaginarios* (*Imaginary Portraits*).
[37]   I am grateful to Enric Tormo, ex-Director of the Book Museum (Museu del Llibre) in Barcelona, for pointing out the dimensions of the text to me.

de Rosenmold' ('Duke Carl of Rosenmold').[38] The title page of the text
announced that the translation of Pater's text was from English and carried a
prologue by J. Farrán y Mayoral, boxwood engravings by Manuel Benet, as
well as sixteen illustrations apart from the text. Below this information and
before the name of the publishing house, Ediciones Aymá, and place of
publication, Barcelona, a coat of arms figures, which is made up of a shield
with a sprig of laurel rising from each side of the shield. The word 'blason'
(coat of arms) is written in white capital letters against a black background
represented as a piece of ribbon below the shield and the central motif on the
shield is the dragon. St George is the patron of Catalonia and, as is well
known, is mythically reputed to have overcome the dragon. It would have
been risky to represent St George in 1942 during the onslaught on
manifestations of Catalan identity (Benet 1979), but it would seem that
Jaume Aymà, now forcefully metamorphosed into Jaime Aymá (that is, his
forename translated into Castilian and the Catalan accented 'à' at the end of
his surname reproduced as an accented 'á' in Castilian), contrived to evoke
Catalonia in so far as he was able. The text is delicately laid out with a motif
of a circle within a circle marking the top and foot of each page in rows of
pink print. The title of the text heads each left-hand page in capital letters
and the title of the particular portrait each right-hand page. The line of
circles at the foot of the page is broken by the page number, centred within
it.

Ediciones Aymá applied for permission to publish *Retratos imaginarios*
(*Imaginary Portraits*) on 3 February 1942 and publication of 2,000 copies of a
text measuring 17 by 23 centimetres and of some 200 pages in length was
authorized on 11 March of the same year. The censorship's reader, Conde,[39]
considered Pater's text to be good in terms of literary or artistic worth and
translated correctly. He had nothing to report as regards its documentary value
or its political tendency and did not recommend anything to be suppressed.
His only comments were the following general ones: 'The work is written in a
highly competent manner and with great sensitivity. It includes four
narratives, which focus on the life of a number of personalities. The
atmosphere of the period in each of them is very well described. Summing up,
the publication of this text may be said to be in our interest.'[40]

Translating from English was not new to Farrán y Mayoral. Farran i
Mayoral [sic] had translated Shakespeare, Goldsmith, Swift and R. L.
Stevenson into Catalan during the Republican years; however, the censor's
judgement that Pater's text was translated correctly is not wholly valid. Farrán
y Mayoral's occasional inaccuracies derive mainly from errors in understanding

---

[38]   These illustrations appear in all the copies which were produced.

[39]   This may be Enrique Conde Gargallo, listed as a specialized reader in the list of
censors for 1954 in Abellán's Appendix 2 (Apéndice 2) (Abellán 1980, 288).

[40]   'La obra está escrita con gran agilidad y sensibilidad. Comprende cuatro
narraciones acerca de la vida de diversas personalidades. Está muy bien descrito el
ambiente de la época de las mismas. En resumen, es interesante su publicación.'
Signed: Conde. (Vice-Secretaria de Educación Popular, Delegación Nacional de
Propaganda, Expediente 21/6827, Archivo General de la Administración, Alcalá
de Henares).

or what would appear to be carelessness, but there are also cases of stylistic interference as well as particular changes, omissions and even additions. In order to exemplify my claims, I shall focus on the first of the four portraits, 'Un príncipe de pintores cortesanos' ('A Prince of Court Painters').

5

the enthusiastic, meticulous – and always troubled – effort of the translator'[41]

The first portrait is a partly fictionalized rendering of the career of the painter Jean-Antoine Watteau (1684–1721) through the diary entries of a young female neighbour, dated between September 1701 and July 1721. The first entry might already be said to be characteristic of Pater's style in that it is a dense block of narrative and carries one of Pater's extended sentences (this one running into fifteen lines in the original English [Pater 1914, 5–6]), many of which are in evidence in *Marius the Epicurean*. Farrán y Mayoral will break the block up into three paragraphs (Pater 1942, 23–4), a practice he will adopt on two other occasions: in the March 1714 and August 1717 entries (Pater 1942, 36, 50). In the first entry, too, Watteau's father is described as having recently built himself 'a new stone house, big and grey and cold' (Pater 1914, 6). The imposing weight of the building and the sterile quality of it, as well as of its owner (totally insensitive to his son's artistic talent) is rendered in English through the monosyllables in the sequence of adjectives – 'new', 'stone', 'big', 'grey', 'cold' – and noun 'house', as well as reinforced through the repetition of the conjunction 'and'. This impact is forfeited in the Castilian: 'una nueva casa de piedra, grande, gris y fría' (Pater 1942, 24) though it might be argued that the pile-up of adjectives 'grande, gris y fría' with the heavy stress falling on the first syllable in the disyllabic 'grande' and 'fría', coupled with the monosyllable in 'gris' and the alliteration in the voiced consonant /g/ in 'grande' and 'gris', do satisfactorily convey a sense of weight. Also here is the first instance of error in comprehension. The financially favourable position of Watteau's father is described by recourse to litotes – 'he is not ill-to-do' (Pater 1924, 6)– rendered by Farrán y Mayoral as his not being badly off: 'no lo pasa mal' (Pater 1942, 24). Another striking one is in the final diary entry where the narrator refers to Watteau's working on a crucifix for the priest, M. Gersaint, since he was not partial to the rough one the priest possessed, as the narrator explains: 'liking little the very rude one he possessed' (Pater 1914, 43–4). The translator confuses the verb, 'to like', modified by the adverb 'little', with the conjunction 'like', producing a totally incorrect translation as well as taking the liberty of introducing 'the latter' instead of the pronoun 'he': 'algo parecido al muy tosco que éste poseía' ('somewhat similar to the very rude one the latter possessed', Pater 1942, 59). Other instances of single words are 'weary' (Pater 1914, 8), introduced to describe soldiers, translated as 'aburridos' (bored, Pater 1942, 26); 'ruffles' (Pater 1914, 9), translated as

---

[41] 'el entusiasta, minucioso – y remordido a cada paso – esfuerzo del traductor' (Farrán y Mayoral 1942, 18).

'mangas' (sleeves, Pater 1942, 27). The ruffles could be a decorative item on sleeves, but also around the collar, therefore, 'volantes' and 'gorgueras' or 'golas' should have been used. In the July 1705 entry, the narrator will refer to her ten-year-old brother, in awe of the young Watteau, as caring only 'to save and possess' (Pater 1942, 12). His preoccupation with possessing is rendered as 'ganar dinero' (to earn money, Pater 1942, 30), which falls short of expressing the more all-embracing idea of possession and, moreover, it is not clear from the original that the young boy wishes to possess by means of earning! In the April 1714 entry, the narrator refers to Watteau as conversing 'very sparingly' (Pater 1914, 21) but Farrán y Mayoral produces a translation which evokes style rather than degree: 'conversación [...] muy sobria' (a very sober conversation or one using great restraint, Pater 1942, 38). Later examples of single lexical items mistranslated are 'habitación' (room, Pater 1942, 46) for 'dwelling-place' (Pater 1914, 30); 'esponjado' (spongy, Pater 1942, 46) for 'dewy' (Pater 1914, 30); 'desasosegado' (restless, Pater 1942, 47) for 'disquieting' (Pater 1914, 31), that is, in the original the narrator is recording Watteau's effect on others rather than his own state; 'prados' (meadows, Pater 1942, 48) for 'lawns' (Pater 1914, 32); 'muy' (very, Pater 1942, 48) for 'wholly' (Pater 1914, 33); 'sin duda' (without a doubt, Pater 1942, 49) for 'perhaps' (Pater 1914, 33). Other errors reflect an ignorance of metaphorical usage in the language or idiomatic expression in English. In the September 1714 entry, the narrator speaks of 'an outburst of watery sunset, which strikes from the far horizon' (Pater 1914, 25). The use of 'strike' here I understand as attempting to convey the impact of the outburst of, albeit, watery sunset. However, Farrán y Mayoral interprets 'strike' as hit and, thus, translates the verb as 'viene a herir' (comes to hit/strike, Pater, 1942, 42). This same verb is used on two other occasions in this first portrait in the sense of something impressing itself upon the speaker or appearing thus to him/her. On both occasions the translator mistranslates. Hence, in the same September 1714 entry, the narrator reflects: 'With myself, how to get through time becomes sometimes the question, – unavoidably; though it strikes me as a thing unspeakably sad in a life so short as ours' (Pater 1914, 25). The subordinate clause is rendered by the translator as: 'aunque esto me aflige como cosa inevitablemente triste para una vida tan corta como la nuestra' (Pater 1942, 41), that is, he conveys 'strike' as afflict, perhaps understanding that if 'strike' means hit, then what strikes/hits my emotions afflicts me. In the October 1717 entry, the narrator refers to the story of 'poor Manon Lescaut' and declares: 'There is a tone about it which strikes me as going well with the grace of these leafless birch-trees' (Pater 1914, 37). Here the translator will render the use of 'strike' in the original as communicating the particular impact of the tone on the narrator, one which frightens: 'Tiene un tono general que me sobrecoge, como si armonizase con la gracia de esos deshojados abedules' (Pater 1942, 53), which is wide of the mark. Finally, I will refer to two other examples of Farrán y Mayoral's failure to grasp the idiomatic use of the language, as becomes clear from the translation. In the February 1712 entry, the narrator reports that Watteau: 'looks to receive more orders for his work' (Pater 1914, 16). The use of 'to look' followed by the infinitive is an alternative way of expressing to 'take an interest in' or 'concern oneself with', followed by the gerund. However, the translator interpreted 'look' as 'seem' and translated accordingly: 'Según parece, recibe más encargos de obras suyas' (It seems/looks as though he receives more orders for his work, Pater 1942, 33). In the February 1715 entry, the narrator expresses Watteau's contempt for the Parisian *beau monde*, declaring: 'he looks down upon it' (Pater 1914, 27). Farrán y Mayoral translates literally: 'la mira desde muy alto' (He looks at it from high above, Pater 1942, 43). On another occasion he will have recourse to idiomatic usage when the text's meaning is literal. In the October 1717 entry, the narrator recalls 'the past summer', when: 'the earth [was] dry enough to sleep on' (Pater 1914, 38). The translator appears not to have grasped the idea that the dry earth provided a surface adequate for sleeping on, like a hard bed or board. Here he seems to have been pondering the use of sleep plus the preposition on, meaning to reflect on or think something over, and connects the thinking with the cold, mentioned by the narrator earlier in the sentence, producing a total distortion of the final part of the sentence: 'la tierra estaba lo suficiente seca para no pensar en él' (the earth was dry enough so as not to have to think about it [the cold])' (Pater 1942, 54).

Apart from the above-mentioned errors, there are some omissions. In the February 1712 entry, the narrator registers a change of manner in Watteau and goes on to comment: 'at variance, methinks, with his own singular gravity and even sadness of mien and mind' (Pater 1914, 16–17). Farrán y Mayoral simplifies in the translation, omitting 'and even sadness', which would lessen the Spanish reader's knowledge of the narrator's perception of the artist's facial expression and his intellect: 'en desavenencia, pienso yo, con su gravedad singular de semblante y de pensamiento' (Pater 1942, 34). In the March 1713 entry, the narrator refers to Watteau's 'most generously' (Pater 1914, 17) offering to take on her brother as his pupil. The superlative of the original is omitted and Watteau's offering qualified as generously: 'generosamente' (Pater 1942, 34). It is a detail but a not unimportant one within the construction of the character of the narrator who consistently expresses a sense of awe before Watteau and the superlative is consonant with her attitude towards the artist. At the end of this entry, the narrator alludes to 'that delightful new life' (Pater 1914, 17) her brother is about to experience as a pupil of Watteau's. The translation omits 'new': 'aquella vida encantadora' (that delightful life, Pater 1942, 35). At the end of the January 1714 entry, the narrator expresses her longing to see Watteau's works: 'those works which I for one so thirst to see' (Pater 1914, 19). The intensity of her longing is diminished in Spanish as 'so' is omitted: 'esas obras que, a lo menos yo, estoy sedienta de ver' (those works which I for one thirst to see, Pater 1942, 36).

There are additions too. In the April 1714 entry, the narrator reflects on the sombre style, an inheritance of the Spanish presence in Flanders, which she sees as not appropriate to the northern clime: 'But in our country, where we must needs economize not the shade but the sun, its grandiosity weighs a little on one's spirits' (Pater 1914, 20–1). Farrán y Mayoral will render the sentence exclamatory by introducing exclamation marks as well as inserting the possessive pronoun so as to avoid the repetition of 'country' with which the previous sentence ends in the original: '¡Pero en el nuestro, donde lo que debemos economizar no es la sombra, sino el sol, esa grandiosidad pesa un poco sobre nuestros espíritus!' (Pater 1942, 37).

And, finally, there are changes. In the July 1714 entry, the narrator refers to a visit to the cathedral church of Cambrai and to the presence there of

Monseigneur le Prince de Cambrai, remarking: 'He appears to be of great age, assists but rarely at the offices of religion, and is never to be seen in Paris; and Antony has much desired to behold him' (Pater 1914, 23). Farrán y Mayoral will transform the clause following the sem-colon into one of consequence: 'por eso Antonio estaba muy deseoso de poder verlo' (so that Antony greatly desired to see him, Pater 1942, 40). In the September 1714 entry 'a long wet day' (Pater 1914, 25) becomes 'un largo día brumoso' (a long misty day, Pater 1942, 41) and a 'watery sunset' (Pater 1914, 25) becomes 'una puesta de sol lluviosa' (a rainy sunset, Pater 1942, 42). In the October 1717 entry, Farrán y Mayoral does not respect a new sentence produced by Pater in the original, introducing a semi-colon to make it a continuation of the previous one, as well as again rendering Pater's use of the conjunction 'and', here at the beginning of the first sentence, into a clause of consequence. Thus Pater:

> And I could fancy myself almost of their condition sitting here alone this evening, in which a premature touch of winter makes the world look but an inhospitable place of entertainment for one's spirit. With so little genial warmth to hold it there, one feels that the merest accident might detach that flighty guest altogether. (Pater 1914, 38)

The translator renders this:

> De modo que yo misma podría imaginarme casi en su situación mientras estoy aquí sola esta tarde, en que un prematuro amago de invierno hace que el mundo no parezca sino un lugar inhóspito para la diversión de nuestro espíritu; con tan poco afable calor para retener aquí el espíritu, que una comprende cómo el menor accidente podría desprender totalmente del cuerpo a este huésped fugaz. (Pater 1942, 53)

In the last entry, dated July 1721, the final paragraph is composed of two sentences which are made into one by Farrán y Mayoral through the introduction of a comma and the conjunction 'and'. Moreover, the nihilism envisaged in the final sentence of the original, that is, that what Watteau sought in the world may not be there, is modified to express a sense of possibility, through the introduction of the adverbs perhaps, 'tal vez', and really, 'en realidad', thus lessening the nihilistic thrust: 'He has been a sick man all his life. He was always a seeker after something in the world that is there in no satisfying measure, or not at all' (Pater 1914, 44); 'Ha sido un enfermo toda su vida, y siempre anduvo buscando en el mundo algo que no existe en él en medida satisfactoria, o que tal vez en realidad no existe' (Pater 1942, 59).[42]

Judging from his initial address to the reader, 'From the translator to the reader' (Del traductor al lector), Farrán y Mayoral would have been mortified to learn of the above-mentioned inaccuracies. His prologue shows an acute concern with adequately rendering the distinction of the original into the foreign language. Thus, he ponders the challenge: 'How to translate, how to succeed in translating into a language so different from the original, something of that life, of this music; of the play of sounds and combinations of rhythms

---

[42] Farrán y Mayoral may have been anticipating disapproval of such nihilism on the part of the reader in the Vice-Secretary's Office for the Education of the People (Vice-Secretaría de Educación Popular) and modified the text accordingly.

and forms, with which the author wrought the rich work of art of his style?'[43] And he asks himself not least because his first contact with Pater was, as he recalls in confessional mode, in the second paragraph of his prologue, through a Mercure de France translation discovered in a crumpled state in a second-hand bookshop. Farrán y Mayoral claims not to have been familiar with Pater at the time but admits to having been seduced by the title of the text and wonders how he could have come to appreciate the 'extraordinary merit' of what he qualifies as a 'monstrous translation: the worst I have read in my life'.[44] Apart from expressing his preoccupation with producing a translation worthy of the original, Farrán y Mayoral uses the prologue to sing the praises of Pater's text, a book, as he claims in his first paragraph, to be read slowly and one which contains 'countless instances of beauty', a book which is 'marvellous'[45] and, as he asserts in the final sentence of the first part of his prologue, which carries 'a vital element of the everlasting, of eternity'.[46] The second section of the prologue continues in a similar superlative vein with Farrán y Mayoral quoting from Arthur Symons to further illustrate Pater's human virtues and literary distinction. Most of the remaining part of the second section of the prologue is taken up with quotations from Pater's work, the climax of which is the frequently cited piece in the penultimate paragraph of the Conclusion to *The Renaissance*: 'To burn always with this hard, gem-like flame, to maintain this ecstasy, is success in life. In a sense it might even be said that our failure is to form habits: for, after all, habit is relative to a stereotyped world, and meantime it is only the roughness of the eye that makes any two persons, things, situations seem alike' (Pater 1998, 152).[47] However, Farrán y Mayoral, product and supporter of a bourgeois society, would recognize the need for a degree of habit, for instance, and, therefore, registers the possibility of disagreement: 'And even if some of our ideas were not in agreement with this aesthetic sense', but ultimately overrules it by asking: 'how can we not recognize the depth, the truth of these penetrations of Walter Pater into the intelligent intuition of the beautiful?', and sees Pater's perception as appealing to 'the most authentic sense of beauty which all men, some to a higher degree, others to a lesser one, carry in their souls'.[48] In the

---

[43]   '¿Cómo traducir, cómo alcanzar en la traducción a una lengua tan distinta de la original, algo de aquella vida, y de esta música; de los juegos de sonidos y combinaciones de ritmos y formas, con que el autor trabaja la rica obra de arte de su estilo?' (Farrán y Mayoral 1942, 18).

[44]   'el mérito extraordinario'; 'monstruosa traducción, la peor que he leído en mi vida' (Farrán y Mayoral 1942, 9).

[45]   'bellezas innumerables'; 'maravilloso' (Farrán y Mayoral 1942, 9).

[46]   'un vivo elemento de perennidad, de eternidad' (Farrán y Mayoral 1942, 10).

[47]   See my comment on Farrán y Mayoral's translation of this piece from the Conclusión to *The Renaissance* in my reference to the Castilian translation of 1945, towards the end of this chapter.

[48]   'Y aun en el caso de que algunas ideas nuestras no estuviesen conformes con semejante estética'; 'cómo no reconocer la profundidad, el acierto de estas penetraciones de Walter Pater en la intuición inteligente de lo bello?'; 'lo más auténtico del sentido de la belleza que todos los hombres, quien más, quien menos, llevan en su alma' (Farrán y Mayoral 1942, 14).

final section of his prologue, Farrán y Mayoral will refer to Pater's work on different artists, both pictorial and literary, and will focus on the four *Imaginary Portraits*, qualifying the second, 'Denys l'Auxerrois' (perhaps the most disturbing of all four), as: '[t]he masterpiece of these four masterpieces'.[49] Furthermore, in referring to this portrait, he will highlight the fusion of the art of antiquity with Christian spirituality, which will lead him to evoke the Renaissance. Herein lies one idea which links *Imaginary Portraits* back to ideas expressed in *The Renaissance* and in *Marius the Epicurean*, which would appear in Spanish translation within two years of the publication of *Retratos imaginarios*.

6

Marius the Epicurean clarifies many things which were only insinuated, perhaps a little obscurely, in the famous Conclusion [to *The Renaissance*].[50]

Just a year before the celebration of the end of the Second World War in Europe, *Marius the Epicurean*, 'Pater's longest and most unified work of fiction' (Knoepflmacher 1970, 169), was brought out in the 'Ave Phoenix' series of Ediciones Lauro, one of the publishing ventures initiated by José Janés from 1940 on (Hurtley 1986; 1992). The phoenix would become the trademark of Janés's publishing house, José Janés, editor, but up until the Allied victory in 1945, he appeared as a director of series rather than a publisher in his own right, under his own name, a penalty for what was assessed by the new regime set up in Spain from April 1939 as his Catalan separatist past. Like the translator of *Marius the Epicurean*, Agustí Esclasans i Folch (1895–1967), Josep Janés i Olivé (1913–59), transformed into José Janés after the Civil War, had been imprisoned and, moreover, condemned to death but, unlike the translator, would now find himself with friends who held positions of sway within the new order, not least Eugenio d'Ors and the Falangists Luys Santamarina and Félix Ros, whose lives Janés had defended during the War (Hurtley 1986, 176–8). Janés used his own good fortune to the advantage of those less in favour than himself, like Agustí Esclasans, about to become Castilianized as Agustín Esclasans. In the second volume of his autobiography, Esclasans, who was imprisoned over a two-year period, between 1939 and 1940, recalls that Janés and his wife were the first to visit him following his release (Esclasans 1957, 157). Esclasans had already been employed by Janés, both as a writer and translator, in the Catalan publishing house the enterprising young publisher, poet and journalist had set up in Barcelona between 1934 and 1938, the Literary Notebooks (Quaderns Literaris). Like so many, Esclasans was now rescued by Janés and set to work:

> New life, new work. Josep Janés was the first to help me in a positive way. Straightaway, he asked me to translate Madame de Lafayette's *La princesse de Clèves*. All the other [publishers] gave me books to translate and so I was

---

[49]　'[l]a obra maestra entre estas cuatro obras maestras' (Farrán y Mayoral 1942, 1).

[50]　'*Màrius l'epicuri* és l'aclariment de moltes coses insinuades potser una mica obscurament, en la Conclusió famosa' (Manent 1938, 11).

able to earn a living and maintain my family for five years, until 1945. [. . .] I had rented a typewriter for sixty pesetas a month. [. . .] And from 4 to 6p.m. I translated.[51]

José Janés applied for permission to publish *Mario el Epicúreo* (*Marius the Epicurean*) on 30 December 1943. On the application form for the Censorship Section of the Vice-Secretary's Office for the Education of the People within the National Delegation for Propaganda (Sección de Censura de Libros de la Vicesecretaria de Educación Popular de la Delegación Nacional de Propaganda), Janés indicated that the text was of a literary nature and possessed no political nuance. The application further stated that the text would have 208 pages and 3,000 copies would be produced. The text was reported on by Reader 3, who considered that the text did not attack dogma, that is the dogma of the Catholic Church, moral values or the institutions of the regime. The reader then went on to assert that it had both literary and documentary value and summed up: 'The work is a study about the personality of a Roman in the period of the Emperor Marcus Aurelius and about the religious environment before the conquest of the Christian Church, when paganism was still the order of the day.'[52] The text was authorized on 19 January 1944 and would be published in May.

Agustí Esclasans was a poet and prose writer, a disciple of Eugeni d'Ors and liable to recreate the latter's worst excesses (Pericay and Toutain 1996, 113). As Agustín Esclasans, he produced a nine-page introduction to the translation and his opening sentence, in which he identifies Pater as 'the author of the philosophical novel *Marius the Epicurean*' (Esclasans in Pater 1944, 7), already suggests that he was familiar with the French translation produced by the palaeographic archivist E. Coppinger, entitled: *Marius l'épicurien: roman philosophique* (Pater 1922). However, if this was the case (and a consideration of Esclasans's 'Prologue' [Prólogo] in the light of Coppinger's 'Foreword' [Avant-propos] confirms that he was aware of it), he did not acknowledge the fact; at the end of his introduction, he refers only to his use of volumes II and III of *The Works of Walter Pater* published by Macmillan and Co. in 1918 (Esclasans 1944, 15). As was the case with Farrán y Mayoral in his opening note to the reader, Esclasans reveals concern with the task of translating Pater, conveying a sense of the challenge constituted by his stylistic idiosyncrasy, as well as revealing his own!

---

[51] 'Vida nova, feina nova. Josep Janés fou el primer d'ajudar-me positivament. M'encarregà tot seguit la traducció de *La princesa de Clèves*, de Madame de Lafayette. Tots els altres m'encarregaren traduccions, i així vaig poder viure i mantenir la familia durant cinc anys, fins al 1945. [. . .] Jo havia llogat una màquina d'escriure, que em costava seixanta pessetes al mes [. . .] i de quatre a set feia traduccions' (Esclasans 1957, 159).

[52] 'La obra es un estudio sobre la personalidad de un romano de la época del emperador Marco Aurelio y del ambiente religioso ante la conquista de la Iglesia Cristiana cuando aun se mantenia [sic] el paganismo'. Signed: Reader (Lector) 3. The accompanying signature appears to read 'Conde' – see note 39 above. (Vice-Secretaría de Educación Popular, Delegación Nacional de Propaganda, Expediente 21/7322, Archivo General de la Administración, Alcalá de Henares).

In this *Marius the Epicurean* I have just translated (passing through how many and what enormous difficulties of interpretation and style, heroically and patiently overcome!), paragraphs stretch themselves out, they wind themselves around in arabesques, they break into highly elegant parenthetic clauses, to round off the strict sonorousness of the period with a master touch of the Greco-Roman humanist. There is repeated abuse of the semi-colon, and of the dash used to underline parenthetic clauses. [. . .] But the translator cannot omit any of this. I have respected it [. . .] To leave it out or modify it would be tantamount to falsifying Pater's noble, complicated humanistic style.[53]

Like Coppinger in his foreword, on occasion with sentences directly translated from the palaeographic archivist's text and in a similar apocalyptic vein, Esclasans further expresses the view that Pater's 'philosophical novel'[54] contains a message for his own age, claiming, in a sentence directly taken from Coppinger, that he was sustained through the time of translation by the hope that those who are searching for a firm base and direction to their lives will be able to find Christian consolation in *Marius the Epicurean*:

I consider this philosophical novel to be very meaningful for our contemporary society, which, in its frivolous and superficial drive to be modern sometimes seems to tend towards an absurd neo-paganism [. . .] *après-la-lettre*. Following Marius in the revision, so sincere and complete, of the most ancient doctrines of the philosophies of Greece and Rome, so that they can serve him as a foundation in the moral and intellectual life he seeks to attain for himself, and the insubstantiality of which he comes to confirm, it must not be difficult for those of sincere spirit to believe and affirm, like him, that only the definitive superiority of Christianity, with its perfect doctrine, can provide solutions to guide humanity along the paths of order and peace.[55]

---

53   'En este *Mario el epicúreo* que acabamos de traducir (¡a través de cuántas y cuán enormes dificultades de interpretación y estilo, heroica y pacientemente vencidas!) los párrafos se prolongan, se tuercen en arabescos, se rompen en incisos elegantísimos, par redondear la estricta sonoridad del período con un toque maestro de humanista grecolatino. Hay un constante abuso del punto y coma, y del guión subrayador de incisos. [. . .] Pero el traductor no puede prescindir de ello. Lo he respetado [. . .] Suprimirlo, o modificarlo, equivaldría a falsear el noble y complicado estilo humanístico de Pater' (Esclasans 1944, 12).

54   'novela filosófica' (Esclasans 1944, 7, 13).

55   'Consideramos la lectura de esta novela filosófica muy sugestiva para nuestra sociedad contemporánea, que en su modernismo frívolo y epidérmico parece, a veces, tender a un absurdo neopaganismo [. . .] *après-la-lettre*. Siguiendo a Mario en la revisión que efectúa, tan sincera y completa, de las doctrinas más antiguas de las filosofías de Grecia y Roma, para que le puedan servir de fundamento en la vida moral e intelectual que se propone realizar para sí mismo, y cuya inanidad acaba comprobando, no ha de ser difícil a los espíritus sinceros creer y afirmar, como él, que solamente la superioridad definitiva del cristianismo, con su doctrina perfecta, puede aportar las soluciones que guíen a la humanidad por los caminos del orden y de la paz' (Eclasans 1944, 13). Compare Coppinger's foreword: 'La lecture de ce livre est tout à fait suggestive pour notre société contemporaine dont les allures par tant de côtés, sont en passe de revenir au paganisme. En suivant

Esclasans heads his introduction to the translation 'Walter Pater' and refers to it as an 'essay on the life and work'[56] of the writer. He certainly provides general information in this connection, going on to place Pater in relation to Ruskin and Swinburne and connecting him as a critic to Hazlitt and Lamb, but he also uses the essay to evoke the cultural movement in which his translation of Pater acquires its significance. Thus, the final paragraph introduces the name of Eugeni d'Ors (now known as Eugenio d'Ors), of the movement of which he was the major exponent, '[the] "novecentista" movement',[57] and cedes the conclusion of his essay to his mentor, quoting at length from him on Pater though without providing the precise source.

Pater's tendency to focus on the '*persona* of a pensive young skeptic' (Knoepflmacher 1970, 154), reiterated in *Imaginary Portraits*, is dwelt on at length through the 'lad' Marius in *Marius the Epicurean* as the youth's development is meticulously traced through his encounters with, and meditation on, diverse pagan philosophies to his final embracing of Christianity. There is much here that would appeal to *noucentista* notions and practice: the aristocratic nature of Marius and the company which surrounds him, his bookish air, the pursuit of intellectual distinction and refined sensation, Flavian's euphuistic style, serenity of spirit, male bonding, most intimately exemplified in Marius's relationships with Flavius and Cornelius, and the ubiquitous idealism. The recognition by Agustí Esclasans's mentor, d'Ors, of Pater, coupled with Esclasans's more rudimentary need to earn his living and provide for his two sisters, would spur him to take on this dense novel, no easy task, even for one who had translated Max Beerbohm's *The Happy Hypocrite* and poetry by Edgar A. Poe in the 1930s and had penned translations of Charlotte Brontë's *The Professor* and Stevenson's *The Strange Case of Dr Jekyll and Mr Hyde* in 1943.

In spite of his claim in the introduction, quoted above, that he had respected the idiosyncrasies of Pater's style, close examination of the translation reveals that Esclasans constructs new paragraphs and sentences and does not always respect those introduced by Pater. Already in chapter 1, there are five new paragraphs and one new sentence.[58] However, examination of Coppinger's translation reveals that all five paragraphs are in the French text[59] and much else in Esclasans's rendering can also be accounted for by consultation of it. I have found inaccuracies, cases of stylistic impoverishment, omissions and additions in the Spanish translation. The examples which follow are taken from 'Part the First'.

Marius l'Epicurien [sic] dans l'enquête si sincère et si complète qu'il mène, sur les doctrines les plus anciennes des philosophies de la Grèce et de Rome, comme pouvant servir de fondement à la vie intellectuelle et morale qu'il cherche à réaliser pour lui et dont il ne peut en définitive que constater l'inanité, il semble bien invraisemblable que les esprits sincères n'aboutissent pas comme lui, a conclure à la supériorité définitive du Christianisme pour les solutions qui doivent ramener l'humanité dans les voies de l'ordre et de la paix.'

[56] 'ensayo sobre la vida y obra' (Eclasans 1944, 13).
[57] 'el movimiento novecentista' (Eclasans 1944, 14).
[58] Esclasans 1944, 20, 21 (paragraphs); 22 (sentence).
[59] Coppinger 1922, 14, 15.

In chapter 1, reference is made to 'the dying Antoninus Pius' (Pater 1918, 4). Esclasans's translation does not capture the moment described by Pater but refers to him carrying out the action in question before he died: 'antes de morir' (Pater 1944, 18), that is, as in the French translation: 'avant de mourir' (Pater 1922, 12). In the same paragraph, in a characteristically lengthy sentence, though half the length or less of a number of others, the narrator comes to focus on Marius:

> The old-fashioned, partly puritanic awe, the power of which Wordsworth noted and valued so highly in a northern peasantry, had its counterpart in the feeling of the Roman lad, as he passed the spot, 'touched of heaven', where the lightning had struck dead an aged labourer in the field: an upright stone, still with mouldering garlands about it, marked the place. (Pater 1918, 5)

In the French translation there is a misprint in the Romantic poet's name and this is reproduced in the Spanish version, thus Wordsworth becomes Woodsworth (Pater 1922, 12; Pater 1944, 18). The colon is not respected in either the French or Spanish translations and Esclasans' rendering of 'awe', 'partly', and the omission of any equivalent for 'mouldering' all follow Coppinger. Thus, Esclasans's 'terror' (Pater 1944, 18) for 'awe' comes from Coppinger's 'terreur' (Pater 1922, 12), where the Spanish 'respeto', French 'respect', would have been more appropriate here. Again, the Spanish 'casi' comes from Coppinger's use of 'quasi' to modify 'puritanic' where 'parcialmente', French 'partialement', would have been accurate. Esclasans translates the 'upright stone' as a 'monumento funerario' (funereal monument, Pater 1944, 18), which is what the stone represents in effect. However, Coppinger remains closer to Pater's diction: 'une pierre erigée' (an upright stone, Pater 1922, 12). When referring to 'the old Roman religion' (Pater 1918, 5) inherited by Marius, the narrator defines it as 'of a year-long burden of forms' (Pater 1918, 6), expressed by Esclasans less precisely as: 'de un formalismo pesado e ininterrumpido' (of a heavy/boring and uninterrupted formalism, Pater 1944, 19). Again, examination of the French translation reveals that this was Coppinger's resolution of the original: 'd'un formalisme encombrant et ininterrompu' (of a cumbersome and uninterrupted formalism, Pater 1922, 13). One other occasion in chapter 1 where Esclasans reveals his debt to Coppinger is in the final sentence of the chapter, which begins: 'The spell of his religion' (Pater 1918, 12). Esclasans's text reads: 'El sitio reservado a su religión' (The place reserved for his religion, Pater 1944, 22). This invention may be traced to Coppinger's French: 'La place réservée à la religion' (Pater 1922, 16). In the final paragraph of the chapter, a description of fire is interpreted as: 'a favourable omen, making it a duty to render the mirth of the evening complete' (Pater 1918, 11). Esclasans's translation omits the concept of duty, reading: 'presagio favourable, que invitaban a una dulce alegría para todo el resto de la jornada' (a favourable omen, which invited a sweet happiness for the rest of the day, Pater 1944, 21). Esclasans places the verb in the plural as he has pluralized 'the flame' which is introduced in the original as rising from the fire. Coppinger uses the gerund but he pluralized the flame, and the omission of the concept of duty as well as the idea of sweet happiness found in the Spanish are obviously taken from him. He does, however, speak of evening rather than day, and is, therefore, more respectful as regards this detail of the original: 'présage favourable, invitant à une douce gaieté pour tout le reste de la soirée' (Pater 1922, 15). Other cases of lack of precision and even invention are solely attributable to Esclasans. Thus, the description of the altars on the day of the private *Ambarvalia* carries reference to 'the more sumptuous sort of blossom' (Pater 1918, 7), which becomes in Spanish 'los más bellos tallos frescos' (the more/most beautiful freshly cut stems, Pater 1944, 7), though a semi-colon introduced in the Spanish text immediately before this phrase, which is preceded by the conjunction 'and', follows Coppinger (Pater 1944, 19; Pater 1922, 13). At this same point in the text, we are told that 'the scent of the bean-fields mingled pleasantly with the cloud of incense' (Pater 1918, 7) whilst Esclasans speaks of the scent of roses and more than one cloud of incense: 'el aroma de las rosas se mezclaba suavemente con las nubes de incienso' (Pater 1944, 19). His use of 'suavemente' (gently) for 'pleasantly' seems reasonable since the Spanish verb he uses for 'mingle', 'mezclar', is 'to mix', so the gentleness conveyed by 'mingle' in the English original is forfeited, and it may be argued that if the scent was mixing gently, it would produce a pleasant effect. Following a quote in Latin a little later in the chapter, the English text carries an adverb, followed by an exclamation mark: 'Perhaps!' Esclasans totally distorts this response to the Latin, declaring: 'Era extraño' (It was strange, Pater 1944, 21). And in the following sentence, where reference is made to the food left for 'the dead genii', 'a morsel of honeycomb' is listed. Esclasans makes the morsel a piece and adds that the honeycomb is dripping with honey: 'un trozo de panal goteando miel' (Pater 1944, 21). This may be accounted for by Coppinger's translation since he makes the morsel a piece 'une tranche' (Pater 1922, 15) and honeycomb is rendered as 'ruche à miel' (Pater 1922, 15). At the end of the chapter, Marius is described as being woken from sleep: 'amid the beating of violent rain on the shutters' (Pater 1918, 12). The shutters become the window in Esclasans: 'la ventana' (Pater 1944, 22).

In chapter 2 other modifications or inaccuracies in the Esclasans translation can be related to the Coppinger version. Thus, Marius's 'singularly pleasant smile' (Pater 1918, 14), rendered by Esclasans as 'su sonrisa particularmente seductora' (Pater 1944, 23), is accountable by consultation of Coppinger's text: 'un sourire particulièrement séduisant' (Pater 1922, 18). The narrator elaborates further on the smile: 'consistent, however, in the younger face, with some degree of sombre expression when the mind within was but slightly moved' (Pater 1918, 14). Esclasans introduces a comma before the adverbial clause of time, as does Coppinger, and goes on to translate: 'cuando el sentimiento no era interiormente profundo' (when the sentiment was not profoundly felt inside, Pater 1944, 23). This is a translation of Coppinger's misunderstanding of the use of 'but' in the original: 'lorsque intérieurement l'impression n'avait pas été profonde' (Pater 1922, 18), faithfully reproduced by Esclasans. A parenthetic clause describing the life of Marius's mother in the wake of her husband's death, in which 'but' is again misinterpreted, gives rise to a totally opposite meaning. The original reads: 'The life of the widow, languid and shadowy enough but for the poignancy of that regret' (Pater 1918, 17), whilst the translation indicates that the 'regret', described a few lines earlier in the original as 'a sustained freshness of regret', is portrayed as responsible for the widow's sorry state instead of as a consolation within it, as conveyed in the English narrative: 'La vida de la viuda, ya melancólica y ensombrecida por la amargura de este sentimiento' (The life of the widow, already melancholic and darkened by the bitterness of this sentiment', Pater 1944, 24), that is, as in the French translation: 'La vie de la veuve, déjà morne et assombrie par l'amertume de ce regret' (Pater 1922, 19). A new paragraph in chapter 2 begins: 'Something pensive, spell-bound' (Pater 1918, 20). Esclasans ignores the new paragraph, as did Coppinger, and his translation also follows the French rendering: 'Algo íntimo, inexpresable' (Something intimate, inexpressible, Pater 1944, 26), 'Quelque chose d'intime, d'inex-primable' (Pater 1922, 21). Later, the conjunction which begins the paragraph, 'And a certain vague fear of evil' (Pater 1918, 22), is replaced by an adverb, 'Todavía más', followed by a colon (Pater 1944, 27). The use of the adverb, though not the colon, appears to be derived from Coppinger's 'Bien plus' (Pater 1922, 22). Within the same paragraph, there is a passing reference to 'an African showman' (Pater 1918, 23) who becomes a juggler or tumbler in the French translation: 'un bateleur d'Afrique' (Pater 1922, 22). I can only think that 'bateleur' misled Esclasans to the French 'bateau' for boat, which would explain his converting the showman into a sailor: 'un marinero africano' (Pater 1944, 28). Finally, the 'dwarf roses' (Pater 1918, 26) on the marsh, referred to in the final paragraph of the chapter, are reduced to 'flores rojas' (red flowers, Pater 1944, 29) and 'the flock of wild birds' (Pater 1918, 26) become 'un vuelo de pájaros libres' (a flight of free birds, Pater 1944, 29) in Esclasans. Certainly, flowers and the description of them appear not to be Esclasans's forte. In chapter 3, 'choice flowering plants' (Pater 1918, 38) become: 'raras plantas floridas' (strange plants in flower, Pater 1944, 35) and in chapter 7, 'rich-scented flowers' (Pater 1918, 112) are 'flores de colores encendidos' (flowers of flaming colour, Pater 1944, 72).

Many more examples might be quoted, but I shall limit myself finally to two examples of stylistic impoverishment. In the park-like enclosure around the temple of Aesculapius, described in chapter 3, 'grass and trees were allowed to grow with a kind of graceful wildness' (Pater 1918, 36). The impact of the oxymoron is forfeited with Esclasans's 'una especie de desorden salvaje y encantador' (a kind of savage and charming disorder, Pater 1944, 34). In chapter 4, where Flavian is introduced and described at some length, we are told: 'there was an attractive piquancy in the poverty of Flavian' (Pater 1918, 50). The tripping quality of the alliteration in 'p' is totally lost in the Spanish translation, which, moreover, cryptically speaks of an 'oculto atractivo' (an attractive hidden quality, Pater 1944, 41).

7

J. Farrán y Mayoral's Castilian translation from the English, as the title page pronounces, of Pater's *The Renaissance, El renacimiento: estudios de arte y poesía* (1945), would come to complete the Pater canon in Castilian. It was published by Joaquín Gil Editores, S.A., that is, the Iberia publishing house (Editorial Iberia), already in existence in Barcelona as a publishing enterprise producing in Castilian in the 1920s, in a series entitled Masterpieces (Obras

Maestras). The translation carries an unsigned prologue which speaks of Pater's life and work and ends with a twenty-seven line quote from 'a distinguished writer',[60] who remains unnamed. Farrán y Mayoral is also referred to in the prologue as 'the distinguished writer'[61] and this should not be overlooked since, if the distinguished writer ever existed, it was as Farran i Mayoral, in Catalan. Spirits were high in Catalonia within nationalist circles in 1945: it was hoped that with the allied victory, General Franco's regime might end, and it seems to me significant that Pater's *The Renaissance* should be brought out at this point. It links back to Manent's translation into Catalan in 1938 and comes to reaffirm the hopes for the establishment of a religious humanism, a Christian democracy, which could constitute the foundation for a new postwar order. The application for permission to publish *El renacimiento* and the reader's report are missing from the Archivo General de la Administración archive in Alcalá de Henares, but since two of Pater's works had already been granted permission for publication, he would not be seen to be controversial initially.

Farrán y Mayoral had shown his familiarity with *The Renaissance* in his opening piece from the translator to the reader in *Retratos imaginarios*, where he quoted at some length from Pater's Conclusion (Farrán y Mayoral 1942, 13–14). Interestingly, his 1945 translation of the pieces he reproduced from the Conclusion for the 1942 preface is not exactly the same. The command of Castilian is greater and, at least as far as these extracts are concerned, the translation is to some degree more precise in relation to the original. For instance, Pater's famous 'To burn always with this hard, gem-like flame, to maintain this ecstasy, is success in life' (Pater 1998, 152) is rendered: 'Arder siempre con esta llama, fuerte y densa como una piedra preciosa, para mantener ese éxtasis, es triunfar en la vida' (To burn always with this flame strong and dense like a precious stone, in order to maintain that ecstasy, is to triumph in life, Pater 1945, 207). As can be appreciated from my translation of Farrán y Mayoral's Spanish, the rendering is not totally precise: 'fuerte y densa' may not be the most appropriate way of expressing Pater's 'hard' and 'to maintain this ecstasy' is in apposition to 'To burn always with this hard, gem-like flame', therefore, the use of 'para' with the infinitive in Spanish, 'para mantener', indicating purpose, is incorrect. In 1942, Farrán y Mayoral had spoken of 'esta poderosa, preciosa llama' (this powerful, beautiful flame, Pater 1942, 13) but had omitted 'gem-like'. However, he had not introduced a clause of purpose, respecting, therefore, the apposition, but had diluted Pater's claim that burning in the way he described was 'success in life', modifying it, perhaps on the grounds of caution, to 'un triunfo en la vida' (one instance of success in life, Pater 1942, 13). In 1945, the Spanish translation, through the use of the infinitive, 'to triumph', respects Pater's text.

---

[60] 'un ilustre escritor' (Pater 1945, 6–7).
[61] 'el ilustre escritor' (Pater 1945).

8

the old puzzle of life had found its solution[62]

England, a master like Rome in the art of government[63]

The pagan Marius, a youth of longing and searching, will encounter peace and fulfilment in Cecilia's Christian household and over the final chapters of the novel a message of hope is reiterated. It seems to me that in Pater's fusion of the classical and Christian, present in the prose writings translated over the 1930s and 1940s, those Catalans who believed in the *noucentista* project or who were nostalgic following the Civil War for what the movement had begun to construct in Catalonia in the earlier part of the century, and who had hopes that the country might pick up from where it had been forcibly removed in 1939, exploited Pater's texts with a view to consolidating their political and cultural ideals. Thus, the quiet fellow of Brasenose, intellectual representative of a nation whose parliamentary democracy was held in high esteem by law-abiding Catalans, not least the first President of the Mancomunitat de Catalunya, Enric Prat de la Riba, was given a not insignificant part to play in the Catalan bourgeoisie's struggle for national liberation in the first half of the twentieth century.

---

[62]   Pater, 1918, vol. 2, 106)
[63]   'Anglaterra, mestra com Roma, en l'art de governar' (Prat de la Riba in Costa Ruibal 2002, 49).

Bibliography

Introduction

Bann, Stephen (2002) 'Pater's Reception in France: A Provisional Account', in Brake, Laurel, Lesley Higgins and Carolyn Williams (eds.) *Walter Pater: Transparencies of Desire*, Greensboro: University of North Carolina Press, pp. 55–62.

Bertocci, Angelo Philip (1949) *Charles Du Bos and English Literature: A Critic and his Orientation*, New York: King's Crown Press, Columbia University.

— (1955) 'French Criticism and the Pater Problem', *Boston University Studies in English*. 1: 178–94.

Bloom, Harold (ed.) (1974) *Selected Writings of Walter Pater*, New York: Columbia University Press.

Brake, Laurel, Lesley Higgins and Carolyn Williams (eds.) (2002) *Walter Pater: Transparencies of Desire*. Greensboro: University of North Carolina Press.

Dodd, Philip (ed) (1981) *Walter Pater: An Imaginative Sense of Fact*, London and Totowa, N. J.

Du Bos, Charles (1946) *Journal 1921–1923*, Paris: Corréa.

— (1965) *Approximations*, Paris: Fayard.

Duthuit, Georges (1974) *Le Rose et le noir* (1923), republished in *Représentation et présence: premiers écrits et travaux 1923–1952*, with an introduction by Yves Bonnefoy, Paris: Flammarion, pp. 38–104.

Levey, Michael (1978) *The Case of Walter Pater*, London: Thames & Hudson.

Oman, Sir Charles (1941) *Memories of Victorian Oxford* (second edition).

Osterkamp, Ernst (2001) 'Art History and Humanist Tradition in the Stefan George Circle', *Comparative Criticism* [Cambridge], 23: 211–30.

Saint, Nigel (2000), *Marguerite Yourcenar: Reading the Visual*, Oxford: Legenda.

Vilain, Robert (2002) 'The Reception of Walter Pater in Germany and Austria', in Brake, Laurel, Lesley Higgins and Carolyn Williams (eds.) *Walter Pater: Transparencies of Desire*, Greensboro: University of North Carolina Press, pp. 63–72.

Yourcenar, Marguerite (1929) 'Abraham France traducteur de Virgil Oscar Wilde', *Revue Bleue*, 20: 621–7.

Chapter 1

Anceschi, Luciano (1976) 'D'Annunzio e il sistema dell'analogia', in Mariano, Emilio (ed.) *D'Annunzio e il simbolismo europeo*, Milan: Il Saggiatore, pp. 65–101.

Angeli, Diego (1930) *Cromache del Caffé Greco*, Milan: Treves.

Angeli, Monica Maria (ed.) (1999) *Le carte di Enrico Nencioni*, Florence: Manent.

Bini, Benedetta (1992) *L'incanto della distanza: ritratti immaginari nella cultura del decadentismo*, Bari: Adriatica.

— (2003) '*Genius loci* e ville italiane: Viterbo e la Tuscia nella cultura anglosassone di fine Ottocento', in Platania, Gaetano (ed.) *Viaggiatori da e per la Tuscia*, Viterbo: Settecittà, pp. 159–82.

— 'L'esilio dorato di William Wetmore Story', in Mancini, Marco (ed.) *Esilio, pellegrinaggio e altri viaggi*, Viterbo: Settecittà, pp. 401–14.

Cambieri Tosi, Mari Jose (1984) *Carlo Placci: maestro di cosmopoli nella Firenze fra Otto e Novecento*, Florence: Vallecchi.

Cicognani, Bruno (ed.) (1943) *Le più belle pagine di Enrico Nencioni*, Milan: Garzanti.

Colby, Vineta (1970) 'The Puritan Aesthete: Vernon Lee', in *The Singular Anomaly: Women Novelists of the Nineteenth Century*, New York: New York University Press.

— (2003) *Vernon Lee: A Literary Biography*, Charlottesville: University of Virginia Press.

Conti, Angelo (1894) *Giorgione*, Florence: Alinari.

— (1900) *La beata riva: trattato dell'oblio. Preceduto da un ragionamento di Gabriele d'Annunzio*, Milan: Treves.

Corrigan, Beatrice (1962) 'Giovanni Ruffini's Letters to Vernon Lee', *English Miscellany*, 13. 179–240.

Damigella, Anna Maria (1981) *La pittura simbolista in Italia: 1885–1900*, Turin: Einaudi.

d'Anna, Riccardo (1996) *Roma preraffaellita: note su Gabriele d'Annunzio, Diego Angeli, G.A. Sartorio*, Rome: Atti dell'Accademia Nazionale dei Lincei.

d'Annunzio, Gabriele

— 'Note su Giorgione e su la critica', *Il Convito*, a.1, 82–85.

— (1900) *The Flame of Life*, trans. Kassandra Vivaria, London: William Heinemann.

— (1989) *Le vergini delle rocce*, in *Prose di romanzi II*, preface by Ezio Raimondi, ed. Annamaria Andreoli and Niva Lorenzini, Milan: Mondadori.

— (1989) *Il fuoco*, in *Prose di romanzi II*, preface by Ezio Raimondi, ed. Annamaria Andreoli and Niva Lorenzini, Milan: Mondadori.

— (1996) 'Un poeta d'autunno', *Scritti giornalistici*, vol. 1, ed. Annamaria Andreoli and Federico Roncoroni, Milan: Mondadori, pp. 935–8.

Fletcher, Ian (1970) 'Herbert Horne: The Earlier Phase', *English Miscellany*, 21: 117–57.

Frandini, Paola (1972) 'Nino Costa e l'ambiente artistico romano fra il 1870 e il 1890', in Durbé, Dario (ed.) *Aspetti dell'arte a Roma dal 1870 al 1914*, Rome: De Luca, pp. 19–33.

Gunn, Peter (1970) *Vernon Lee: Violet Paget, 1856–1935*, London: Oxford University Press.

Horne, Herbert P. (1908) *Botticelli*, London: Bell (rpb. 1980: Princeton: Princeton University Press).

James, Henry (1984) 'Gabriele d'Annunzio' (1904), in *Selected Literary Criticism*, ed. by Morris Shapira, prefaced with a note on 'James as Critic' by F.R. Leavis, Harmondsworth: Penguin Books, pp. 309–42.

Kermode, Frank (1985) *Forms of Attention*, Chicago: University of Chicago Press.

Lee, Vernon (1880) *Studies of the Eighteenth Century in Italy*, London: W. Satchell.

— (1881) *Il Settecento in Italia: letteratura, teatro, musica*, preface by A. Arnaboldi, Milan: Fratelli Dumolard.

— (1881) *Belcaro: Being Essays on Sundry Aesthetical Questions*, London: W. Satchell.

— (1884) *Euphorion: Being Studies of the Antique and the Medieval in the Renaissance*, London: T. Fisher Unwin.

— (1885) 'La morale nell'estetica: appunti sul nuovo libro di Walter Pater', *Fanfulla della domenica* [Rome], 10 May, 1–2.

— (1887) *Juvenilia: Being a Second Series of Essays on Sundry Aesthetical Questions*, London: T. Fisher Unwin.

— (1895) *Renaissance Fancies and Studies*, London: Smith, Elder & Co.

— (1937) *Letters*, ed. Irene Cooper Willis, London: privately printed.

Lorenzini, Niva (1989) 'Note' to d'Annunzio, Gabriele (1989) *Le vergini delle rocce* and *Il fuoco*, in *Prose di romanzi II*, ed. Annamaria Andreoli and Niva Lorenzini: Milan: Mondadori, pp. 1089–314.

Marabini Moevs, Maria Teresa (1976) *Gabriele d'Annunzio e le estetiche della fine del secolo*, L'Aquila: L. U. Japadre Editore.

McComb, A. K. (1966) 'The Anglo-Americans in Florence', *English Miscellany*, 17: 279–310.

Nencioni, Enrico (1897) *Saggi critici di letteratura inglese*, Florence: LeMonnier.

Oliva, Gianni (1979) *I nobili spiriti: Pascoli, d'Annunzio e le riviste dell'estetismo fiorentino*, Bergamo: Minerva Italica.

Olivero, Federico (1914) *Studi sul romanticismo inglese*, Bari: Laterza.

— (1918) *Nuovi saggi di letteratura inglese*, Turin: Libreria Editrice Internazionale.

Pantazzi, Sybille (1959) 'Enrico Nencioni, W.W. Story e Vernon Lee', *English Miscellany*, 10: 249–60.

— (1961) 'Carlo Placci and Vernon Lee: Their Letters and Their Friends', *English Miscellany*, 12: 97–122.

Pater, Walter (1970), *Letters*, ed. Lawrence Evans, Oxford: Clarendon Press.

— (1980) *The Renaissance: Studies in Art and Poetry*, ed. Donald L. Hill, Berkeley, Los Angeles and London: University of California Press.

Piantoni, Gianna (1972) 'La *Cronaca bizantina*, il *Convito* e la fortuna dei preraffaelliti a Roma', in Durbé, Dario (ed.) *Aspetti dell'arte a Roma dal 1870 al 1914*, Rome: De Luca, pp. 35–42.

Placci, Carlo (1884) 'Euphorion: a proposito del recente libro di Vernon Lee', *Fanfulla della domenica*, 31 August, 1–2.

— (1892) *Un furto*, Milan: Treves.

Praz, Mario (1937) 'Vernon Lee', in *Studi e svaghi inglesi*, Florence: Sansoni, pp. 315–36.

— (1944) 'Un cortegiano moderno' (1941), in *Fiori freschi*, Florence: Sansoni, pp. 209–16.

— (1995) 'Enrico Nencioni' (1943), in *Il patto col serpente*, Milan: Leonardo, pp. 336–40.

Raimondi, E. (1989) 'Introduzione' a d'Annunzio, Gabriele (1989) *Le Vergini delle rocce*, in *Prose di Romanzi II*, a cura di Ezio Raimondi e Annamania Andreoli, Milan: Mondadori, pp. xiii–l.

Ruffini, Giovanni (1855) *Doctor Antonio*, Edinburgh: T. Constable & Co.

Samuels, Ernest (1979) *Bernard Berenson: The Making of a Connoisseur*, Cambridge, MA. and London: Harvard University Press.

Sborgi, Franco (1990) 'Gabriele d'Annunzio e la cultura figurativa inglese del XIX secolo', in Nerozzi Bellman, Patrizia (ed.) *Gabriele d'Annunzio e la cultura inglese e americana*, Chieti: Marino Solfanelli, pp. 71–91.

Sormani, Elisa (1875) *Bizantini e decadenti nell'Italia umbertina*, Bari: Laterza.

Tamassia Mazzarotto, Bianca (1949) *Le arti figurative nell'arte di Gabriele d'Annunzio*, Milan: Boccia.

Vita-Finzi, Paolo (1978) 'Chi era il poeta d'autunno?', in *Quaderni del Vittoriale*, May–June 1978.

Wellek, René (1970) 'Vernon Lee, Bernard Berenson and Aesthetics', in *Discriminations: Further Concepts of Criticism*, New Haven, CT: Yale University Press, pp. 164–87.

Zorn, Christa (2003) *Vernon Lee: Aesthetics, History, and the Victorian Female Intellectual*, Athens: Ohio University Press.

Chapter 2

Bardi, Pietro (1912) *Scrittori inglesi dell'Ottocento*, Bari: Laterza.

Bettini, Sergio (1942) *Botticelli*, Bergamo; Milan; Rome: Istituto italiano d'arti grafiche.

Cecchi, Emilio (1912) 'L'ebreo errante', in *Studi critici*, Ancona: Giovanni Puccini e Figli.

Conti, Angelo (1894) *Giorgione*, Florence: Alinari.

— (1900) *La beata riva: trattato dell'oblio*, Milan: Treves.

— (1910) 'Leonardo pittore', in AA. VV., *Leonardo da Vinci: conferenze fiorentine*, Milan: Treves, pp. 81–103.

Cozzani, Ettore (1914) *Vita di Sandro Botticelli*, Florence: Bemporad.

Croce, Benedetto (1910) *Problemi di estetica e contributi alla storia dell'estetica italiana*, Bari: Laterza.

d'Annunzio, Gabriele (1895) 'Note su Giorgione e su la critica', *Il Convito* [Rome], 1: 69–86.

de Rensis, Raffaello (1910) *Anime musicali: introduzione ai poeti musici – G. d'Annunzio, N. Lenau, E. Nencioni, I.V. Tarchetti*, Rome: Musica.

— (1927) *Anime musicali: la sensibilità musicale nei poeti, letterati, filosofi – Leonardo, d'Annunzio, Lenau, Giorgio Sand, Nencioni, Trachetti, Oriani, Walter Pater*, Rome: Maglione & Strini.

de Rinaldis, Aldo (1919) 'Il sorriso di Leonardo', in AA. VV., *Per il IV centenario della morte di Leonardo da Vinci*, Bergamo: Istituto italiano di arti grafiche, pp. 263–73.

Gargano, Giuseppe Saverio (1912) 'Walter Pater', *Il Marzocco* [Florence], (4 August): 2–3.

Gengaro, Marialuisa (1943) 'La "critica immaginativa" di Walter Pater (1839–1894)', *La Nuova Italia* [Florence], 2: 3–7.

Gibellini, Pietro (2000) Introduction in Angelo Conti, *La beata riva*, ed. Pietro Gibellini, Venice: Marsilio, pp. ix–xxii.

Golzio, Vincenzo (1925) 'Walter Pater critico d'arte', *L'arte*, 28: 63–8.

James, Henry (1909) *The Novels and Tales of Henry James*, vol. 15, New York: Charles Scribner's Sons.

Lee, Vernon (1885) 'La morale nell'estetica: appunti sul nuovo libro di Walter Pater', *Fanfulla della domenica* [Rome], (10 May): 1–2.

Longhi, Roberto (1912) 'Recensione a W. Pater, *Il Rinascimento: studi d'arte e di poesia', La Voce* [Florence], 39: 902.

Marangoni, Matteo (1933) *Saper vedere*, Milan: Treves – Treccani – Tuminelli.

Olivero, Federico (1909) 'Walter Pater e i suoi studi sul Rinascimento', Pavia: Tipografia successori fratelli Fusi.

— (1939) *Il pensiero religioso ed estetico di Walter Pater*, Turin: SEI.

Ortensi, Ulisse (1902) 'Letterati contemporanei: Walter Horatio Pater', *Emporium* [Bergamo], 15 (January): 23–28.

Pater, Walter (1893) *The Renaissance: Studies in Art and Poetry*, London and New York: Macmillan.

— (1912) *Il Rinascimento: studi d'arte e di poesia*, trans. Aldo de Rinaldis, Naples: Ricciardi.

— (1944), *Pater*, ed. Mario Praz, Milan: Garzanti.

Raimondi, Ezio (1986) *Il silenzio della Gorgone*, Bologna: Zanichelli.

Ricorda, Ricciarda (1990) Introduction to Angelo Conti, *Leonardo pittore*, Padua: Programma.

Solmi, Edmondo (1910) 'La resurrezione dell'opera di Leonardo', in AA. VV., *Leonardo da Vinci: conferenze fiorentine*, Milan: Treves, pp. 3–48.

Supino, Igino Benvenuto (1909) *Sandro Botticelli*, Bologna and Modena: Formiggini.

Venturi, Lionello (1919) *La critica e l'arte di Leonardo da Vinci*, Bologna: Zanichelli.

— (1913) *Giorgione e il giorgionismo*, Milan: Hoepli.

— (1948) *Storia della critica d'arte*, Florence: Edizioni U.

Wilde, Oscar (1966) 'The Critic as Artist', in *The Complete Works*, ed. Vyvyan Holland, London and Glasgow: Collins, pp. 1009–59.

Zanetti, Giorgio (1996) *Estetismo e modernità: saggio su Angelo Conti*, Bologna: Il Mulino.

Chapter 3

Anon. (1940) 'Cronaca', *Giornale storico della letteratura italiana* [Turin], 115 (April-June): 251.

Anon. (1941) 'Bibliografia', *La civiltà cattolica* [Rome], 42: 66–7.

Ascari, Maurizio (1999) 'The Mask Without the Face: Walter Pater's *Imaginary Portraits*', *Textus* [Genoa], 12: 97–112.

— (2001) 'Walter Pater in Italy at the Postmodern Fin de Siècle', *The Pater Newsletter*, 42: 18–23.

Barbolini, Roberto (1975) 'Socrate e le pertinenti brame di Nietzsche, Pater e d'Annunzio', *Il Verri* [Turin], 9: 68–91.

— (1981) *Il sileno capovolto. Socrate nella cultura fin de siècle: Nietzsche, Pater e d'Annunzio*, Bologna: Il Mulino.

Bini, Benedetta (1992) *L'incanto della distanza: ritratti immaginari nella cultura del decadentismo*, Bari: Adriatica.

— (1993) 'Alle origini del ritratto: "An English Poet" di Walter Pater', in Billi, Mirella and Massimo Ferrari Zumbini (eds.) *Percorsi: studi dedicati ad Angela Giannitrapani*, Viterbo: Betagramma, pp. 47–64.

Bizzotto Elisa (1998a) 'Echi di Giorgione nella narrativa di Walter Pater', *Paragone* [Florence], 17–18 (June-August): 86–96.

— (1998b) 'Madri e amanti. Le figure femminili negli *Imaginary Portraits* di Pater', *Il lettore di provincia* [Ravenna], 29 (December): 37–44.

— (2000) 'The Legend of the Returning Gods in Pater and Wilde', in Marucci, Franco and Emma Sdegno (eds.) *Athena's Shuttle: Myth, Religion, Ideology from Romanticism to Modernism*, Milan: Cisalpino, pp. 161–74.

— (2001) *La mano e l'anima: il ritratto immaginario fin de siècle*, Milan: Cisalpino.

Bizzotto, Elisa and Franco Marucci (eds.) (1996) *Walter Pater (1839–1894). Le forme della modernità. The Forms of Modernity*, Milan: Cisalpino.

Caprin, Giulio (1913) 'Critica e immaginazione: i *Ritratti immaginari* di W. Pater', *Il Marzocco* [Florence], 27 July: 3.

Cecchi, Emilio (1912) 'Walter Horatio Pater', *La Tribuna* [Rome], 3 July.

— (1913) '*Ritratti immaginari* di W. H. Pater', *La Tribuna* [Rome], 5 August, republished in *Scrittori inglesi e americani*, vol. 1, Milan: Garzanti, 1976, pp. 151–4.

— (1963) 'Splendori e miserie del decadentismo inglese', *Corriere della sera* [Milan], 11 May, republished *Scrittori inglesi e americani*, vol. 2, Milan: Garzanti, 1976, pp. 379–83.

Conti, Angelo (1894) *Giorgione: studio*, Florence: Alinari.

— (1900) *La beata riva: trattato dell'oblio*, Milan: Treves.

— (1910) 'Leonardo pittore', in AA. VV., *Leonardo da Vinci: conferenze fiorentine*, Milan: Treves, republished in Ricorda, Ricciarda (ed.) *Leonardo pittore*, Padua: Editoriale Programma, 1990.

d'Annunzio, Gabriele (1895) 'Note su Giorgione e su la critica', *Il Convito* [Rome], 1(January): 69–86.

d'Elia, Gaetano (1996) 'Pater tra saggismo e intento storiografico', *Corriere del giorno* [Taranto], 12 January: 3.

del Sapio, Maria (1995) 'La Sfinge e la Chimera: miraggi di pienezza nella biblioteca *fin de siècle*', in Chialant, Maria Teresa and Eleonora Rao (eds.) *Per una topografia dell'altrove*, Naples: Liguori, pp. 161–82.

de Rinaldis, Aldo (1919) 'Il sorriso di Leonardo', in AA. VV., *Per il IV centenario della morte di Leonardo da Vinci*, Bergamo: Istituto italiano d'arti grafiche, pp. 263–73.

Eco, Umberto (1966) *Le poetiche di Joyce*, Milan: Bompiani.

Fumagalli, Giuseppina (1954) 'Leonardo: ieri e oggi', in Marazza, Achille (ed.) *Leonardo: saggi e ricerche*, Rome: Istituto Poligrafico di Stato, pp. 393–411.

Galletti, Alfredo (1918) 'Dante Gabriele Rossetti e il Romanticismo Preraffaellita', in *Studi di letteratura inglese*, Bologna: Zanichelli, pp. 10–237.

Gargano, Giuseppe Saverio (1912) 'Walter Pater', *Il Marzocco* [Florence], 4 August: 2–3.

Gazzoni-Pisani, Dario (1963) *Walter Pater: critico d'arte. Con particolare riguardo agli 'Studi sul Rinascimento'*, Rome: Pioda.

Gentili, Sandro (1981) 'Il ruolo di Angelo Conti', in *Trionfo e crisi del modello dannunziano*, Florence: Vallecchi, pp. 87–142.

Golzio, Vincenzo (1925) 'Walter Pater critico d'arte', *L'arte* [Rome], 28 (January-April): 63–8.

Grassi, Luigi (1948), 'Walter Pater e il Rinascimento', *Emporium* [Bergamo], 107: 637 (January): 11–14.

Lee, Vernon (1885) 'La morale nell'estetica: appunti sul nuovo libro di Walter Pater', *Fanfulla della domenica* [Rome], 10 May: 1–2.

Longhi, Roberto (1912) 'Walter Pater: *Il Rinascimento: studi d'arte e di poesia*, Traduz. de Rinaldis, Napoli, 1912', *La Voce* [Florence], 39: 902.

Lugli, Vittorio (1927) 'Una visita a Ronsard', *Il Baretti* [Turin], 4, 8 (August), 41–42, rpt in *Jules Renard ed altri amici*, Messina: D'Anna, 1948, pp. 137–52.

Marabini Moevs, Maria Teresa (1976) *Gabriele D'Annunzio e le estetiche della fine del secolo*, L'Aquila: Japadre.

Marucci, Franco (1994) 'Ruskin, Pater e il Rinascimento sfaccettato', in Clegg, Jeanne and Paul Tucker (eds.) *The Dominion of Daedalus: Papers from the Ruskin Workshop Held in Pisa and Lucca, 13–14 May 1993*, St Albans, Hertfordshire: Brentham Press, pp. 130–42.

— (1996) 'Alcune considerazioni sul ritrattismo letterario', *Comparatistica* [Florence], 7: 17–26.

— (1997) 'L'aforisma nel secondo ottocento inglese: Arnold, Pater e Wilde', *Annali di Ca' Foscari* [Venice], 36: 135–45.

— (2001) 'Bellezza, modernità', *Alias* [Rome], 20 (26 May): 19.

Melchiori, Giorgio (1956) *The Tightrope Walkers: Studies of Mannerism in Modern English Literature*, London: Routledge & Kegan Paul.

Micks La Regina, Gabriella (1982) 'Dante Gabriel Rossetti e Walter Pater: House of Life e House Beautiful nella *Waste Land* vittoriana', in Oliva, Gianni (ed.) *I Rossetti tra Italia e Inghilterra*, Rome: Bulzoni, pp. 271–307.

— (1984) '"All Things Give Way, Nothing Remaineth": Walter Pater and the Heraclitean Flux', in Rossetti, Livio (ed.) *Atti del Symposium Heracliteum 1981*, vol. 2, Rome: Edizioni dell'Ateneo, pp. 191–208.

Migliore, Sandra (1994) 'Walter Pater e la fondazione del mito', in *Tra Hermes e Prometeo. Il mito di Leonardo nel decadentismo europeo*, Florence: Olschki, pp. 17–43.

Nardi, Isabella (1985) *Un critico vittoriano: Enrico Nencioni*, Naples: Edizioni Scientifiche Italiane.

Nencioni, Enrico (1889) 'Due nuovi romanzi: *Il piacere* di Gabriele d'Annunzio. *All'erta sentinella* di Matilde Serao', *Nuova antologia* [Rome], 105 (16 June): 660–71.

— (1890) 'W. Pater. *Appreciations*', *Nuova antologia* [Rome], 109 (16 February): 702.

— (1893) 'La lirica del Rinascimento', in AA. VV., *La vita italiana nel Rinascimento*, Milan: Treves, pp. 267–304.

Olivero, Federico (1909) 'Walter Pater ed i suoi studi sul Rinascimento', *Studium* [Pavia]: 3–11.

— (1930) *Letteratura inglese moderna*, Turin: Edizioni de 'L'Erma'.

— (1939) *Il pensiero religioso ed estetico di Walter Pater*, Turin: Società Editrice Internazionale.

Ortensi, Ulisse (1902) 'Letterati contemporanei: Walter Horatio Pater', *Emporium* [Bergamo], (January), 23–5.

Pater, Walter (1912) *Il rinascimento*, ed. and trans. Aldo de Rinaldis, Naples: Ricciardi, republished in 1925.

— (1913) *Ritratti immaginari*, trans. Aldo de Rinaldis, Naples: Ricciardi.

— (1939) *Mario l'epicureo*, ed. and trans. Lidia Storoni Mazzolani, Turin: Einaudi.

— (1944a) *Pater: scelta e traduzione*, ed. and trans. Mario Praz, Milan: Garzanti.

— (1944b) *Ritratti immaginari*, ed. and trans. Mario Praz, Rome: De Luigi.

— (1946) *Il rinascimento*, ed. and trans. Mario Praz, Naples: Edizioni Scientifiche Italiane.

— (1994a) *Studi greci*, ed. Paola Colaiacomo, trans. Vittoria Caterina Caratozzolo, Rome: Editori Riuniti.

— (1994b) *Ritratti immaginari*, ed. and trans. Franco Marucci, Florence: Giunti.

— (1995) *Gaston de Latour*, ed. and trans. Franco Marucci, Venice: Marsilio.

— (1999) *Walter Pater critico di Shakespeare*, ed. and trans. Maria Luisa de Rinaldis, Lecce: Milella.

— (2001) *Mario l'epicureo*, ed. Viola Papetti, trans. Alberto Rossatti, Milan: Rizzoli.

Praz, Mario (1930) *La carne, la morte e il diavolo nella letteratura romantica*, Milan: Roma: Società editrice la Cultura.

— (1962) 'Due padri del Decadentismo', in *Cronache letterarie anglosassoni III*, Rome: Edizioni di storia e letteratura, pp. 576–81.

— (1972) *Il patto col serpente*, Milan: Mondadori.

Ricorda, Ricciarda (1993) *Dalla parte di Ariele: Angelo Conti nella cultura di fine secolo*, Rome: Bulzoni.

Rognoni, Francesco (1996) 'Nel nome del Pater', *La rivista dei libri* [Milan], 6 (June): 39–41.

Sdegno, Emma (1996) '*Walter Pater (1839–1894): le forme della modernità*, a cura di Franco Marucci e Elisa Bizzotto, Milano, Cisalpino, 1996', *Comparatistica* [Florence], 8: 210–14.

Severi, Rita (1989) 'Words for Pictures: Notes on Iconic Description in Pater, Wilde, and Firbank', *Comparatistica* [Florence], 1: 83–102.

— (1992) 'The Myth of Leonardo in English Decadent Writers', *Achademia Leonardi Vinci* [Florence], 5: 96–104.

Tucker, Paul (1991) 'Pater as a "Moralist"', in Brake, Laurel and Ian Small (eds.) *Pater in the 1990s*, Greensboro: ELT Press, pp. 107–25.

Villa, Luisa (1988) 'Verso/Attraverso *The Hill of Dreams*: Walter Pater, Arthur Machen, l'oggetto estetico e la decadenza', *Textus* [Genoa], 1: 101–45.

— (1996) 'Walter Pater: *Studi greci* et al.', *L'indice* [Milan], 5 (May): 20–1.

Zanetti, Giorgio (1996) *Estetismo e modernità: saggio su Angelo Conti*, Bologna: Il Mulino.

Chapter 4

'A Cosmopolitan Frenchman' (1896), [unsigned article on de Wyzewa], *The Saturday Review* [London], 82 (1 August): 106–7.

Ainslie, Douglas (1923) 'Témoignage d'un ami', in *Hommage à Marcel Proust: La Nouvelle Revue française* [Paris], (1 January): 259–61.

André, Robert (1963) 'Walter Pater et Marcel Proust', *La Nouvelle Revue française* [Paris], (1 June): 1082–9.

Baker, Joseph E. (1959) 'Ivory Tower as Laboratory: Pater and Proust', *Accent: A Quarterly of New Literature* [Urbana, Illinois], 19 (Autumn): 204–16.

Bann, Stephen (2002) 'Pater's Reception in France: A Provisional Account', in Brake, Laurel, Lesley Higgins and Carolyn Williams (eds.) *Walter Pater: Transparencies of Desire*, University of North Carolina at Greensboro: ELT Press, pp. 55–62.

Benson, Arthur Christopher (1906) *Walter Pater*, London and New York: Macmillan.

Billy, Robert de (1930) *Lettres et conversations avec Marcel Proust*, Paris: Editions des Portiques.

Bourget, Paul (1906) *Etudes et Portraits*, Paris: Plon-Nourrit.

— (1912) *Pages de critique et de doctrine*, vol. 1, Paris: Plon-Nourrit.

Cazamian, Madeleine L. (1924) [review article of the French translations of *La Renaissance* and *Platon et le Platonisme*], *Revue anglo-américaine* [Paris], 1: 5 (June): 443–5.

Cecil, Lord David (1955) *The Scholar-Artist*, Cambridge: Cambridge University Press.

Conlon, John J. (1982) *Walter Pater and the French Tradition*, Lewisburg: Bucknell University Press.

Court, Franklin E. (1980) *Walter Pater: An Annotated Bibliography of Writings About Him*, De Kalb, Illinois: Northern Illinois University Press.

Davray, Henry-D. (1910) [review article of Laurent 1910], *Mercure de France* [Paris], 88 (1 November): 172–3.

Duclaux, Mary (1925) 'Souvenirs sur Walter Pater', *La Revue de Paris* (15 January): 339–58.

Duthuit, Georges (1923) *Le Rose et le noir, de Walter Pater à Oscar Wilde*, Paris: La Renaissance du livre.

Eells, Emily (2002) *Proust's Cup of Tea: Homoeroticism and Victorian Culture*, Aldershot: Ashgate.

Fernandez, Ramon (1924) [review article of Emmanuel Coppinger's translation *Marius l'Epicurien*, Dr Samuel Jankélévitch's translation *Platon et le Platonisme* and Georges Duthuit's *Le Rose et le noir*], *La Nouvelle Revue française* [Paris], (1 February): 247–51.

— (1928) 'Note sur l'esthétique de Proust', *La Nouvelle Revue française* [Paris], (1 August): 272–80.

Frank, Ellen Eve (1979) *Literary Architecture: Essays Toward a Tradition: Walter Pater, Gerard Manley Hopkins, Marcel Proust, Henry James*, Berkeley, Los Angeles and London: University of California Press.

Fraser, Robert (1994) *Proust and the Victorians: The Lamp of Memory*, London: Macmillan.

Goichot, Emile (1982) *Henri Bremond, historien du sentiment religieux: genèse et stratégie d'une entreprise Littéraire*, Paris: Ophrys.

Gosse, Edmund (1894) 'Walter Pater: a Portrait', *The Contemporary Review* [London], 66 (December): 795–810.

— (1916) 'France et Angleterre: l'avenir de leurs relations intellectuelles', *Revue des deux mondes* [Paris], 35 (1 October): 526–41.

Hafley, James (1957) 'Walter Pater's *Marius* and the Technique of Modern Fiction', *Modern Fiction Studies* [Lafayette, Indiana], 3:2 (Summer): 99–109.

Hangest, Germain d' (1961) *Walter Pater, l'homme et l'œuvre*, 2 vols., Paris: Didier.

Henry, Anne (1981) *Marcel Proust: théories pour une esthétique*, Paris: Klincksieck.

Jaloux, Edmond (1923) 'Walter Pater', *Les Nouvelles littéraires* [Paris], 8 (September): 2.

Johnson, Lee McKay (1980) *The Metaphor of Painting: Essays on Baudelaire, Ruskin, Proust and Pater*, Ann Arbor, Michigan: UMI.

Lalou, René (1926) *Panorama de la littérature anglaise contemporaine*, Paris: Krä.

Laurent, Raymond (1910) *Etudes anglaises*, Paris: Bernard Grasset.

Lauro, Carlo (1995) *Proust e la cultura anglosassone*, Rome: Bulzoni Editore.

Mallarmé, Stéphane (1897) *Divagations*, Paris: E. Fasquelle.

Maranini, Lorenza (1933) *Proust: Arte e Conoscenza*, Florence: Novissima editrice.

Michaud, Régis (1918) *Mystiques et réalistes anglo-saxons,* Paris: Armand Colin.

Miller, J. Hillis (1976) 'Walter Pater: A Partial Portrait', *Daedalus* [Cambridge, MA], 105 (Winter): 97–113.

Monsman, Gerald (1980) *Walter Pater's Art of Autobiography*, New Haven and London: Yale University Press.

Mourey, Gabriel (1926) 'Marcel Proust, John Ruskin et Walter Pater', 2 parts, *Le Monde nouveau* [Paris], (15 August–15 September): 702–14 and (15 October); 896–909.

Pater, Walter (1887) *Imaginary Portaits*, London: Macmillan.

— (1889) *Appreciations*, London: Macmillan.

— (1895) *Greek Studies*, London: Macmillan.

— (1895) *Miscellaneous Studies*, London: Macmillan.

— (1898) 'Sebastien van Storck', trans. Georges Khnopff, *Mercure de France* [Paris], 27 (July 1898): 42–70.

— (1899a) *Portraits imaginaires*, trans. Georges Khnopff, Paris: Mercure de France.

— (1899b) 'Léonardo de Vinci', trans. Richard Irvine Best and Robert Darles, *Mercure de France* [Paris], 31 (September): 577–606.

— (1902) *The Renaissance: Studies in Art and Poetry*, London: Macmillan.

— (1917) *La Renaissance*, trans. Firmin Roger-Cornaz, Paris: Payot.

— (1922) *Marius l'Epicurien*, trans. Emmanuel Coppinger, Paris: Perrin et Cie.

— (1924) 'Vézelay: essai d'histoire d'art religieux', trans. Dr L. Vignes, Avallon: Imprimerie de la Revue de l'Yonne.

— (1930) *Portraits imaginaires*, trans. Philippe Neel, Paris: Stock, Delamain et Boutelleau. Reprinted in 1985 with a postface by Mario Praz, Paris: Christian Bourgois.

— (1961) *The Renaissance: Studies in Art and Poetry*, ed. Kenneth Clark, London: Collins.

— (1963) 'L'Ecole de Giorgione', trans. Robert André, *La Nouvelle Revue française* [Paris], (1 June): 1156–62.

— (1985) *Essais sur l'art et la Renaissance*, trans. Anne Henry, Paris: Klincksieck.

— (1992) *L'Enfant dans la maison*, trans. Pierre Leyris, Paris: José Corti.

Proust, Marcel (1970–93) *Correspondance*, ed. Philip Kolb, 21 vols, Paris: Plon.

— (1971) *Contre Sainte-Beuve, précédé de 'Pastiches et mélanges' et suivi de 'Essais et articles'*, ed. Pierre Clarac and Yves Sandre, Paris: Bibliothèque de la Pléiade, Gallimard.

— (1983) *Selected Letters*, vol. 1, 1880–1903, ed. Philip Kolb, trans. Ralph Manheim, London: Collins.

— (1987–89) *A la recherche du temps perdu*, ed. Jean-Yves Tadié and others, 4 vols., Paris: Bibliothèque de la Pléiade, Gallimard.

— (1988) *Against Sainte-Beuve and other Essays*, trans. John Sturrock, London: Penguin.

— (1989) *Selected Letters*, vol. 2, 1904–1909, ed. Philip Kolb, trans. Terence Kilmartin, London: Collins.

— (1992) *In Search of Lost Time*, 6 vols., trans. C. K. Scott Moncrieff and Terence Kilmartin, rev. D. J. Enright, London: Chatto & Windus.

Raffalovich, Marc-André (1928a) [under pseudonym Alexander Michaelson] 'Giles and Miles and Isabeau', *Blackfriars* [Oxford], 9: 94 (January): 18–29.

— (1928b) [under pseudonym Alexander Michaelson] 'Walter Pater: In Memoriam', *Blackfriars* [Oxford], 9: 101 (August): 463–71.

Robert, Pierre-Edmond (1976) *Marcel Proust: Lecteur des Anglo-Saxons*, Paris: A.-G. Nizet.

Roz, Firmin (1904) 'Une bibliographie du roman historique', *Revue des deux mondes* [Paris], 22 (1 July): 209–18.

Ruskin, John (1904) *La Bible d'Amiens*, trans. Marcel Proust, Paris: Mercure de France.

— (1906) *Sésame et les lys*, trans. Marcel Proust, Paris: Mercure de France.

Séailles, Gabriel (1892) *Léonard de Vinci, l'artiste et le savant: 1452–1519: Essai de biographie psychologique*, Paris: Perrin.

Schwob, Marcel (1896) *Vies imaginaires*, Paris: G. Charpentier et E. Fasquelle.

Seiler, R. M. (1980) *Walter Pater: The Critical Heritage*, London, Boston and Henley: Routledge & Kegan Paul.

Souday, Paul (1918) '*La Renaissance*', *Le Temps* (31 January): 3. Reprinted in a slightly modified form in Paul Souday, *La Société des grands esprits* (Paris: E. Hazan, 1929): 85–93.

Symons, Arthur (1897) 'Walter Pater', in *Studies in Two Literatures*, London: Leonard Smithers, 169–85. Trans. Georges Khnopff, *Mercure de France* [Paris], 25 (February 1898): 450–62. Khnopff's translation was reprinted in Arthur Symons (1907) *Portraits anglais*, Bruges: A. Herbert: 77–102.

Tyrrell, George (1971) *Lettres de George Tyrrell à Henri Bremond*, ed. A. Louis-David, Paris: Aubier Montaigne.

Vernon, Peter J. (1983) 'Pater's Letters to André Raffalovich', *English Literature in Transition 1880–1920*, 26.3: 192–7.

Wyzewa, Théodore de (1890) 'La Renaissance du roman historique en Angleterre', *Revue des deux mondes* [Paris], 97 (1 January): 184–201.

— (1894) 'Les derniers articles de Walter Pater', *Revue des deux mondes* [Paris], 124 (15 August): 935–38.

— (1895) 'Deux figures d'écrivains anglais: Walter Pater et James Anthony Froude', *Revue des deux mondes* [Paris], 127 (1 January): 219–23.

— (1896) 'Un roman posthume de Walter Pater', *Revue des deux mondes* [Paris], 138 (15 November): 458–68.

Chapter 5

André, Robert (1963a) 'L'Ecole de Giorgione', *Nouvelle revue française* [Paris], 11: 1156–62 (translates a part of 'The School of Giorgione').

— (1963b) 'Walter Pater et Marcel Proust', *Nouvelle revue française* [Paris], 11: 1082–109.

Bokanowski, Hélène (1992) 'Introduction', in *Walter Pater: La Renaissance et l'esprit de la modernité*, Paris: Corti (translates the 'Preface' and the Conclusion', pp. 33–93).

Bourdieu, Pierre (1999) *Les Règles de l'art*, Paris: Seuil.

Bourget, Paul (1993) 'Baudelaire', in *Essais de psychologie contemporaine*, Paris: Gallimard, pp. 3–18. Orig. pub. 1883.

Cassagne, Albert (1998) *La Théorie de l'art pour l'art en France*, Seyssel: Champ Vallon. Orig. pub.1906.

Chastel, André (2001) *Fables, formes, figures I*, Paris: Champs-Flammarion. First published 1978.

Conlon, John (1981) *Pater and the French Tradition*, Lewisburg, PA: Bucknell University Press.

Coppinger, Emmanuel (1922) *Marius l'Epicurien : Roman philosphique: Traduit par E. Coppinger, archiviste-paléographe*, Paris: Perrin.

Dellamora, Richard (1990) *Masculine Desire: The Sexual Politics of Victorian Aestheticism*, Chapel Hill: The University of North Carolina Press.

Dowling, Linda (1986) *Language and Decadence*, Princeton: Princeton University Press.

Du Bos, Charles (1930) 'Sur *Marius l'Epicurien* et Walter Pater', *Le Roseau d'or* [Paris], 9: 39–81.

Dufrenne, Mikaël (1953) *Phénoménologie et esthétique*, Paris: Presses Universitaires de France.

Farmer, Albert (1931a) *Le Mouvement 'esthétique' et décadent en Angleterre, 1873–1900*, Paris: Champion.

— (1931b) *Walter Pater as a Critic of English Literature: A Study of 'Appreciations'*, Grenoble: Didier et Richard.

Hangest, Germain d' (1961) *Walter Pater: L'homme et l'œuvre*, 2 vols., Paris: Didier.

— (1974) 'La Place de Walter Pater dans le mouvement esthétique', *Etudes anglaises* [Paris], 37.2: 158–71.

— (2000) Review of *Walter Pater: Platon et le platonisme: Conférences de 1893. Introduction, traduction et notes de J. B. Picy*, *Etudes anglaises* [Paris], 53.2: 224.

Henry, Anne (1983) *Marcel Proust: théories pour une esthétique*, Paris: Klincksieck.

— (1985a) 'Walter Pater ou le plaisir esthétique', preface to *Essais sur l'art et la Renaissance*, Paris: Klincksieck, pp. 9–43.

— (1985b) *Essais sur l'art et la Renaissance*, Paris: Klincksieck (excerpts from the 'Conclusion', the 'Preface', 'The School of Giorgione', 'Winckelmann', 'Coleridge', 'Leonardo da Vinci', 'Sandro Botticelli', 'The Poetry of Michelangelo', 'Luca della Robbia', 'The Myth of Demeter and Persephone', 'The Beginnings of Greek Sculpture', 'The Marbles of Aegina', *Plato and Platonism*, 'Style').

Hill, Charles G. (1967) 'Walter Pater and the Gide-Du Bos Controversy', *Revue de littérature comparée* [Paris], 41: 367–84.

Inman, Billie (1994) 'Estrangement and Connection: Walter Pater, Benjamin Jowett and William M. Hardinge', in Brake, Laurel and Ian Small (eds.) *Pater in the Nineties*, Greensboro: University of North Carolina Press.

Jankélévitch, Samuel (1923) *Platon et le platonisme*, Paris: Payot.

Jankélévitch, Vladimir (1950) 'La Décadence', *Revue de métaphysique et de morale* [Paris], 4: 337–89.

Khnopff, Georges (1899) *Portraits imaginaires*, Paris: Mercure de France.

Lacan, Jacques (1966) 'Remarques sur le rapport de Daniel Lagache', in *Ecrits*, Paris: Seuil, pp. 647–84.

Lambert, Martine (1999) 'Miroirs de la culture et images du moi: du portrait au portrait imaginaire chez Walter Pater', 2 vols. (unpublished doctoral thesis, University of Paris).

Levey, Michael (1978) *The Case of Walter Pater*, London: Thames & Hudson.

Leyris, Pierre (1992) *L'Enfant dans la maison*, Paris: Corti (translates 'The Child in the House', 'Emerald Uthwart', 'Hippolytus Veiled' and 'Apollo in Picardy').

Mallarmé, Stéphane (1897) *Divagations*, Paris: E. Fasquelle.

Michaud, Régis (1918) *Réalistes et mystiques anglo-saxons*, Paris: Colin.

Monsman, Gerald (1980) *Walter Pater's Art of Autobiography*, New Haven; London: Yale University Press.

Neel, Philippe (1930) *Portraits imaginaires*, Paris: Stock, Librairie cosmopolite. Repr. (1985) as *Portraits imaginaires*, trans. Philippe Neel with an introduction by Mario Praz, Paris: Bourgois.

Palacio, Jean de (1993) *Figures et formes de la décadence*, Paris: Séguier.

Pater, Walter (1895) *Miscellaneous Studies*, ed. C. L. Shadwell, London: Macmillan.

Picy, Jean-Baptiste (1998) *Platon et le platonisme: Conférences de 1893*, Introduction, trans. and notes by J. B. Picy, Paris: Vrin.

Roger-Cornaz, Firmin (1917) *La Renaissance*, Paris: Payot (translates the 1893 edn).

Rosenblatt, Louise (1931) *L'Idée de l'art pour l'art dans la littérature anglaise pendant la période victorienne*, Paris: Champion.

Seiler, Robert (ed.) (1980) *Walter Pater: The Critical Heritage*, London: Routledge & Kegan Paul.

Shuter, William (1971) 'The History as Palingenesis in Pater and Hegel', *Publications of the Modern Language Association of America* [New York], 86: 411–21.

Villeneuve, Guillaume de (1992) *Walter Pater: Marius l'Epicurien*, Paris: Bourgois.

Ward, Anthony (1966) *Walter Pater: The Idea in Nature*, London: MacGibbon & Kee.

Williams, Carolyn (1990) *Transfigured World: Pater's Aesthetic Historicism*, London and Ithaca: Cornell University Press.

Wright, Thomas (1907) *The Life of Walter Pater*, 2 vols., London: Lane.

Yeats, W. B. (ed.) (1936) *The Oxford Book of Modern Poetry*, Oxford: Oxford University Press.

Chapter 6

Baumann, Gerhart (1961) *Rudolf Kassner – Hugo von Hofmannsthal*, Stuttgart: Kohlhammer.

Borchardt, Rudolf (1960) *Gesammelte Werke in Einzelbänden. Prosa III*, ed. Marie Luise Borchardt and Ernst Zinn, Stuttgart: Klett.

— (1987) *Das Gespräch über Formen und Platons Lysis Deutsch*, Stuttgart: Klett.

Breuer, Stephan (1995) *Ästhetischer Fundamentalismus*, Darmstadt: Wissenschaftliche Buchgesellschaft.

Brie, Friedrich (1921) *Ästhetische Weltanschauung in der Literatur des XIX. Jahrhunderts*, Freiburg im Breisgau: Boltze.

Burdorf, Dieter (2001) *Die Poetik der Form*, Stuttgart: Metzler.

Cecil, Lord David (1955) *Walter Pater: The Scholar-Artist*, Cambridge: Cambridge University Press.

Curtius, Ernst Robert (1948) *Europäische Literatur und Lateinisches Mittelalter*, Bern: Franke.

Eliot, T. S. (1953) *Selected Essays*, London: Faber & Faber.

Friedrich, Hugo (1949) *Montaigne*, Bern: Franke.

Hecht, Hans (1927) 'Walter Pater: Eine Würdigung', *Deutsche Vierteljahrsschrift für Literaturwissenschaft und Geistesgeschichte* (Halle) 5: 550–82.

Hofmannsthal, Hugo von (1956) *Gesammelte Werke in Einzelausgaben. Prosa I* ed. Herbert Steiner, Frankfurt am Main: Fischer.

Hummel, Hildegard (1987) 'Reflexe der ästhetischen Konzeption Walter Paters im Werk Rudolf Borchardt's: Borchardt's Lysis-Übersetzung', *Germanisch-Romanische Monatsschrift* [Heidelberg], 37: 166–86.

Hutton, J. A. (1906) *Pilgrims in the Religion of Faith*, Edinburgh: Oliphant, Anderson and Ferrier.

Iser, Wolfgang (1960) *Walter Pater: die Autonomie des Ästhetischen*, Tübingen: Niemeyer.

— (1987) *Walter Pater: The Aesthetic Moment*, Cambridge: Cambridge University Press (English translation of 1960 German original).

— (1995) 'Enfoldings in Paterian Discourse: Modes of Translatability', *Comparative Criticism* [Cambridge], 17: 41–60.

Kassner, Rudolf (1949) *Sämtliche Werke* IX, ed. Ernst Zinn und Klaus E. Bohnenkamp, Pfullingen: Neske.

— (1957) *Sämtliche Werke* X

— (1969) *Sämtliche Werke* I

— (1976) *Sämtliche Werke* III

— (1982) *Sämtliche Werke* VI

— (1984) *Sämtliche Werke* VII
— (1992) *Gesicht und Gegengesicht. Aus den Schriften*, ed. Gerhart Baumann, Frankfurt am Main: Insel.
Lukács, Georg (1982) *Briefwechsel 1902–1927*, ed. Eva Karád and Eva Fekete, Budapest: Corvina.
Mattenklott, Gert (1987) 'Der Ästhetische Mensch', in Werner Busch and Peter Schmook (eds.) *Kunst: die Geschichte ihrer Funktionen*, Werinheim and Berlin: Belz.
Obenauer, K. J. (1933) *Die Problematik des Ästhetischen Menschen in der deutschen Literatur*, Munich: Beck.
Pater, Walter (1919) *The Renaissance: Studies in Art and Poetry*, London: Macmillan.
— (1920a) *Appreciations: With an Essay on Style*, London: Macmillan.
— (1920b) *Plato and Platonism: A Series of Lectures*, London: Macmillan.
Schmidt, Ernst A. (2003) *Die Augusteische Literatur: System im Bewegung* (Schriften der Philosophisch-historischen Klasse der Heidelberger Akademic der Wissenschaft 18), Heidelberg: Winter.
Smith, Logan Pearsall (1936) *Reperusals and Recollections*, London: Constable.
Stamm, Ulrike (1997) *'Ein Kritiker aus dem Willen der Natur': Hugo von Hofmannsthal und das Werk Walter Paters*, Würzburg: Königshausen & Neumann.

Chapter 7

Borchardt, Rudolf (1960) 'Walter Pater zu seinem hundertsten Geburtstag', in *Gesammelte Werke in Einzelbänden, Prosa III*, ed. Marie Luise Borchardt and Ernst Zinn, Stuttgart: Ernst Klett, pp. 402–23.
Böschenstein, Renate (1990) 'Das Ich und seine Teile. Überlegungen zum anthropologischen Gehalt einiger lyrischer Texte', in Buhr, Gerhard, Friedrich Kittler and Horst Turk (eds.) *Das Subjekt der Dichtung: Festschrift für Gerhard Kaiser*, Würzburg: Königshausen & Neumann, pp. 73–98.
Du Bos, Charles (1929) 'Avant-propos pour les Ecrits en prose de Hofmannsthal', in *Approximations III*, Paris: Le Rouge et le Noir, pp. 285–313.
Exner, Richard (1976) *Index Nominum zu Hugo von Hofmannsthals Gesammelten Werken*, Heidelberg: Stiehm.
Fülleborn, Ulrich (1992) '"Zwei Antinomien waren zu lösen…"': Werden und Sein, Individuum und Gemeinschaft im Werk Hugo von Hofmannsthals', in *Wir sind aus solchem Zeug wie das zu Träumen: kritische Beiträge zum Werk Hugo von Hofmannsthals*, ed. Joseph P. Strelka, Bern: Lang, pp. 169–97.
Hamburger, Michael (1961) 'Hofmannsthal's Bibliothek: Ein Bericht', *Euphorion*, 55.1: 15–76.
Hofmannsthal, Hugo von (1935) *Briefe 1890–1901*, Berlin: Fischer.
— (1961) *Poems and Verse Plays*, Bilingual Edition, ed. Michael Hamburger, trans. Michael Hamburger and others, New York: Bollingen Foundation.
— (1968) *Briefwechsel mit Leopold von Andrian*, ed. Walter H. Perl, Frankfurt am Main: Fischer.

— (1979) *Gesammelte Werke: Reden und Aufsätze I*, ed. Rudolf Schoeller, Frankfurt am Main: Fischer.

— (1980) *Gesammelte Werke: Reden und Aufsätze III 1925–1929*, ed. Bernd Schoeller, Frankfurt am Main: Fischer.

— (1984) *Sämtliche Werke: Gedichte I*, ed. Eugene Weber, Frankfurt am Main: Fischer.

— (1993) *Sämtliche Werke, XII, Dramen 10: Der Schwierige*, ed. Martin Stern, Frankfurt am Main: Fischer.

Kohlschmidt, Werner (1965) 'Der Dichter vor der Zeit. Zur Problematik des Zeitbewußtseins seit der Romantik', in *Dichter, Tradition und Zeitgeist: Gesammelte Studien zur Literaturgeschichte*, Bern: Francke, pp. 35–53.

Kümmel, Friedrich (1962) 'Bergsons Begriff der Dauer (durée)', in *Über den Begriff der Zeit*, Tübingen: Niemeyer.

Pater, Walter (1902) *The Renaissance. Studies in Art and Poetry*, London: Macmillan.

— (1914) *Marius the Epicurean*, vol. 1, London: Macmillan.

Sondrup, Steven (1989) 'Terzinen', in Resch, Margit (ed.) *Seltene Augenblicke: Interpretations of Poems by Hugo von Hofmannsthal*, Columbia, SC: Camden House.

Stamm, Ulrike (1997a) *Ein Kritiker aus dem Willen der Natur: Hugo von Hofmannsthal und das Werk Walter Paters*, Würzburg: Königshausen & Neumann.

— (1997b) 'Walter Pater's Essay "Diaphaneitè" as a Bridge Between Romanticism and Modernism', *Nineteenth-Century Prose*, 24.2: 88–108.

Stoupy, Joëlle (1989) '"Il faut glisser la vie…"': ein Zitat und seine Wandlungen im Werk Hugo von Hofmannsthals', *Hofmannsthal-Blätter*, 39: 9–43.

Weiss, Winfried (1973) 'Ruskin, Pater and Hofmannsthal', *Colloquia Germanica* 6: 162–70.

Wendorff, Rudolf (1980) *Zeit und Kultur: Geschichte des Zeitbewußtseins in Europa*, Opladen: Westdeutscher Verlag.

Williams, Carolyn (1989) *Transfigured World: Walter Pater's Aesthetic Historicism*, Ithaca and London: Cornell University Press.

— (1997) 'On Pater's Late Style', *Nineteenth-Century Prose*, 24.2: 143–61.

Chapter 8

Bernauer, Markus (2001) 'Borchardt und Pound im faschistischen Italien', in Kauffmann, Kai (ed.) *Dichterische Politik: Studien zu Rudolf Borchardt*, Bern, Berlin and Brussels: Lang, pp. 115–45.

Borchardt, Rudolf (1905), *Das Gespräch über Formen und Platons Lysis deutsch*, Leipzig: Zeitler.

— (1909) 'Swinburne', written for the journal *Hyperion*; unpublished. First publication 1952 in *Neue Literarische Welt: Zeitung der Deutschen Akademie für Sprache und Dichtung* [Darmstadt], 9 (10 June).

— (1923) 'Walter Savage Landor', written as a postscript for *Imaginäre Unterhaltungen*, unpublished; in *Gesammelte Werke in Einzelbänden: Prosa III*, ed. Marie Luise Borchardt and others, Stuttgart: Klett, pp. 353–64.

— (1928) 'Dante Gabriel Rossetti. Zum 100. Geburtstag (12. Mai)', *Deutsche allgemeine Zeitung* [Berlin], 219 (11 May), Beiblatt and *Neue Zürcher Zeitung, Mittagsausgabe* [Zurich], 889 (15 May), [pp. 1–2].

— (1931) 'Führung', Munich: G. Müller.

— (1935) *Schriften*, manuscript print, Bremen: Aschoff.

— (1935) 'Vernon Lee: Ein Gedenkblatt', *Sonntagsblatt der Basler Nachrichten* [Basel], 29.23 (9 June), 93–94.

— (1936) *Englische Dichter: Deutsch von Rudolf Borchardt*, Vienna: Phaidon.

— (1939) 'Walter Pater: zu seinem hundertsten Geburtstage', *Sonntagsblatt der Basler Nachrichten*, 33.33 (13 August), 129–32.

— (1955) *Gesammelte Werke in Einzelbänden: Reden*, ed. Marie Luise Borchardt and others, Stuttgart: Klett.

— (1957) *Gesammelte Werke in Einzelbänden: Prosa I*, ed. Marie Luise Borchardt, Stuttgart: Klett.

— (1960) *Gesammelte Werke in Einzelbänden: Prosa III*, ed. Marie Luise Borchardt and others, Stuttgart: Klett.

— (1966) *Kindheit und Jugend. Von ihm selbst erzählt*, Hamburg: Maximilian-Gesellschaft.

— (1968) *Ausgewählte Gedichte*, ed. Theodor W. Adorno, Frankfurt am Main: Suhrkamp.

Burckhardt, Jacob (1859) *Die Cultur der Renaissance in Italien: ein Versuch*, Basel: Schweighauser, 1860 [recte 1859].

— (1878) *The Civilization of the Period of the Renaissance in Italy*, trans. S. G. C. Middlemore [from the 3rd edn, Leipzig, 1877–8], London: Kegan & Paul.

Burdorf, Dieter (1999) 'Gespräche über Kunst: zur Konjunktur einer literarischen Form um 1900', in Beyer, Andreas and Dieter Burdorf (eds.), *Jugendstil und Kulturkritik: zur Literatur und Kunst um 1900*, Heidelberg: Winter, pp. 29–50.

Eilert, Heide (1999) '"… daß man über die Künste überhaupt fast gar nicht reden soll": zum Kunst-Essay um 1900 und zur Pater-Rezeption bei Hofmannsthal, Rilke und Borchardt', in Beyer, Andreas and Dieter Burdorf (eds.), *Jugendstil und Kulturkritik: zur Literatur und Kunst um 1900*, Heidelberg: Winter, pp. 51–72.

Goethe, Johann Wolfgang (1964) *Selected Verse: With Plain Prose Translations of Each Poem*, trans. David Luke, Harmondsworth: Penguin.

Hofmannsthal, Hugo von (1894a) [Loris, pseud.] 'Über moderne englische Malerei', *Neue Revue* [Vienna], 5.1, no. 26 (13 June), 811–16.

— (1894b) [Archibald O'Hagan, pseud.] 'Walter Pater', *Die Zeit: Wiener Wochenschrift für Politik, Volkswirthschaft, Wissenschaft und Kunst* [Vienna and Leipzig] 1.7 (17 November), 104–05.

— (1902) 'Ein Brief', *Der Tag* [Berlin], 489 (18 October) [pp. 1–3] and 491 (19 October) [pp. 1–3].

— (1942) 'The Letter', trans. Francis C. Golffing, *Rocky Mountain Review* [Cedar City, Utah], 6.3–4 (Spring-Summer), 1; 3; 11–13.

— (1952) 'The Letter of Lord Chandos', trans. Tania and James Stern, in Hofmannsthal, Hugo von, *Selected Writings: Selected Prose*, vol. 1, New York: Pantheon Books, 129–41.

— (1956) *Gesammelte Werke in Einzelausgaben: Prosa I*, ed. Herbert Steiner, Frankfurt am Main: Fischer.

— (1991) *Sämtliche Werke: Erfundene Gespräche und Briefe*, vol. 31, ed. Rudolf Hirsch and others, Frankfurt am Main: Fischer.

Hummel, Hildegard (1987) 'Reflexe der ästhetischen Konzeption Walter Paters im Werk Rudolf Borchardts', *Germanisch-Romanische Monatsschrift* n.s. 37: 166–86.

Kassner, Rudolf (1900) *Die Mystik, die Künstler und das Leben: Über englische Dichter und Maler im 19. Jahrhundert: Accorde*, Leipzig: Diederichs.

— (1969) *Sämtliche Werke*, vol. 1, ed. Ernst Zinn, Pfullingen: Neske.

Landor, Walter Savage (1923) *Walter Savage Landor: Imaginäre Unterhaltungen*, trans. Rudolf Borchardt, Berlin: Rowohlt.

Lauster, Martina (1992) 'Englishness in Essays of Hugo von Hofmannsthal, Rudolf Borchardt and Rudolf Kassner', in Byrn, R. F. M. and K. G. Knight (eds.), *Anglo-German Studies*, Leeds: The Leeds Philosophical and Literary Society, pp. 116–47.

— (1993) 'Stone Imagery and the Sonnet Form: Petrarch, Michelangelo, Baudelaire, Rilke', *Comparative Literature* [Eugene, Oregon], 45.2: 146–74.

Lönker, Fred (1997) 'Die Sprache der Restauration: Zu Rudolf Borchardts Dichtungstheorie', in Huntemann, Willi and Lutz Rühling (eds.), *Fremdheit als Problem und Programm: die literarische Übersetzung zwischen Tradition und Moderne*, Berlin: Erich Schmidt, pp. 206–19.

Ott, Ulrich (2001) 'Die *Jamben* als politische Dichtung', in Kauffmann, Kai (ed.) *Dichterische Politik: Studien zu Rudolf Borchardt*, Berne, Berlin and Brussels: Lang, pp. 147–61.

Pater, Walter (1902) *Die Renaissance: Studien in Kunst und Poesie*, trans. Wilhelm Schölermann, Leipzig: Eugen Diederichs.

— (1904) *Plato und der Platonismus: Vorlesungen*, trans. Hans Hecht, Jena; Leipzig: Eugen Diederichs.

— (1925) *The Renaissance: Studies in Art and Poetry*, London: Macmillan Pocket Edition.

Petzinna, Berthold (2001) 'Wilheminische Intellektuelle: Rudolf Borchardt und die Anliegen des "Ring"-Kreises', in Kauffmann, Kai (ed.) *Dichterische Politik: Studien zu Rudolf Borchardt*, Berne, Berlin and Brussels: Lang, pp. 63–79.

Rilke, Rainer Maria (1902) 'Ein neues Buch von der Renaissance' [review of Schölermann's translation of Pater's *The Renaissance*], *Bremer Tageblatt und General-Anzeiger* [Bremen], 6 (27 July).

— (1996) *Werke: Kommentierte Ausgabe in vier Bänden: Schriften*, vol. 4, ed. Manfred Engel and others, Frankfurt am Main; Leipzig: Insel.

Rizza, Stephen (1997) *Rudolf Kassner and Hugo von Hofmannsthal: Criticism as Art: The Reception of Pre-Raphaelitism in fin-de-siècle Vienna*, Frankfurt am Main: Lang.

Stamm, Ulrike (1997) *'Ein Kritiker aus dem Willen der Natur': Hugo von Hofmannsthal und das Werk Walter Paters*, Würzburg: Königshausen & Neumann.

Swinburne, Algernon Charles (1919) *Swinburne, Deutsch*, trans. Rudolf Borchardt, Berlin: Rowohlt.

Vilain, Robert (2002) 'The Reception of Walter Pater in Germany and Austria', in Brake, Laurel, Lesley Higgons and Carolyn Williams (eds.), *Walter Pater: Transparencies of Desire*, Greensboro, University of North California Press, pp. 63–72.

Chapter 9

Babits, Mihály (1935) *Az európai irodalom története*, Budapest: Nyugat.
— (1978a) *Az európai irodalom olvasókönyve: Töredék és vázlat*, Budapest: Magvető.
— (1978b) *Esszék, tanulmányok*, 2 vols., Budapest: Szépirodalmi.
Bendl, Júlia (1994) *Lukács György élete a századfordulótól 1918-ig*, Budapest: Scientia Humana.
Czeke, Marianne (1915) 'Walter Pater: görög tanulmányok', *Egyetemes Philologiai Közlöny*, 747–51.
Gellér, Katalin (1990) 'Hungarian Art Nouveau and its English Sources', *Hungarian Studies*, 6: 155–65.
Hevesi, Sándor (1904) 'Új görög renaissance', *Magyar Szemle*, 16: 338–9, 346–47, 354–55.
James, Henry (1957) *Literary Reviews and Essays*, ed. Albert Mordell. New Haven: Yale University Press.
Justh, Zsigmond (1941) *Napló*, Budapest: Athenaeum.
Kőszegi, László (1914). 'Walter Pater: A Renaissance', *Egyetemes Philologiai Közlöny*, 374–7.
Kriesch, Aladár (1904). *Ruskinről és az angol preraffaelitákról*, Budapest: Műbarátok Köre.
Latkóczy, Mihály (1906) 'Walter Pater: griechische Studien', *Egyetemes Philologiai Közlöny*, 30: 146–9.
Lukács, György (1965) *Az esztétikum sajátossága*, trans. István Eörsi, 2 vols. Budapest: Akadémiai.
— (1975) *A heidelbergi művészetfilozófia és esztétika – a regény elmélete*, Budapest: Magvető.
— (1977) *Ifjúkori művek (1902–1918)*, Budapest: Magvető.
Pater, Walter (1912) 'Sebastian van Storck', trans. Piroska Reichard, *Budapesti Szemle* 151: 280–99.
— (1913) trans. Károly Sebestyén, Budapest.
— (1914) *Görög tanulmanyok*, trans. László Kőszegi, Budapest: Magyar Tudományos Akadémia.
— (1941a) 'La Gioconda', trans. József Szigeti in Halász, Gábor (ed.) *Az angol irodalom kincsesháza*, Budapest: Athenaeum, pp. 290–2.
— (1941b) 'Watteau a szülővárosában', trans. Piroska Reichard in Halász, Gábor (ed.) *Az angol irodalom kincsesháza*, Budapest: Athenaeum, pp. 292–3.
— (1967) 'Leonardo da Vinci', trans. István Jánosy in *Hagyomány és egyéniség: az angol esszé klasszikusai*, Budapest: Európa, pp. 390–412.
'Pater Walter: A Renaissance' (1913) *Egyetemes Philologiai Közlöny*, 293.
Rába, György (1981) *Babits Mihály költészete 1903–1920*, Budapest: Szépirodalmi.

Reichard, Piroska (1912) 'Walter Pater', *Budapesti Szemle* 150: 408–23.
Rózsa, Dezső (1927) 'Pater, Walter', in *Irodalmi lexikon*, ed. Marcell Benedek, Budapest: Győző Andor.
Sarbu, Aladár (1999) 'The Lace of Lacedaemon: A Note on Pater and Modernism', in Szaffkó, Péter and Tamás Bényei (eds.) *Happy Returns: Essays for Professor István Pálffy*, Debrecen: KLTE, pp. 91–109.
— (2002) Electronic letter to Mihály Szegedy-Maszák, 10 September 2002.
Szegedy-Maszák, Mihály (2002) 'Egy műfaj kockázatai', *Alföld* 53 (February): 17–27.
Szerb, Antal (1971) *Gondolatok a könyvtárban*. Budapest: Magvető.
— (2001). *Naplójegyzetek (1914–1943)*. Budapest: Magvető.
Szini, Gyula (1922) *Írói arcképek: Essayk*, Budapest: Világirodalom.

Chapter 10

Forst, Vladimír (ed.) (1985) *Lexikon české literatury 1 (A-G)*, Prague: Academia.
Pater, Walter (1907) *Imaginární portraity* trans. Jiří Živný, Prague: Kamilla Neumannová.
— (1910) *The Renaissance*, London: Macmillan and Co.
— (1911) *Dojmy a myšlenky Maria Epikurejce – román*, trans. Anna Fišerová, Prague: Kamilla Neumannová.
Stříbrný, Zdeněk (1987) *Dějiny anglické literatury*, 2 vols., Prague: Academia.

Chapter 11

Brzozowski, Stanisław (1913) *Pamiętnik*, Lvov: Księgarnia Polska B. Połonieckiego.
— (1990a) 'Nasze "ja" i historia', in 'Legenda Młodej Polski', in Markiewicz, Henryk (ed.) *Eseje i studia o literaturze*, Wrocław: Zakład Narodowy im. Ossolińskich, pp. 699–718.
— (1990b) 'Skarga to rzecz straszna. (Rzecz o "*Róży*" Józefa Katerli)', in Markiewicz, Henryk (ed.) *Eseje i studia o literaturze*, Wrocław: Zakład Narodowy im. Ossolińskich, pp. 1061–79.
Boniecki, Edward (1993) *Struktura nagiej duszy: studium o Stanisławie Przybyszewskim*, Warsaw: Instytut Badań Literackich.
Dale, Peter A. (1977) 'Historicism as Weltanschauung', in *The Victorian Critic and the Idea of History*, Cambridge, MA, and London: Harvard University Press, pp. 171–205.
Głowiński, Michał (1997) *Ekspresja i empatia: Studia o młodopolskiej krytyce literackiej*, Cracow: Wydawnictwo Literackie.
Grabowski, Zbigniew (1929) *Walter Pater: Życie – dzieło – styl*, Poznań: Poznańskie Towarzystwo Przyjaciół Nauk.
C. J. [Jellenta, Cezary] (1909a) 'Z Przed-Renesansu', *Literatura i Sztuka* [Poznań] 17: 257–9.

— (1909b) 'Z Po-Renesansu', *Literatura i Sztuka* [Poznań] 19: 289–92.
Juszczak, Wiesław (1965) *Wojtkiewicz i Nowa Sztuka*, Warsaw: Państwowy Instytut Wydawniczy.
Krajewska, Wanda (1972), *Recepcja literatury angielskiej w Polsce okresu modernizmu (1887–1918): Informacje. Sądy. Przekłady*, Wrocław: Zakład Narodowy im. Ossolińskich.
Lack, Stanisław (1979a) 'Krytyka–bojkot–impresja', in Głowala, Wojciech (ed.) *Wybór pism krytycznych*, Cracow: Wydawnictwo Literackie, pp. 305–13.
— (1979b) 'Przegląd przeglądów', in Głowala, Wojciech (ed.) *Wybór pism krytycznych*, Cracow: Wydawnictwo Literackie, pp. 477–78.
— (1979c) 'Luźne uwagi o krytyce literackiej', in Głowala, Wojciech (ed.) *Wybór pism krytycznych*, Cracow: Wydawnictwo Literackie, pp. 314–21.
Maciejewska, Irena (1965) *Leopold Staff: Lwowski okres twórczości*, Warsaw: Państwowy Instytut Wydawniczy.
Matuszewski, Ignacy (1897) 'Subjektywizm w krytyce', *Biblioteka Warszawska*, 2: 76–103.
Pater, Walter (1906) *Die Renaissance: Studien in Kunst und Poesie*, trans. Wilhelm Schölermann, Jena and Leipzig: Diederichs.
— (1909a), *Wybór pism*, trans. Stanisław Lack, Lvov: Księgarnia Polska B. Połonieckiego.
— (1909b) 'Luca della Robbia', trans. Maria Rakowska, *Sfinks* [Warsaw] 6: 413–21.
— (1909c) 'Leonardo da Vinci', trans. unknown, *Literatura i Sztuka* [Poznań] 9; 10; 11; 12: 1.
— (1910) 'Pico della Mirandola: z cyklu szkiców P. T. Odrodzenie,' trans. Maria Rakowska, *Sfinks* [Warsaw] 11: 334–51.
— (1998) *Renesans. Rozważania o sztuce i poezji*, trans. Piotr Kopszak, Warsaw: Aletheia.
Podraza-Kwiatkowska, Maria (1985) '"Żyjąc w pięknie" (O Miriamie krytyku)', in *Somnambulicy – dekadenci – herosi*, Cracow: Wydawnictwo Literackie, pp. 390–424.
Przesmycki, Zenon (1973), 'Walka ze sztuką', in Podraza-Kwiatkowska, Maria (ed.) *Programy i dyskusje literackie okresu Młodej Polski*, Wrocław and Cracow: Zakład Narodowy im. Ossolińskich, pp. 297–328.
Przybyszewski, Stanisław (1973), 'Confiteor', in Podraza-Kwiatkowska, Maria (ed.) *Programy i dyskusje literackie okresu Młodej Polski*, Wrocław and Cracow: Zakład Narodowy im. Ossolińskich, pp. 235–43.
Staff, Leopold (1966) *W kręgu literackich przyjaźni: listy*, ed. Janina Czachowska and Irena Maciejewska, Warsaw: Państwowy Instytut Wydawniczy.
Winiarski, Leon (1896/1897) 'Walter Pater', *Prawda* [Warsaw] 17.1: 8–9.
— (1897) 'Walter Pater', *Prawda* [Warsaw] 17.2: 20.
— (1899a) 'Walter Pater: "Imaginary Portraits – Denys l'Auxerrois"', *Prawda* [Warsaw] 19.38: 452–3.
— (1899b) 'Walter Pater: "Imaginary Portraits – Carl von Rosenmold"', *Prawda* [Warsaw] 19.40: 478–9.
— (1901) 'Walter Pater: "Imaginary Portraits – Sebastyan van Storck"', *Prawda* [Warsaw] 21.33: 402–3.

Witkiewicz, Stanisław (1949) *Sztuka i krytyka u nas*, ed. Jan Zygmunt Jakubowski, Warszawa: Książka i Wiedza.

Chapter 12

Almeida, Teresa Sousa de (1983) 'Athena ou a Encenação Necessária', *Athena. Edição Facsimilada*, Lisbon: Contexto Editora, pp. [v–xv].
Fernandes, Aníbal (org.) (1989) *Raul Leal: Sodoma Divinizada. Uma polémica iniciada por Fernando Pessoa a propósito de António Botto, e também por ele terminada, com ajuda de Álvaro Maia e Pedro Teotónio Pereira (da Liga de Acção dos Estudantes de Lisboa)*, Lisbon: Hiena Editora.
Lopes, Teresa Rita (coord.) (1993) *Pessoa inédito*, Lisbon: Livros Horizonte.
— (1990) *Pessoa por conhecer*, Lisbon: Editorial Estampa, 2 vols.
Malafaia, Maria Teresa (1985) 'Walter Pater: o relativismo estético e a função do crítico', unpublished MA thesis, University of Lisbon, 130pp.
— (1987) '*Marius the Epicurean: his sensations and ideas* – Marius e Psyché ou a reconciliação das polaridades', *Anglo-Saxónica*, 2: 93–105.
— (1993) 'Cultura e identidade: ou a forma como Edward Said nos recorda Walter Pater', *Actas do XVI Encontro da Associação Portuguesa de Estudos Anglo-Americanos*, Vila Real: Universidade de Vila Real, 281–85.
Pater, Walter (1901) *The Renaissance: Studies in Art and Poetry*, London: Macmillan.
— (1922) *Marius l'épicurien*, Paris: Perrin.
— (1923) *Platon et le platonisme*, Paris: Payot.
— (1924) 'La Gioconda', transl. Fernando Pessoa, *Athena: Revista de Arte* [Lisbon], 1. 2, I November, 58.
— (1927) *Marius the Epicurean*, London: Macmillan.
— (1931) *Appreciations: with an Essay on Style*, London: Macmillan.
— (1944a) *Mário, el Epicúreo: sus sensaciones y sus ideas*, Barcelona: Ediciones Lauro.
— (1944b) *El Renacimiento*, Buenos Aires: Hachette.
— (1968) *Marius the Epicurean*, London: Dent.
— (1973) *Essays on Literature and Art*, London: Dent.
— (1985) *Essais sur l'art et la Renaissance*, Paris: Klincksieck.
— (1990a) *Essays on Literature and Art*, London: Everyman's Library.
— (1990b) *The Renaissance: Studies in Art and Poetry*, with an introduction by Adam Philips, Oxford and New York: Oxford University Press.
Pessoa, Fernando (1966) *Páginas íntimas e de auto-interpretação*, ed. Georg Rudolf Lind and Jacinto do Prado Coelho, Lisbon: Edições Ática.
— (2000) *Crítica: ensaios, artigos e entrevistas*, ed. Fernando Cabral Martins, Lisbon: Assírio & Alvim.
— (2002) *Obras de António Mora*, ed. Luís Filipe B. Teixeira, n.p.: Imprensa Nacional – Casa da Moeda.
Saraiva, Arnaldo (1996) *Fernando Pessoa poeta – tradutor de poetas: os poemas traduzidos e o respectivo original*, Porto: Lello Editores.
Silva, E. J. Moreira da (1993) 'Concordância das obras de Walter Pater', unpublished work, Ponta Delgada, 3 vols.
— (1997) 'Walter Pater e Kant', unpublished PhD thesis, University of the Azores, 2 vols.

Chapter 13

Abellán, Manuel L. (1980) *Censura y creación literaria en España (1939–1976)*, Barcelona: Ediciones Península.

Aznar, M. (1940) 'Ha muerto la teoría de las pequeñas nacionalidades: los imperios germánico, italiano y español, fuerzas vitales de la nueva Europa', *Solidaridad Nacional* [Barcelona], 29 June. Cited in J. Benet (1979, 403–4).

Baras, Montserrat (1984) *Acció Catalana 1922–1936*, Barcelona: Edicions Curial.

Benet, Josep (1979) *Catalunya sota el règim franquista*, Barcelona: Editorial Blume. First publ. 1973.

Berga, Miguel (1987) *John Langdon-Davies: La Setmana Tràgica de 1937*, Barcelona: Edicions 62.

— (1991) *John Langdon-Davies (1897–1971): una biografia anglo-catalana*, Barcelona: Editorial Pòrtic, S.A.

Campillo, Maria (1999) 'Les lletres catalanes durant la Guerra Civil', in Bordons, Glòria and Jaume Subirana (eds.) *Literatura catalana contemporània*, Barcelona: Edicions de la Universitat Oberta de Catalunya/Proa, 201–5.

Campillo, Maria (2003) 'La primera Institució de les Lletres Catalanes: situació i sentit d'un compromís amb la cultura' at *http://cultura.gencat.es/ilc/docs/antecedent.doc*

Castellanos, Jordi (1987) 'El noucentisme: ideologia i estètica' in *El noucentisme; cicle de conferències fet a la Institució Cultural del CIC de Terrassa: curs 1984–85*, Barcelona: Abadia de Montserrat, pp. 19–39.

Comadira, Narcís (1999) 'El noucentisme: un esbós d'aproximació', in Bordons, Glòria and Jaume Subirana (eds.) *Literatura catalana contemporània*, Barcelona: Edicions de la Universitat Oberta de Catalunya/Proa, 107–114.

Coppinger, Emmanuel (1922) 'Avant-propos', in Pater, Walter, *Marius l'épicurien*. Paris: Librairie Académique Perrin & Cie., no page number.

Costa Ruibal, Òscar (2002) *L'imaginari imperial: el noucentisme càtala i la política internacional*, Barcelona: Institut Cambó.

D'Ors, Eugeni (1919) 'Pròleg', in *Sonets i Odes de John Keats*, trans. M. Manent, Barcelona: Publicacions de la Revista, reproduced in *Homentage a Marià Manent* (1979), *Delta 4. Revista de Literatura* [Barcelona]: 59–60.

— (1950) *Obra Catalana Completa. Glosari 1906–1910*, Barcelona: Editorial Selecta, S.A.

Edwards, Jill (1979) *The British Government and the Spanish Civil War*, London and Basingstoke: Macmillan.

Esclasans, Agustín (1944) 'Prólogo', in Pater, Walter, *Mario el epicúreo*, Barcelona: Ediciones Lauro, 7–15.

— (1957) *La meva vida (1920–1945)*, Barcelona: Editorial Selecta.

Farrán y Mayoral, J. (1942) 'El traductor al lector', in Pater, Walter, *Retratos imaginarios*, Barcelona: Ediciones Aymá, pp. 9–18.

Fuster, Joan (1980) *Literatura Catalana Contemporània*, Barcelona: Curial. First publ. 1971.

Gran Enciclopèdia Catalana, vol. 7 (1981), Barcelona: Enciclopèdia Catalana, S.A. First publ. 1974.

Gran Enciclopèdia Catalana, vol. 8 (1981), Barcelona: Enciclopèdia Catalana, S.A. First publ. 1976.

Hill, Donald L. (ed.) (1980) *Walter Pater. The Renaissance: Studies in Art and Poetry. The 1893 Text*, Berkeley, Los Angeles, London: University of California Press.

Hurtley, Jacqueline Anne (1986) *Josep Janés: el combat per la cultura*, Barcelona: Edicions Curial.

— (1992) *José Janés: editor de literatura inglesa*, Barcelona: Promociones y Publicaciones Universitarias, S.A.

Jardí, Enric (1967) *Eugeni D'Ors*, Barcelona: Aymà, S.A. Editora.

Keats, John (1919) *Sonets i Odes*, trans. Marià Manent, Barcelona: Edicions de La Revista.

Knoepflmacher, Ulrich C. (1970) *Religious Humanism and the Victorian Novel: George Eliot, Walter Pater and Samuel Butler*, Princeton, NJ: Princeton University Press. First publ. 1965.

Malé, Jordi (1999) 'Carles Riba', in Bordons, Glòria and Jaume Subirana (eds.) *Literatura catalana contemporània*, Barcelona: Edicions de la Universitat Oberta de Catalunya/Proa, pp. 157–62.

Manent, Albert (1989) 'Ha mort Jaume Aymà, pioner de les edicions en llengua catalana', *La Vanguardia* [Barcelona], 23 May.

Manent, Marià (1918) *La branca*, Barcelona: [Joan Sallent].

— (1934) *Notes sobre literatura estrangera*, Barcelona: Edicions de La Revista.

— (1938a) *Versions de l'anglès*, Barcelona: Edicions de la Residència d'Estudiants.

— (1938b) 'Nota preliminar', in Pater, Walter, *El Renaixement: estudis d'art i poesia*, Barcelona: Institució de les Lletres Catalanes, 9–12.

— (1975) *El Vel de Maia*, Barcelona: Edicions Destino.

Medina, Jaume (1987) 'Noucentisme i Humanisme', in *El noucentisme; cicle de conferències fet a la Institució Cultural del CIC de Terrassa: curs 1984–85*, Barcelona: Abadia de Montserrat, pp. 79–98.

— (2000) *Estudis sobre Carles Riba*, Barcelona: Publicacions de l'Abadia de Montserrat.

Oliva, Salvador and Angela Buxton (1986) *Diccionari Català-Anglès*, Barcelona: Enciclopèdia Catalana.

Parcerisas, Francesc (1997) 'Marià Manent and translation', *Catalan Writing* [Barcelona], 15: 57–62.

Pater, Walter (1914) *Imaginary Portraits*, London: Macmillan & Co., Ltd.

— (1917) *La Renaissance*, trans. F. Roger-Cornaz, Paris: Librairie Payot et Cie.

— (1918) *Marius the Epicurean. His Sensations and Ideas*, 2 vols., London: Macmillan & Co., Ltd.

— (1922) *Marius l'épicurien*, trans. Emmanuel Coppinger, Paris: Librairie Académique Perrin & Cie.

— (1938) *El Renaixement: estudis d'art i poesia*, trans. Marià Manent, Barcelona: Institució de les Lletres Catalanes.

— (1942) *Retratos imaginarios*, trans. J. Farrán y Mayoral, Barcelona: Ediciones Aymá.

— (1944) *Mario el epicúreo*, trans. Agustín Esclasans, Barcelona: Ediciones Lauro.
— (1945) *El Renacimiento*, trans. J. Farrán y Mayoral, Barcelona: Editorial Iberia.
— (1946) *Platón y el platonismo*, trans. Vicente P. Quintero, Buenos Aires: Emecé.
— (1982) *El Renacimiento*, no translator acknowledged, Barcelona: Icaria Editorial, S.A.
— (1998) *The Renaissance: Studies in Art and Poetry*, Oxford: Oxford University Press.
— (1999) *El Renacimiento: estudios sobre arte y poesía*, trans. Marta Salís. Barcelona: Alba.
Pericay, Xavier and Ferran Toutain (1996) *El malentès del noucentisme*, Barcelona: Proa.
Riba, Carles (1919) *Primer Llibre d'estances*, Barcelona: Publicacions de La Revista, 28.
— (1931) 'Pròleg', in Brooke, Rupert, *Poemes*, trans. Marià Manent, Barcelona: Publicacions de La Revista, 9–14.
Santaeulàlia, J. N. (1999) 'Noucentisme i literatura', in Bordons Glòria, and Jaume Subirana (eds.) *Literatura Catalana Contemporània*, Barcelona: Edicions de la Universitat Oberta de Catalunya/Proa, pp. 120–6.
Vallcorba, Jaume (1994) *Noucentisme, Mediterraneisme i Classicisme: apunts per a l'història d'una estètica*, Barcelona: Quaderns Crema.

The Reception of Walter Pater in Russia: Bibliography

Translations

Muratov, P. (trans. and introd.) (1908) *Voobrazhaemye portrety; Rebenok v dome* [*Imaginary Portraits; The Child in the House*] Moscow: Sablin.
— (trans. and introd.) (1916) *Voobrazhaemye portrety* 2nd edition, revised and supplemented, Moscow: K. F. Nekrasov [includes excerpts from *Marius the Epicurean*].
Zaimovskii, S. G. (trans.) (1912) *Renessans; ocherki iskusstva i poezii* [*Studies in the History of The Renaissance*] Moscow: Problemy estetiki.

Major articles (including those showing Pater's direct influence)

Kuzmin, M. (1910) 'O prekrasnoi yasnosti: zametki o proze' ['On Beautiful Clarity: Remarks on Prose'], *Apollon* 4: 5–10
Vengerova, Z. A. (1895) 'Sandro Bottichelli', *Vestnik Evropy* 12: 767–802, republished (1897) as 'Bottichelli' in Vengerova, Z. A., *Literaturnye kharakteristiki*, St Petersburg: A. E. Vineke, 3 vols., vol. I, 344–92.
— (1897) 'Val'ter Peter', *Cosmopolis* 2: 107–18, republished (1905) in *Literaturnye kharakteristiki*, St Petersburg: A. E. Vineke, 3 vols., vol. II, 267–77.
Z. V. [Z. A. Vengerova] (1898) 'Val'ter Pater, 1839–94', *Entsiklopedicheskii slovar'*, ed. K. K. Arseniev et al. St Petersburg: Brockhaus and Efron, vol. XXV, 930–1.

Secondary literature

Polonsky, Rachel (1998) *English Literature and the Russian Aesthetic Renaissance*, Cambridge: Cambridge University Press, pp. 26–7; 170–87; passim.

Index